THE
METROPOLITAN MUSEUM
OF ART
GUIDE

THE METROPOLITAN MUSEUM OF ART GUIDE

WORKS OF ART SELECTED BY
PHILIPPE DE MONTEBELLO, DIRECTOR

DESCRIPTIVE TEXTS WRITTEN BY
THE CURATORIAL STAFF OF THE MUSEUM

EDITED BY KATHLEEN HOWARD

THE METROPOLITAN MUSEUM OF ART
NEW YORK

Fourth Printing, 1987

Published by The Metropolitan Museum of Art
John P. O'Neill, Editor in Chief

Designed by Irwin Glusker; page layout by
    Kristen Reilly, assisted by Sara Jane Goodman

Floor plans by H. Shaw Borst, Inc., Mount Kisco, N.Y.
Type set by U.S. Lithograph Inc., New York
Printed by Colorcraft Lithographers, Inc., New York
Bound by Sendor Bindery, Inc., New York

LIBRARY OF CONGRESS CATALOGING IN PUBLICATION DATA
Metropolitan Museum of Art (New York, N.Y.)
    The Metropolitan Museum of Art guide.
    Art works selected by Philippe de Montebello; text by the curatorial staff of
The Metropolitan Museum of Art.
    Includes index. 1. Art—New York (N.Y.)—Catalogs.
2. Metropolitan Museum of Art (New York, N.Y.)—Catalogs. I. De Montebello, Philippe.
II. Howard, Kathleen.
III. Title.
N610.A6743 1983   708.147'1   83-13097
ISBN 0-87099-348-8
ISBN 0-87099-346-1 (pbk.)
ISBN 0-8109-1443-3 (HNA)

CONTENTS

INTRODUCTION

The Metropolitan Museum is a living encyclopedia of world art. Every culture from every part of the world—from Florence to Thebes to Papua New Guinea—from the earliest times to the present and in every medium is represented, frequently at the highest levels of quality and invention. The Metropolitan's 1.4 million square feet houses what is in fact a collection of collections; several of its departments could and would be major independent museums almost anywhere else. But here musical instruments adjoin arms and armor, and forty thousand Egyptian objects are displayed on the floor directly above a collection of forty-five thousand costumes.

A guide to the Museum's immense holdings—more than three million works of art, of which several hundred thousand are on public view—can only be the briefest of anthologies. Through a selection of some of the finest works in every department we have attempted to give a balanced picture of the collection. Inevitably many legitimate candidates had to be excluded, and it is no empty boast to say that the guide could have been twice as long with scarcely a loss of quality or éclat in the works presented. For example, out of more than thirty paintings by Monet we show four, and only fifty-five examples of Greek and Roman art must stand for the thousands of objects in that department's galleries. And how many museums could omit two works by so rare and supreme a painter as Vermeer while still including three?

The difficulty we faced in these choices makes it clear that the works of art reproduced here are only signposts to direct and introduce the visitor to the various parts of the Metropolitan. I hope those who come to the Museum often will use this book to plan their visits, creating itineraries to suit a time or a mood (they may find, as I have, that a short, focused visit is perhaps the most rewarding way to experience the Museum). This guide can, of course, be used as a basis for a tour of highlights, serving as an articulate companion to elucidate the visit as well as direct the visitor's steps. I should add that the random stroll, the unexpected discovery often bring as much pleasure as the satisfaction of locating a specific object.

Selecting the works of art for this guide helped to remind us that some degree of humility is called for, as there remain many gaps in the Metropolitan's collections—where is Donatello; where are the poetic church interiors of Saenredam; and where, in our superlative holdings of Impressionism, is Bazille? Still this guide could not fail to fill us with pride; it underscores the crucial role played by donors in the Museum's growth, and to all of them we extend our profound gratitude and admiration.

The Museum has long recognized that a guide like this one was urgently needed, but it lacked the requisite financial resources to produce it. Thus without the extraordinary generosity of Saul P. Steinberg of Reliance Group Holdings this book would not exist, and to him the Museum expresses its deepest thanks.

Philippe de Montebello
Director

The works of art in a great museum are the visible inheritance passed on to us by preceding generations. The more that we know about the motivations and the aspirations that inspired these works, the more clearly they can speak to us of the past; this deepened understanding of the past may allow us to see the present in a new perspective.

The passionate pursuit of collectors and the skills of scholars have assembled at the Metropolitan Museum an encyclopedic treasure. Reliance Group Holdings, Inc. is pleased to have been able to assist in publishing a comprehensive survey of the Museum's collections.

Saul P. Steinberg
Chairman of the Board
Reliance Group Holdings, Inc.

GENERAL INFORMATION

In Paris in 1866 a group of Americans gathered to celebrate the Fourth of July at a restaurant in the Bois de Boulogne. John Jay, the grandson of the eminent jurist and himself a distinguished public man, delivered the after-dinner speech, proposing that he and his compatriots create a "National Institution and Gallery of Art." This suggestion was enthusiastically received, and during the next years the Union League Club in New York, under Jay's presidency, rallied civic leaders, art collectors, and philanthropists to the cause. The project moved ahead swiftly, and The Metropolitan Museum of Art was incorporated on April 13, 1870. During the 1870s the Museum was located first in the Dodworth Building at 681 Fifth Avenue and then in the Douglas Mansion at 128 West 14th Street; finally, on March 30, 1880, it moved to Central Park at 82nd Street and Fifth Avenue. Its first building, a Ruskinian Gothic structure, was designed by Calvert Vaux and Jacob Wrey Mould; its west facade is still visible in the Lehman Wing. The Museum's Neoclassical facade on Fifth Avenue was erected during the early years of this century. The central pavilion (1902) was designed by Richard Morris Hunt; after his death in 1895 work continued under the supervision of his son, Richard Howland Hunt. The north and south wings (1911 and 1913) were the work of McKim, Mead and White. The Robert Lehman Wing (1975), The Sackler Wing (1978), The American Wing (1980), The Michael C. Rockefeller Wing (1982), and the Lila Acheson Wallace Wing (1987) were designed by Kevin Roche John Dinkeloo and Associates.

Admission: $5.00 suggested for adults, $2.50 suggested for students and senior citizens; free for members and children under twelve, accompanied by an adult. Some contribution is required, but the amount of the tax-deductible admission fee is voluntary.

The Main Building: Located on Fifth Avenue at 82nd Street. Open Tuesday from 9:30 to 8:45; Wednesday through Sunday from 9:30 to 5:15. Closed every Monday and January 1, Thanksgiving Day, and December 25. For recorded information, call 535-7710. For information about The Thomas J. Watson Library, The Photograph and Slide Library, and the study rooms for drawings, prints and photographs, and textiles, call 879-5500.

Museum Parking Garage: The entrance driveway is at 80th Street and Fifth Avenue. The Museum garage is open seven days a week, twenty-four hours a day. Parking fees are competitive for the area.

Visitors' Center: The Visitors' Center is located at the Information Desk in the Great Hall and is staffed by Museum volunteers, who provide information about the Museum and about exhibitions at other cultural institutions in New York.

Wheelchairs: Available upon request at Coat Check areas. Exhibitions and galleries are accessible by wheelchair.

Handicapped Visitors: For activities for the sight-impaired, call 879–5500, ext. 3561. For access to the Telephone for the Deaf (TTY), call 879–0421.

Strollers: Permitted on weekdays only in all galleries except Egyptian and special exhibitions.

Museum Cafeteria: Open Tuesday from 9:30 to 10:30 (continental breakfast), from 11:00 to 4:30, and from 5:00 to 8:00; Wednesday through Sunday from 9:30 to 10:30 (continental breakfast) and from 11:00 to 4:30.

Museum Restaurant with Waiter Service: Open Tuesday from 11:30 to 8:00; Wednesday through Sunday from 11:30 to 3:30. For reservations, call 570–3964.

Museum Bar: Open Tuesday from 11:30 to 8:00; Wednesday through Sunday from 11:30 to 4:30.

Museum Dining Room with Waiter Service: Open for brunch *only* on Saturday and Sunday from 11:30 to 2:30. For reservations, call 879–5500, ext. 3614.

Museum Shops: Located off the Great Hall, these shops offer a large selection of books, children's publications, postcards, prints, posters, and reproductions of sculpture, jewelry, and other works from the Museum's collections.

Recorded Tours: Recorded tours of the Museum's collections and special exhibitions are available for rent. See the floor plans on pp. 10–14 for locations of Audioguide desks.

Gallery Tours: Tours in English take place daily; tours in Spanish are held weekly. Inquire at the Visitors' Center for schedule, topics, and meeting places.

Concerts and Lectures: For subscription concerts and lectures, call the Concerts and Lectures Office at 570–3949. Open for ticket sales: Tuesday through Friday from 1:00 to 4:00; Saturday and Sunday from 11:00 to 4:00 (closed Saturday and Sunday from June through September). For recorded information, call 744–9120.

Calendar/News: This bimonthly publication lists special exhibitions, lectures, concerts, films, and other activities. It is available at the Information Desk in the Great Hall.

The Cloisters: The Metropolitan Museum's branch for medieval art is located in Fort Tryon Park at the northern tip of Manhattan. Open Tuesday through Sunday (March–October) from 9:30 to 5:15; Tuesday through Sunday (November–February) from 9:30 to 4:45. Closed every Monday and January 1, Thanksgiving Day, and December 25. Tours for individual visitors are offered several times a week. Reservations for all group visits must be made in advance. For information, call 923–3700.

GROUND FLOOR

Key to Maps

Information	Men's Room	Telephone
Elevator	Women's Room	Smoking
Escalator	Handicapped	Restaurant
Coat Check	Audioguides	Bicycles

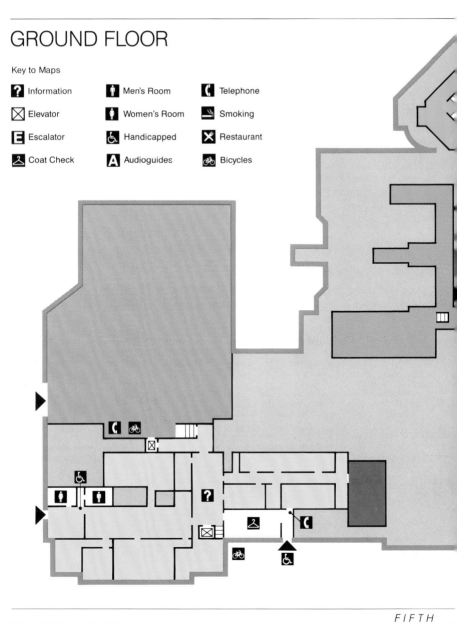

FIFTH

COSTUME INSTITUTE
including The Irene Lewisohn Costume
Reference Library

RUTH AND HAROLD D. URIS
CENTER FOR EDUCATION

EUROPEAN SCULPTURE AND
DECORATIVE ARTS

THE PHOTOGRAPH AND
SLIDE LIBRARY

ROBERT LEHMAN COLLECTION

GARAGE

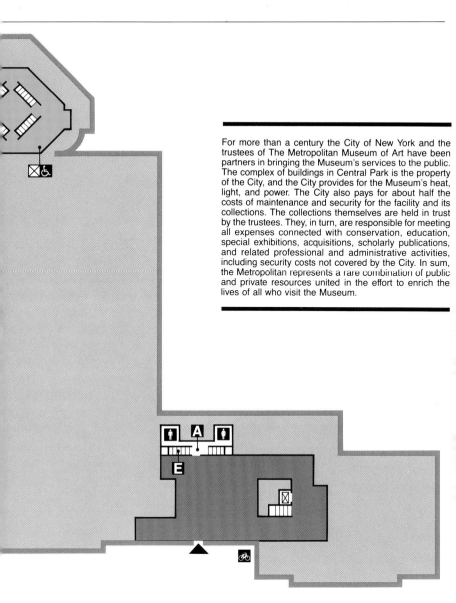

For more than a century the City of New York and the trustees of The Metropolitan Museum of Art have been partners in bringing the Museum's services to the public. The complex of buildings in Central Park is the property of the City, and the City provides for the Museum's heat, light, and power. The City also pays for about half the costs of maintenance and security for the facility and its collections. The collections themselves are held in trust by the trustees. They, in turn, are responsible for meeting all expenses connected with conservation, education, special exhibitions, acquisitions, scholarly publications, and related professional and administrative activities, including security costs not covered by the City. In sum, the Metropolitan represents a rare combination of public and private resources united in the effort to enrich the lives of all who visit the Museum.

AVENUE

RUTH AND HAROLD D. URIS CENTER FOR EDUCATION

Approximately one-third of all visitors, some 1.3 million people each year, participate in the many education programs offered by the Museum, such as public lectures, films, gallery talks, school tours, children's classes, and various professional training programs. Information about education services is available in the Uris Center, a large education facility operated by the Division of Education Services. The center features a visitor information area with information on the collections, an orientation theater for continuously shown films on the Museum, an exhibition gallery, a library, and a media center, in addition to classrooms and an auditorium. Also located in the center are offices for the Volunteer Organization and the Division of Education Services, which include the departments of Young Peoples' Programs, High School Programs, Public Education, Community Education, and Academic Affairs.

FIRST FLOOR

FIFTH

THE AMERICAN WING
including James and Margaret Carter Federal Gallery, The Charles Engelhard Court, The Lawrence and Barbara Fleischman Gallery, The Martha and Rebecca Fleischman Pre-Civil-War Decorative Arts Gallery, The George M. and Linda H. Kaufman Galleries, The Richard and Gloria Manney Rooms, The Israel Sack Galleries, and The Erving and Joyce Wolf Gallery

ARMS AND ARMOR
including Bashford Dean Gallery

EGYPTIAN ART
including The Lila Acheson Wallace Galleries of Egyptian Art, The Sackler Gallery for Egyptian Art, and The Sackler Wing

EUROPEAN SCULPTURE AND DECORATIVE ARTS
including Blumenthal Patio, Josephine Mercy Heathcote Gallery, Josephine Bay Paul Gallery, and The Wrightsman Galleries

GREEK AND ROMAN ART

ROBERT LEHMAN COLLECTION

THE JACK AND BELLE LINSKY GALLERIES

MEDIEVAL ART
including The Lawrence A. and Barbara Fleischman Gallery of Late Medieval Secular Art

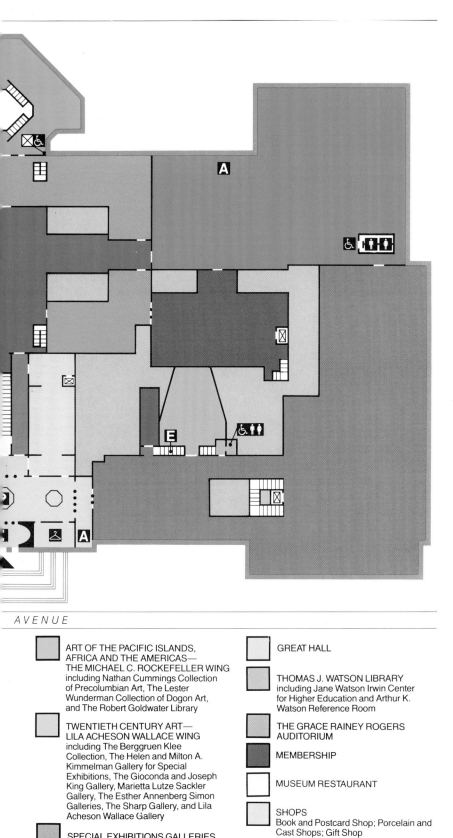

AVENUE

ART OF THE PACIFIC ISLANDS, AFRICA AND THE AMERICAS—THE MICHAEL C. ROCKEFELLER WING including Nathan Cummings Collection of Precolumbian Art, The Lester Wunderman Collection of Dogon Art, and The Robert Goldwater Library

TWENTIETH CENTURY ART—LILA ACHESON WALLACE WING including The Berggruen Klee Collection, The Helen and Milton A. Kimmelman Gallery for Special Exhibitions, The Gioconda and Joseph King Gallery, Marietta Lutze Sackler Gallery, The Esther Annenberg Simon Galleries, The Sharp Gallery, and Lila Acheson Wallace Gallery

SPECIAL EXHIBITIONS GALLERIES

GREAT HALL

THOMAS J. WATSON LIBRARY including Jane Watson Irwin Center for Higher Education and Arthur K. Watson Reference Room

THE GRACE RAINEY ROGERS AUDITORIUM

MEMBERSHIP

MUSEUM RESTAURANT

SHOPS
Book and Postcard Shop; Porcelain and Cast Shops; Gift Shop

SECOND FLOOR

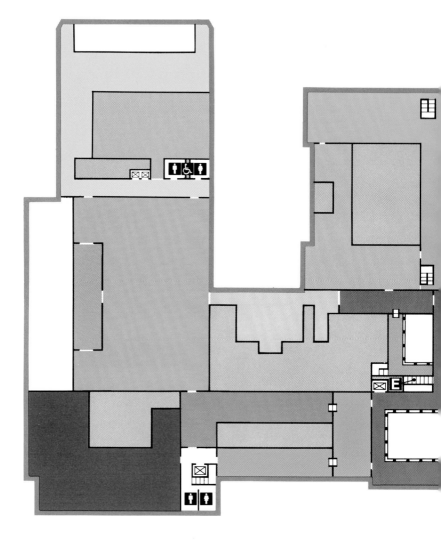

 THE AMERICAN WING
including The Charles Engelhard
Court and The Joan Whitney Payson
Galleries

 ANCIENT NEAR EASTERN ART
including Raymond and Beverly Sackler
Gallery for Assyrian Art

ASIAN ART
including The Astor Court, Douglas
Dillon Galleries, The Arthur Sackler
Gallery, and The Sackler Galleries for
Asian Art

DRAWINGS;
PRINTS AND PHOTOGRAPHS
including The Charles Z. Offin Gallery
and the Print Study Room

 EUROPEAN PAINTINGS
including Benjamin Altman Galleries,
Harry Payne Bingham Galleries, Stephen C.
Clark Galleries, The R. H. Macy Gallery,
The André Meyer Galleries, C. Michael
Paul Gallery, and Dr. Mortimer D. Sackler
and Theresa Sackler Gallery

 EUROPEAN SCULPTURE AND
DECORATIVE ARTS
including Blumenthal Patio balcony and
B. Gerald Cantor Sculpture Galleries

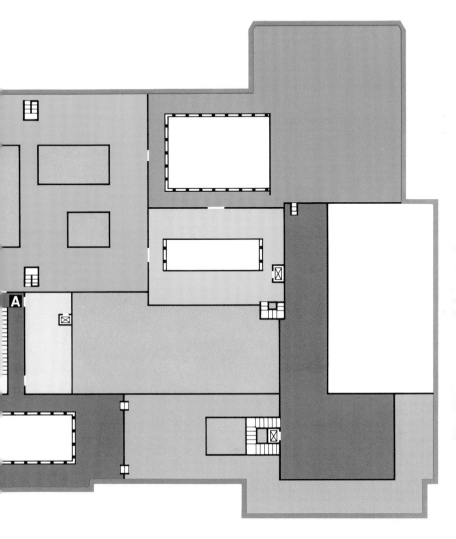

A V E N U E

GREEK AND ROMAN ART

ISLAMIC ART
including The Hagop Kevorkian Fund
Special Exhibitions Gallery

MUSICAL INSTRUMENTS
The André Mertens Galleries
for Musical Instruments

TWENTIETH CENTURY ART—
LILA ACHESON WALLACE WING
including The Iris and B. Gerald Cantor
Roof Garden

ROBERT WOOD JOHNSON JR.
RECENT ACQUISITIONS GALLERY

SPECIAL EXHIBITIONS GALLERIES
including Iris and B. Gerald Cantor
Exhibition Hall

SHOPS
Print and Poster Shop; Children's Book
Shop. The Mezzanine Gallery is located
between the first and second floors.

FIRST FLOOR

SECOND FLOOR

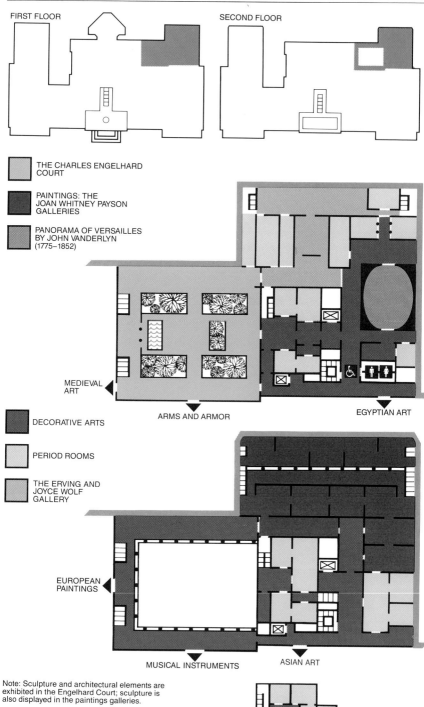

THE CHARLES ENGELHARD COURT

PAINTINGS: THE JOAN WHITNEY PAYSON GALLERIES

PANORAMA OF VERSAILLES BY JOHN VANDERLYN (1775–1852)

MEDIEVAL ART

ARMS AND ARMOR

EGYPTIAN ART

DECORATIVE ARTS

PERIOD ROOMS

THE ERVING AND JOYCE WOLF GALLERY

EUROPEAN PAINTINGS

MUSICAL INSTRUMENTS

ASIAN ART

Note: Sculpture and architectural elements are exhibited in the Engelhard Court; sculpture is also displayed in the paintings galleries.

COURT

Note: These galleries are located above the second floor.

THE AMERICAN WING

From its establishment in 1870, the Museum has acquired important examples of American art. The collection, one of the finest and most comprehensive in existence, is housed in The American Wing and is supervised by the departments of American Paintings and Sculpture, established in 1948, and American Decorative Arts, organized in 1934. Comprehensive in scope and high in quality, the collection of paintings illustrates almost all phases of the history of American art from the late eighteenth to the early twentieth century. The collection of sculpture is equally distinguished and is especially strong in Neoclassical and Beaux-Arts works. (Paintings and sculpture by artists born after 1876, as well as decorative arts created after 1916, are exhibited by the Department of Twentieth Century Art.)

The collection of decorative arts extends from the late seventeenth to the early twentieth century and includes furniture, silver, glass, ceramics, and textiles. Of special interest are the period rooms; when fully installed, twenty-five rooms with original woodwork and furnishings will offer an unequaled view of American art history and domestic life.

1 JOHN SINGLETON COPLEY, 1738–1815
Daniel Crommelin Verplanck
Oil on canvas; 49½ × 40 in. (125.7 × 101.6 cm.)

Copley was America's foremost painter of the eighteenth century. This portrait of Daniel Verplanck, painted in 1771 when the subject was nine years old, represents Copley at the height of his power. Daniel holds a pet squirrel on a golden leash, a motif that the artist used several times in portraits of young people. The picturesque landscape has traditionally been called a view from the Verplanck country estate at Fishkill, New York, looking toward Mount Gulian. *Gift of Bayard Verplanck, 1949, 49.12*

3 RALPH EARL, 1751–1801
Elijah Boardman
Oil on canvas; 83 × 51 in. (210.9 × 129.6 cm.)

Boardman is pictured in a room of the dry-goods store he operated with his brother in Connecticut. A door open to an adjoining room reveals shelves holding bolts of plain and printed stuffs. The young merchant stands in front of an unusual piece of furniture, which probably served as a stand-up desk. This portrait, painted in 1789 during the years which are generally regarded as the finest period of Earl's work, blends truth with grace, and it embodies the whole spirit of the age and place in which it was painted. *Bequest of Susan W. Tyler, 1979, 1979.395*

2 RUFUS HATHAWAY, 1770?–1822
Lady with Her Pets
Oil on canvas; 34¼ × 32 in. (87 × 81.3 cm.)

This work, executed in 1790 by Rufus Hathaway, an itinerant Massachusetts artist, is one of the finest American primitive paintings. It exhibits the curious dichotomy characteristic of works of the self-taught: a naive, all-inclusive narrative element combined with an almost abstract use of line, color, and pattern in a sophisticated composition. The reduction of drapery folds to linear, rhythmical designs reaffirms the work's two-dimensional, decorative quality. The painting shows an allover crackle, or alligatoring, the result of an improper combination of materials. *Gift of Edgar William and Bernice Chrysler Garbisch, 1963, 63.201.1*

4   MATTHEW PRATT, 1734–1805
The American School
Oil on canvas; 36 × 50¼ in. (91.4 × 127.6 cm.)

One of the great documents of colonial painting, *The American School* was done by Pratt in 1765, when he was in London studying with his countryman Benjamin West. Subdued in color, hard in finish, painstakingly drawn, and somewhat awkwardly composed, it is a rare attempt by an American at the informal group portrait, or "conversation piece," a staple of eighteenth-century English painting. The painting represents a group of young American artists working in West's studio under the direct supervision of the master, who stands, palette in hand, criticizing work by a young man who is probably Pratt. The picture speaks eloquently of the youthful eagerness of Pratt and his companions as they listen to West, who taught virtually every major artist of the fledgling United States until his death in 1820. *Gift of Samuel P. Avery, 1897, 97.29.3*

5   JOHN TRUMBULL, 1756–1843
The Sortie Made by the Garrison of Gibraltar
Oil on canvas; 70½ × 106 in. (179.1 × 269.2 cm.)

Trumbull wanted to excel at history painting in the grand manner, to create pictures large in scale and heroic in import. Possibly his most successful work in this manner is *The Sortie Made by the Garrison of Gibraltar,* painted in 1789 when he was in London. It depicts an episode during the three-year siege of the English fortress by French and Spanish forces. In 1781 the British under General Eliott destroyed an entire line of the enemy's counterworks in a nighttime foray. Trumbull chose to dramatize the moment when a gallant Spaniard, Don José Barboza, although mortally wounded, refused British help because that would have meant complete surrender to the enemy. *Purchase, Pauline V. Fullerton Bequest, Mr. and Mrs. James Walter Carter Gift, Mr. and Mrs. Raymond J. Horowitz Gift, Erving Wolf Foundation Gift, Vain and Harry Fish Foundation, Inc. Gift, Gift of Hanson K. Corning, by exchange, and Maria DeWitt Jesup and Morris K. Jesup Funds, 1976, 1976.332*

6 GILBERT STUART, 1755–1828
George Washington
Oil on canvas; 30¼ × 25¼ in. (76.8 × 64.1 cm.)

In Philadelphia in 1795, two years after returning to the United States from Great Britain, Stuart painted his first portrait of George Washington from life. The picture, which established Stuart as the leading American portrait painter of his time, is one of the best-known images in American art. Thirty-nine replicas were commissioned, but few of them have the vitality and immediate quality of this version, which suggests that it must have been painted at least in part from life. The rich, vibrant flesh tones, set off by the green drapery, and the freely expressive brushwork contrast effectively with the simple composition and austere dignity of the subject. Stuart's work had a strong influence on many American portrait painters of the early nineteenth century. *Rogers Fund, 1907, 07.160*

7 GEORGE CALEB BINGHAM, 1811–79
Fur Traders Descending the Missouri
Oil on canvas; 29 × 36½ in. (73.7 × 92.7 cm.)

A unique document of river life in the Midwest, this work is one of the masterpieces of American genre painting. Bingham has raised anecdote to the level of poetic drama by setting up a tension between the suspicious stare of the old trader, the unconcerned reverie of his sprawling son, and the compact, enigmatic silhouette of their pet fox. Parallel planes receding into deep space suggest the artist's familiarity with engravings from classical European paintings, yet the strict formality is softened by the exquisitely luminous atmosphere. Painted about 1845, this work is an early example of Luminism, a meticulous realism concerned with light and atmosphere. *Morris K. Jesup Fund, 1933, 33.61*

8   JAMES PEALE, 1749–1831
Still Life: Balsam Apple and Vegetables
Oil on canvas; 20¼ × 26½ in. (51.4 × 67.3 cm.)

This remarkable still life, probably dating from the 1820s, is a surprising departure from James Peale's usual work in this genre. Instead of the more familiar formal composition of tightly drawn pieces of fruit falling out of a Chinese export porcelain basket, we have here a freely painted, casually arranged assortment of vegetables—okra, blue-green cabbage, crinkly Savoy cabbage, hubbard squash, eggplant, purple-red cabbage, and tomatoes—and a balsam apple. In place of the somber coloring characteristic of his still lifes, Peale used the blonde palette that is often encountered in his portraits. His unusual, rather juicy handling of pigment in this picture seems especially well suited to the richly textured vegetables. *Maria DeWitt Jesup Fund, 1939, 39.52*

9   THOMAS COLE, 1801–1848
View from Mount Holyoke, Northampton, Massachusetts, After a Thunderstorm (The Oxbow)
Oil on canvas; 51½ × 76 in. (130.8 × 193 cm.)

"I would not live where tempests never come, for they bring beauty in their train." So wrote Cole in his diary in 1835, the year before he painted this magnificent panorama of the Connecticut River valley. It is thus not surprising to find that he selected the moment following a cloudburst, when all nature seems freshened, and foliage, still wet, glitters in the crisp light. There is a marvelous wealth of detail —especially in the rocks and vegetation along the foreground promontory. Cole is often called the father of the Hudson River School of landscape painters. *Gift of Mrs. Russell Sage, 1908, 08.228*

10 FREDERIC EDWIN CHURCH, 1826–1900
Heart of the Andes
Oil on canvas; 66½ × 119¼ in. (168.9 × 302.9 cm.)

Church, Thomas Cole's major pupil, headed the second generation of the Hudson River School. He gained fame for his large views of near and distant places. Church's panorama of the Ecuadorian Andes was a sensation when it was exhibited in the artist's studio in New York in 1859. This huge canvas is a dazzling compen-

dium of minutely rendered wildlife, vegetation, and terrain. To heighten the sense of reality, *Heart of the Andes* was exhibited in a darkened gallery, placed in a window-like frame that was flanked by tropical foliage and illuminated by gas jets. After experiencing the total grandeur of the painting, the visitor was given a viewing tube to explore, bit by bit, the marvelously rendered details. *Bequest of Margaret E. Dows, 1909, 09.95*

11 ALBERT BIERSTADT, 1830–1902
The Rocky Mountains, Lander's Peak
Oil on canvas; 73¼ × 120¾ in. (186.1 × 306.7 cm.)

Bierstadt specialized in panoramic depictions of the American West, typified by *The Rocky Mountains,* painted in 1863. The peaceful encampment of Shoshone Indians, bathed in soft morning light, is an Edenic image of the unset-

tled American West. Bierstadt's vision of soaring snowcapped mountains and broad fertile valleys reflects the prevailing belief in manifest destiny—the assumption that divine will paralleled national interest in the country's westward expansion. Bierstadt used sketches and photographs made during trips west to paint finished pictures in his studio. *Rogers Fund, 1907, 07.123*

12 MARTIN JOHNSON HEADE, 1819–1904
The Coming Storm
Oil on canvas; 28 × 44 in. (71.1 × 111.8 cm.)

A preoccupation with the effects of light and atmosphere earned a group of painters the name of Luminists, among them John Frederick Kensett, Fitz Hugh Lane, and Martin Johnson Heade. In *The Coming Storm* (1859) Heade reveals his intense love of nature and light.

Land and sea are hushed before the ominous approaching storm. Isolated figures and a single white sail under the threatening cloud produce an almost surrealistic impression, which is typical of his work. Heade's eerie pictures of sky and water achieve their compelling moody spells with an exciting suffusion of enveloping light. *Gift of Erving Wolf Foundation and Mr. and Mrs. Erving Wolf, 1975, 1975.160*

13 WINSLOW HOMER, 1836–1910
Northeaster
Oil on canvas; 34⅜ × 50¼ in. (87.3 × 127.6 cm.)

Northeaster, painted in 1895, is an outstanding example of the late work of Homer, one of America's indisputable masters. In this painting the thrust of the storm is concentrated in a single heaving wave, and the composition has been simplified to one sweeping diagonal. Two areas of sharp contrast between light and dark heighten the drama, as does the fear generated by the ominous pull of undertow toward the

lower right corner. These effects are made possible by Homer's great breadth and freedom of brushstroke.

Homer produced a series of distinctive images of the sea unparalleled in American art. His commitment to the evidence of his own observations, his development of a direct technique largely unencumbered by the constraints of extensive academic training, and his unconventional, inventive imagery contribute to the originality that distinguishes his work. (See also no. 23.) *Gift of George A. Hearn, 1910, 10.64.5*

14 EMANUEL GOTTLIEB LEUTZE, 1816–68
Washington Crossing the Delaware
Oil on canvas; 149 × 255 in. (378.5 × 647.7 cm.)

Many nineteenth-century painters, sculptors, and novelists created sentimentalized reconstructions of American colonial history. Inaccurate in many historical details, this painting is a conspicuous example of such Romantic imagery. The style is highly representative of a school of Romantic painting that flourished in Düsseldorf, where Leutze was living when he painted this picture in 1851. Worthington Whittredge, one of the American artists present while Leutze was working in Germany, posed for the figures of both Washington and the steersman. *Gift of John S. Kennedy, 1897, 97.34*

16 WILLIAM MICHAEL HARNETT, 1848–92
Still Life—Violin and Music
Oil on canvas; 40 × 30 in. (101.6 × 76.2 cm.)

In this work of 1888, Harnett pushes trompe-l'oeil painting to its limits, presenting objects in a daring range of spatial planes: the sheet music and calling card are shown with edges bent, not flat; the partly open door suggests depth behind it; heavy items are suspended on strings or balanced precariously on nails. Harnett delights in the textures and subdued colors of the old violin and its gleaming strings; in the silver, ivory, and granadilla piccolo; in the metal hinges, horseshoe, hasp, and lock. His technical brilliance and popular subject matter made him the most emulated American still-life painter of his generation. *Wolfe Fund, Catharine Lorillard Wolfe Collection, 1963, 63.85*

15 THOMAS EAKINS, 1844–1916
Max Schmitt in a Single Scull, or
The Champion Single Sculls
Oil on canvas; 32½ × 46¼ in. (82.6 × 117.5 cm.)

In this haunting work, painted in 1871, the artist's passion for sports is suffused with a lyrical response to subtle qualities of light and to the rhythmic placement of forms in deep space. In a serene and spacious setting, provided by the Schuylkill River flowing through Philadelphia's Fairmount Park, Eakins's friend Max Schmitt turns toward us; just beyond, the artist himself pulls away in a shell. Accents in the distance are created by other oarsmen, a train approaching the near bridge, and a steamboat. Most of the details are crystal clear, yet here and there passages are more freely painted, such as the stone house and leafy shore at the left. *Purchase, The Alfred N. Punnett Endowment Fund and George D. Pratt Gift, 1934, 34.92*

17   JOHN SINGER SARGENT, 1856–1925
Madame X (Madame Pierre Gautreau)
*Oil on canvas; 82⅛ × 43¼ in. (208.6 ×
109.9 cm.)*

Mme Gautreau, born Judith Avegno in New
Orleans, married a French banker and became
one of Paris's notorious beauties during the
1880s. Sargent probably met her in 1881, and
impressed by her charm and theatrical use of
heavy lavender makeup, he determined to paint
her. Work began the following year but was
attended by delays and numerous reworkings
of the canvas. The picture was shown at the
1884 Paris Salon with the title *Portrait de
Mme . . . ,* to avoid the indelicacy of mentioning
the sitter's name. It was given a scathing reception by reviewers critical of the character of
Mme Gautreau, the lavender coloring of her
skin, and the impropriety of her dress, with its
revealing décolletage and slipped strap which
bared her right shoulder (this strap was later
painted over).

The portrait lacks the bravura brushwork of
many of Sargent's major paintings, partly because of the many reworkings, but the elegant
pose and outline of the figure, recalling his debt
to Velázquez, make it one of his most striking
canvases. When he sold it to the Museum in
1916, Sargent wrote, "I suppose it is the best
thing I have done." *Purchase, Arthur Hoppock
Hearn Fund, 1916, 16.53*

18   MARY CASSATT, 1844–1926
Lady at the Tea Table
Oil on canvas; 29 × 24 in. (73.7 × 61 cm.)

Cassatt was the only American artist who became an established member of the Impressionist group in Paris. In this painting of 1885 she
places the imposing figure in an ambiguous
setting where foreground and background—
virtually the same color—nearly merge. This
departure from traditional spatial relationships
shows Cassatt's debt to Degas and Manet and
her growing awareness of Japanese prints in
the early 1880s. The picture is enlivened by
the blue-and-gold Canton tea set and the fluid
brushwork of the delicate lace near the sensitively portrayed face. In Cassatt's well-
constructed design, the sitter is framed in a
series of rectangles, which increase in intensity as they diminish in size. *Gift of Mary
Cassatt, 1923, 23.101*

19 JAMES MCNEILL WHISTLER, 1834–1903
**Arrangement in Flesh Colour and Black:
Portrait of Théodore Duret**
Oil on canvas; 76⅛ × 35¾ in. (193.4 × 90.8 cm.)

This painting, of about 1883, demonstrates
Whistler's use of portraiture as a vehicle for the
investigation of formal problems of design and
color. It also reflects his preoccupation with
subtle color effects. Into a palette of white, gray,
and black he introduced color only in the flesh,
pink domino, and stylized butterfly (his signature).
The dark, full-length figure on a neutral ground
has precedents in the works of Velázquez and
Courbet. The reduction of content to the most
essential and expressive forms, the subtle asymmetrical placement of the figure, the strong
silhouette, and the monogram itself show
Whistler's interest in Japanese art. These characteristics of his style made Whistler one of the
most avant-garde and controversial painters of
the nineteenth century. *Wolfe Fund, Catharine
Lorillard Wolfe Collection, 1913, 13.20*

20 JOHN H. TWACHTMAN, 1853–1902
Arques-la-Bataille
Oil on canvas; 60 × 78⅞ in. (152.4 × 200.3 cm.)

Twachtman was an influential member of the
American Impressionist group popularly called
"The Ten." This work, painted in Paris in 1885,
pictures a river scene near Dieppe on the Normandy coast in a subtle orchestration of subdued colors. Its restricted palette (delicate grays,
greens, and blues), thinly and broadly applied
paint, subtle tonal transitions, and strong calligraphic motifs reflect the influences of French
Impressionism, Japanese art, and Whistler's
tonal studies. This work stands today as one of
the masterpieces of nineteenth-century American painting. *Morris K. Jesup Fund, 1968, 68.52*

21 WILLIAM MERRITT CHASE, 1849–1916
For the Little One
Oil on canvas; 40 × 35¼ in. (101.6 × 89.5 cm.)

This peaceful scene (ca. 1895) shows Chase's wife sewing in their Long Island home. Sunlight through the window caresses the folds of her white dress and pink blouse and enlivens wood surfaces. Ignoring detail, Chase revels in the fluidity of his pigments, in texture and contour. His composition, arranged on a diagonal, relegates the figure and furniture to the middle ground, leaving the foreground bare except for a white scrap. An American Impressionist, Chase executed many superb oils but few equal this one in intimacy, glowing light, and fresh composition. *Amelia B. Lazarus Fund, by exchange, 1917, 13.90*

WATERCOLORS

22 WILLIAM GUY WALL, 1792–after 1864
New York from Heights near Brooklyn
Watercolor with white on paper; 16 × 25½ in. (40.6 × 64.8 cm.)

A native of Dublin, Wall arrived in the United States in 1818. During the 1820s the publication of a series of aquatints from twenty of his watercolors in the *Hudson River Portfolio* established his reputation and satisfied a growing demand for representations of American scenery. This work was published as an aquatint in 1823. It shows an old windmill once used by a distillery with Brooklyn Heights on the right and Manhattan in the distance. An eloquent example of Wall's skill as a watercolorist, this rare early nineteenth-century view of the city demonstrates his keen sense of light, color, and descriptive detail. *The Edward W. C. Arnold Collection of New York Prints, Maps and Pictures. Bequest of Edward W. C. Arnold, 1954, 54.90.301*

23 WINSLOW HOMER, 1836–1910
Inside the Bar
*Watercolor and pencil on paper; 15⅜ × 28½ in.
(39.1 × 72.4 cm.)*

In 1881 and 1882 Homer spent several months in the English fishing village of Cullercoats rethinking his approach to watercolor. Already a leader in the American watercolor movement, he returned to surprise his New York contemporaries with a technique and content transformed by his exposure to modern British watercolor. Where previously he had studied novel American subjects in a personal and impressionistic manner, his English work showed a more conventional notion of the picturesque, delivered in a monumental and deliberate style. *Inside the Bar* (1883), one of the most powerful of his Cullercoats works, demonstrates the disciplined complexity of Homer's new technique and its heroic concept of the struggle between humans and their environment. *Gift of Louise Ryals Arkell, in memory of her husband, Bartlett Arkell, 1954, 54.183*

24 JOHN SINGER SARGENT, 1856–1925
In the Generalife
*Pencil and watercolor on paper; 14¾ × 17⅞ in.
(37.5 × 45.4 cm.)*

This scene (ca. 1912) depicts Sargent's sister, at the easel, and two companions in the gardens of the Generalife, the former residence of the sultans in Granada, Spain. Sargent vividly demonstrates the versatility of his medium in a technique ranging from transparent washes, with little articulation of form, to well-worked, heavily saturated areas in which vigorous brushstrokes create deep, rich shadows. He achieves brilliant highlights by exposing the white paper and enlivens fluid surfaces with chalky calligraphic lines. Sargent placed his figures in an oblique, close-up view, which seems to draw the spectator into the cool mysterious shadows. *Purchase, Joseph Pulitzer Bequest, 1915, 15.142.8*

25 ERASTUS DOW PALMER, 1817–1904
The White Captive
Marble: h. 66 in. (167.6 cm.)

The Neoclassical style dominated American
sculpture during the second quarter of the nineteenth century, and works in white marble were
especially popular because of the medium's
strong classical associations. Although the Neoclassical spirit is evident in this graceful life-
size nude, this figure was probably inspired by
tales of the Indians' captives along the colonial
frontier. An upstate New Yorker, Palmer was
self-taught and, unlike most of his contemporaries, did not go abroad to study. He worked
directly from live models; these were often his
daughters, one of whom may have posed for
this statue, which was completed in 1859.
Palmer's first attempt at an undraped figure,
this work is one of the finest nudes produced in
the United States during the nineteenth century.
Bequest of Hamilton Fish, 1894, 94.9.3

26 JOHN QUINCY ADAMS WARD, 1830–1910
The Indian Hunter
Bronze; h. 16 in. (40.6 cm.)

Ward was one of the leading sculptors in the
United States in the second half of the nineteenth century. This statuette, dated 1860, was
modeled from life sketches made in the Dakotas,
where Ward had gone to study the Indians. A
few years later he made an enlarged version of
The Indian Hunter, which is in New York's
Central Park. Ward's work marked the beginning of a half century in which naturalism dominated American sculpture. *Morris K. Jesup Fund,
1973, 1973.257*

27   AUGUSTUS SAINT-GAUDENS, 1848–1907
Victory
Gilded bronze; h. 41¾ in. (106 cm.)

One of the foremost nineteenth-century American sculptors, Saint-Gaudens was among the first generation of artists from the United States to study in Paris at the École des Beaux-Arts, the official French academy. This figure derives from his bronze equestrian statue of General William Tecumseh Sherman, which was placed at the southeast corner of Central Park in New York in 1903. With her right arm outstretched, she leads the mounted general forward. In her left hand she holds a laurel branch, the symbol of honor. This reduced Victory is a brilliant reminder of the Sherman monument, which was also gilded. *Rogers Fund, 1917, 17.90.1*

28   DANIEL CHESTER FRENCH, 1850–1931
The Melvin Memorial
Marble; h. 146 in. (345.4 cm.)

French's finest funerary monument, *The Melvin Memorial* commemorates three brothers who died while serving in the Union army during the Civil War. The original marble of 1908 is located in Sleepy Hollow Cemetery, Concord, Massachusetts; the Museum's replica was made in 1915. French enjoyed a long and illustrious career. In 1874 he had executed the bronze *Minute Man,* also in Concord, which won him immediate fame; forty-eight years later he created the statue of Abraham Lincoln for that president's memorial in Washington, D.C.

The Melvin Memorial, also known as *Mourning Victory,* projects the duality of melancholy (the downcast eyes and somber expression) and triumph (the laurel hold high). In this moving work French has captured the sense of calm after the storm of battle. *Gift of James C. Melvin, 1912, 15.75*

29 FREDERIC REMINGTON, 1861–1909
The Mountain Man
Bronze; h. 28 in. (71.1 cm.)

The Mountain Man is one of four statuettes purchased directly by the Museum from Remington in 1907. It was described by the artist as "one of these old Iriquois [*sic*] Trappers who followed the Fur Companies in the Rocky Mountains in the '30 and '40ties." Encumbered with all his equipment—bear traps, ax, bedroll, and rifle—the mountain man guides his horse down a precariously steep path. Remington has masterfully captured the breathless moment of descent. *Rogers Fund, 1907, 07.79*

30 FREDERICK WILLIAM MACMONNIES,
1863–1937
Bacchante and Infant Faun
Bronze; h. 83 in. (210.8 cm.)

The *Bacchante* of MacMonnies epitomizes the jubilance of the Beaux-Arts style of sculpture. Her spiraling form, joyous mouth, and richly textured surfaces help to create a most gleeful image. MacMonnies gave the statue to the architect Charles McKim, who placed it in the courtyard of the Boston Public Library, designed by his firm. After protests against the figure's "drunken indecency," the sculpture was removed. McKim then presented it to the Museum. *Gift of Charles Follen McKim, 1897, 97.19*

1 Chest
Ipswich, Massachusetts, 1660–80
Red and white oak; 29³/₄ × 49¹/₈ × 21³/₈ in.
(75.6 × 124.8 × 72.1 cm.)

The richest and most vigorous early colonial carving is that associated with the work of William Searle (1634–67) and Thomas Dennis (d. 1706) of Ipswich. Paired leaves, with a naturalistic, three-dimensional quality rare in American furniture of the period, dominate the panels of this chest; the panels are carved in the popular seventeenth-century design of a stalk of flowers and leaves emerging from an urn, of which only the opening is indicated here. Varied geometric and plant forms appear on the stiles and rails. Searle and Dennis came from Devonshire, England, where a tradition of florid carving, using many of the motifs seen on this chest, flourished in the early seventeenth century. *Gift of Mrs. Russell Sage, 1909, 10.125.685*

3 High Chest of Drawers
Probably New York, 1700–1730
Walnut veneer, maple and cedar banding,
maple, and walnut; 65 × 37¹/₂ × 22 in.
(165.1 × 95.3 × 55.9 cm.)

The William and Mary style, introduced into the colonies in the 1690s, remained the ruling fashion until the 1730s. Among the new forms that became popular during this period was the high chest which replaced the cupboard as the most important piece of case furniture in the household. The early eighteenth-century high chest, raised up on six boldly turned legs, featured trim lines and large smooth surfaces decorated with figured veneers. Chests of known New York origin have a pulvinated drawer under the cornice and three drawers in the top tier, as seen in this example, rather than two. Also characteristic of New York workmanship is the prominent banding that visually divides each drawer into smaller units. *Gift of Mrs. J. Insley Blair, 1950, 50.228.2*

2 CORNELIUS KIERSTEDE, New York, 1675–1757
Two-Handled Bowl, ca. 1700–1710
Silver; h. 5³/₈ in. (13.7 cm.), diam. 10 in.
(25.4 cm.)

A uniquely New York form, this lavishly decorated six-lobed bowl attests to the skill of the city's early silversmiths and the luxurious taste of its prosperous burghers. It was made by Cornelius Kierstede, an outstanding early New York craftsman of Dutch descent. Following Dutch custom, the bowl was most likely filled with a drink of brandy and raisins and passed to guests, who helped themselves with silver spoons. It combines the horizontal shape, caryatid handles, stamped baseband, and naturalistic flowers of the late seventeenth century with the strong, repetitive Baroque rhythms and extravagant ornament of the William and Mary style. *Samuel D. Lee Fund, 1938, 38.63*

4   Room from the Hewlett House
Woodbury, New York, 1740–60
*h. 9 ft. (2.78 m.), l. 17½ ft. (5.33 m.),
w. 14 ft. (4.27 m.)*

The woodwork of this room, painted a bright blue based on traces of the original color, came from a Long Island farmhouse. The wall opposite the door is fully paneled and contains the fireplace and a shell-carved cupboard. In the mid-Atlantic colonies, where the furniture shown in this room was made, English styles mingled with those from other European countries during the seventeenth and early eighteenth centuries. The painted cupboard, or kas, in the corner, which was made about 1690–1720, came from the Hewlett family for whom the house was built. Cupboards of this form and with this distinctive grisaille decoration of heavy fruit and foliage are found exclusively in the areas of New York and New Jersey settled by the Dutch, who carried on a tradition of painting designs on furniture to simulate carving. *Gift of Mrs. Robert W. de Forest, 1910, 10.83*

5   Armchair
Philadelphia, 1740–60
Walnut; 41 × 32 × 18½ in. (135.1 × 81.3 × 47 cm.)

The Queen Anne style, characterized by continuous flowing curves, became popular in the colonies during the second quarter of the eighteenth century. Boston, Newport, New York, and Philadelphia developed distinctive interpretations of this style, but its purest and most elegant renditions are in the seating furniture of Philadelphia. This stately Queen Anne armchair, made inviting by the broad, ample seat and the outsplayed arms with crisply scrolled armrests, is a symphony of curves. It perfectly exemplifies William Hogarth's famous description of the serpentine curve as the "line of beauty." *Rogers Fund, 1925, 25.115.36*

6 High Chest of Drawers
Philadelphia, 1762–90
*Mahogany, mahogany veneer; 91½ ×
46¾ × 24¼ in. (232.4 × 118.7 × 62.2 cm.)*

This high chest, an unsurpassed example of
the Philadelphia Chippendale style, is popularly
known as the "Pompadour," owing to the fanciful
idea that the finial bust represents Louis XV's
mistress Madame de Pompadour. Although the
basic form of double chest on high cabriole legs
is a distinctively American innovation, the pediment and carving are drawn from English pattern books. The representation on the large
bottom drawer of two swans and a serpent
spewing water is taken directly from Thomas
Johnson's *New Book of Ornament* (1762). The
entire top of the piece—the continuous cornice
with scroll pediment above—is adapted from a
secretary desk in Thomas Chippendale's
Gentleman and Cabinet Maker's Director (1754);
the urn finials flanking the pediment are reduced versions of one on a bookcase also in
the *Director*. This chest of drawers is unequaled
among American pieces in its perfect proportions and masterful execution. *John Stewart
Kennedy Fund, 1918, 18.110.4*

7 JOSEPH SMITH POTTERY, Wrightstown,
Bucks County, Pennsylvania
Tea Canister, ca. 1769
Earthenware; h. 7½ in. (19 cm.)

This tea canister, one of the earliest examples
of American pottery known, is a departure from
the decorative red earthenware typical of
Pennsylvania-Germans. Although decorated in
the German sgraffito manner, whereby a design was scratched through the cream-colored
slip, or outer coating, to expose the red body
beneath, it reflects Joseph Smith's English heritage in both its function and decorative motifs.
The tea canister, or caddy, was part of the
fashionable tea equipage, which was usually
made of fine English pottery or porcelain. This
canister represents an attempt by the potter to
emulate an elegant, high-style form, specifically
that of the English salt-glazed stoneware tea
caddy of the 1740s and 1750s. *Purchase, Peter
H. B. Frelinghuysen and Anonymous Gifts, and
Friends of the American Wing Fund, 1981,
1981.46*

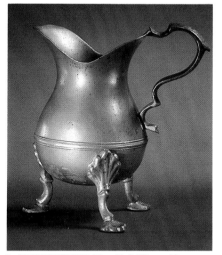

8 PETER YOUNG, New York City or Albany,
New York, act. 1775–95
Creamer
Pewter; h. 4½ in. (11.4 cm.)

This diminutive pewter pitcher, or creamer, has
a robustness of form and an elegance and
assurance of line that were seldom equaled in
larger vessels. It is stamped PY in a serrated
rectangle, the mark of Peter Young, one of the
most gifted of American pewterers.

Pewter, which was widely used for eating and
drinking utensils in colonial America, is about
90 percent tin with copper or bismuth added for
hardness. It was cast in brass molds and then
scraped by hand or skimmed on a lathe. Since
the molds were very costly, pewterers continued
to use them long after their shapes went out of
fashion. Thus it is not surprising that, in the last
quarter of the eighteenth century, Young was
producing these masterful creamers (half a
dozen are known) whose baluster shape and
cabriole legs with shell feet stylistically match
silver creamers made in the Queen Anne style
in the 1750s. *Purchase, Anonymous Gift, 1981,
1981.117*

9 NEW BREMEN GLASS MANUFACTORY,
Frederick County, Maryland, 1784–95
Covered Goblet, 1788
Glass; h. with cover 11¼ in. (28.6 cm.)

This goblet, or pokal, is dated 1788 and is engraved with the arms of Bremen, Germany. It was very likely presented by John Frederick Amelung (fl. 1784–95) to merchants from Germany who had invested in his glassworks at New Bremen, Maryland. Typical of Amelung's glass is the superb engraving, the inverted baluster stem, and the domed foot with plain rim. In style, the goblet looks back to the Baroque and Rococo rather than to the newly popular Neoclassical taste. *Rogers Fund, 1928, 28.52*

10   Room from the Williams House
Richmond, Virginia, 1810
h. 13 ft. (3.96 m.), l. 19 ft. 10 in. (6.05 m.), w. 19 ft. 6 in. (5.94 m.)

This parlor is from the William C. Williams house in Richmond. The influence of the French Empire style is evident in the massive proportions of the doorways, the palmettes decorating their friezes, the simple but heavy moldings, and the inclusion of a paneled dado. Highly unusual, but in tune with this aesthetic, is the use of somber mahogany woodwork and of King of Prussia marble for the baseboard. The woodwork is signed "Theo. Nash, Executor," presumably the joiner. The walls are covered with facsimiles of a colorful French scenic wallpaper—a popular embellishment of Federal American homes from New England to Virginia. Published in 1814 by the Dufour firm of Paris, this paper celebrates the monuments of Paris. The room displays furniture by the two most prominent New York cabinetmakers of the period, Duncan Phyfe (1768–1854) and Charles Honoré Lannuier (1779–1819). *Gift of Joe Kindig, Jr., 1968, 68.137*

11   Desk and Bookcase
Baltimore, ca. 1811
*Mahogany, satinwood, églomisé; 91 × 72 ×
19⅛ in. (231.1 × 162.9 × 48.6 cm.)*

The design of this large, elaborate, and colorful
combination desk and bookcase was taken
from a plate in Thomas Sheraton's *Cabinet
Dictionary* (1803), where it is termed the "Sister's
Cylinder Bookcase," but it has been artfully and
originally reworked. The inlaid satinwood ovals
and banding and, more conspicuously, the two
flanking panels of glass with Neoclassical painted
decorations are devices associated with Baltimore Federal furniture. A pencil inscription on
the bottom of one drawer reads "M Oliver
Married the 5 of October 1811 Baltimore." *Gift
of Mrs. Russell Sage and various other donors,
by exchange, 1969, 69.203*

12   JOSEPH B. BARRY (act. 1794–d. 1838)
AND SON, Philadelphia
Pier Table, 1810–15
*Mahogany, satinwood, amboyna, gilt brass;
38⅝ × 54 × 23¾ in. (98.1 × 137.2 × 60.3 cm.)*

The pier table was made for the Philadelphia
merchant Louis Clapier by one of Philadelphia's greatest Federal period cabinetmakers,
Joseph B. Barry and Son. The total design of this
extraordinarily rich table is a unique American
interpretation of classical taste that demonstrates the cabinetmaker's training in the English
Neoclassical mode and the distinct influence of
the French Directoire and Empire styles. The
carved and pierced griffin panel is based on
Thomas Sheraton's "Ornament for a Frieze or
Tablet," from his *Drawing-Book* (1793). *Pur-
chase, Friends of the American Wing Fund,
Anonymous Gift, George M. Kaufman Gift,
Sansbury-Mills Fund, and Gift of Mrs. Russell
Sage, Gift of the Members of the Committee of
the Bertha King Benkard Memorial Fund, John
Stewart Kennedy Fund, Bequest of Martha S.
Tiedeman, Gift of Mrs. Frederick Wildman,
F. Ethel Wickham, Edgar William and Bernice
Chrysler Garbisch, and Mrs. F. M. Townsend
and Bequest of W. Gedney Beatty, by exchange,
1976, 1976.324*

13   FLETCHER & GARDINER, Philadelphia,
1808–ca. 1827
Presentation Vase, 1824
Silver; 23½ × 20½ in. (59.7 × 52.1 cm.)

Thomas Fletcher and Sidney Gardiner, who
produced this magnificent vase, were the foremost designers and makers of the large presentation pieces that became an important form in
late Federal silver. This vase is one of a pair
presented in 1825 to DeWitt Clinton, the governor of New York, by a group of New York City
merchants for his role in the building of the Erie
Canal. The shape of the vessel and the vine
handles which continue into a grape border are
based directly on a classical model; the decoration combines American motifs such as the
eagle finial with ornament derived from antique
sources. On the front, Mercury (commerce) and
Ceres (agriculture) flank a view of the canal at
Albany; another canal scene appears on the
back of the vase. *Purchase, Louis V. Bell and
Rogers Funds; Anonymous and Robert G. Goelet
Gifts; and Gifts of Fenton L. B. Brown and of the
grandchildren of Mrs. Ranson Spaford Hooker,
in her memory, by exchange, 1982, 1982.4*

14 THE AMERICAN CHAIR COMPANY, Troy,
New York, 1829–58
Centripetal Spring Chair, ca. 1849
*Cast iron, wood, upholstery; 31⅛ × 17¾ in.
(79.1 × 45.1 cm.)*

Innovations in design, materials, and function,
all characteristics of nineteenth-century furniture,
are nowhere better illustrated than in this cast-
iron and upholstered centripetal spring chair.
The prototype of twentieth-century desk chairs
that revolve and tilt to facilitate movement and
give maximum comfort, it was manufactured
after the designs of Thomas Warren, who first
patented its central spring in 1849. *Gift of Elinor
Merrell, 1977, 1977.255*

15 Tête-à-tête
New York, 1850s
*Rosewood; 44½ × 52 × 43 in. (101.3 × 132.1 ×
109.2 cm.)*

The Victorian love of innovation resulted in a
number of new furniture forms, among them the
tête-à-tête, or love seat. This Rococo Revival
example in laminated rosewood was made in
New York, possibly in the factory of John Henry
Belter (1804–1863). Bold S- and C-scrolls outline the backs and form the seat rail and cabriole legs; the decoration is carved flowers, leaves,
vines, acorns, and grapes. The sinuous shape
illustrates the importance of lamination and
bending. This piece has eight layers; the wood
was pressed in steam molds to achieve its
curves. *Gift of Mrs. Charles Reginald Leonard,
in memory of Edgar Welch Leonard, Robert
Jarvis Leonard, and Charles Reginald Leonard,
1957, 57.130.7*

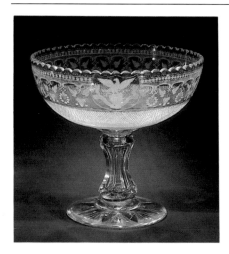

16 GREENPOINT FLINT GLASS WORKS,
Brooklyn, New York, 1852–63
Compote, ca. 1861
Glass; h. 7½ in. (19.1 cm.)

This elegantly designed compote shows the
restraint and predilection for engraving and
shallow cutting typical of fine glassware of the
1860s. It bears the United States coat of arms
in the center of an engraved border of leaves,
scrolls, and flowers. The compote was part of
the state service ordered by President and Mrs.
Lincoln for the White House from Christian
Dorflinger (1828–1915), the French émigré who
established his first Brooklyn glass factory in
1852. *Gift of Kathryn Hait Dorflinger Manchee,
1972, 1972.232.1*

17   ALEXANDER ROUX, New York, act.
1837–81
Cabinet, ca. 1866
*Rosewood, ebony, porcelain, gilt bronze;
53⅜ × 73⅜ × 18⅜ in. (135.6 × 186.4 ×
46.7 cm.)*

The Renaissance Revival of the mid-1860s was
often characterized by the eclectic combination
of historical styles. In this cabinet, labeled by
the maker, Louis XVI ornament has been joined
to a Renaissance Revival form. In the Louis XVI
manner are the ormolu moldings and mounts,
metal plaque with a classical figure, painted
porcelain plaques on the doors, and marquetry.
The heavy form, however, is typical of the Renaissance Revival, as are the architectural qualities:
three pseudo-Ionic pilasters across the front,
extensive paneling through use of moldings
and contrasting woods, and an unusual flat
pediment. *Purchase, The Edgar J. Kaufmann
Foundation Gift, 1968, 68.100.1*

18   HERTER BROTHERS, New York
Wardrobe, ca. 1880
*Cherry, ebonized and inlaid; 78½ × 49½ ×
26 in. (199.4 × 125.7 × 66 cm.)*

Herter Brothers was one of the most influential
New York interior decorators and furniture-
makers in the second half of the nineteenth
century. Although they were trained on the
Continent, Christian and Gustav Herter were
influenced by English reformers such as William Burges and Richard Norman Shaw who at
midcentury rebelled against the exuberant historical revival furniture styles and advocated designs that featured rectilinear shapes and flat
surface decoration. This wardrobe, part of a
bedroom suite made for Jay Gould, is deceptively simple in its straight lines and sparse
ornament but is actually a studied composition.
The "Japonaise" marquetry gives movement to
the static rectangle. The thoughtful relating of
ornament to structure, with emphasis on blank
space, shows the new vision of reform furniture,
of which this is the finest example in the Japanese taste. *Gift of Kenneth O. Smith, 1969,
69.140*

19 GORHAM MANUFACTURING COMPANY,
Providence, Rhode Island, 1865–1961
Ewer with Plateau, 1901–1905
*Silver; h. with plateau 21½ in. (54.6 cm.),
diam. of plateau 17⅛ in. (43.5 cm.)*

Martelé was a term applied to a line of art silver
introduced by Gorham and considered the
finest expression of the Art Nouveau style in
the United States. This ewer is a particularly
successful example of Martelé silver, hand-
hammered into undulating forms and decorated
with swirling repoussé waves, plants, and
female figures. *Gift of Mr. and Mrs. Hugh J.
Grant, 1974, 1974.214.26a,b*

20 LOUIS COMFORT TIFFANY, New York,
1848–1933
Favrile Glass Bottle and Vases
*Blown glass; h. (left to right) 2⅞ in. (7.3 cm.),
15½ in. (39.4 cm.), 18¹¹⁄₁₆ in. (47.5 cm.), 4¹⁄₁₆ in.
(10.4 cm.)*

Louis Comfort Tiffany, America's leading designer in the Art Nouveau style, gained international renown for his work in glass. The son of
Charles L. Tiffany, founder of the well-known
New York silver store, he studied landscape
painting and then pursued a career in the decorative arts. In 1893, after working with stained
glass for almost fifteen years, Tiffany began to
experiment with free-blown glass at his Corona,
New York, furnaces. Rejecting mechanical production in favor of quality handcrafting, he named
his pieces "Favrile," a variant of the Old English
fabrile (of the craftsman). Natural forms pre-
dominate in Favrile glass—willowy flower-form
vases, leafy designs embedded in glass, peacock feathers captured in gleaming color. Also
noteworthy is the iridescent surface, which imitates that found on long-buried ancient glass.
*Gift of H. O. Havemeyer, 1896, 96.17.46; Gift
of Louis Comfort Tiffany Foundation, 1951,
51.121.17; Anonymous Gift, 1955, 55.213.11, 27*

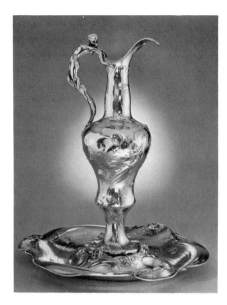

21 GRUEBY FAIENCE COMPANY, Boston, ▶
1894–1911
Vase, 1899–1910
*Earthenware; h. 11 in. (27.9 cm.), diam. 6 in.
(15.2 cm.)*

Art pottery (a term that loosely refers to ceramics made with aesthetic intent and respect for
the handcrafted object) was produced from
about 1875 to the 1920s by commercial enter-
prises throughout the United States. Much of
the Grueby Company's art pottery seems to
have been influenced by Egyptian forms, and
this yellow vase, with its small scrolls and flat
leaves, is typical in that respect. Typical too
is the mat glaze which William Grueby
(1867–1925) developed in the late 1890s.
*Purchase, The Edgar J. Kaufmann Foundation
Gift, 1969, 69.91.2*

22   FRANK LLOYD WRIGHT, 1867–1959
Living Room from the Little House, Wayzata,
Minnesota, 1912–15
*h. 13 ft. 8 in. (4.17 m.), l. 46 ft. (14 m.), w. 28 ft.
(8.53 m.)*

The living room of the Little house is an extension of Wright's earlier Prairie Style houses,
where he first developed his concept of total
design for his interiors. Characteristically, the
room has a strong architectural quality in its
finishes and furnishings. A wonderful harmony
is achieved in the combination of the ocher
plaster walls, the natural oak flooring and trim,
the reddish-brown bricks of the fireplace (a
repetition of the exterior brickwork), and the
electroplated copper finish of the leaded
windows. The bold forms of the oak furniture
were conceived as an integral part of the
composition, and the arrangement of the furniture reflects Wright's architectural bent. The
center of the room is empty with groupings to
the side; chairs and tables are arranged in
pinwheels to enliven the space. Many of the
accessories are original to the room, and others have been duplicated from period photographs. The use of Japanese prints and natural
flower arrangements are characteristic Wright
touches. *Purchase, Emily C. Chadbourne
Bequest, 1972, 1972.60.1*

SECOND FLOOR

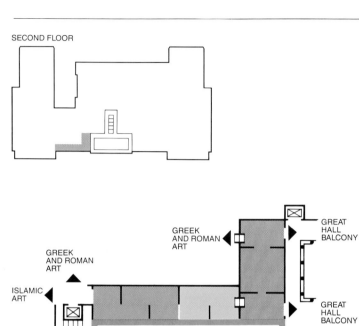

GREEK
AND ROMAN
ART

GREAT
HALL
BALCONY

GREEK
AND ROMAN
ART

ISLAMIC
ART

GREAT
HALL
BALCONY

RAYMOND AND BEVERLY SACKLER
GALLERY FOR ASSYRIAN ART

MESOPOTAMIAN, SYRIAN,
AND ANATOLIAN ART

IRANIAN, ACHAEMENIAN, PARTHIAN,
AND SASANIAN ART

ANCIENT NEAR EASTERN ART

This department, formed in 1956, covers both a lengthy chronological span and a vast geographical area. The works of art in the collection range in date from the sixth millennium B.C. to the time of the Arab conquest in A.D. 626, almost seven thousand years later. They were created in ancient Mesopotamia, Iran, Syria, Anatolia, and other lands in the region that extends from the Caucasus in the north to the Gulf of Aden in the south and from the westernmost borders of Turkey to the valley of the Indus River in central Pakistan. In the earliest periods the cultures that developed in this area were often isolated from each other; contacts gradually increased, however, and these interconnections can be traced through the material remains.

The department's collection has been acquired by gift, by purchase, and by participation in excavations in the Near East; its strengths include Sumerian stone sculptures, Anatolian ivories, Iranian bronzes, and Achaemenian and Sasanian works in silver and in gold. An extraordinary group of Assyrian reliefs and statues from the palace of Ashurnasirpal II (r. 883–859 B.C.) at Nimrud can be seen in the Raymond and Beverly Sackler Gallery for Assyrian Art.

IRAN

1 Jar
Iranian, ca. 3500 B.C.
Terracotta; h. 20⅞ in. (53 cm.), diam. 19⅛ in. (48.6 cm.)

This ovoid vessel is a masterpiece of the art of early pottery. On the upper two-thirds of the vessel three ibexes, painted dark brown, appear against a buff background. Each ibex is placed in the center of a large panel and is shown in silhouette facing right. The panels are bordered at the top and bottom by several thin bands and at the sides by zones of neatly drawn vertical zigzags framed within thick vertical bands. *Purchase, Joseph Pulitzer Bequest, 1959, 59.52*

2 Bull Holding a Vase
Proto-Elamite, ca. 2900 B.C.
Silver; h. 6⅜ in. (16.2 cm.)

This figurine of a kneeling bull is magnificently sculpted in silver. It is clothed as a human, in a textile decorated with a stepped pattern, and holds a tall, spouted vessel in its outstretched hooves in the posture of a supplicant. We know nothing of the religious rituals of Iran from the beginning of the third millennium B.C. Contemporary Proto-Elamite cylinder seals do, however, show animals in human posture that may be engaged in some kind of ritual activity. *Purchase, Joseph Pulitzer Bequest, 1966, 66.173*

3 Recumbent Mouflon
Mature Harappan(?), second half of 3rd millennium B.C.
Marble; l. 11 in. (28 cm.)

This powerful sculpture represents a mouflon, a wild sheep native to the highland regions of the Near East. The entire body is contained within a single unbroken outline. The horns, ears and tail, and muscles were clearly modeled in relief, although time and secondary use have somewhat softened the contours. Incised lines define the eye and brow and mark the horizontal striations on the horns. This combination of a closed outline with broadly modeled masses and a minimum of incised detail is characteristic of animal sculptures from Harappan-period levels at the site of Mohenjo Daro in the lower reaches of the Indus River. The function of animal sculptures such as this is unknown, but findspots of excavated examples suggest that they were primarily religious objects. It is likely that such images were deposited in sacred places as offerings to ensure an abundance of wild game. *Anonymous gift and Rogers Fund, 1978, 1978.58*

4 Head of a Man with Curled Beard

Elamite, ca. 2200 B.C.
Bronze; h. 13½ in. (34.3 cm.)

Although this life-size head has suffered the
ravages of time, it still represents magnificently
what is almost certainly an important personage,
perhaps a ruler. Although it is said to have been
found in either central or northwestern Iran, it is
usually identified as an Elamite work of art, presumably from the environs of Susa. It is quite
possible that both ideas are correct, because
there is proof that important objects even larger
than this head were moved in ancient times
from their original location to other sites, where
they were subsequently discovered. *Rogers
Fund, 1947, 47.100.80*

5 Cup with Four Gazelles

Iranian, ca. 1000 B.C.
Gold; h. 2½ in. (6.4 cm.)

The tradition of making vessels decorated with
animals whose heads project in relief has a long
history in the Near East, and a number of cups
similar to this one have been excavated in Iran
at Marlik in the north and Susa in the southwest.
On this cup, which is probably from the southwest Caspian region, four gazelles framed by
guilloche bands walk to the left. Their bodies
are in repoussé with finely chased details; the
heads are in the round and were added separately by skillful working of the metal. The horns
and ears were added to the heads. The base of
the cup is decorated with a chased pattern of
seven overlapping six-petaled rosettes against
a dotted background. *Rogers Fund, 1962, 62.84*

6   Plaque with Fantastic Creatures

Iranian, ca. 700 B.C.

Gold; 8⅜ × 10⅜ in. (21.3 × 27 cm.)

This gold plaque was part of a treasure allegedly found in 1947 at Ziwiyeh, in northwestern Iran, the site of a first-millennium hill-fortress. At the time of its discovery, this plaque was cut into three parts. It is thin metal and now consists of five registers (the lowest, sixth register is missing) decorated in repoussé and chasing with fantastic winged beasts—griffins, lions with horns and scorpion tails, human-headed bulls—striding from left and right toward a sacred tree in the center. Between each register and around the plaque's edges are beautifully executed guilloche patterns. This plaque was perhaps sewn on the garment of a wealthy lord. Although it was undoubtedly made in Iran, its style shows the influence of both the Assyrians and the Urarteans, who vied for the domination of northern Iran during the first part of the first millennium B.C. *Rogers Fund, 1962, 62.78.1*

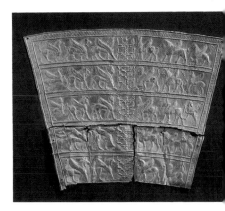

7   Vessel Ending in the Forepart of a Lion

Achaemenian, ca. 6th–5th c. B.C.

Gold; h. 7 in. (17.8 cm.), diam. of rim 5⅜ in. (13.7 cm.)

Horn-shaped vessels or cups, terminating in an animal's head, have a long history in Iran and the Near East as well as in Greece and Italy. In the early first millennium B.C., this type of vessel occurs at Hasanlu in northwestern Iran. These early Iranian examples are straight, having the cup and animal head made in the same plane. Later, in the Achaemenian period, the head or animal protome was often placed at a right angle to the cup, as on this example. The vessel illustrated here was made of a number of pieces; the cup and the lion's body and its legs were made separately and then joined. The animal's tongue, some of its teeth, and the roof of its mouth, which is finely ribbed, were decorative additions. *Fletcher Fund, 1954, 54.3.3*

8   Head of a Horned Animal

Achaemenian, 6th–5th c. B.C.
Bronze; h. 13 ⅜ in. (34 cm.), w. at horns about 9 in. (23 cm.)

The stylization of all forms, human, plant, and animal, is a striking characteristic of the art of the ancient Near East, typified by this head. The patterns for the eyes, brows, horns, beard, and curls are those used again and again by artists of the Achaemenian period. The massive size and weight of this head suggest that it was used to decorate a throne or some part of a royal building. The head was cast in a number of parts, which were joined by fusion welding. This piece is an eloquent example of Iranian art of the Achaemenian period, still untouched by the influence of classical Greece. *Fletcher Fund, 1956, 56.45*

9   Servants Bearing a Wineskin and a Covered Bowl

Achaemenian, Persepolis, 4th c. B.C.
Limestone; 34 × 25½ in. (86.4 × 64.8 cm.)

Achaemenian art and architecture are best exemplified by the vast ruins of Persepolis, the ceremonial capital of the empire under Darius I and his successors. (These ruins lie thirty miles from Shiraz in southwest Iran.) Column capitals were decorated with the foreparts of bulls, lions, and griffins carved in the round. The most characteristic Achaemenian sculptures, however, are stone reliefs such as this fragment from a staircase at Persepolis. The sculptures are essentially symbolic; while detail is exquisitely rendered, the forms and composition tend to be formal and abstract. *Harris Brisbane Dick Fund, 1934, 34.158*

10   Plate with a King Hunting Antelopes

Sasanian, ca. 5th c. A.D.
Silver, niello, mercury gilding; h. 1⅝ in. (4.1 cm.), diam. 8⅝ in. (21.9 cm.)

On this silver plate, alleged to have come from Qazvin in northwestern Iran, a king mounted on horseback is depicted as an archer. The animals are shown in two pairs: one pair alive and running before the king; the other pair dead beneath the horse's hooves. Similar hunting scenes appear on a large number of Sasanian silver vessels. The raised design, which is covered with mercury gilding, consists of a number of separate pieces fitted into lips which have been cut up from the background of the plate. It is impossible to identify the king precisely, but judging from comparisons with the coins of the period, he is either Peroz or Kavad I, both of whom ruled Iran in the second half of the fifth century A.D. This plate is superior in style—notably in the naturalism of the forms and in the delicate modeling of the bodies—to most Sasanian silver objects. *Fletcher Fund, 1934, 34.33*

11 Head of a King
Sasanian, late 4th c. A.D.
Silver; h. 15⅛ in. (38.4 cm.)

The prestige of the Sasanian dynasty, which ruled over northwestern Iran from the third to the mid-seventh century, was so great that its art was widely imitated in the East and the West. Silver-gilt plates and vases decorated with hunting, ritual, and banquet scenes are among the best-known Sasanian works of art (nos. 10 and 12). Magnificent weapons also exist, with handles and scabbards of gold and silver and blades of iron (no. 13).

This powerful head, which may depict the Sasanian king Shapur II (310–379), is raised from a single piece of silver with details chased and in repoussé. A true sculpture in silver, it demonstrates the technical proficiency and aesthetic eloquence of Sasanian metalworkers. *Fletcher Fund, 1965, 65.126*

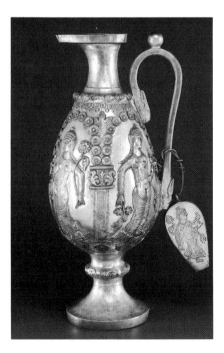

12 Ewer
Sasanian, ca. 6th c. A.D.
Silver, mercury gilding; h. 13⁷⁄₁₆ in. (34.1 cm.)

Late Sasanian silver vessels, particularly bottles and ewers, were often decorated with female figures. Although they suggest the Dionysiac representations of the Roman West, these scenes may relate to the cult of an Iranian deity, perhaps the goddess Anahita, or to Iranian festivals. Sasanian artists frequently used Greco-Roman designs as models for the works of art they created. Here birds peck at fruit and a small panther drinks from a ewer; framed by arcades, the female figures, like maenads, are in a dancing pose and hold branches and flowers. Few ewer lids have survived; this one is decorated with a female figure holding a branch and a bird. The handle terminates at both ends in onager heads. Made in separate parts, this vessel is close in shape to late Roman and Byzantine ewers. *Purchase, Mr. and Mrs. C. Douglas Dillon Gift and Rogers Fund, 1967, 67.10ab*

13 Sword

Iranian, 6th–7th c. A.D.
Iron and gold; l. 39½ in. (100.3 cm.)

This splendid iron sword with gold-covered scabbard and hilt, dating from the sixth or seventh century A.D., is an excellent example of the swords used by the Hunnish nomads who roamed Europe and Asia at that time. It is a type adopted by the Sasanians from these nomads shortly before the beginning of the Islamic era. The sword has a long pommelless grip with two finger rests and a very short quillon bar; its scabbard has a pair of large cufflike mounts with irregularly P-shaped flanges, which are fixtures for the two straps—a short one and a long one—that held the sword suspended from the waist belt. The different lengths of the straps caused the sword to hang at a convenient "quick draw" angle. This way of carrying a sword was particularly practical for a horseman. The gold on the scabbard replaced leather, which was normally used for the sheath. Several other swords of this type are known—some mounted in gold, some in silver. Stylistically and technically, they are all very similar, although the Museum's sword is by far the most elaborate of the group. *Rogers Fund, 1965, 65.28*

14 Standing Male Figure

MESOPOTAMIA

Sumerian, Tell Asmar, ca. 2750–2600 B.C.
White gypsum; h. 11 7/16 in. (29 cm.)

This male figure, which is from the Square Temple at Tell Asmar, illustrates the abstract geometric style of some Sumerian sculpture of the Early Dynastic period. The large head has a dominant triangular nose and prominent eyes made of shell set in bitumen; the one pupil that is preserved is cut from black limestone. Traces of the bitumen that once heavily colored the long hair, mustache, and beard are still to be seen, recalling that the Sumerians referred to themselves as the "black-headed people." In characteristic Sumerian style, the bare-chested male figure is clad in a long skirt. For all its abstraction, or perhaps even because of it, the statuette seems to exude life and power. *Fletcher Fund, 1940, 40.156*

15 Man Carrying a Box on His Head

Sumerian, ca. 2700 B.C.
Bronze; h. 15 in. (38.1 cm.)

Most materials used by Sumerian artists—gold, silver, copper, and fine stone—had to be imported. Despite this limitation, the Sumerians created works of art of high quality. A notable example in metal is this vigorous bronze statuette of a man bearing a heavy burden on his head. This may have been part of a foundation deposit commemorating the construction of a building; however, no other deposit figures closely resemble this unusual piece. *Harris Brisbane Dick Fund, 1955, 55.142*

16 Chaplet of Gold Leaves
Mesopotamian, ca. 2600–2500 B.C.
Gold, lapis lazuli, carnelian; l. 15³/₁₆ in.
(38.5 cm.)

This chaplet is part of an important collection of Sumerian jewelry found in the royal tombs of the Early Dynastic period at the site of Ur, excavated in 1927–28. It came from one of the graves of Queen Pu-abi's handmaidens, who were interred at the same time as the queen. This wreath of gold beech leaves, suspended from strings of little lapis and carnelian beads, encircled the crown of the head. *Dodge Fund, 1933, 33.35.3*

17 Ibex on Stand
Sumerian, ca. 2600 B.C.
Arsenical copper; h. 15¹¹/₁₆ in. (39.8 cm.)

During the Early Dynastic period (2900–2370 B.C.), the Sumerian civilization developed in southern Mesopotamia. Government was based on the city-state unit. Each city had a patron deity, although many other gods were also worshiped; the life of the city was organized around the temple of the patron deity and the palace of the king.

The upper part of this stand, with its four rings, may have been used to support offering bowls. The lower stand, to which the ibex is fastened by tenons, is similar in form to others found in excavations in the region of the Diyala River. *Rogers Fund, 1974, 1974.190*

seal

impression

18 Cylinder Seal
Mesopotamian, late Akkadian period,
2250–2154 B.C.
Green serpentine; h. 1¹/₈ in. (2.8 cm.),
diam. ³/₄ in. (1.8 cm.)

The scene engraved around the edge of this seal shows a spear-bearing hunter grasping a rampant mountain goat by the horn. This lively hunt scene is set in a mountain landscape in which two similar goats are shown, each perched on a towering peak surrounded by high-topped conifers. Above the scene of capture is a two-

line Akkadian inscription in cuneiform, which identifies the owner of this seal as "Balu-ilu, cup bearer."

During the Akkadian period (2334–2154 B.C.) the iconographic repertory of the seal engraver expanded to include a variety of mythological and narrative scenes that were unknown in earlier periods. The artist also rendered images in a realistic style that occasionally includes specific details of landscape, a rare feature in the Near East. *Bequest of W. Gedney Beatty, 1941, 41.160.192*

19   Foundation Figure
Northern Mesopotamian, reportedly Urkish,
ca. 2200 B.C.
Bronze; h. 4⅝ in. (11.7 cm.)

From the northern reaches of the Akkadian
empire comes this bronze foundation figure in
the form of a snarling lion; its forelegs are outstretched to hold an inscribed tablet (now
missing). Although attributed to the Hurrians, a
people whose role in third-millennium Mesopotamia is still obscure, this piece parallels the art of
Akkad in its stirring realism. *Purchase, Joseph
Pulitzer Bequest, 1948, 48.180*

20   Seated Gudea
Neo-Sumerian, ca. 2150 B.C.
Diorite; h. 17⁵⁄₁₆ in. (44 cm.)

Between 2144 and 2004 B.C., under the leadership of the kings of Lagash and the rulers of the
Third Dynasty of Ur, Sumerian culture experi-
enced a renaissance that matched
a revival of Sumerian political power.
During this period, while Gudea and
his son Ur-Ningirsu (no. 21) were
governors of the city-state of Lagash,
many fine works of art were produced, among them this statue of
Gudea.
   This is the only complete statue
of Gudea in the United States, and
it is almost identical to another
now in the Louvre. The Museum's
figure is broken; the perfect join
between the head and body, however, leaves no doubt that they belong together. Gudea sits on a low
chair in a formal attitude of conscious piety, conveyed by the steady
forward gaze of the eyes, the tightly
clasped hands with their very long
fingers, the precisely rendered feet,
and the neatly draped garment. Like
most Gudea statues, it has a cuneiform inscription that names the statue:
"It is of Gudea, the man who built
the temple: may it make his life long."
*Harris Brisbane Dick Fund, 1959,
59.2*

23 Winged Bird-Headed Divinity

Neo-Assyrian, Nimrud, 883–859 B.C.
Limestone, 94 × 66 in. (238.8 × 167.6 cm.)

The kings of the Neo-Assyrian empire ruled over a vast area from the ninth to the seventh century B.C. The heart of the kingdom lay in northern Iraq where the capital cities were located. The first great Assyrian king in this era was Ashur-nasirpal II (r. 883–859 B.C.). His capital was at Nimrud (ancient Kalhu), near modern Mosul, and he undertook a vast building program at that site. The palace rooms were decorated in a new fashion with immense stone reliefs and gate figures. While the door guardians (no. 24) are cut partially in high relief and partially in the round, wall reliefs such as this one, which were originally painted in different colors, are always low and flat. This bird-headed divinity resembles the *apkallu* of Babylonian ritual texts, which carries in its right hand a purifier and in its left hand a ritual cup; the creature protected the house from evil spirits. This relief originally decorated a doorjamb of the palace at Nimrud. *Gift of John D. Rockefeller, Jr., 1932, 32.143.7*

22 Necklace with Pendants

Mesopotamian, 18th–16th c. B.C.
Gold; l. 15¾ in. (40 cm.)

This elaborate gold necklace, allegedly from the region of Babylon, is difficult to date. The extensive use of granulation and the form of the beads as well as the shape of the divine symbols are almost identical to jewelry elements found in a house at the site of Larsa of the Isin Larsa period (nineteenth–eighteenth century B.C.). However, jewelry of similar appearance and technique was in use as late as the mid-second millennium B.C.

The pendants include the lightning fork of the god Adad, the crescent of Sin (the moon-god), and a medallion with rays, perhaps signifying the sun-god, Shamash. Two complete figures represent the goddess Lama, who acted as a mediator between humans and the gods. These goddesses, although minute in size, are carefully delineated. Their flounced robes, horned crowns of divinity, and heavy necklaces with counterweights behind are all depicted in fine detail. *Fletcher Fund, 1947, 47.1a–n*

21 Ur-Ningirsu, Son of Gudea

Neo-Sumerian, ca. 2100 B.C.
Chlorite; h. of head 4½ in. (11.4 cm.), h. of body 18½ in. (46 cm.)

This statue of Ur-Ningirsu, son of Gudea (no. 20), shows the competence of the Neo-Sumerian sculptor. Although this is not a monumental work, it has a sense of great dignity. The scene on the base shows tribute being borne to the ruler by figures wearing distinctive plumed head-dresses. The head of Ur-Ningirsu belongs to the Metropolitan Museum, and the body belongs to the Musée du Louvre. In 1974 they were joined as a result of an unprecedented agreement between the two institutions, and the entire statue is now exhibited at each institution for alternating three-year periods. Head of Ur-Ningirsu: *Rogers Fund, 1947, 47.100.86;* body and base: *lent by Musée du Louvre, Département des Antiquités Orientales (Inv. A. O. 9504), L.1977.23.1*

24 Human-Headed Winged Lion
Neo-Assyrian, Nimrud, 883–859 B.C.
Limestone; h. 122½ in. (311.2 cm.)

In the palace of Ashurnasirpal II (no. 23), pairs of human-headed winged lions and bulls decorated the gateways and supported the arches above them. This lion creature wears the horned cap of divinity and a belt signifying his super-human power. The Neo-Assyrian sculptor gave these guardian figures five legs. Viewed from the front, the animal stands firmly in place; from the side he appears to stride forward. *Gift of John D. Rockefeller, Jr., 1932, 32.143.2*

25 Nubian Tribute Bearer

Neo-Assyrian, Nimrud, 8th c. B.C.
Ivory; h. 5⁵/₁₆ in. (13.5 cm.)

In contrast to the massive stone reliefs and winged animals (nos. 23 and 24), the Museum's other important group of objects from Nimrud consists of carved ivories, delicate in material, size, and execution. This statuette is one of four that may have ornamented a piece of royal furniture. Many of the ivories found at Nimrud were brought there as booty or tribute from vassal states to the west of Assyria, where elephants were native and ivory carving was a long-established craft. This masterpiece may have been sent from Phoenicia as tribute, or it may have been carved in Nimrud by Phoenician craftsmen. The Phoenician ivory-carvers were strongly influenced by Egyptian art, and the Egyptianizing style of this piece has caused it to be associated with Phoenicia. *Rogers Fund, 1960, 60.145.11*

27 Walking Lion

Babylonian, 6th c. B.C.
Glazed brick; 89½ × 38¼ in. (227.3 × 97.2 cm.)

The Assyrian dynasty fell before the combined onslaughts of the Babylonians, Scythians, and Medes in 612 B.C. In the dying days of the empire, Nabopolassar, who had been in Assyrian service, became king in Babylon, and in the reign of his son Nebuchadnezzar the Neo-Babylonian empire reached its peak. During this period an amazing amount of building activity took place in southern Mesopotamia. Babylon became a city of brilliant color through the use of molded glazed bricks—white, blue, red, and yellow—which decorated the gates and buildings of the city. This relief comes from the Processional Way which passed through the city to the Festival House; the walls of this street between the Ishtar Gate and the Festival House were decorated with these striding lions. *Fletcher Fund, 1931, 31.13.1*

28 Door Lintel

Northern Iraq, Hatra, ca. 2nd c. A.D.
Stone; l. 67¾ in. (172.2 cm.)

Originally part of a decorated doorway in the north hall of the so-called Palace Building at Hatra, this lintel stone was positioned so that the carved surface faced the floor. The two fantastic creatures have feline bodies, long ears, and bird's wings and crest feathers, a combination of animal and bird elements typical of Near Eastern lion-griffins. Between the two figures is a vase containing a stylized lotus leaf and two curling tendrils. The naturalistic modeling of the creatures' bodies and the form of the central vase reflect Roman influence. However, the rigid symmetry of the composition, the pronounced simplification of the plant forms, and the lion-griffin motif are all characteristic Near Eastern features. *Purchase, Joseph Pulitzer Bequest, 1932, 32.145*

26 Median Bringing Horses to King Sargon
Neo-Assyrian, Khorsabad, 8th c. B.C.
Limestone; 20 × 32 in. (50.8 × 81.3 cm.)

Divine and fantastic creatures (nos. 23 and 24) were not the only subjects that engaged Assyrian sculptors; they were also concerned with depicting the victories of their monarchs in war and in the chase. Full of vitality and extraordinarily detailed, these scenes expressing regal power and triumph are among the masterworks of Assyrian art. This fragment is from the palace at Khorsabad of Sargon II (r. 722–705 B.C.); it shows a mountaineer of Media bringing two gaily caparisoned horses as tribute to the king. *Gift of John D. Rockefeller, Jr., 1933, 33.16.1*

ANATOLIA

29 Ewer
Anatolian, ca. 2100 B.C.
Gold; h. 7 in. (17.8 cm.)

Before the second millennium B.C., Anatolia was home to a people whom we know only as predecessors of the Hittites. Material evidence of their flourishing culture has been scarce until recent years, but it amply illustrates the skill of the pre-Hittite metalworker. The form of this gold ewer was achieved by raising—that is, shaping the gold through hammering; the decoration was made by repoussé. The long spout that would have risen at an oblique angle from the neck of this ewer was cut away in modern times, but the vessel's form can be reconstructed from the many surviving pottery and metal examples. The elaborate geometric decoration is characteristic of Anatolian art of this period. *Harris Brisbane Dick Fund, 1957, 57.67*

30 Sistrum with Bird and Finials
Anatolian, ca. 2300–2000 B.C.
Bronze; h. 13 in. (33 cm.)

A sistrum is an elaborate noisemaker used in religious ceremonies or in performances of music. This example from Anatolia has a handle and two upright prongs, which are decorated with projecting bull's horns and capped with stylized plants. A crossbar at the top is adorned with a standing bird of prey with outstretched wings. The fork, crossbar, and ornaments appear to have been cast together, but the three wires, each holding loose disks, were inserted through holes in the prongs. Both bull's horns and birds of prey played symbolic roles in the religions of Anatolian peoples for several millennia. It is therefore possible that this sistrum was used by priests in a religious ceremony, as accompaniment to singing or dancing in honor of the gods. *Purchase, Joseph Pulitzer Bequest, 1955, 55.137.1*

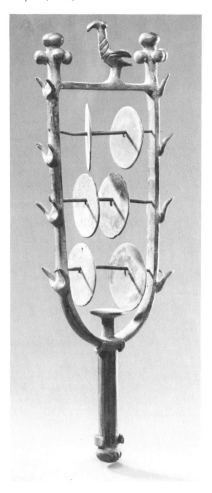

31 Female Sphinx
Anatolian, ca. 18th c. B.C.
Ivory; h. 5⅜ in. (13.7 cm.)

This is one of three ivory female sphinxes from central Anatolia in the Museum's collection. In all probability these ivories came from Acemhöyük, a huge mound near the Turkish town of Aksaray on the Konya plain. Recent excavation has revealed a burned building on the highest part of the mound; this structure contained ivories related to those in the Museum's collection. The heat of the fire that destroyed the building is reflected in the vitrification, warping, and discoloration of the Museum's ivories. The sphinxes were undoubtedly set into some object of furniture. Deep sockets are carved in the head and sometimes the base to anchor them in place. Traces of gold leaf remain on the heads and hair of some of the sphinxes. The spiral locks of the sculptures ultimately derive from the female hair fashion of the Middle Kingdom in Egypt, and the heads are precursors of those of the fourteenth-century gate sculptures at Boghazkeui, the capital of the Hittite empire. *Gift of George D. Pratt, 1932, 32.161.46*

32 Sphinx
North Syrian, 9th–8th c. B.C.
Bronze; h. 5¼ in. (13.3 cm.)

This plaque, one of a pair in the Museum, was hammered from a thick sheet of bronze. Parallels for the stance and facial features of this fantastic creature can be found in similar North Syrian works in bronze and ivory from the same period. The flamelike pattern on the hind legs was common at this time and appears on ivories from Hama, Nimrud, and Ziwiyeh. The Museum's plaques may have been used as inlays in an object of furniture, or they may have been set into a wall or door. Whatever their use, the plaques are fine examples of North Syrian metalwork. *Rogers Fund, 1953, 53.120.2*

33 Hunting Scene
Neo-Hittite, Tell Halaf, 9th c. B.C.
Basalt; 22 × 27 in. (55.9 × 68.6 cm.)

During the Neo-Assyrian period (883–612 B.C.), much was happening in the peripheral areas around Assyria. The two regions of greatest power and importance lay directly to the west in North Syria and to the southeast in Elam. In the west a number of small Aramean city-states, which acted as a barrier between Assyria and the Mediterranean coast, were gradually brought under Assyrian domination. Although in the beginning the art of this western region was independent of that of Assyria, it soon came to reflect the cultural influence of this powerful neighbor. Stone reliefs decorated the walls of the Neo-Hittite palaces and temples; these sculptures are often extremely crude, but the influence of Assyrian prototypes can be detected in the choice of scene and in such details as the types of chariots and horse trappings (see nos. 23–26). *Rogers Fund, 1943, 43.135.2*

34 Beaker
Danubian region, ca. 4th c. B.C.
Silver; h. 11 in. (27.9 cm.)

This beaker, raised from a single piece of silver, has a repoussé, stamped, and chased design of stags and goats, birds and fishes. Small scales, surmounted by a running spiral, are represented beneath the feet of the animals. The fantastic decorative fashion in which the animals are represented, the addition of bird's heads to the animal horns, and the pendent position of the hooves are all characteristics of the art of the nomadic peoples who spread across the steppes of southern Russia into Europe in the first millennium B.C.

The area from which the Museum's beaker comes, ancient Thrace, was occupied by various tribes in the fourth century B.C. Objects related in form and style to this vessel have been found in graves at sites in Romania and Bulgaria and can be associated with the Getae and Triballi tribes who ruled in northern Thrace. *Rogers Fund, 1947, 47.100.88*

FIRST FLOOR

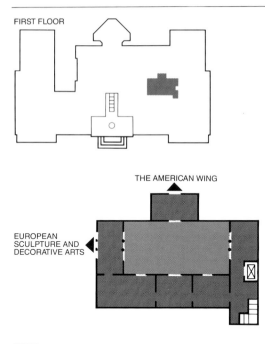

THE AMERICAN WING

EUROPEAN
SCULPTURE AND
DECORATIVE ARTS

 ARMS AND ARMOR

EQUESTRIAN COURT

ARMS AND ARMOR

The Arms and Armor Department, established in 1912, preserves and exhibits distinguished examples of the art of the armorer, swordsmith, and gunmaker. The collection concentrates on offensive and defensive arms of outstanding design and decoration—arms often intended more for display than actual use—rather than on arms of purely military or technical interest. Unlike the great dynastic accumulations of arms and armor still preserved in Vienna, Madrid, Dresden, and the Tower of London, the Museum's collection is a modern one that reflects collectors' and curators' tastes throughout the past century. One of the most encyclopedic in the world, the collection includes fourteen thousand objects from Europe, the Near East, the Far East, and the Americas that range from small arrowheads to full suits of armor consisting of hundreds of separate elements. The strength of the department lies in the extraordinary diversity and quality of its holdings.

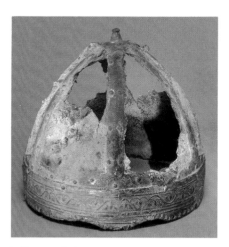

1 Spangenhelm
Germanic, early 6th c.
*Steel, bronze, gilt; h. 8⁹/₁₆ in. (21.7 cm.),
wt. 2 lb. (0.9 kg.)*

During the Migration period and Dark Ages the
spangenhelm was the helmet type characteristic
of the barbarian warriors who brought about
the Fall of Rome. The structural features of this
helmet type—triangular steel segments mounted
into a framework of bronze browband and straps
—are a translation into metal of the felt cap worn
by Eastern steppe nomads. It was probably the
invasion of Europe by the Huns (375–453)
which brought the spangenhelm to the West.
The twenty-odd spangenhelms known, most of
which were found in graves of Germanic chieftains, are so closely linked in style and workmanship that it is safe to assume that they all came
from a common workshop. Most likely they
were made at the court armory of the Ostro-
gothic kings, who ruled Italy from Ravenna (ca.
500–550). These helmets were apparently prized
regalia, which were presented to allied princes
and chieftains as diplomatic gifts.

Originally this helmet would have had two
shield-shaped cheekpieces and a mail curtain
as a neckguard hanging from its browband; a
horsehair plume would have been attached to the
apical spike. This helmet is the only spangenhelm in the Western Hemisphere. *Gift of
Stephen V. Grancsay, 1942, 42.50.1*

2 Composite "Brigandine" Armor
Italian, ca. 1400
Steel, brass, velvet; wt. 41 lb. (18.7 kg.)

The appearance of "the knight in shining armor"
was actually a gradual process. It began in the
thirteenth century when stiffened leather or
metal plates were added to the knight's armor
of mail (a fabric of interlinked iron rings) at such
vulnerable points as the elbows, knees, and
shins. This process culminated around 1400,
when the knight was encased cap-a-pie in
articulated steel plates held together and made
flexible by rivets and leather straps. The armor
shown here, the Museum's earliest complete

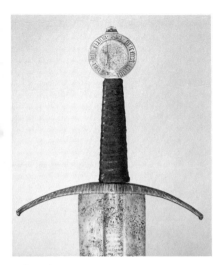

3 Sword
Western European, ca. 1400
*Steel, silver, wood, leather; l. 40¼ in.
(102.3 cm.)*

This impressive sword with its extraordinarily wide blade is a knightly battle weapon designed for both cut and thrust. This sword is distinguished from most other contemporary swords, which were quite plain and unadorned, by heavy silver decoration wound around its guard and wide silver borders around its disk-shaped pommel. These silver rims are engraved with a Latin inscription in Gothic letters: *sunt.hic.etiam.sua. praemia.laudi.* (Here, too, virtue has its due reward), a quotation from Vergil's *Aeneid* (I, 461). This is presumably a dedicatory inscription, indicating that this sword was a present from a feudal lord to one of his loyal knights; it is also the motto of the old French family de Beufvier, seneschals of Poitou. The blade is stamped with two armorer's marks and bears an illegible etched inscription in its groove. *The collection of Giovanni P. Morosini, presented by his daughter Giulia, 1932, 32.75.225*

4 Armet
North Italian, ca. 1440
Steel; wt. 9 lb. 4 oz. (4.2 kg.)

This is one of the earliest examples of the armet, the typical helmet of the fifteenth-century Italian knight. It is a tight-fitting helmet, and hinged cheek plates allow it to be opened at the chin; a pivoted visor protects the face. This armet's smooth streamlining exemplifies the lifesaving skill of the armorer, who carefully fashioned the plates so as to deflect the blows of a lance or sword. The helmet would originally have been worn with a separate chin defense (bevor) of plate and a mail curtain (camail) attached through the projecting studs at the base of the helmet. The helmet is stamped in several places with the armorer's marks, one of them including his Christian name, Lionardo. *Gift of Stephen V. Grancsay, 1942, 42.50.2*

armor, represents this last stage, though the cuirass is not yet formed of a solid breastplate and back. Instead, the torso is covered by a "brigandine," a tight-fitting sleeveless jacket lined with small steel plates riveted to the fabric, with the decorative rivet heads visible on the outside. With the exception of the helmet, this armor is composed of plates found in the ruins of the Venetian fortress of Chalcis, on the Greek island of Euboea, which was overrun by the Turks in 1470. *The Bashford Dean Memorial Collection, Gift of Helen Fahnestock Hubbard, in memory of her father, Harris C. Fahnestock, 1929, 29.154.3*

5 Parade Sallet
Italian, ca. 1460
Steel, bronze, gilded and partly silvered, semi-precious stones; h. 11⅛ in. (28.3 cm.), wt. 8 lb. 4 oz. (3.7 kg.)

Under the splendid covering of gilt bronze, cast in the form of a lion's head, is hidden a real battle helmet of polished steel painted red around the face opening to simulate the gaping maw of the animal; the teeth of the lion are silvered and its eyes inset with semiprecious stones, apparently carnelian. This parade helmet—imitating the headdress of Hercules, who wore the skin of the Nemean lion—is a striking example of the impact of the rediscovered classical world on the unfolding Renaissance. A practically identical helmet is to be found on one of the figures accompanying King Alfonso on his triumphal arch at the Castel Nuovo in Naples. *Harris Brisbane Dick Fund, 1923, 23.141*

6 Shield
German, Nürnberg, late 15th c.
Wood, covered with pigskin; gesso, paint; 21 × 18 in. (53.5 × 46 cm.)

While the knightly shield of the High Middle Ages was triangular, with its lower tip extended to protect the rider's knee, the shield of the Late Gothic period, after 1350, was the targe, almost square in outline with a cutout in its dexter side to accommodate the couched lance. This targe is richly painted with the figure of a lady supporting the full arms of the Behaim von Schwarzbach family. The black background is enlivened with floral scrolls in silver and bordered with a wavy cloud motif. By the late fifteenth century targes like this were reserved for use in the tournaments that were held during Shrovetide festivals, patrician weddings, state visits of foreign dignitaries, and similar joyous occasions. A famous jouster might have his tournament shield hung in a church or chapel over his tomb; this is how most surviving shields have come down to us. *Gift of Mrs. Florence Blumenthal, 1925, 25.26.6*

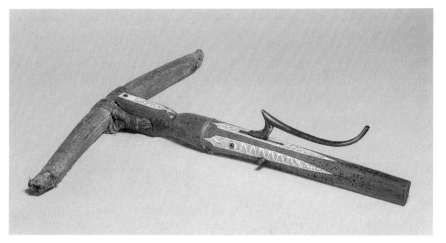

7 Hunting Crossbow

German, dated 1460

Wood, horn, whalebone, birchbark, bone, hemp cord, steel; l. 28¼ in. (72.5 cm.), wt. 6½ lb. (2.95 kg.)

With several times the "pull" of a longbow, the crossbow was the most powerful missile weapon carried by a single man before the introduction of firearms. Its heavy bow—built up from carefully glued-together strips of horn and whalebone, covered with waterproof birchbark—could not be bent by hand; it had to be spanned by means of a mechanical device, the cranequin, operating on the principle of the autojack. Because of its silent release and absence of a recoil, the crossbow was an ideal hunting weapon, and it remained in favor up to the beginning of the eighteenth century, long after the perfection of the rifle.

This crossbow, dated 1460, bears the arms of Ulrich V, count of Württemberg, and of his wife, Marguerite of Savoy. There are three inlaid plaques with religious invocations, two in Latin and one, most interestingly, in Hebrew letters (Hebrew was thought to have been the language God spoke to Adam in Paradise). *Rogers Fund, 1904, 04.3.36*

---

8 Helm for the German Joust

German, Nürnberg, ca. 1500

Steel, brass; wt. 18.7 lb. (8.5 kg.)

The main event of a tournament was the joust, when two champions on horseback ran against each other with lances. In western Europe the jousters were separated by a barrier, in order to avoid collisions, but east of the Rhine the "German joust" in the open field, without a barrier, was preferred. Elaborate protection was necessary for this very dangerous sport. The body of the jouster was strapped into a tight-fitting cuirass, onto which the large "frog mouthed" jousting helm was bolted. Eyelets on the helm's sides and top were used to attach its thickly padded lining. The plates used on breastplate and front of the helm were up to half an inch thick. Because of its tremendous weight German jousting armor was worn only on the upper body (it was a foul to hit below the belt). Even so, it could weigh up to 120 pounds—twice as much as a battle armor.

This helmet was one of a number kept in the city arsenal of Nürnberg, to be rented to young patricians eager for a tournament in the market square. *Bashford Dean Memorial Collection, Gift of Edward S. Harkness, 1929, 29.156.67*

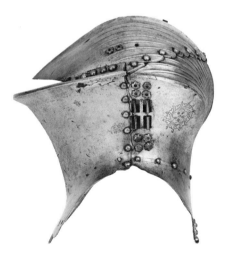

9   Armor for Man and Horse
German, ca. 1510
Steel

The knight on horseback, the principal unit of a medieval army, is today appreciated as the quintessential symbol of the bygone age of chivalry. The steel surfaces of this armor are fluted, giving a rippling, light-catching effect. This treatment, fashionable in the early sixteenth century, was more than decorative: it added extra strength to the plates without additional weight. This essentially German style of armor is commonly called "Maximilian" after the Holy Roman Emperor Maximilian I (r. 1493–1519), who is frequently depicted in art wearing armor of this type. Part of the associated horse armor, fluted like that of the rider, comes from the collection of the princes Radziwill in Poland. *The Bashford Dean Memorial Collection, Funds from various donors, 1929, 29.158.4*

10   Armor
English, Greenwich, 1527
Steel, etched and gilded, brass, leather, velvet

This armor is the earliest dated work of the Royal English Court Workshop, established by Henry VIII at Greenwich in 1514. Its master armorer was the workshop's first master, Martin van Royne (act. until 1540), who evidently had been trained in Burgundy.

This armor is known as the "Genouilhac" armor, because of a nineteenth-century attribution to Galiot de Genouilhac, maître d'artillerie of Francis I of France. However, it is now thought to be the armor "like the king's own" given by Henry VIII to the French ambassador François de la Tour, vicomte de Turenne, in 1527. A few months earlier Henry VIII had appeared at a joust in an armor "the like of [which] had not been seen before." Since there is no trace of a similar armor for Henry VIII, some scholars claim that this was our armor; possibly the overall etching and gilding was the novel effect that so astounded the spectators at that tournament. Henry VIII may have given his own armor to the ambassador, perhaps to avoid the expense of having a new armor made. In any case this armor has royal connections of the highest order. The etched decoration, incidentally, seems to be based on sketches by Henry VIII's court painter, Hans Holbein the Younger. *William H. Riggs Gift and Rogers Fund, 1919, 19.131.1*

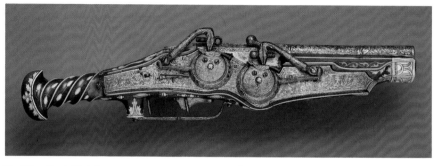

11 Wheellock Pistol

German, Munich, ca. 1540
Steel, gold, walnut, bone; l. 19⅜ in. (49.2 cm.)

Portable firearms are recorded in Europe in the fourteenth century, first as hand-cannon, later as match-fired guns. It was not until the early sixteenth century that the first automatic ignition system, the wheellock, was invented. The wheellock mechanism allowed a gun to be loaded and primed in advance, ready for instant use, and thus was ideally suited for troops on horseback. The shorter version, the pistol, did not appear until the 1530s. Made about 1540, this pistol is the masterpiece of the Munich watchmaker and gunsmith Peter Peck (ca. 1500/1510–d. 1596); it combines mechanical ingenuity with sophisticated design and decoration. The etched and gilded barrels and locks are decorated with the coat of arms and devices (the Pillars of Hercules and the motto "Plus Ultra") of the Holy Roman Emperor Charles V (r. 1519–56), one of the first and most lavish patrons of the gunmaker's art. *Gift of William H. Riggs, 1913, 14.25.1425*

12 Parade Burgonet

Milanese, 1543
Steel, gold; greatest w. 7⁵⁄₁₆ in. (18.5 cm.), wt. 4 lb. 2 oz. (1.9 kg.)

The design and decoration of this helmet justify the fame of Filippo Negroli (ca. 1500–d. 1561) as one of the best of the Milanese clan of armorers. The helmet bowl is hammered in a bold sweeping design from a single piece of steel; its rich luster makes it look as if it was cast in black bronze. A browband, built in for an exact fit on the wearer's head, is damascened in gold with an inscription giving the maker's name and the date. The embossed decoration is in a classicizing Renaissance taste with motifs derived from the decorations—*grotteschi*—in the recently rediscovered ruins of the Golden House of Nero at Rome. A mermaid, her fishtail scaly with acanthus, forms the crest of the helmet. Reclining, she holds in her uplifted arms a head of Medusa, which stares over the helmet's umbril. *Gift of J. Pierpont Morgan, 1917, 17.190.1720*

13 Armor
French, ca. 1550–59
*Steel, embossed and gilded, damascened
with gold and silver; brass, leather, red velvet;
h. approximately 69 in. (175.3 cm.), wt. 53 lb.
4 oz. (24.1 kg.)*

Designed by the noted engraver Étienne Delaune
(1518/19–1583), this armor was meant for dress
or parade wear. It has been estimated that it
would have taken a skilled metalworker about
two years to fashion this armor. However, there
are at least three different hands recognizable in
the decoration alone, which would have speeded
up the process considerably, and much of the
decoration must have been done by a goldsmith.
The iconographical details of the decoration—
bound captives, female genii presenting weapons wreathed with laurel to a hero, and other
similar motifs—illustrate the theme of Triumph
and Fame. This armor was made for the French
king Henry II (1519–59), who, incidentally, died
in a tournament accident. There is a tradition
that it was presented by Louis XIII (1601–1643)
to Bernhard, duke of Saxe-Weimar (1604–1639),
a famous general of the Thirty Years' War (1618–
48). *Harris Brisbane Dick Fund, 1939, 39.121*

14 Dagger *(Schweizerdolch)*
Swiss, 1567
*Steel, gilt bronze, wood, velvet; l. 17½ in.
(43.3 cm.)*

These daggers of characteristic shape—the
I-shaped hilt was jealously considered a Swiss
national trait—and with silver or bronze-gilt
scabbards sumptuously decorated in relief were
badges of rank for officers in the citizens' mili-
tias of Switzerland during the sixteenth century.
In western Europe these daggers were named
"baselards" after the city of Basel. It is possible
that the painter Hans Holbein the Younger
(1497?–1543), a citizen of Basel, created the
luxury type with ornamental scabbard, because
one of the earliest surviving drawings for such
a dagger is by him. The very appropriately
chosen theme of this drawing is the Dance of
Death, which was also of local importance because *Der Tod von Basel* was a famous mural
of the *danse macabre* in a Basel cemetery.

The twenty-odd themes to be found as reliefs
on Swiss daggers are biblical, such as the last
battle of King Saul (as shown here), or from
classical mythology, such as the Judgment of
Paris, or of a purely patriotic nature, such as
the story of William Tell. *Gift of Jean Jacques
Reubell, in memory of his mother Julia C. Coster
and his wife Adeline E. Post, both of New York
City, 1926, 26.145.47a–d*

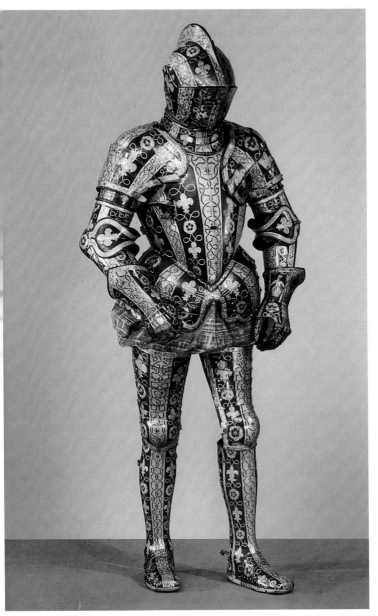

15 Armor with Exchange Pieces
English, Greenwich, ca. 1590
*Steel, blued, etched, and gilded; brass, leather,
velvet; h. as mounted 69½ in. (176.5 cm.), wt.
as mounted about 60 lb. (27.2 kg.)*

This armor is thought to be the one worn by Sir
George Clifford (1558–1605), the 3rd earl of
Cumberland, when he took over the office of
champion of Queen Elizabeth in 1590. The chief
duty of that office appears to have been presid-
ing over the jousts and tournaments held every
Queen's Day, November 17, at Westminster. Sir
George Clifford was the prototype of the Eliza-
bethan gentleman-courtier, soldier, scholar, and
pirate. He studied mathematics and geography
at Cambridge and Oxford, and he fitted out ten
expeditions against the Spaniards, personally
leading four of them.

This armor was made under the direction of
Jakob Halder (act. 1555–1607), master of the
Royal Workshop at Greenwich, which was established by Henry VIII for his personal use and
for the manufacture of presentation pieces of
princely magnificence (see no. 10). For a knight
to have his armor made in this workshop was a
special privilege granted by the sovereign. The
earl of Cumberland's armor is the best preserved and most complete Greenwich armor in
existence.

The main motifs of the decoration are Tudor
roses and fleur-de-lis tied together by double
knots and, repeated on the ornamental gilded
bands filled with strapwork, a cipher of two
addorsed *E*'s (for Elizabeth) interlaced with
annulets (a Clifford badge). *Rogers Fund, 1932,
32.130.6a–y*

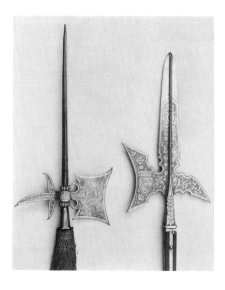

16   Two Halberds

German, dated 1584 and 1632
Steel, wood

Decorated polearms like these were carried by the palace guards of princely houses. Depending on local custom and on the taste of the lord of the castle, these guards might be equipped with partizans, bills, couses, or, as is the case here, halberds. All these staff weapons were designed for mortal combat. The halberd was one of the most efficient types among them; with its ax-blade, sharp spike, and apical hook it was suited for hacking, stabbing, and grappling (as in pulling a knight off his horse). Halberds were also well suited for parade weapons and arms for a palace guard—the large surface of the ax-blade afforded space for the display of heraldic devices, emblems, or monograms.

The earlier halberd (left) bears the arms of Ferdinand IX, duke of Bavaria; the later one (right) bears the arms of the princes of Liechtenstein. *Bashford Dean Memorial Collection; Gift of Edward S. Harkness, 1929, 29.156.33. Gift of Mary Alice Dyckman Dean, 1949, in memory of Alexander McMillan Welch, 1949, 49.120.12*

17   Parade Rapier

German, Dresden, 1606
Steel, gilt bronze, various jewels and seed pearls, traces of enamel; l. 48 in. (121.9 cm.), greatest w. 6¾ in. (17.1 cm.)

Israel Schuech (act. ca. 1590–1610), swordcutler and hiltmaker to the electoral court of Saxony, fashioned the magnificently cast and chiseled bronze hilt of this rapier for Christian II, duke of Saxony and elector of the Holy Roman Empire. Lavishly covered with decorative detail of elaborate strapwork and exquisite allegorical figurines and sparkling with jewels and pearls, the hilt gives us a fitting impression of the pomp and circumstance of the early Baroque. However, as if to indicate that under all this pageantry lurked the religious and dynastic troubles that led to the Thirty Years' War (1618–48), as if to show that in these troubled times a man, even a rich and powerful man, might have to use the edge of the sword to defend his life, there is attached to the splendidly overdecorated hilt a blade by Juan Martinez (act. late sixteenth century), bladesmith to the king of Spain and the most renowned of the celebrated swordsmiths of Toledo. *Rogers Fund, 1970, 1970.77*

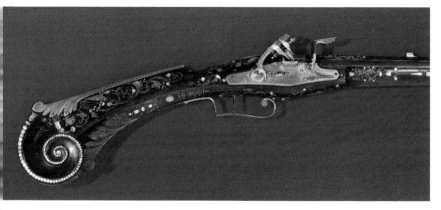

18 Flintlock Fowling Piece
French, Lisieux, ca. 1615
Steel, gilt bronze, silver, wood, mother-of-pearl; l. 55 in. (139.7 cm.)

One of the earliest known flintlocks, this fowling piece bears the mark of Pierre Le Bourgeoys, who worked with his brothers Marin and Jean in a family shop which is credited with the invention of this ignition system. It also bears the crowned cipher of Louis XIII (1601–1643) and the inventory number 134 of his *cabinet d'armes*. Two other flintlock guns from the Le Bourgeoys workshop survive, one in the Musée de l'Armée, Paris, and the other in the State Hermitage Museum, Leningrad. *Rogers and Harris Brisbane Dick Funds, 1972, 1972.223*

19 Smallsword
English, London, 1798
Steel, gold, enamel; l. 38½ in. (97.8 cm.)

The smallsword was an indispensable accessory of costume for the eighteenth-century gentleman. In the hands of a trained fencer, this light thrusting sword could be a deadly weapon, well suited for self-defense. On the other hand, many of these swords are mounted with hilts of gold or silver embellished with porcelain, tortoiseshell, even rhinestones. Such precious and delicate materials betray a purely ornamental purpose as masculine jewelry and as status symbols. A distinctive series of richly decorated smallswords was produced in England around 1800 as gifts to honor distinguished naval and military commanders. This one, made by the goldsmith James Morisset (recorded 1767–1815), was presented to Captain W. E. Cracraft of the H.M.S. *Severn* in 1798. It has a hilt of gold set with plaques of translucent enamels painted with maritime scenes, trophies, and the recipient's coat of arms and monogram. *Gift of Stephen V. Grancsay, 1942, 42.50.35*

20 Flintlock Fowling Piece
French, Versailles, ca. 1820
Steel, gold, walnut; l. 47⅜ in. (120.3 cm.)

The author of this hunting gun was Nicolas Noël Boutet (1761–1833), the most renowned gunmaker in Napoleonic France. From 1794 until 1818 Boutet was directeur-artiste of the National Arms Factory at Versailles, which produced not only regulation arms for the French army, but also lavishly decorated arms for presentation by the government to national heroes, foreign diplomats, and esteemed members of the emperor's court. This fowling piece, one of Boutet's last works, ranks as one of his masterpieces. The decoration includes subject matter appropriate to the hunt—dogs and wolves appear on the blued and gilt steel barrels and locks; hares, squirrels, and birds are shown on the gold inlaid stocks. No owner for this splendid weapon is indicated on the blank escutcheon, but a trophy of oriental arms on one of the gold mounts suggests it may have been made for some eastern European or Near Eastern prince. *Gift of Stephen V. Grancsay, 1942, 42.50.7*

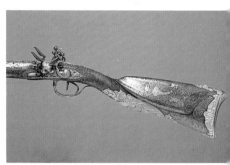

SECOND FLOOR

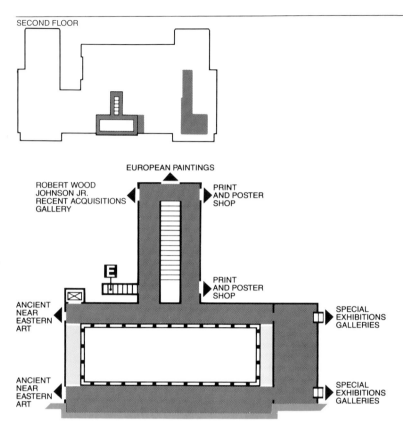

EUROPEAN PAINTINGS

ROBERT WOOD
JOHNSON JR.
RECENT ACQUISITIONS
GALLERY

PRINT
AND POSTER
SHOP

E

PRINT
AND POSTER
SHOP

ANCIENT
NEAR
EASTERN
ART

SPECIAL
EXHIBITIONS
GALLERIES

ANCIENT
NEAR
EASTERN
ART

SPECIAL
EXHIBITIONS
GALLERIES

THE AMERICAN WING

CHINESE ART, INCLUDING
DOUGLAS DILLON GALLERIES
AND THE ARTHUR SACKLER GALLERY

THE ASTOR COURT
(CHINESE GARDEN COURT)

JAPANESE ART, INCLUDING
THE SACKLER GALLERIES
FOR ASIAN ART

INDIAN AND SOUTHEAST ASIAN ART

ASIAN ART

The arts of China, Japan, Korea, India, and Southeast Asia are the responsibility of the Department of Asian Art, which was established in 1915. The collections range from the second millennium B.C. into the twentieth century A.D. and include paintings, sculpture, ceramics, bronzes, jades, decorative arts, and textiles. The collection of monumental Chinese Buddhist sculpture ranks among the finest outside China, and a major Chinese painting collection is being built through the generous support of the Honorable Douglas Dillon and The Dillon Fund. The department also has notable holdings of Ming dynasty furniture; Japanese screens, lacquer ware, and prints; and Indian and Southeast Asian bronze sculpture.

In recent years the department has embarked on a new installation of its collections. The Astor Court and Douglas Dillon Galleries for Chinese painting opened to the public in 1981. The arts of Japan are on view in The Sackler Galleries for Asian Art which opened in 1987. New exhibition areas are planned for Korean, Indian, and Southeast Asian art.

JAPAN

1 Jar
Middle Jōmon period, ca. 3000–2000 B.C.
*Clay with applied, incised, and cord-marked
decoration; h. 27½ in. (69.8 cm.)*

Cord-marked pottery is the characteristic ware
of the earliest inhabitants of Japan. These Neo-
lithic people, known as the Jōmon (cord marking)
culture, existed on the abundant fishing and
hunting of the Japanese islands from at least
the fifth millennium B.C., surviving in some areas
until the third century A.D. During this period
handmade utilitarian wares were treated with
inventive, often extravagant artistry, and regional separations between groups resulted in
a wide range of types and styles. This earthenware food vessel, which came from the Aomori
prefecture in northeastern Japan, is remarkable
for the fine quality of its clay and for its sophisticated decoration. The cord-marked herring-
bone pattern was produced by cords knotted
together and twisted in opposite directions. *The
Harry G. C. Packard Collection of Asian Art,
Gift of Harry G. C. Packard and Purchase,
Fletcher, Rogers, Harris Brisbane Dick and
Louis V. Bell Funds, Joseph Pulitzer Bequest
and The Annenberg Fund, Inc. Gift, 1975,
1975.268.182*

2 Talisman ▶
Prehistoric, 4th–5th c.
Steatite; 2½ × ½ in. (6.5 × 1.2 cm.)

This irregular disk with smooth radial fluting is a
fine example of a type of carved stone object
found in the keyhole-shaped burial mounds of
central Japan of the fourth and fifth centuries.
Works in this shape are called *sharinseki*
(carriage-wheel stones), and they are sometimes identified as stone bracelets. They seem,
however, to be talismans with magical or religious significance. They do not appear in burials of the later Kofun period; perhaps their special
meaning faded with the influx of Chinese and
subsequently Buddhist culture that began in the
sixth century. *The Harry G. C. Packard Collection of Asian Art, Gift of Harry G. C. Packard
and Purchase, Fletcher, Rogers, Harris Brisbane Dick, and Louis V. Bell Funds, Joseph
Pulitzer Bequest, and The Annenberg Fund,
Inc. Gift, 1975, 1975.268.338*

4 Zaō Gongen
Late Heian period, 11th c.
Bronze; h. 14¾ in. (37.5 cm.)

This is a rare example of Zaō Gongen, a uniquely Japanese deity, who is represented here in the strong active pose conventional for a Buddhist guardian figure. A local Shinto kami, Zaō Gongen is the tutelary deity of Mount Kimpu in the Yoshino Mountains south of Nara. During the eleventh century, when this image was cast, he became the object of an important cult that incorporated Shinto and Buddhist beliefs. Zaō was identified as a local manifestation of the Buddha, and Mount Kimpu came to be revered as a sacred mountain associated with the Pure Land of Buddhist salvation. Venerated by Heian aristocrats, Zaō was also regarded as a patron by adherents of Shugendo, an ascetic sect. While expressing an intense spirituality, this image is a fine example of the elegance of the aristocratic Heian style. *The Harry G. C. Packard Collection of Asian Art, Gift of Harry G. C. Packard and Purchase, Fletcher, Rogers, Harris Brisbane Dick, and Louis V. Bell Funds, Joseph Pulitzer Bequest, and The Annenberg Fund, Inc. Gift, 1975, 1975.268.155*

3 Segment of the *Kegon-kyō*
Nara period, ca. 744
Segment of handscroll (calligraphy) mounted as hanging scroll; silver ink on indigo paper; 9¾ × 20⅛ in. (24.8 × 53.7 cm.)

This manuscript is a fragment of a Buddhist text, the *Kegon-kyō*, or *Avatamsaka-sutra*, the story of a young boy's travels through India in search of supreme truth. Written in India, the text was translated into Chinese (the language used in this scroll) in the fifth century. This scripture is one of the longest in the Buddhist canon, comprising sixty scrolls. The set to which this segment belongs came from the Nigatsu-dō, a hall within the Tōdai-ji compound, a vast temple complex that dominated the capital city of Nara in the eighth century. The quality of the writing on this scroll—the finest of its day—is impressive, as is the combination of silver against vibrant blue. The silver is an alloy and has not tarnished—the Buddhist Law was meant to last forever. *Purchase, Mrs. Jackson Burke Gift, 1981, 1981.75*

5 Fudō Myō-ō
Late Heian period, 12th c.
Wood with color and gold leaf; 80 × 30 in.
(203.2 × 76.2 cm.)

Fudō, whose name means "immovable," is a staunch guardian of the faith, warding off enemies of the Buddha with his sword of wisdom and binding evil forces with his lasso. Here his youthful, chubby body and his skirt and scarf are modeled with the restrained gentle curves typical of late Heian sculpture. Fudō's halo of red flames has been lost, and his rock pedestal is a nineteenth-century replacement. Enough pigment remains to show that his hair was once painted red and his flesh dark blue-green. His clothing was covered with delicate patterns of cut gold leaf.

The statue was the central icon of the Kuhonji Gomadō in Funasaka, some twenty miles northwest of Kyoto. A gomadō is a small auxiliary hall attached to temples of the Shingon, or Esoteric, sect of Buddhism and intended specifically for the ritual worship of Fudō with fire-burning ceremonies. *The Harry G. C. Packard Collection of Asian Art, Gift of Harry G. C. Packard and Purchase, Fletcher, Rogers, Harris Brisbane Dick, and Louis V. Bell Funds, Joseph Pulitzer Bequest, and The Annenberg Fund, Inc. Gift, 1975, 1975.268.163*

6 Miracles of Kannon (Avalokiteshvara)
Kamakura period, 1257
Handscroll; color and gold on paper;
9½ in. × 32 ft. (24.1 cm. × 9.76 m.)

In this handscroll (*emaki*) from the middle of the Kamakura period both the sacred text (sutra) and the illustrations are modeled after a Chinese printed scroll said to have been made in the Sung dynasty. The sutra text was transcribed by Sugawara Mitsushige, a thirteenth-century calligrapher, who signed and dated it 1257. We do not, however, know the name of the painter who illustrated with superb color and gold each section of the thirty-three texts describing the many miracles performed by Kannon in saving people from fire, flood, and other calamities.

The bodhisattva Kannon is the god of mercy who delayed his own attainment of buddhahood in order to bring salvation to humankind. Known in China as Kuan Yin and in India as Avalokiteshvara, he is one of the most popular deities in the Buddhist pantheon. Here, in the lower right, traders are being waylaid by bandits; they will, however, be rescued because they have invoked the name of Kannon (who appears in the upper left). (See also nos. 8 and 32.) *Purchase, Louisa Eldridge McBurney Gift, 1953, 53.7.3*

7 Tenjin Engi

Kamakura period, late 13th c.
*Handscroll; ink and color on paper; w. 12¼ in.
(31.1 cm.)*

This illustration is from a set of three scrolls
(now remounted as five) that present the legendary origins of the Shinto cult of the deified
Sugawara no Michizane (845–903), a distinguished poet, statesman, and scholar. These
scrolls, which contain thirty-seven lively and
evocative illustrations, were painted in the late
thirteenth century for didactic use in one of the
many Tenjin shrines dedicated to this patron of
agriculture and learning. In its combination of
landscape, narrative, and fantastic vision, this
work is a prime example of the classic *yamato-e*
style of painting. The Museum's version of the
Tenjin Engi is unique in its elaboration of the
priest Nichizō's journey through hell. Here
Nichizō is depicted entering the caves of hell.
Fletcher Fund, 1925, 25.224d

8 Eleven-Headed Avalokiteshvara (Jūichimen Kannon) atop Mount Potalaka

Late Kamakura period, ca. 1300
*Hanging scroll; ink, color, gold pigment, and gold
leaf on silk; 42¾ × 16¼ in. (108.6 × 41.2 cm.)*

This strikingly lyrical painting shows an Eleven-
Headed Kannon on his mountain-island paradise,
Potalaka, where glorious palaces and lakes lie
amid fragrant trees and flowers. A bodhisattva
renowned for his infinite compassion and mercy,
Kannon here sits on a lotus throne, his right
hand making the gift-giving gesture (*varada-
mudra*) and his left holding a vase out of which
lotus flowers emerge. (See also nos. 6 and 32.)
*The Harry G. C. Packard Collection of Asian
Art, Gift of Harry G. C. Packard and Purchase,
Fletcher, Rogers, Harris Brisbane Dick and
Louis V. Bell Funds, Joseph Pulitzer Bequest,
and The Annenberg Fund, Inc. Gift, 1975,
1975.268.20*

11 OGATA KŌRIN, Edo period, 1658–1716 ▶
Waves
Two-fold screen; ink, color, and gold leaf on paper; 57⁷/₈ × 65¹/₈ in. (147 × 165.4 cm.)

Ogata Kōrin was born into a wealthy merchant-class family in Kyoto. After squandering his inheritance, he turned to painting as a serious vocation. This screen was painted at a period when Japan was enjoying peace and prosperity. Having assimilated foreign influences, Japan was ready to pursue its own artistic progress. The Japanese feeling for nature is obvious here, as is Kōrin's ability to transpose it into a rhythmic bold stylization. The design is really the abstract essence of a wave, and Kōrin expresses this imaginative design with supremely controlled brushwork. The subtle gradations of color, with gold and blue predominating, enhance the extraordinary ink strokes; the result is a remarkable fusion of decorative and realistic elements. (See also no. 12.) *Fletcher Fund, 1926, 26.117*

9 Battles of the Hogen and Heiji Eras
Momoyama period, ca. 1600
Pair of six-fold screens; ink, color, and gold leaf on paper; each 60⁷/₈ × 140¹/₈ in. (154.6 × 355.6 cm.)

The Momoyama period saw the reestablishment of warrior control of Japan. Although these men were not interested in the refinements of court life, they did decorate their large dark castles with warm color. This is the period when the Japanese screen came into its own. Strong thick colors against a ground of gold leaf were the fashion.

In these screens the drama of the two insurrec-tions is set before us, scene by scene. The locale for most of the action is Kyoto, but the artist did not hesitate to switch to Mount Fuji. Nor are the scenes placed chronologically; rather the artist distributed his incidents as suited him best. The viewer gets a bird's-eye view of the action because of the Japanese technique of looking from above at an oblique angle. Sliding doors and roofs are pulled back so that we see the scene inside the palace as well as outside. The painting is meticulous in detail, making use of strong greens, reds, and blues against the gold. *Rogers Fund, 1957, 57.156.4,5*

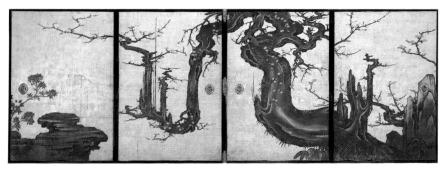

10 The Old Plum
Early Edo period, ca. 1650
Ink, color, and gold leaf on paper; 68 × 191¹/₂ in. (172.7 × 486.4 cm.)

Even the oldest plum puts out green shoots in spring, and thus the tree is a symbol of fortitude and rejuvenation. *The Old Plum* was probably painted for one of the reception rooms of the abbot's residence in the Tenshō-in, built in 1647, which adjoined the Tenkyū-in, a small temple in Kyoto. It formed part of a continuous painting that probably featured one dramatically enlarged tree on each of the four sides of the room. The artist is thought to be Kanō Sansetsu (1590–1651), whose late works are characterized by abstraction and a stylized mannerism. *The Harry G. C. Packard Collection of Asian Art, Gift of Harry G. C. Packard and Purchase, Fletcher, Rogers, Harris Brisbane Dick, and Louis V. Bell Funds, Joseph Pulitzer Bequest, and The Annenberg Fund, Inc. Gift, 1975, 1975.268.48*

12 OGATA KŌRIN, Edo period, 1658–1716
Yatsuhashi
Six-fold screen; ink, color, and gold leaf on paper; 70½ × 146¼ in. (179.1 × 371.5 cm.)

Ogata Kōrin (no. 11) was fascinated by irises, which he painted often in many media. Here, however, the bridge is the clue to the painting's subject, one immediately familiar to a Japanese viewer. It alludes to a passage from the tenth-century *Tales of Ise,* a collection of poetic episodes about the courtier Narihira. Banished from Kyoto to the eastern provinces after an indiscretion with a high-ranking lady of the court, Narihira stopped en route at Yatsuhashi (Eight-

Plank Bridge). There the sight of the irises blooming brought him nostalgic regret for friends left behind in the capital. Kōrin may have seen in this story a parallel to his own condition. In search of clients, he was forced to leave Kyoto in 1704 and travel east to Edo. There, restless and unhappy, he longed for the refined life of the capital.

This screen is one of a pair; the left screen, which is also in the Museum's collection, is identical in size and completes the representation of Yatsuhashi. *Purchase, Louisa Eldridge McBurney Gift, 1953, 53.7.2*

13   Wine Container

Momoyama period, ca. 1596–1600
*Lacquered wood; h. 9⅞ in. (25 cm.), diam.
7 in. (17.8 cm.)*

This sake container (*chōshi*) may have been used by the Momoyama general Toyotomi Hideyoshi (1536–98), the flamboyant ruler who unified Japan in the 1590s. His mausoleum, the Kōdaiji in Kyoto, was furnished with the finest-quality lacquer prepared by the Kōami family. Works in this style, called Kōdaiji lacquers, are characterized by close-ups of autumn plants painted in simple gold designs. Hideyoshi's chrysanthemum and paulownia-leaf crests are also prominent motifs. The diagonally bisected pattern, half against a sprinkled gold ground and half on a black ground, is typical of Kōdaiji lacquers. The stunning contrast of the two areas was a design invention called *katami-gawari* (alternating sides) that was favored about 1600 by artists working not only in lacquer but also in ceramics and textiles. *Purchase, Gift of Mrs. Russell Sage, by exchange, 1980, 1980.6*

14   Bowl with Lid

Early Edo period, late 17th c.
Arita ware, Kakiemon type; porcelain painted in underglaze blue and overglaze enamels; h. 13¾ in. (35 cm.), diam. 12⅜ in. (31.4 cm.)

At least eight of these deep bowls, some missing their lids, are known at present. Like this one, most have been found in Europe. They were no doubt produced for the export market toward the end of the seventeenth century under the influence of K'ang-hsi famille verte (no. 58), and all probably originated from the same kiln. The symmetrical design painted on the lid and bowl, although slightly varied on each piece, is coordinated to show a pair of birds with chrysanthemums on one side and a pair of birds with peonies on the other. *The Harry G. C. Packard Collection of Asian Art, Gift of Harry G. C. Packard and Purchase, Fletcher, Rogers, Harris Brisbane Dick, and Louis V. Bell Funds, Joseph Pulitzer Bequest, and The Annenberg Fund, Inc. Gift, 1975, 1975.268.526*

15   Nō Costume

Edo period, early 18th c.
Silk and gold brocade; l. 59⅜ in. (150.9 cm.)

The rich color and subtle design of this extraordinarily beautiful costume would have been heightened by the austere setting of the small wooden Nō stage. The silk ground is woven in a pattern of alternate bands of pale orange and cream by binding off the warp threads to reserve them for the dye. Loose binding allowed some of the dye to seep into adjacent areas, creating a softly shaded effect in the woven cloth. A felicitous design of pine and bamboo is woven in glossed green silk on the cream-colored bands of unglossed silk. The technique, known as *karaori* (Chinese weaving), is distinguished from embroidery by the uniform direction of all the weft floats, which lie in long "stitches" across the surface. *Karaori* is unique to Nō costumes and is used for the outer robe worn by female characters. *Purchase, Gift of Mrs. Russell Sage, by exchange, 1979, 1979.408*

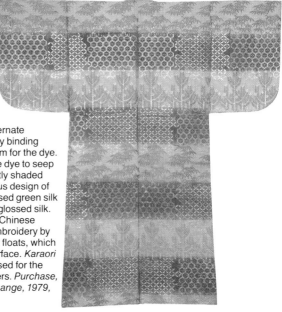

16 HISHIKAWA MORONOBU, Edo period, 1625–94
Lovers in the Garden
Ink printed on paper; 10¾ × 15½ in. (27.3 × 39.4 cm.)

Considered to be the originator of the Japanese single-sheet print, Hishikawa Moronobu was also an extraordinary book-illustrator and painter. This print is thought to be the first page of a series of twelve *shunga,* or erotic prints, which date from 1676–83.

Here a young couple embrace ecstatically in a garden corner. In the left foreground autumn plants in full bloom are drawn so large that they almost envelop the lovers. In contrast to the fine lines of the plants, however, the lovers' hair and garments are drawn in large masses, thus focusing the viewer's attention on the couple. The

flowing lines of the lovers' garments are repeated in the rock and the water, uniting the figures both physically and spiritually with the natural setting. *Harris Brisbane Dick Fund and Rogers Fund, 1949, JP 3069*

INDIA AND PAKISTAN

17 Pair of Royal Earrings
Indian, perhaps Andhra Pradesh, ca. 1st c. B.C.
Gold; left: l. 3 in. (7.7 cm.); right: l. 3⅛ in. (7.9 cm.)

Body adornment in ancient India was not merely self-embellishment but had very real social and religious significance. Jewelry, aside from its intrinsic value, was considered a major art form. These earrings are designed as organic, concepualized, vegetative motifs. Each is composed of two rectangular, budlike forms growing outward from a central double-stemmed tendril. A winged lion and an elephant, both royal animals, occur on each earring. The animals are of repoussé gold, completely covered in granulation and then consummately detailed, using granules, snippets of wire and sheet, and individually forged and hammered pieces of gold. These earrings are the most superb examples of Indian jewelry known. Their size, weight, craftsmanship, and use of royal emblems leave little doubt that they were royal commissions.
Gift of The Kronos Collections, 1981, 1981.398.3,4

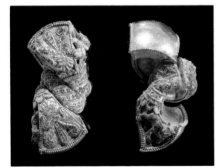

18 Stele with Scenes from the Life of the Buddha
Indian, Andhra Pradesh, Nagarjunakonda, first half of 4th c.
Limestone; h. 56¾ in. (144.1 cm.)

This stele shows the Great Departure—Prince Siddhartha (later to become the Buddha) leaving his family and the palace at Kapilavastu in the dark of night. Renouncing his noble life, he embarks on his search for enlightenment. This event became a standard part of the Buddhist pictorial repertory with little variation in the dramatis personae. Siddhartha's horse and groom are usually present, as well as the gods who rejoice at Siddhartha's decision. Dwarflike figures often support the horse to muffle the sound of its hooves and thus prevent the palace occupants from awakening. In this depiction, the great Vedic god Indra holds a parasol, the symbol of royalty, over the departing Siddhartha. The second scene on the stele depicts Siddhartha at Bodhgaya, where he attained enlightenment and became the Buddha. *Fletcher Fund, 1928, 28.105*

19 Standing Buddha

Indian, Mathura, Gupta period, 5th c.
Mottled red sandstone; h. 33⅝ in. (85.5 cm.)

The Gupta period (the early fourth through the early seventh century) was India's Golden Age, when the arts and the sciences flourished under lavish imperial patronage. In sculpture a new naturalism emerged; a highly refined system of aesthetics produced softer, gentler curves and smoothly flowing forms. As practiced at its two greatest centers, the holy cities of Mathura and Sarnath, the Gupta style had an immense and wide-ranging influence.

This well-modeled and elegantly proportioned Buddha is of the type most often represented in south Asian art: standing, with the right hand (now missing) raised in the fear-allaying or protective gesture (*abhayamudra*) and the lowered left hand holding a portion of the garment. The immutable composure and the calm magnificence of this statue are characteristic of the finest early south Asian sculpture. *Purchase, Enid A. Haupt Gift, 1979, 1979.6*

20 Standing Buddha

Pakistani, Gandharan style, ca. 6th c.
Bronze; h. 13¼ in. (33.6 cm.)

The sculptural styles of the ancient Gandhara region of northwest India and northern Pakistan are well preserved by rich remains of stone and stucco. A few rare small bronzes, almost always representations of the standing Buddha, have also survived. Since the Gandharan-style Buddha was of seminal importance, serving as one of the prototypes for early Buddhist images and iconography throughout the Far East and south Asia, the importance of these small, portable bronze images cannot be overestimated.

Standing on a stepped pedestal, the Buddha raises his right hand in the fear-allaying gesture (*abhayamudra*). His lowered left hand holds a portion of his garment. The mandorla is a complete body halo whose perimeter represents stylized flames. Representing the Gandharan style in its most mature form, this standing Buddha is one of the most important bronze sculptures of the ancient Buddhist world. *Purchase, Rogers, Fletcher, Pfeiffer and Harris Brisbane Dick Funds, and Joseph Pulitzer Bequest, 1981, 1981.188*

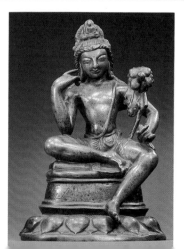

21 Padmapani Lokeshvara Seated in Meditation

Pakistani, Swat Valley region (or Kashmir), first half of 7th c.
Gilded bronze inlaid with silver and copper; h. 8¾ in. (22.2 cm.)

This superb sculpture, one of the finest and earliest Swat Valley bronzes known, closely reflects the inspiration of the Gupta idiom of northern India during the sixth century. It occupies a pivotal position in Indian art, illustrating the transition between the sixth-century Gupta style and the great sculptural traditions of the eighth century in Kashmir and the Swat Valley region. *Harris Brisbane Dick and Fletcher Funds, 1974, 1974.273*

22 Standing Parvati

Indian, Tamilnadu, Chola dynasty, 10th c.
Bronze; h. 27⅜ in. (69.5 cm.)

Parvati, the consort of Shiva, stands in the *tribhanga* (thrice-bent) pose. Her lithe left arm rests at her side, and her right hand is partly raised (at one time it may have held a lotus). Her hair is piled high into a conical crown decorated with elaborate ornaments. Curls fall across the back of her shoulders in a loose fan shape. She wears more than the usual amount of jewelry; a rich girdle with two long tassels holds the form-revealing dhoti, beautifully stylized in a symphony of ridged folds. The lyrical and rhythmic carriage of her body, especially the hips and lower limbs, is characteristic of the masterly achievement of the great South Indian bronzes of the early tenth century when the Chola dynasty began to gain power. This beautiful image was cast by the lost-wax process. *Bequest of Cora Timken Burnett, 1957, 57.51.3*

23 Standing Vishnu

Indian, Tamilnadu, Chola dynasty, 10th c.
Bronze with greenish-blue patination; h. 33¾ in. (85.7 cm.)

This four-armed Vishnu stands on a double-lotus base supported by a plinth. His upper right hand holds a flaming disk, the upper left hand a conch shell. His lower right hand is in the fear-allaying gesture (*abhayamudra*), while the lower left hand, with extended fingers, points diagonally downward. The figure wears a cylindrical tapering crown and is heavily decked with earrings, necklaces, bracelets, anklets, rings on fingers and toes, all symbolic of Vishnu's qualities and attributes. The sacred cord consists of three threads, said to represent the three letters of the mystic syllable "om." Poles could have been inserted through the rings at the four corners of the base, allowing the image to be carried in ceremonial processions.

The monumental style and superb casting of this piece exemplify the high achievement of early Chola art. *Purchase, John D. Rockefeller 3rd Gift, 1962, 62.265*

24 Standing Hanuman
Indian, Tamilnadu, Chola dynasty, 11th c.
Bronze; h. 25⅜ in. (64.5 cm.)

Hanuman, the leader of the great monkey clan, was an ally of Rama (an avatar of Vishnu). His story is one of the most charming in all Hindu theology; it is also of great didactic and moral value—in *The Ramayana,* the bravery, courage, and loyalty of Hanuman serve as a supreme example to all. In Chola bronze sculpture Hanuman is almost always depicted standing slightly bent over as if in obeisance before Rama; he is usually part of a larger group that includes Rama and Rama's brother (Lakshmana) and wife (Sita). Except for his thick tail and simian face Hanuman is represented as human. Here he leans forward slightly, appearing to be engrossed in conversation. Chola representations of Hanuman are rare, and this example is probably the finest known. *Purchase, 1982, 1982.220.9*

25 Yashoda and Krishna ▶
Indian, Karnataka, Vijayanagar period, ca. 14th c.
Copper; h. 13⅛ in. (33.3 cm.)

The Krishna legend is recounted in books ten and eleven of *The Bhagavata Purana,* a great Hindu epic. As an infant, Krishna was exchanged for a daughter born to a cowherding couple to prevent his being killed by the wicked king Kamsa. The stories of Krishna's heroic exploits are well known and revered by the Indian peoples, but the legends concerning his infancy and youth are especially beloved. The subject of the cowherdess Yashoda holding her foster son, Krishna, is very rare in Indian art, particularly in sculpture. Here she is nursing the infant god; with her left hand she cradles the head of Krishna, and with her right she holds him below his waist. This depiction is surely one of the most intimate and tender portrayals in the history of Indian art. *Purchase, Lita Annenberg Hazen Charitable Trust Gift, in honor of Cynthia Hazen and Leon Bernard Polsky, 1982, 1982.220.8*

AFGHANISTAN

26 Linga with One Face (*Ekamukhalinga*)
Afghani, Shahi period, 9th c.
White marble; h. 22⁷⁄₁₆ in. (57 cm.)

In Hindu theology worship of the linga (phallic emblem) is understood to be worship of the great generative principle of the universe conceptualized as one aspect of the Lord Shiva. The linga is usually the most sacrosanct icon of a Shaivite temple, housed in the main sanctum.

The phallic symbol can be plain or have carved on it one to five faces. The lower shaft of the linga was set into a stone pedestal, the *pitha* or *pindika,* which theoretically corresponded to the female genitalia, though not in actual form. This sculpture shows the orthodox representation of a linga with a single face of Shiva, an *ekamukhalinga*. In traditional fashion Shiva wears the crescent moon in his double-bun hairdo; he also wears earrings and a necklace, his usual adornments. The vertical third eye appears on his forehead. This work is a masterpiece of the Shahi school, which worked almost exclusively in white marble. *Rogers Fund, 1980, 1980.415*

27 Standing Bodhisattva
Nepali, 8th–9th c.
Gilded bronze; h. 12 in. (30.4 cm.)

This majestic sculpture is one of the finest extant early Nepali bronzes. Skillfully modeled, the bare-chested bodhisattva stands in a subtle contrapuntal posture, the right leg slightly relaxed, with the weight of the body resting on the rigid left leg. He holds a fly whisk in his raised right hand and the stem of a lotus, the upper portion of which has not survived, in his left hand. The deity is dressed in the orthodox fashion of the period, wearing the usual complement of jewelries; the sacred thread goes from the left shoulder to the right knee, and a sash, slung diagonally across the abdomen, terminates in full drapery folds with pointed ends. The complex arrangement of the garments balances the elaborate lower portion of the lotus stem. The elegant proportions of this tall figure are emphasized by the high chignon and tripartite tiara.
Gift of Margery and Harry Kahn, 1981, 1981.59

28 Standing Maitreya
Nepali, 9th–10th c.
Gilt copper with polychrome; h. 26 in. (66 cm.)

Ninth-century Nepali art clearly exhibits the influences of the art of India. In this sculpture the elegance of the Pala style at Nalanda is combined with a wholly Nepali aesthetic. This large image of Maitreya, the messianic bodhisattva, stands in a pronounced *tribhanga* (thrice-bent) posture. The sensual exaggeration of the pose is most unusual for Nepali art of this early period. This is an extraordinarily radiant and sensuous sculpture. Not only is it one of the largest of the early Nepali bronzes in the West, it is also the only example of such refined elegance combined with an almost austere economy of surface decoration. A master sculptor has produced an image combining a deep spiritual presence with a most beautifully arranged system of volumes. *Purchase, 1982, 1982.220.12*

29 Hari-Hara

Cambodian, Pre-Angkor period, ca. late 7th–early 8th c.

Calcareous sandstone; h. 35½ in. (90.1 cm.)

Among the rarest and most beautiful south Asian sculptures, Pre-Angkor statues are characterized by a rather naturalistic treatment of the body and, often, a polished surface. The stylistic allegiance is to the aesthetic systems of the Gupta period in India (no. 19), and the iconography is usually Hindu. Hari-Hara is a syncretic Hindu deity in whom the aspects and powers of Shiva and Vishnu are combined. This iconography was popular in Southeast Asia during the sixth through the ninth centuries, and the Museum's standing four-armed Hari-Hara follows orthodox traditions. His hairdo is split down the center, one side displaying Shiva's piled-up locks and the other Vishnu's high, undecorated miter. Half of Shiva's vertical third eye is incised on the forehead. The raised left hand probably held a conch, and the lowered left hand probably rested on a mace—both attributes of Vishnu. The raised right hand would have held Shiva's trident, and the lowered right may have been extended toward the worshiper. *Purchase, Laurance S. Rockefeller Gift and Anonymous Gift, 1977, 1977.241*

30 Standing Ganesha

Cambodian, Pre-Angkor period, ca. late 7th–early 8th c.

Calcareous sandstone; h. 17¼ in. (43.8 cm.)

Ganesha, the elephant-headed Hindu god of auspiciousness, is popularly accepted as being the first son of Shiva and Parvati. He is the deity who controls obstacles—inventing them or removing them—and he is worshiped before beginning any serious undertaking. Like the Museum's Hari-Hara (no. 29), this sculpture is from the Pre-Angkor period (sixth–early ninth century). This charming small Ganesha is well modeled, with an emphasis on the full volumes of the body and head. The sculptural quality is so outstanding, and the spirit of this delightful god so well captured, that it ranks very high among the few extant Pre-Angkor stone Ganeshas. *Louis V. Bell and Fletcher Funds, 1982, 1982.220.7*

31 Presentation Bowl
Malaysian(?), ca. 7th–8th c.
Bronze; h. 8¼ in. (20.9 cm.)

The top section of this extraordinary bronze vessel is cast with a continuous frieze depicting two scenes: a procession leaving a walled city, and a palace courtyard with musicians and a dancer performing for a nobleman and his consort, who are seated on a raised platform with attendants and spectators. The vessel is clearly the product of an advanced and very accomplished workshop with a strongly developed narrative style, but the function or purpose of the bowl is not known. With its elaborate narrative frieze it seems inappropriate for use as either a relic casket or a foundation casket for a religious edifice; perhaps it was intended as an important presentation piece. The scenes represented have not been identified. *Rogers Fund, 1975, 1975.419*

33 Brahma
Cambodian, Bakheng style, late 9th–early 10th c.
Limestone; h. 47½ in. (120.7 cm.)

This four-headed, four-armed figure of the Hindu deity Brahma is reportedly from Prasat Prei. That temple, however, belongs to the reign of Jayavarman II (first half of the ninth century), whereas this sculpture is executed in a pure Bakheng style. Therefore, if the information that it comes from Prasat Prei is correct, it must belong to a later phase of this building.

Brahma wears a *sampot*; the manner in which this garment is arranged is typical of the Bakheng style. Also characteristic of this period is a certain rigidity and stiffness in the figure. *Fletcher Fund, 1935, 36.96.3*

32 Four-Armed Avalokiteshvara
Thai, Pra Kon Chai, ca. second quarter of 8th c.
Bronze; eyes inlaid with silver and black glass or obsidian; h. 56 in. (142.2 cm.)

In 1964 a group of Buddhist bronzes was discovered at Pra Kon Chai, Buriram province, Thailand. Reflecting Cambodian, Indian, and Mon influences in an unequal admixture, they are the mature products of important workshops with obvious connections to Shri Deb and Lopburi, major centers for sculpture in central Thailand. This piece, the largest and one of the finest of the trove, depicts Avalokiteshvara, the bodhisattva of infinite compassion. (See also nos. 6 and 8.) *Rogers Fund, 1967, 67.234*

34 Kneeling Queen
Cambodian, Baphuon style, ca. mid-11th c.
Bronze with traces of gold; eyes inlaid with silver; h. about 17 in. (43.2 cm.)

This may well be the single most beautiful Khmer bronze outside Cambodia. In this magnificently poised and balanced figure, the forms and vol-umes blend harmoniously at every viewing angle. It was once part of what must have been a spectacular bronze group, produced by impe-rial workshops and perhaps housed in one of the temples at the great Angkor complex.
Purchase, Bequest of Joseph H. Durkee, by exchange, 1972, 1972.147

INDIAN PAINTING

35 Manuscript Cover
Indian, 9th c.
Ink and colors on wood; metal insets; h. 2¼ in. (5.7 cm.)

The format and iconography of this manuscript cover relate it to eleventh-century Pala-Nepali manuscript paintings, but the style of painting is not only considerably earlier but is allied to the western cave-painting tradition at Ajanta, Bagh, and Ellora. This cover is the only work known that links these traditions. The scenes depicted on the inside of the cover, except that of the central panel, are from the life of the Buddha. The central panel (a detail of which is shown here) depicts the seated Prajnaparamita, the Buddhist goddess of Transcendent Wisdom, flanked by bodhisattvas. This almost certainly indicates that the palm-leaf manuscript protected by this cover was the *Ashtasahasrika Prajna-paramita* (The Perfection of Wisdom in Eight Thousand Verses), one of the most important Buddhist texts of the period. *Gift of The Kronos Collections and Mr. and Mrs. Peter Findlay, 1979, 1979.511*

CHINA

36 Tuan Fang Altar Set
Shang and Early Chou dynasties, mid-2nd–early 1st millennium B.C.
Bronze; altar table 7⅓ × 35⅜ × 18¼ in. (18.7 × 89.9 × 46.4 cm.)

This ritual bronze altar set, comprising fourteen objects, is extraordinary for its completeness as well as for the quality and vitality of the individual pieces. Tuan Fang, viceroy of Shensi province, purchased the set when it first came to light in 1901. The Museum acquired it from his heirs in 1924. The excavation of these bronzes is undocumented, but they are believed to have come from an early Chou tomb at Tou-chi T'ai in Shensi. The vessels themselves probably date from the Shang and Early Chou periods. Cast with superb control of the bronze technique, they are clearly the product of a culture at its peak. These vessels are related to ancestor worship, but the exact nature of their sacrificial and ritual functions is not entirely clear. The wealth of motifs (particularly the *t'ao-t'ieh* masks, dragons, and birds) shows a complete mastery of the art of decorating bronze forms. *Munsey Fund, 1924, 24.72.1–14*

37 Standing Buddha
Northern Wei dynasty, 477
Gilt bronze; 55¼ × 19½ in. (140.3 × 48.9 cm.)

This figure is the largest and most important Northern Wei gilt-bronze statue yet discovered. The Buddha, standing with outstretched arms on a lotus pedestal, seems to be welcoming worshipers. His monastic robe clings in the "wet drapery" manner, its folds swirling around the chest and shoulders and falling in ever-widening ripples. The cranial protuberance (*usnisha*), the elongated arms, and the large webbed hands are supernatural attributes of the Buddha. An inscription around the base dates the piece to 477 and identifies it as Maitreya, the Buddha of the Future, but some doubt has been expressed about the authenticity of this inscription. This great image, however, is certainly of the fifth century. *John Stewart Kennedy Fund, 1926, 26.123*

38 Altar Shrine with Maitreya
Northern Wei dynasty, 524
Gilt bronze; h. 30¼ in. (76.8 cm.)

This elaborate and nearly complete Buddhist shrine of the early sixth century is said to have been excavated in 1924 in a small village near Cheng-ting fu in Hopei province. It is a masterful grouping of many separate elements in a shimmering Buddhist pantheon. The central figure, the Future Buddha, Maitreya, stands in front of a leaf-shaped mandorla whose openwork surface gives the effect of flickering flame. Apsarases, their draperies fluttering upward, alight on rosettes that decorate the edge of the mandorla; each plays a musical instrument. The Buddha is flanked by two standing bodhisattvas. At his feet sit two others; on either side of these seated figures are a pair of donors. At the center front, a genie supports an incense burner protected by lions and guardians. The inscription on the back of the stand gives the date of the altarpiece, which corresponds to 524, and reveals that the image was made at the order of a father to commemorate his dead son. *Rogers Fund, 1938, 38.158.1a–n*

39 Seated Buddha
T'ang dynasty, 7th c.
Dry lacquer; h. 38 in. (96.5 cm.)

Few early Chinese dry-lacquer figures have been preserved. In this technique numerous layers of lacquer-soaked cloth are molded over a wooden armature to the desired thickness and form; the figure is then painted in gesso, polychrome, and gilt.

This Buddha is said to be from Hopei province. The simplicity of the cranial protuberance, the squared-off hairline, and the sharply defined facial features all indicate a seventh-century date. Remnants of orange and gold still brighten the gray surface of the figure. *Rogers Fund, 1919, 19.186*

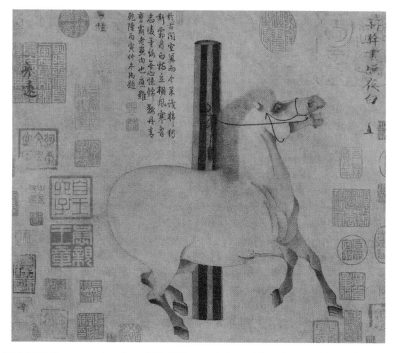

40 HAN KAN, T'ang dynasty, act. ca. 742–756
Night-Shining White
*Handscroll; ink on paper; 12¹⁄₈ × 13³⁄₈ in.
(30.8 × 34 cm.)*

Han Kan's portrait of Night-Shining White, one of the favorite horses of the T'ang emperor Ming-huang (r. 712–756), may be the best-known horse painting in Chinese art. Recorded by eminent critics almost continuously from the ninth century on, the short handscroll also has a formidable pedigree in the form of seals and colophons. The animal, with its wild eye, flaring nostrils, and prancing hooves, epitomizes Chinese myths about "celestial steeds" that were dragons in disguise. Although the horse is tethered to a sturdy post, *Night-Shining White* radiates supernatural energy. At the same time it presents an accurate portrayal of a strong, restless animal. The sensitive contour lines are reinforced by pale ink-wash modeling in a style known as *pai-hua*, or "white painting." *Purchase, The Dillon Fund Gift, 1977, 1977.78*

41 Summer Mountains
Northern Sung dynasty, 11th c.
*Handscroll; ink and light color on silk;
17³⁄₄ × 45¹⁄₄ in. (45.1 × 114.9 cm.)*

The monumental landscape style, in the ascendant since the first half of the tenth century, reached its apogee around the middle of the eleventh century. In landscape painting the subject was creation itself. Mountains and trees contrast with and complement each other according to Yin and Yang concepts in various relationships of high and low, hard and soft, light and dark—to create infinite change, variety, and interest in a timeless landscape. *Summer Mountains*, attributed to Ch'ü Ting (act. ca. 1023–1056), depicts the vastness and multiplicity of the natural world. The best way to appreciate such a painting is to look closely and identify oneself with a human figure or a man-made object in the scene. The vastness of the view surrounding the tiny travelers is as convincing as it is staggering. Strife and concern seem far away from a world of such visual splendor. *Gift of The Dillon Fund, 1973, 1973.120.1*

42   KUO HSI, Northern Sung dynasty, ca. 1000–ca. 1090
Trees Against a Flat Vista
Handscroll; ink and pale color on silk; 13¾ × 41¼ in. (34.9 × 104.8 cm.)

During the late eleventh century, landscape painters began to turn away from minutely descriptive portrayals of nature to explore evocations of a specific mood, a past style, or temporal phenomena—the changing seasons, the hours of the day, or the varied effects of weather. In this painting the bare branches of the trees and the dense mist suggest an autumnal evening; the travelers emphasize the transitory quality of the moment. The panorama is depicted in blurred ink washes and freely brushed outline strokes that impart the illusion of moisture-laden atmosphere and contribute to the introspective mood of the scene. The "billowing cloud" rocks and "crab claw" branches of the trees add to the painting's dreamlike quality and are hallmarks of Kuo Hsi, the preeminent late eleventh-century landscapist. *Gift of John M. Crawford, Jr. in honor of Douglas Dillon, 1981, 1981.276*

43   EMPEROR HUI-TSUNG, Sung dynasty, 1082–1135
Finches and Bamboo
Handscroll; ink and colors on silk; 11 × 18 in. (27.9 × 45.7 cm.)

"What good fortune for these insignificant birds to have been painted by this sage," mused the famous connoisseur Chao Meng-fu (1254–1322) in a colophon attached to this gemlike painting. The sage he refers to is Hui-tsung, the eighth emperor of the Sung dynasty and the most artistically accomplished of his imperial line. During his reign (1101–1125) he spent vast sums in the pursuit of fine calligraphy, of great paintings, and of spectacular rocks for his garden-parks.

Finches and Bamboo illustrates the supra-realistic style of bird and flower painting practiced at Hui-tsung's Painting Academy. The painting is signed at the right with the emperor's cipher over a seal that reads "imperial writing." Over one hundred other seals of subsequent owners and connoisseurs dot the scroll. The scroll is also valued for the superb calligraphy in the form of appreciative comments that follow the painting. *John M. Crawford, Jr. Collection, Purchase, Douglas Dillon Gift, 1981, 1981.278*

44 Emperor Ming-huang's Flight to Shu
Southern Sung dynasty, 12th c.
Hanging scroll; ink and colors on silk;
32⅝ × 44¾ in. (82.9 × 113.7 cm.)

In 745, after thirty-three years of able rule, the T'ang emperor Ming-huang (r. 712–756) fell in love with the concubine Yang Kuei-fei. As he grew indifferent to his duties, court intrigues flourished, and in 755 Yang Kuei-fei came under attack. Fleeing from the capital at Sian to the safety of Shu (Szechuan province), the emperor was confronted by mutinous troops who forced him to assent to the execution of Yang Kuei-fei. Ming-huang looked on with horror and shame and soon after abdicated. This painting depicts the imperial entourage moving through a somber landscape after the execution. Yang Kuei-fei's richly caparisoned white horse is followed by a palace guard who grins at the absence of the rider. The disconsolate emperor, dressed in a red robe, follows at the right. (This painting was called *The Tribute Horse* in earlier Museum publications.) *Rogers Fund, 1941, 41.138*

45 CH'IEN HSUAN, late Southern Sung–early Yuan dynasty, ca. 1235–after 1301
Wang Hsi-chih Watching Geese
Handscroll; ink, color, and gold on paper;
9⅛ × 36½ in. (23.2 × 92.7 cm.)

Ch'ien Hsuan's life was half over when the Mongols completed their conquest of China, and after 1279 he chose to live as an *i-min,* a "forgotten citizen" of the Sung dynasty. His "blue-and-green" style is a consciously "primitive" manner. The "blue-and-green" idiom originated in the T'ang period (618–907), and its characteris-tic features are the "iron-wire" outline technique and the use of flat mineral green and blue colors. In *Watching Geese* we see this archaic idiom used as the perfect nonrealistic mode for depicting a classic art-historical story. Wang Hsi-chih (321–379), the calligraphic master of legendary fame, derived inspiration from natural forms; he was said to have solved difficult technical problems of writing by observing the graceful movements of geese. *Gift of The Dillon Fund, 1973, 1973.120.6*

46 CHAO MENG-FU, Yüan dynasty, 1254–1322
Twin Pines Against a Flat Vista
Handscroll; ink on paper; 10½ × 42 in.
(26.7 × 106.7 cm.)

A minor member of the Sung imperial clan,
Chao Meng-fu was a young man when the Southern Sung fell to the Mongols. He went north in
1286 to serve at the Mongol court; there he
came in contact with the Northern Sung tradition of landscape painting. In Southern Sung
painting a brushstroke's primary function is to
represent form, either as an outline or as a
modeling stroke. Chao, however, advised that
calligraphic techniques be used in painting, stating that "calligraphy and painting have always
been the same." Rocks and pines, a subject
made popular by Northern Sung masters (no.
42), here act as the vehicle for the expressive
brushwork of a master calligrapher. Chao's approach influenced succeeding painters, allowing them to "write out" their feelings in pictorial
form. *Gift of The Dillon Fund, 1973, 1973.120.5*

47 NI TSAN, late Yüan–early Ming
dynasty, 1301–1374
Woods and Valleys of Yü-shan
Hanging scroll; ink on paper; 37½ × 14⅛ in.
(95.3 × 35.9 cm.)

The late Yüan period—the years from 1333 to
1368 that saw the overthrow of the Mongols
—was among the most chaotic in China's history.
One of the Four Great Masters of this era, Ni
Tsan developed only one basic landscape composition: sparse trees, sometimes with an empty
pavilion, standing on a riverbank, with distant
mountains on the opposite shore. In this hanging scroll, dated 1372, the trees, like lonely
friends, huddle together against an otherwise
bleak background. The stillness of the trees
and rocks becomes even more alluring when
they are seen as symbols of deep and melancholy thoughts. *Gift of The Dillon Fund, 1973,
1973.120.8*

49 T'ANG YIN, Ming dynasty, 1470–1524
The Moon Goddess Ch'ang O
Hanging scroll; ink and colors on paper;
53½ × 23 in. (135.3 × 58.4 cm.)

A supremely gifted scholar and painter, T'ang
Yin forfeited all chances of an official career
after being involved in an examination scandal
in 1499. Turning to painting and poetry for his
subsistence, he led the life of a dissolute scholar
and died in poverty. This brilliantly executed
painting (ca. 1510) is a poignant reminder of
T'ang Yin's dashed dreams for success in the
official examinations—symbolized by the cassia branch in the goddess's left hand. (The word
"cassia" [*kuei*] is a pun on the word "nobility,"
which has the same pronunciation.) T'ang Yin's
poem, in bold calligraphy, reads in part: "Ch'ang
O, in love with the gifted scholar,/Presents him
with the topmost branch of the cassia tree."
The flat, oval face and elegant fluttering drapery
of the moon goddess reflect the Ming emphasis
on beautiful calligraphic line rather than three-
dimensional form. *Gift of Douglas Dillon, 1981,*
1981.4.2

48 The Assembly of the Buddha Shakyamuni
Shansi province, ca. second quarter of 14th c.
Water-base pigments over clay mixed with mud-and-straw foundation; 24 ft. 8 in. × 49 ft. 7 in. (7.52 × 15.12 m.)

The northern province of Shansi is a region rich in monuments of Buddhist art. A distinctive school of wall painting, containing both Buddhist and Taoist examples, flourished in Shansi along the lower reaches of the Fen River in the thirteenth and fourteenth centuries. This monumental mural epitomizes the mannered, elegant approach of the Fen River artists. Buddhist assemblies are arranged symmetrically about a large central image of the Buddha in one of his aspects or manifestations. Here Shakyamuni (the historical Buddha) is flanked by two major bodhisattvas, and the triad is in turn surrounded by a host of divine, mythological, or symbolic figures. Murals such as this one were intended to provide illiterate believers with a visual expression of Mahayana Buddhist metaphysics. They were not, in this period, the principal objects of devotion but were designed as a background for sculpture. *Gift of Arthur M. Sackler in honor of his parents, Isaac and Sophie Sackler, 1965, 65.29.2*

50 HUNG-JEN, late Ming–early Ch'ing dynasty, 1610–64
Dragon Pine on Mount Huang
Hanging scroll; ink and slight color on paper; 75⅞ × 31¼ in. (192.7 × 79.4 cm.)

Hung-jen was the central figure of the Anhwei school of painters, whose common bond was a fascination with Huang-shan (Yellow Mountain) in Anhwei province. This monumental work is one of the monk-painter's many "portraits" of the eccentric pines that cling to the sheer granite peaks of the mountain. While Hung-jen's paintings seem dominated by an aloof moral intelligence, intense emotion often lurks just below the surface. Here the tenacity of the tortuously bent pine reflects the artist's convictions as a Ming loyalist. Like the pine, he has a precarious existence (Hung-jen chose to become a Buddhist monk, rejecting the comfort and safety of an official position under the Ch'ing dynasty). *Gift of Douglas Dillon, 1976, 1976.1.2*

51 WANG HUI, Ch'ing dynasty, 1632–1717
The K'ang-hsi Emperor's Second Tour of the South
Scroll no. 3; ink and colors on silk; 2 ft. 2¹¹/₁₆ in. × 45 ft. 8½ in. (0.68 × 13.93 m.)

In 1689 the K'ang-hsi emperor (r. 1662–1722) made a grand tour of southern China to inspect his domains. Wang Hui was commissioned to record the momentous journey in painting, and a series of twelve sumptuous handscrolls was produced by Wang and his assistants between 1691 and 1698. Wang Hui designed the series; he also painted many of the landscape passages, leaving figures, architectural drawings, and the more routine work to his assistants. This scroll—*From Chi-nan to T'ai-an and Ascent of Mount T'ai*—is the third in the set. It shows the emperor's journey through Shantung province and culminates with a view of Mount T'ai, the famous "cosmic peak of the East," where he conducted a ceremony of worshiping heaven. The landscape background, painted in ink and cool colors with blue and green predominating, is typical of the style of Wang Hui's later years. *Purchase, The Dillon Fund Gift, 1979, 1979.5*

52 The Astor Court
The Astor Court is modeled on a scholar's court in the Garden of the Master of the Fishing Nets in Soochow, a city renowned for its garden architecture. Chinese gardens were meant to be lived in as well as viewed. The formula for domestic architecture, repeated over thousands of years, was to build rooms around a central courtyard that provided light, air, and a view of the outdoors to each room. The scholar's garden began with domestic architectural forms and added to them the wildness of nature. By enlarging courtyards and buildings, by increasing the plantings, by adding rocks and water,

the scholar created a microcosm of the natural world. In the scholar's garden, as in the Astor Court, complexity of space is achieved through an orderly use of Yin and Yang opposites: darkness and light; hardness and softness.

This garden court represents the first permanent cultural exchange between the United States and the People's Republic of China. The materials needed for construction were gathered and manufactured in China, and the court was built almost entirely by Chinese craftsmen. The Vincent Astor Foundation provided the funds for the Astor Court, which includes the Ming Hall at its north end.

53 Vessel

Six Dynasties, late Northern dynasties—Sui dynasty, ca. second half of 6th—early 7th c., probably of northern origin
Porcelaneous stoneware with celadon glaze; l. 11⅞ in. (30.2 cm.)

This magnificently sculpted crouching animal epitomizes the great affection and charm with which the Chinese have always represented animals. The pale olive glaze is an interesting example of a major category of high-fired green glazes generally called "celadons" in the West.

An extremely important group of celadon-glazed stonewares was produced in numerous kilns in northern Chekiang and southern Kiangsu provinces from as early as the Han dynasty into the Sung era; these ceramics are frequently called proto-Yüeh and Yüeh wares, probably after an administrative capital once known as Yüeh Chou.

Recent tomb finds suggest that another tradition of green-glazed stonewares was established in northern China during the Six Dynasties, probably by the mid-sixth century. Analysis of the composition of this vessel indicates that it may be assigned with some confidence to this lesser-known group of northern wares. *Harris Brisbane Dick Fund, 1960, 60.75.2*

54 Flask

T'ang dynasty, ca. 9th c., probably from Huang-tao kilns, Honan province
Stoneware with suffused glaze; h. 11½ in. (29.2 cm.)

Among the most dramatic T'ang stonewares are those with fairly thick, opaque dark-brown or black glazes, which seem to add extra power to already energetic shapes. Sometimes, as on this stunning flask, the dark glazes are suffused with bold splashes of contrasting color, including shades of cream, gray, blue, and lavender. These patches of color generally appear to have been applied at random and to have been permitted to run at will over the glaze. The unusual shape of this exceptionally fine flask was probably based on a leather prototype. As on the leather original, a cord can be passed up the sides and through two loops; the back is flat, allowing the flask to lie securely when carried. *Gift of Mr. and Mrs. John R. Menke, 1972, 1972.274*

55 Bowl

Five Dynasties, 10th c., Yüeh ware, probably from a kiln in the vicinity of Shang-lin Hu, Chekiang province
Porcelaneous stoneware with celadon glaze; diam. 10⅝ in. (27 cm.)

The celadon-glazed wares that had been the pride of the Yüeh kilns for centuries reached their high point during the Five Dynasties period (907–960), when Yüeh potters produced some of the finest ceramics in the history of the region. An important part of their output, known as *pi-se yao,* "prohibited-color wares," was reserved for the princes of Wu-Yüeh, who controlled the area. This special ware is probably represented by one of the great treasures of the collection—this bowl with a splendidly carved design of three high-spirited dragons under a lustrous, translucent soft-green glaze. The agile grace displayed by these dragons as they race across a background of waves is a tribute to the peerless technique of the carver, who, by pressing a stylus against damp clay, has virtually created perpetual motion. (One dragon's tail is tucked under his hind leg, a Yüeh trademark.) *Rogers Fund, 1917, 18.56.36*

56 Ewer

Northern Sung dynasty, 11th–12th c., probably from Huang-pao Chen (Yao Chou) kilns, Shensi province
Porcelaneous stoneware with celadon glaze; h. 8¼ in. (21 cm.)

This magnificent ewer demonstrates the special talent of Sung potters for stressing shape and glaze, relegating ornament—no matter how complex—to the lesser role of complementing rather than dominating the object. The body is brilliantly carved with two phoenixes flying amid a ground of scrolls with conventionalized flowers and sickle-shaped leaves. The bold design is emphasized by the translucent olive-green glaze, which accumulates in the recessed areas, intensifying in tone and accenting the pattern. Standing on three scowling-mask legs that terminate in paws, the ewer is topped by a high arched handle in the form of a serpent-like dragon, whose head forms the spout; a small figure crouches on his back. This ewer exemplifies the group of wares, generically known as Northern celadons, produced at several kiln-complexes in northern China during the Northern Sung, Chin, and Yüan periods. *Gift of Mrs. Samuel T. Peters, 1926, 26.292.73*

57 Jar

Ming dynasty, Hsüan-te mark and period, 1426–35, from kilns at Ching-te Chen, Kiangsi province
Porcelain painted in underglaze blue; h. 19 in. (48.3 cm.)

The porcelains of the Ming dynasty have attained such recognition in the West that "Ming" has almost become the generic name for anything ceramic fabricated in China before the twentieth century. While, unhappily, many of the pieces called "Ming" have no claim to that attribution, the porcelains that were produced during the period are among the most beautiful and exciting to emerge from China's kilns. In many respects the blue-and-white porcelains of the early fifteenth century illustrate these wares at their apogee. They combine the freedom and energy of a newly ripened art form with the sophistication of concept and mastery of execution that come with maturity. The highest traditions of early Ming dynasty brushwork are represented in the bristling dragon on this marvelous jar. Flying amid cloud forms, he moves around the jar with total power and consummate grace. Flanked by the heads of fearsome monsters is an inscription with the reign title of the incumbent emperor, Hsüan-te (1426–35). *Gift of Robert E. Tod, 1937, 37.191.1*

58 The God of Wealth in Civil Aspect

Ch'ing dynasty, probably K'ang-hsi period, late 17th–early 18th c., from kilns at Ching-te Chen, Kiangsi province
Porcelain painted in polychrome enamels on the biscuit; h. 23⅞ in. (60.6 cm.)

Seated on a gilded silver throne, his filigreed hat set with pearls, jade, and kingfisher feathers, this figure is truly gorgeous. One of a pair, he is possibly the God of Wealth in Civil Aspect (the other may be the God of Wealth in Military Aspect); he wears elaborately fashioned robes, sumptuously embroidered with a panoply of flowers and auspicious symbols. The figure is decorated in the famille verte palette of enamels, but rather than using them over a glaze—which would tend to fill in and blunt the sharp modeling of the features and contours of the garments—the painter has applied them directly onto the unglazed, prefired (or biscuited) porcelain body. *Bequest of John D. Rockefeller, Jr., 1961, 61.200.11*

TEXTILES

59 Lay Aristocrat's Robe (*Chuba*)

Tibetan, 18th–19th c.
Silk yarns and silk yarns wrapped with gold (k'o-ssu); *62 × 75 in. (157.5 × 190.5 cm.)*

A robe like this, composed of an early Ch'ing five-clawed dragon robe (and fragments of other Chinese silks), could be worn, in accord with Lhasa sumptuary laws, only by princes of the church and certain lay aristocrats. The Tibetans, through friendly association with the Manchus long before the latter invaded China in 1644, had a well-developed taste for the Chinese dragon robes and silks passed on to them by these neighbors on the northeast border of China. Tibetan taste seems to have been for early styles (or later copies of them); thus Tibetan robes are of special interest in the study of Chinese dragon robes, of which few early examples remain. *Rogers Fund, 1962, 62.206*

60 *Yogi* Coverlet
Japanese, 19th c.
*Cotton with cone-painted resist, hand-painted
pigments; h. 63½ in. (161.3 cm.), greatest
w. 58½ in. (148.5 cm.)*

A *yogi* coverlet is ceremonial bedding in the
form of a robe. On this one, the New Year is
symbolized by striking ornaments—the straw
rope with its prescribed strips of seaweed at
intervals and traditional auspicious objects (the
lobster, the fern and *yuzuriha* leaves, and the
mandarin orange). These decorative elements
are resist-dyed and, except for the rope which
is left white, are painted with bright-colored
pigments. The large family crest at the top is
composed of three cloves in a fine clear-dyed
blue. *Seymour Fund, 1966, 66.239.3*

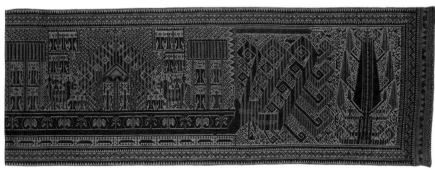

61 Ship Cloth
Sumatran, southern Lampong region, late
19th c.
Woven textile; 27 × 113½ in. (68.5 × 288.3 cm.)

Among the most remarkable textiles of the Indonesian archipelago are the so-called ship
cloths, which were woven on the south coast of
Sumatra. One group was decorated with a long
ship or a pair of ships in profile, usually carrying
animals and riders, trees, birds, buildings, and
human figures. The Museum's fine example (a
detail of which is illustrated) belongs, in the
designation of the Sumatrans, to the long ship
cloths (*palepai*). These cloths were hung as
backdrops in ceremonies of transition, such as
weddings and the presentation of the first grand-
child to its maternal grandparents. They have
not been made for at least seventy-five years,
and their origins and the reasons for their
decline are still only conjectural. *Gift of Alice
Lewisohn Crowley, 1939, 1979.173*

62 Woman's Robe (*Kosode*)

Japanese, Edo period, late 17th c.
Satin, tie-dyed, stitch-resisted, embroidered with silks, couched with silk yarns wrapped in gold; l. 53½ in. (135.9 cm.), w. at sleeves 53 in. (134.6 cm.)

This *kosode* reflects the taste of the Genroku era (1680–1700), when the wealthy merchant class was beginning to dominate society and artists such as Ogata Kōrin (nos. 9 and 10) were active. The bold design and soft, sumptuous colors are typical, as is the use of a variety of techniques to create a single garment. A branch with enormous cherry blossoms in tie-dye and stitch-resist hangs in the center of the robe's back. Below this branch cherry blossoms float in front of zigzags suggesting the cypress slats of a garden fence. A section of a waterwheel appears on one sleeve, cherry blossoms on the other. The combination of cherry blossoms with the waterwheel and the garden fence undoubtedly has poetic or literary overtones. *Purchase, Mary Livingston Griggs and Mary Griggs Burke Foundation Gift, 1980, 1980.222*

63 Welcoming the New Year

Chinese, Yüan dynasty, late 13th or early 14th c.
Panel; silk embroidery and plant fiber (some originally gold wrapped) on silk gauze; 85 × 25³/₁₆ in. (215.7 × 64 cm.)

During the Sung and Yüan dynasties, the art of embroidery reached a peak of refinement and complexity, with decorative compositions frequently imitating paintings both in format and in subject matter. Embroidered hangings were displayed in palace halls or residences to mark the changing seasons or to celebrate a birthday or the New Year. This large embroidered panel combines a number of auspicious symbols appropriate to the New Year's celebration. Young male children, here in Mongol costume, promise new life and the continuation of the family line; sheep and goats are emblems of good fortune. Since the word for sheep and goats (*yang*) also suggests that aspect of the Yin-Yang dichotomy associated with growth, warmth, and light, the embroidery may be read as a visual pun conveying a wish for a sunny and prosperous New Year. Technically, the panel is extraordinary for its unusual and painstaking workmanship. *Purchase, The Dillon Fund Gift, 1981, 1981.410*

GROUND FLOOR

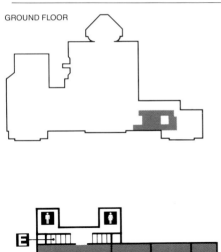

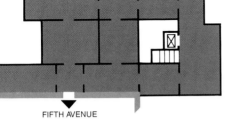

FIFTH AVENUE

COSTUME INSTITUTE

Founded in 1937, the Costume Institute collects, preserves, and exhibits clothing from the seventeenth century to the present. The exceptionally comprehensive collection includes both fashionable dress and regional costumes from Europe, Asia, Africa, and the Americas; its archives include accessories and photographs, and there is an extensive costume library. The annual exhibition mounted by the Institute has become an important event in the cultural and social life of New York.

The Costume Institute also serves as a research center where designers from the theater and the clothing industry, as well as students, scholars, and other professionals in the field of design, can study costumes and related materials. The library and storage facilities are available by appointment for consultation by scholars and professionals.

1 Man's Doublet

Spanish, late 16th c.

Silk velvet with patterned silver-gilt bands; l. at center back 23 in. (58.4 cm.)

Paintings, which are the primary visual source for research of costume before the eighteenth century, cannot furnish the kind of information that actual garments provide. For example, from a careful look at the front panels of this doublet we learn that it is the use of the grain of the fabric, cut on the bias, that helps it to fit smoothly and gives it its fashionably elongated protruding center front, called a peascod belly.

For several centuries the doublet was an indispensable article of gentlemen's apparel. It evolved from the protective padded shirts worn under armor during the Middle Ages. To fit comfortably, particularly under plate armor, it had to be shaped closely to the body. For this reason doublets are probably the earliest examples of "tailor made" clothing. In the latter part of the seventeenth century they grew longer and became waistcoats. Today's men's vests are descendants of the doublet. *Anonymous Gift, 1978, 1978.128*

2 Chopines
Venetian, ca. 1600
Leather decorated with stamped and pierced designs and silk-floss pom-poms; l. 8¾ in. (22.2 cm.)

Chopines—a fashionable version of shoes or sandals on platforms or stilts—arrived in Venice from the Orient in the late fifteenth century. Women found them so appealing that their popularity, which was to last for almost two centuries, spread rapidly from Italy to France and from there to other countries throughout Europe. The height of the platforms varied from three to eighteen inches. High chopines made walking so precarious that to keep from toppling, ladies had to be supported by servants or escorts. Thus wearing chopines was looked on as a status symbol, a privilege of rich upper classes who could afford such dependence. Chopines are an interesting example of the vagaries of fashion. Since earliest times, shoes on raised soles have been worn in many places as a protection against muddy roads and fields. When fashion translated this form of footwear into chopines, a practical article of wearing apparel evolved into an essentially impractical accessory serving primarily to enhance the wearer's worth in the eyes of society. *Purchase, Irene Lewisohn Bequest, 1973, 1973.114.4ab*

3 É. PINGAT & CIE, Paris, ca. 1855–ca. 1893
Ballgowns
(Left) *Satin, various other materials; l. at center back: bodice 11½ in. (29.2 cm.), skirt 70 in. (177.8 cm.)*
(Right) *Silk faille, various other materials; l. at center back: bodice 13 in. (33 cm.), skirt 62¾ in. (159.4 cm.)*

These two ballgowns are beautiful examples of the elegant designs of Émile Pingat, one of the first couturiers. They date from about 1866 and were worn by Margaretta Willoughby Pierrepont (1827–1902), the wife of Edwards Pierrepont (1817–92) whose distinguished career included service as attorney general of the United States and foreign minister to Great Britain. Little is known of the designer except his name and the address of his shop. The labels on these two dresses read: É. Pingat & Cie, no. 30 rue Louis le Grand, Paris. Both of these gowns show his work at its most sophisticated; especially notable is the embellishment of the wide expanse of the skirts. The dress on the left is of white satin trimmed with ruched tulle, white velvet ribbon, loops of white satin studded with tiny gold beads, and white satin bows. The dress on the right is of white silk faille trimmed with bands of black lace dotted in gilt, black velvet ribbon, white satin appliqués, and black chenille fringe. *Gift of Mary Pierrepont Beckwith, 1969, CI 69.33.1ab (left), CI 69.33.12ab (right)*

4   HOUSE OF WORTH, Paris, 1858–1956
Evening Gown
Silk satin and velvet; l. of bodice 17 in. (43 cm.),
l. of skirt 42½ in. (107.5 cm.)

Few garments better demonstrate the relationship
of haute couture to a major artistic movement than
does this Worth evening gown (ca. 1898–1900).
The dynamic linear motion associated with Art
Nouveau is clearly evident in the design of the
fabric as well as in the curvilinear volumes of the
silhouette. The luxury of the gown, made of heavy

white silk satin voided with black velvet in an
Art Nouveau scroll design, exemplifies the elegance of the late 1890s. The House of Worth
was the first of the great couture houses of Paris;
under its founder, Charles Frederick Worth
(1825–95), it was known for the high quality of its
design and craftsmanship. These standards were
maintained by Worth's sons, Jean Philippe and
Gaston, after the death of their father. *Gift of Eva*
Drexel Dahlgren, 1976, 1976.258.1ab

5 MARY QUANT, British, b. 1934
Minidress (left)
Wool; l. at center back 33½ in. (85.1 cm.)
ANDRÉ COURRÈGES, French, b. 1923
Coatdress (center)
Wool and grosgrain silk; l. at center back 37½ in. (95.3 cm.)
YVES SAINT LAURENT, French, b. 1936
Day Dress (right)
Wool; l. at center back 36 in. (91.4 cm.)

The 1960s saw revolutions in politics, art, music, education, and fashion, initiated in large part by the young. The minidress caused a radical change in the fashionable silhouette; it evolved from a popular sleeveless chemise dress of the early 1960s, becoming progressively higher in the waistline and shorter in the skirt. London was the center of the youth culture, and the minis of the English girls ("birds") influenced the American Mod Look and the French *style anglais*. Mary Quant was in the forefront of British design, and her minidress (1966–67) is characteristic of her exuberant clothing. In Paris André Courrèges was designing functional young clothes, distinguished by vibrant colors and unusual cut. He studied architecture before apprenticing with Balenciaga, and his impeccable tailoring, seen in his coatdress (1965), lifted the mini into couture. Yves Saint Laurent, another young designer, had to leave Dior because his avant-garde collection was rejected by that house's staid clientele. He created some of the most wearable mini fashions; his day dress (1965), constructed in geometric segments à la Mondrian, shows his qualities of wit, taste, and fine tailoring. Left: *Gift of Maxine McKendry, 1969, CI 69.10.1;* center: *Gift of Kimberly Knitwear Inc., 1974, 1974.136.3;* right: *Gift of Mrs. William Rand, 1969, CI 69.23*

6 Woman's Costume: Blouse, Skirt, Apron, and Kerchief
Yugoslavian, early 20th c.
Handwoven cotton, embroidered in silk and cotton floss and trimmed with lace; l. of blouse 25½ in. (64.8 cm.), l. of skirt 28½ in. (72.4 cm.), l. of apron 27½ in. (69.9 cm.), kerchief 25½ x 16⅝ in. (64.8 x 42.2 cm.)

This costume from Donja Kupčina is characteristic of those worn in the Panonian Plain region of northern Croatia. Unlike the clothing worn in urban areas, where fashions accent change, regional costumes reflect a preference for maintaining a traditional manner of dress that is unique to an ethnic group. As a result, these costumes reflect their geographical origin rather than the date they were made. The fact that this costume has a separate blouse and skirt—instead of the long one-piece chemise worn in most of the southern Balkan states—suggests that it is related to the central-eastern European group of costumes. Details such as the high collar, embroidered bib, deep sleeve cuffs, and system of pleating help to place this costume south of Zagreb in northern Croatia. One of the six republics of Yugoslavia, Croatia had closer ties to Austria-Hungary than to the Ottoman Empire. Costumes from this region therefore have a distinct European flavor, while those from the lower republics show a strong Turkish influence. *Purchase, Irene Lewisohn Bequest, 1979, 1979.132.1a–c*

SECOND FLOOR

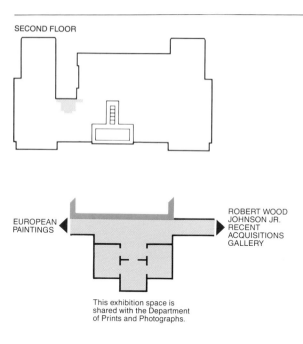

EUROPEAN
PAINTINGS

ROBERT WOOD
JOHNSON JR.
RECENT
ACQUISITIONS
GALLERY

This exhibition space is
shared with the Department
of Prints and Photographs.

DRAWINGS

In 1880, ten years after the incorporation of the Museum, Cornelius Vanderbilt purchased 670 drawings from the pioneering American collector James Jackson Jarves; he then presented these works, which were attributed to European Old Masters, to the Museum. The exhibition of the Vanderbilt drawings seems to have been the first full-scale presentation of drawings by European masters in any American museum. By 1906 the uneven quality of this near-permanent display became apparent, and one of the tasks undertaken by the English critic Roger Fry, who had been called to the Museum as curator of paintings, was the acquisition of representative examples of European draftsmanship. He served as curator in New York for only a year, but he continued for several years thereafter to advise the Museum on purchases. He was succeeded in this consultative role by another English critic, R. Langton Douglas.

In the third, fourth, and fifth decades of the century, the collection of drawings, then auxiliary to the Department of Paintings, grew slowly, enriched from time to time by gift, bequest, or purchase. Since 1960, when the department was set up as a separate curatorial division, a concentrated effort has been made to enrich its holdings. The collection now includes close to four thousand drawings; this growth has been paralleled by an extraordinary increase in the collection's quality and importance. The department is especially known for its Italian and French drawings from the fifteenth through the nineteenth century.

Since drawings are extremely susceptible to damage from prolonged exposure to light, none of the collection is on permanent view. The department does, however, present a varied program of exhibitions, reflecting every aspect of its holdings. The department's study room is open by appointment to qualified scholars.

1 LEONARDO DA VINCI, Italian, 1452–1519
Studies for a Nativity
*Pen and brown ink, over preliminary sketches
in metalpoint on pink prepared paper; 7⅝ ×
6⁷/₁₆ in. (19.3 × 16.2 cm.)*

In these sketches of the Virgin kneeling before the Christ Child, who lies on the ground,
Leonardo explored a theme that was to emerge
as the *Madonna of the Rocks*, where the Virgin
kneels facing the spectator, her right hand raised
in benediction over the seated Infant Jesus.
The sketches at the center and at the lower left
corner of the sheet, where the Virgin raises
both arms in devotional wonder, are related to a
design by Leonardo that must have been developed at least to the stage of a complete cartoon,
for several painted copies have survived. The
controversy about the dating of Leonardo's two
paintings of the *Madonna of the Rocks* (Louvre,
Paris; National Gallery, London) makes it difficult
to decide whether the drawing is to be dated
1483 or considerably earlier, during Leonardo's
first Florentine period. *Rogers Fund, 1917, 17.142.1*

2 MICHELANGELO BUONARROTI, Italian,
1475–1564
Studies for the Libyan Sibyl
Red chalk; 11⅜ × 8⅜ in. (28.9 × 21.4 cm.)

This celebrated sheet bears on the recto a
series of studies from a nude male model for
the figure of the Libyan Sibyl that appears on
the frescoed ceiling of the Sistine Chapel, commissioned in 1508 and finally unveiled in 1512.
In the principal and highly finished drawing
dominating the sheet, Michelangelo has studied
the turn of the sibyl's body, the position of the
head and arms. The left hand of the figure is
studied again below, as are the left foot and
toes. A study of the sibyl's head, possibly the
first drawing made on the sheet, appears at the
lower left, and a rough sketch of the torso and
shoulders is immediately above it. *Purchase,
Joseph Pulitzer Bequest, 1924, 24.197.2*

3 RAPHAEL, Italian, 1483–1520
Nude Male Figure
Pen and brown ink; 8¹³/₁₆ × 6¹/₄ in. (22.4 × 15.9 cm.)

This nude male figure has been drawn with a forceful pen line and sharp anatomical observation from a model in the studio. The figure, with his head hanging limply forward and his arms raised behind his back by cords that are hardly indicated, may well be a study for one of the thieves crucified with Christ.

On the other side of this sheet is a composition study in red chalk for the *Madonna in the Meadow* (Kunsthistorisches Museum, Vienna), which bears a date that can be read as 1505 or 1506. (See also European Paintings, nos. 17 and 18.) *Rogers Fund, 1964, 64.47*

5 J. A. D. INGRES, French, 1780–1867
Three Studies of a Male Nude
All four corners rounded. Pencil; 7³/₄ × 14³/₈ in.
(19.7 × 36.5 cm.)

A few years after his arrival in Rome in 1806,
Ingres was commissioned by the French military governor to supply pictures for the Palazzo
del Quirinale, which was then destined to serve
as Napoleon's Roman residence. One of the
subjects was from Plutarch: Romulus Victorious over Acron, King of the Caeninenses, Carries the Spolia Opima to the Temple of Jupiter.
Working in his studio in the church of the Trinità
dei Monti, Ingres finished the picture in 1812.

Ingres made a number of magnificent studies
from the nude for the figures of Romulus and
his soldiers, as well as for the dead body of
Acron. None of the solutions proposed in this
drawing for the position of Acron's arms and feet
was adopted in the picture, where the corpse is
turned toward the spectator, with the right arm
over the chest. (See also European Paintings,
no. 121, and Robert Lehman Collection, nos. 26
and 45.) *Rogers Fund, 1919, 19.125.2*

6 EDGAR DEGAS, French, 1834–1917
Portrait of Édouard Manet
Pencil and charcoal; 13 × 9¹/₈ in. (33 × 23.2 cm.)

About 1864 Degas made two etched portraits of
the painter Édouard Manet. In the first of these
Manet is seated with his top hat in hand. The
present drawing and another sketch in the
Museum, both purchased at the sale of the
contents of Degas's studio in 1918, are preparatory studies for this etching. Manet and Degas
seem to have been good friends, in spite of the
latter's rather irascible nature and a mutual
professional suspicion. About the time these
drawings were made, Degas painted Manet
listening to Madame Manet playing the piano.
Manet, to whom Degas presented the picture,
was dissatisfied with his wife's likeness and cut
her off the canvas—a mutilation that quite under-
standably enraged Degas. (See also European
Paintings, nos. 137–139; European Sculpture
and Decorative Arts, no. 24; and Robert Lehman Collection, no. 31.) *Rogers Fund, 1919,
19.51.7*

4 GIOVANNI BATTISTA TIEPOLO, Italian,
1696–1770
River God and Nymph
*Pen and brown ink, brown wash, over a little
black chalk; 9¹/₄ × 12⁵/₁₆ in. (23.5 × 31.3 cm.)*

This river god and his attendant nymph appear
on the edge of a painted cornice at one end of
the ceiling Tiepolo painted in fresco in the
Palazzo Clerici at Milan in 1740. Some twelve
years later Tiepolo used the same figures reclining on the edge of the frescoed ceiling of the
Kaisersaal at the Würzburg Residenz (see European Paintings, no. 32). Only in his early years
did Tiepolo produce drawings for sale; the drawings of his maturity seem to have been kept in
his studio, where they served as a repertory of
compositional motifs. *Rogers Fund, 1937,
37.165.32*

7 GEORGES SEURAT, French, 1859–91
Portrait of the Artist's Mother
Conté crayon; 12⁵/₁₆ × 9⁷/₁₆ in. (31.2 × 24 cm.)

Using reserves of the white paper for his high-lights, Seurat has built up in graduated passages of velvety conté crayon a subtle but massive form that seems to shimmer in the light. Technically the drawing is simple but the results have a masterful plastic authority. The drawing was entered by Seurat in the Salon des Artistes Français of 1883 and is listed in the catalogue of the exhibition. At the last moment it was replaced by the much larger portrait of the painter Aman-Jean, a drawing also now in the Museum. (See also European Paintings, nos. 155 and 156.) *Purchase, Joseph Pulitzer Bequest, 1955, 55.21.1*

8 PETER PAUL RUBENS, Flemish, 1577–1640
Study for a Standing Female Saint
Brush and light brown wash over traces of black chalk; certain contours reinforced in pen and dark brown ink; 18³/₈ × 12¹/₈ in. (46.7 × 30.9 cm.)

This full-length female figure resembles in both dress and attitude classical marble statues of Roman empresses. The addition of the sword, however, suggests that the figure is intended to be a saint or martyr. This is, in fact, a drawing for Saint Domitilla, made in connection with the preparation of the first version, now at Grenoble, of Rubens's most important Roman commission, the high altarpiece for the Chiesa Nuova. This rapidly drawn sketch records the artist's initial and later largely rejected ideas for the disposition and poses of the saints that were to be ranged in the picture before the archway, over which hangs an image of the Virgin and Child. (See also European Paintings, nos. 65 and 66.) *Rogers Fund, 1965, 65.175*

9 REMBRANDT, Dutch, 1606–1669
Seated Man Wearing a Flat Cap
Pen and brown ink, brown wash, and white gouache; 5¹³/₁₆ × 5⁷/₁₆ in. (14.8 × 13.8 cm.)

Rembrandt has drawn this seated male figure with great authority, enriching the energetic pen outlines with summary but masterful indications of shadow. This sad-faced man wearing a broad flat cap, who has cast his coat down beside him on the steps, may be an actor. The drawing has been dated about 1636; at this time Rembrandt made other stylistically comparable drawings of theatrical figures. In a drawing in the Masson Collection at the École des Beaux-Arts in Paris, a seated male figure, who may also be an actor, wears a similar flat cap and rests the knuckles of his hand on his knee, as does the model in the present drawing. (See also European Paintings, nos. 74–77; Robert Lehman Collection, nos. 24 and 44; and Prints and Photographs, no. 2.) *Bequest of Mrs. H. O. Havemeyer, 1929. H. O. Havemeyer Collection, 29.100.935*

10 FRANCISCO GOYA, Spanish, 1746–1828
Portrait of the Artist
Point of brush and gray wash; 6 × 3⁹/₁₆ in. (15.3 × 9.1 cm.)

The artist, who wears on his lapel a locket inscribed with his name, stares at the spectator with an intensity that suggests that the portrait is a mirror image. Goya reveals in this small and powerful work a technical virtuosity that was later to enable him to dash off an extraordinary series of miniatures on ivory. The drawing is the first page of an album of fifty Goya drawings dating from several periods of the artist's activity, purchased by the Museum in 1935. (See also European Paintings, nos. 51 and 52; Robert Lehman Collection, no. 23; and Prints and Photographs, no. 3.) *Harris Brisbane Dick Fund, 1935, 35.103.1*

FIRST FLOOR

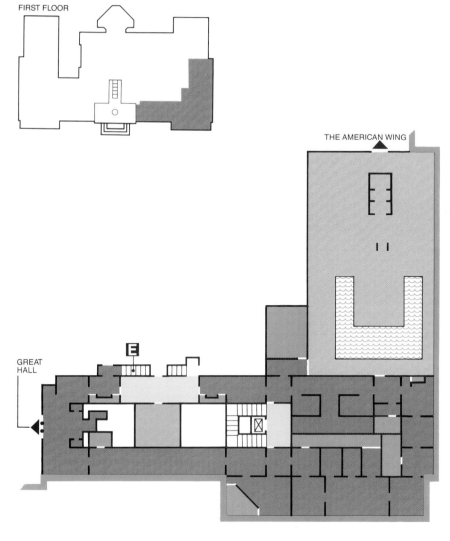

THE AMERICAN WING

GREAT
HALL

**THE LILA ACHESON WALLACE
GALLERIES OF EGYPTIAN ART**

 EGYPTIAN ART

 STUDY GALLERIES

FACSIMILES OF WALL PAINTINGS

 SPECIAL EXHIBITIONS GALLERY

 TEMPLE OF DENDUR: THE SACKLER WING

EGYPTIAN ART

The Department of Egyptian Art documents the life and culture of Egypt from the Prehistoric Period (before 3100 B.C.) to the Byzantine Period (8th century A.D.). Founded in 1906, this department was inaugurated with a program of excavations that lasted more than forty years and yielded vast holdings of archaeological material. The richness of the department's collection is due in part to this excavated material, comprising thousands of objects with recorded histories. The acquisition of numerous other important pieces has resulted in a collection that is one of the finest and most complete outside Cairo. Architectural monuments are included, notably the Tomb of Perneb and the Temple of Dendur. The collection's most renowned groups are its Mekutra models, jewelry from the Middle to New Kingdom, portrait sculpture from the Middle Kingdom, and sculpture depicting Queen Hatshepsut. The richness and depth of the collection is enhanced by extensive holdings in royal and private objects of Dynasties 11, 12, and 18 and funerary remains of Dynasties 19–26.

For the last decade the department's energies have been focused on a new installation of the entire collection. Now completed, these galleries occupy the entire northeast wing of the Museum's main floor and present a chronological panorama of ancient Egypt's art, history, and culture. Virtually every object of the collection is on view, either in the primary exhibition galleries or in auxiliary study rooms.

1 Elephant
Predynastic Period, ca. 3600–3400 B.C.
Pottery; l. 3⁷/₈ in. (9.8 cm.)

At first glance the Egyptian artist of the Predynastic Period appears to have been more realistic in his representations of animals and birds than of human beings. This belief is based primarily on the modern perception of these animal depictions as being more "natural" than those of human beings (and therefore less the result of deliberate artistic abstraction). Even at this early period, however, the simple carvings and drawings of birds and beasts testify to a conscious creative process by which the artist emphasized the salient features of a species so that the identity of the creature is hardly ever in doubt. This handmade clay elephant probably comes from Upper Egypt and is ascribed to the Amratian culture of Egyptian prehistory. *Rogers Fund, 1907, 07.228.74*

2 Comb
Predynastic Period, ca. 3400–3200 B.C.
Ivory; 2¹/₈ × 1¹/₂ in. (5.5 × 4 cm.)

The tendency to decorate utilitarian objects appeared very early in Egyptian culture. Among the earliest of such pieces was a series of finely carved ivory combs and knife handles produced in Upper Egypt during the period of the Gerzean culture. This comb, whose teeth are now missing, is adorned with rows of wild and domestic animals carved in raised relief: elephants, wading birds, hyenas, bovines, and (possibly) boars. Similar arrangements of these creatures occur on some other carved ivory pieces, an indication that the pattern and choice of animals were not haphazard; they may represent the emblems of some Predynastic towns or districts. *Bequest of Theodore M. Davis, 1915, 30.8.224*

3 Vessel
Late Predynastic–Early Dynastic Period,
ca. 3200–3000 B.C.
Painted pottery; h. 11¹³/₁₆ in. (30 cm.)

This type of decorated ware was produced toward the end of the Predynastic Period, when Egypt was becoming unified into a single kingdom. During this time artists began to represent important social and religious events, the precise significance of which has unfortunately remained obscure. The scenes on this red-on-buff vessel are among the most elaborate that have survived. The overall decoration is organized into four panels, each with a self-contained scene. Certain fundamental characteristics of Egyptian art are already evident: each scene depicts a single frozen event, and the more important participants (or objects) are rendered in larger scale than the others. The panel illustrated here features a many-oared galley, apparently drawn up on land, and several female figures in long skirts, who may be goddesses or priestesses. *Rogers Fund, 1920, 20.1.10*

4 Cosmetic Palette

Protodynastic, ca. 3200–3100 B.C.
Green schist; 7 × 2½ in. (17.8 × 6.3 cm.)

The Predynastic slate palette was originally developed for the grinding of eye paint and other cosmetics and was ultimately interred in the grave of its deceased owner. By the end of this period, however, these objects were adapted for votive or commemorative purposes, largely by the addition of incised and sculpted decoration to both sides of the palette. The decorative motifs included heraldic or magical designs as well as depictions of specific episodes in early Egyptian history. The largest and most elaborate examples of these palettes were discovered in excavations of the temples in which they were dedicated. This palette fragment shows part of the sculpted image of a bitch nursing her puppies. The back of the mother forms part of the exterior edge of the palette and is thus part of the frame for the interior design.
Gift of Henry G. Fischer, 1962, 62.230

5 Lion

Gebelein(?), Dynasty 0, ca. 3100 B.C.
Quartzite; l. 9¹⁵⁄₁₆ in. (25.2 cm.)

This powerful figure, which depicts a crouching lion, belongs to the beginning of Egypt's historic period, when, while all of Upper Egypt was unified under one rule, Lower Egypt remained a separate entity. A simplified sculptural treatment is characteristic of the time, and here it was also demanded by the hardness of the stone. The form was first pounded out of the quartzite with hammers of even harder stone, then polished with abrasives. This statuette may have been a votive offering for a temple, probably given by one of the first Egyptian kings. *Purchase, Fletcher Fund and The Guide Foundation, Inc. Gift, 1966, 66.99.2*

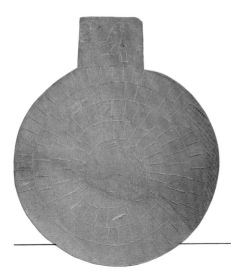

6   Game Board

Abydos(?), Dynasty 1, ca. 3100 B.C. or later
Green schist; 15¼ × 10⅝ in. (38.8 × 27 cm.)

The *mehen* game was played on a board in the shape of a coiled serpent whose body segments form the squares along which the playing pieces were advanced. The game was depicted in Old Kingdom tomb reliefs but had apparently dropped out of favor by the end of that period. Since the name of Horus Aha, the second king of Dynasty 1, is inscribed on the rectangular projection, this board may have been a votive or funerary gift. Like the better-known *senet* game, the snake game embodied religious associations, perhaps reinforced by the lion-shaped playing pieces, found in some tombs of the Early Dynastic Period, which may have been used in this game. *Harris Brisbane Dick Fund, 1958, 58.125.1*

7   Woman

Abydos, Dynasty 1, ca. 3100–2890 B.C.
Ivory; h. 1⅞ in. (4.7 cm.)

The relatively few extant pieces of figure sculpture from the earliest dynasties are generally small in size. The ivory and faience figures of this period in the Museum's collection are from the monuments of the kings of Dynasty 1 and the ancient temple of Osiris at Abydos. Some of these figures reveal a sophisticated modeling that accurately reproduces natural forms. An impression of naturalism, plus a surprising wealth of detail, appears in this ivory statuette of a woman with long hair dressed in parallel locks or braids. Despite the small scale of these early statues, some of them display a dignity and monumental quality often associated with the great sculptured figures of the Old Kingdom. *Gift of Egypt Exploration Fund, 1904, 04.18.50*

8   Cattle of Khufu

Lisht, Dynasty 4, ca. 2589–2566 B.C.
Limestone; 20 × 55½ in. (51 × 141 cm.)

The Museum's Egyptian expedition to Lisht (1906–34) recovered several blocks of fine limestone relief from the pyramid complex of Amenemhat I, the first king of Dynasty 12. These blocks had once adorned the walls of a monument of Khufu (Cheops), the second king of Dynasty 4. Together with many other blocks from Old Kingdom structures in the Memphite area, these limestone blocks had been transported from Giza to Lisht in a conscious effort to associate the new dynasty with the pyramid builders of the Old Kingdom. On one of these relief fragments, illustrated here, there are four long-horned bulls belonging to Khufu's royal estates. Short labels that describe the animals are written over their backs and are compounded with the names of the pharaoh. The fine low relief is an achievement of the classic art of Dynasty 4. (See also no. 9.) *Rogers Fund, 1922, 22.1.3a,b*

Archers

isht, Dynasty 4, ca. 2613–2494 B.C.
ainted limestone; 14½ × 9⅞ in. (37 × 25 cm.)

)ne of the most artistically interesting of the
eused limestone blocks uncovered at Lisht in
ower Egypt (see no. 8) is this fragment from
ie core of the North Pyramid. Portions of five
gyptian archers are preserved. Such complex-
y in the overlapping of figures is rarely found in
gyptian reliefs at any period. The carving is of
ie highest quality, flat but with subtle modeling;

only the ears stand out in a higher relief. The
twisted bowstrings and arrow feathering are
indicated with fine attention to detail. In style
this work matches the best examples of Dynasty 4, although no exact iconographic parallels of such an early date are extant. It is
unusual to find a distinct hooked shape to the
men's noses, a form usually, though not exclusively, reserved for foreigners. *Rogers Fund,
1922, 22.1.23*

10 Sahura and a Deity
Dynasty 5, ca. 2487–2473 B.C.
Gneiss; h. 24¾ in. (62.9 cm.)

This is the only known three-dimensional representation of Sahura, the second ruler of
Dynasty 5. Seated on a throne, the king is
accompanied by a smaller male figure person-
ifying Koptos, the fifth nome (province) of Upper
Egypt, who offers the king an ankh (symbol of
life) with his outstretched left hand. The nome
standard with its double falcon emblem is carved
above the god's head. While Sahura wears the
nemes headdress and square beard associated with kingship, the nome god wears an
archaic wig and curled beard, which are divine
attributes. The blocklike proportions of both
figures echo the overall rectangular shape of
the sculpture. Similar statue groups of King
Menkaura (Mycerinus) of Dynasty 4 were found
in his Valley Temple at Giza. *Rogers Fund,
1917, 18.2.4*

11 Tomb of Perneb
Saqqara, Dynasty 5, ca. 2450 B.C.
Partially painted limestone; h. of facade (recon-structed) 17 ft. (5.2 m.)

Toward the end of Dynasty 5 the lord chamber-lain Perneb built his tomb in the Old Kingdom cemetery of Saqqara west of the pyramid of Userkaef, founder of the dynasty. The tomb consisted of a limestone building (mastaba) and an underground chamber in which the body was placed. The mastaba, comprising a chapel and statue chamber, was purchased in 1913 from the Egyptian government; the recon-structed monument is one of the most interest-ing works in the Museum's Egyptian collection.

The artistic focal point of the tomb is the completely decorated offering chapel, where Perneb is several times depicted seated at an offering table, receiving sustenance from rela-tives and retainers. The offerings were placed on a slab set in front of the false door, through which Perneb's ka was able to partake of them. (See also nos. 14 and 23.) *Gift of Edward S. Harkness, 1913, 13.183.3*

12 Bound Prisoner
Saqqara, Dynasty 5, ca. 2400 B.C.
Limestone; h. 34⅛ in. (86.7 cm.)

This figure of a kneeling prisoner portrays a native of the Libyan Desert west of the Nile. Figures of this type belonged to a series repre-senting various peoples inhabiting the lands adjacent to Egypt; placed in royal pyramid tem-ples of the later Old Kingdom, they symbolized the king's control over the strife and disorder that they embodied. The deep facial furrows and the slanted eyes were devices by which the Egyptian artist characterized foreigners. All of these statues have been deliberately broken, possibly as part of the dedication ritual of the temple (or at the funeral of the king) or, alterna-tively, during a period of civil disorder that fol-lowed the Old Kingdom. *Louis V. Bell Fund, 1964, 64.260*

13 Memisabu and His Wife
Giza(?), Dynasty 5, ca. 2360 B.C.
Painted limestone; h. 24⅜ in. (62 cm.)

Dynasty 5 saw a growth in government bureau-cracy, both in its actual size and in the number of social strata represented by the officeholders. Statues such as this one depicting Memisabu, a steward and keeper of the king's property, and his wife were commissioned by officials of middle rank for placement in their tombs. This pair statue can be linked stylistically with monuments from the cemetery west of the Great Pyramid of Khufu (Cheops) at Giza. This work shows Memisabu and his wife in a rare type of embrace, which suggests that she—and not her husband—was the tomb owner; the pose has one known parallel in a statue depicting two female royal relatives. *Rogers Fund, 1948, 48.111*

14 False Door of Mechechi
Saqqara(?), Dynasty 6, ca. 2345–2181 B.C.
Limestone; 43 × 24⅜ in. (109 × 66.5 cm.)

The false-door stela, placed in the chapel of the Old Kingdom mastaba, served as a magic door through which the deceased in the next life received nourishment in material or ritual form. This impressive false-door stela bears ten sunken-relief inscriptions that include the name of Mechechi, an overseer of the palace staff. The texts request offerings and beneficences on Mechechi's behalf. Several of the inscriptions describe the deceased as being "revered before Unis," the last king of Dynasty 5, perhaps an indication that Mechechi's tomb was located near that of the king at Saqqara. The fine quality of this piece is especially apparent in the sharp carving of the inscriptions and the eight portrayals of the deceased, whose elongated proportions and minimal modeling are typical of Dynasty 6 relief sculpture. *Gift of Mr. and Mrs. J. J. Klejman, 1964, 64.100*

15 Headrest of Khentykai

Saqqara, Dynasty 6, ca. 2330 B.C.
Alabaster; h. 7⅝ in. (19.4 cm.)

The Egyptians preferred a rigid support for their heads while sleeping. The headrest was usually of wood and often consisted of three parts—a curved pillow, which supported the neck rather than the head, a fluted shaft, and a rectangular base. In contrast to pieces of furniture for everyday use, which were made of perishable materials, reproductions designed specifically for the dead were frequently of stone. This alabaster headrest was found in the mastaba tomb of the powerful official Khentykai, who held extremely important positions, including that of vizier, under Teti and Pepy I, two kings of Dynasty 6. The tomb itself was plundered, but the headrest, which was overlooked, suggests the luxurious manner in which an upper-class Old Kingdom mastaba was furnished. *Rogers Fund, 1926, 26.2.11*

16 Young Woman

Dynasty 6, ca. 2345–2181 B.C.
Painted wood; h. 11⅜ in. (28.8 cm.)

This late Old Kingdom wood figure was probably placed either in the sealed statue chamber of a mastaba tomb—along with other representations of the tomb owner and his family—or in the burial chamber of the young woman's own tomb. The face with its large eyes and deeply incised lines is lively rather than beautiful; the cranium, accentuated by the closely cropped hair, is unusually elongated; and the proportions of the slightly modeled body have been greatly attenuated in a manner characteristic of the late Old Kingdom. The arms and hands were formed from separate pieces and joined to the body. This carved statuette is one of the few extant objects of its kind convincingly dated to this early period. *Harris Brisbane Dick Fund, 1958, 58.125.3*

17 Funerary Stela of Inyotef ▶

Dynasty 11, ca. 2060–2010 B.C.
Limestone; 30¾ × 55⅞ in. (78 × 142 cm.)

The most common type of stela was the funerary slab placed in tomb chapels. These monuments were carved with hymns, prayers for offerings and other beneficences, and autobiographical texts (royal stelae, on the other hand, were public notices that extolled the king's deeds or announced official decrees). This refined private-tomb stela was made during the reign of the Theban ruler Mentuhotpe II. It shows characteristics that reflect the iconography and style of earlier monuments at Memphis, the capital of Egypt in the Old Kingdom. The stela (purchased in Western Thebes) was probably made after Mentuhotpe II united the Two Lands in 2040 B.C., thus providing access to those earlier northern monuments from which the sculptor apparently drew artistic inspiration. *Harris Brisbane Dick Fund, 1957, 57.95*

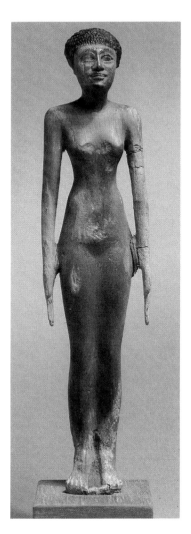

18 Model of House and Garden

Thebes, Dynasty 11, ca. 2009–1998 B.C.
Gessoed and painted wood and copper;
l. 33 in. (84 cm.)

Tomb reliefs of the Old Kingdom present picturesque glimpses of life on the great farms of
ancient Egypt, but the painted wooden models
placed in Middle Kingdom tombs offer even
more intimate views of wealthy landowners'
estates. The Museum possesses thirteen of the
models from the tomb of the chancellor Mekutra,
which show the organization of his property,
including the stables, storehouses, kitchens,
and shops, all filled with servants and craftsmen
at their tasks. This model of Mekutra's house
and garden shows the front veranda with its
gaily painted columns. In the center of the
garden is a copper-lined pond surrounded by
sycamore trees. *Purchase, Rogers Fund and
Edward S. Harkness Gift, 1920, 20.3.13*

19 Spear Thrower

Lisht, Dynasty 12, ca. 1971–1928 B.C.
Painted limestone; h. 8¾ in. (22 cm.)

This relief fragment was excavated at Lisht from
the South Pyramid complex of Senwosret I, the
second king of Dynasty 12. It shows a small
portion of a scene portraying the king's triumph
over foreign enemies, a subject that has rarely
survived from this period. An enemy soldier is
shown launching his spear; the short pointed
beard reveals his non-Egyptian origin, and the
traces of yellow paint on his body and what
appears to be red in his thick matted locks may
identify him as a Libyan. This relief therefore
would have come from the north wall of either
the causeway or the entrance vestibule of the
mortuary temple on which the king was traditionally portrayed destroying his Libyan and Asiatic
foes. On the south wall he would have been
depicted vanquishing Nubians. *Rogers Fund,
1913, 13.235.3*

20 Sphinx of Senwosret III
Dynasty 12, ca. 1878–1843 B.C.
Diorite; l. 28¾ in. (73 cm.)

While the standing sphinx was viewed as a conqueror by the Egyptians, the crouching sphinx was a guardian of sacred places. Thus pairs of such images flanked avenues or entrances to important buildings. This magnificent sphinx of Senwosret III, one of Egypt's greatest soldiers and administrators, is carved from a single block of beautifully grained diorite gneiss from quarries in Nubia. The sculptor's attention has been focused on the deeply lined face of the pharaoh. The proud yet careworn features reflect the philosophy of kingship prevalent at this period, when the ruler was felt to be morally responsible for his governance of the land. *Gift of Edward S. Harkness, 1917, 17.9.2*

21 Cowrie Girdle
Lahun, Dynasty 12, ca. 1897–1797 B.C.
Gold, carnelian, and green feldspar; l. 33 in. (84 cm.)

The personal jewelry and some other possessions of Princess Sithathoryunet—daughter of Senwosret II, sister of Senwosret III, and aunt of Amenemhat III—were found in the tomb of the princess, which was excavated within the pyramid complex of her father at Lahun (between Memphis and the Fayum). The Museum possesses all except four pieces of this treasure, the beauty and technical perfection of which have rarely been equaled in Egyptian art. This splendid girdle, which Sithathoryunet wore around her hips, is composed of eight large cowrie shells of hollow gold, one of which is split to form a sliding clasp. A double strand of small gold, carnelian, and green feldspar beads in the shape of acacia seeds separates the shells. Each of the seven whole cowries contains metal pellets, so that the girdle tinkled softly as the princess walked or danced. *Purchase, Rogers Fund and Henry Walters Gift, 1916, 16.1.5*

22 Young Nubian
Dynasty 12, ca. 1991–1786 B.C.
Ivory and bronze; h. 4½ in. (11.5 cm.)

Although diminutive in size, this figurine of a Nubian girl is robust in its proportions and modeling. The arms, now missing, were attached by dowels at the shoulders and hung down at the sides. The hair, represented by incised dots as well as plugs inserted into the flattened cranium, imitated the partly shaven and partly tufted hairstyles of Egyptian and Nubian children. Although the inlays for the eyes and nipples are missing, the inlaid navel and the large bronze earrings are extant. The feet were never carved. Although nude apodal statuettes have been sometimes interpreted as dolls, it seems possible that they were concubines or erotic figures placed in the tomb to stimulate the deceased's virility in the afterlife. *Gift of Mrs. William Sergeant Kendall and Mrs. Daniel Crena de Iongh, 1966, 66.78*

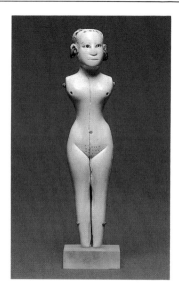

23 Senbi

Meir, Middle Dynasty 12, ca. 1929–1870 B.C.
*Painted wood, stone, and copper; h. 16⅛ in.
(41 cm.)*

In ancient Egypt it was believed that the ka, the individual's vital energy or personality, survived death and could reside in an image (particularly a statue) that preserved an idealized and unchanging version of the individual's features. This sensitively modeled ka statue of the steward Senbi was probably obtained from the clearance of his pit tomb in the necropolis at Meir in Middle Egypt. Although typical of its genre and period, the statuette is distinguished by the quality of both craftsmanship and materials. Made of costly imported wood, it was left unpainted to reveal the grain. The only additions of color are the painted and inlaid eyes and nipples and the long white kilt. The body of the figure was carved from one piece of wood, with the arms and front parts of the feet attached separately. *Rogers Fund, 1911, 11.150.27*

24 Coffin of Khnumnakht

Meir, Dynasty 12, ca. 1897–1843 B.C.
Painted wood; l. 82 in. (208.3 cm.)

The brilliantly painted exterior of the coffin of Khnumnakht, an individual unidentified except for his inscribed name, displays the multiplicity of texts and panels characteristic of coffin decoration of the late Middle Kingdom. It has at least one feature—the figure of a goddess on the head end—that is rare before Dynasty 13. Painted on the side opposite the face of the mummy within is an architectural facade (shown in this detail) with a doorway for the passage of the soul and an opening from which two eyes look forth onto the world of the living. The rest of the exterior is divided into panels framed between inscribed invocations to, and recitations by, various primeval deities and gods—particularly those associated with death and rebirth, such as Osiris, primary god of the dead, and Anubis, god of embalming. *Rogers Fund, 1915, 15.2.2*

25   Funerary Stela of Sehetepibra

Abydos(?), Late Dynasty 12–Early Dynasty 13,
ca. 1798–1700 B.C.
Painted limestone; 12 × 18⁷⁄₈ in. (30.5 × 48 cm.)

According to its inscription, this private-tomb
stela, which belonged to Sehetepibra, an overseer of troops, may have come from Abydos,
the important pilgrimage center of the god Osiris.
The stela's most arresting feature is the niche
in the lower half of the front which holds seven
mummiform figures, each inscribed with the
name of a family member of Sehetepibra,
whose own figure is the large one at the right.
(Sehetepibra is again shown at the upper left,
seated at a table heaped with offerings.) The
similarity of the seven figures to contemporary
shawabtys— magical mummiform figurines
placed in the tomb as substitutes to perform
labor for the deceased in the afterworld—is
strengthened by religious texts of the period,
which guarantee the deceased the eternal
companionship of his family and the services
of his servants in the afterlife. *Rogers Fund,
1965, 65.120.2*

26   Anonymous Official

Dynasty 13, ca. 1786–1668 B.C.
Quartzite; h. 7³⁄₄ in. (19.5 cm.)

The complete statuette of which this is a fragment depicted a man sitting cross-legged on
the ground, wearing only a kilt and a full shoulder-
length wig. The minimum amount of detail is
consistent with the grainy texture of the stone,
but the impression of a somewhat flabby torso
has been adequately conveyed. Although this
piece cannot be dated precisely, the curve of
the almond-shaped eyes below a natural brow-
line, the straight nose with its downturned tip,
the protruding mouth and narrow chin, and the
solemn expression are characteristic of sculpture produced in the late Middle Kingdom.
*Purchase, Frederick P. Huntley Bequest, 1959,
59.26.2*

27   Head of Hatshepsut

Thebes, Asasif, Dynasty 18, ca. 1503–1482 B.C.
Red granite; h. 13³⁄₄ in. (35 cm.)

The most prominent queen regnant in ancient
Egypt, Hatshepsut proclaimed herself king between the second and seventh year of the reign
of Tuthmosis III, her stepson and nephew. She
ruled in her own name for nearly twenty-two
years. Among the many monuments she erected
throughout Egypt was her imposing funerary
temple at Deir el Bahri in Western Thebes,
where the statue of which this head was originally a part once probably stood. Excavated by
the Museum's Egyptian Expedition from a
Ramesside temple built over the lower end of
the causeway to the queen's temple complex
(and therefore initially ascribed to that later
period), this royal head wearing the *nemes*
headdress has now been recognized as portraying Hatshepsut herself. This attribution is based
on its close stylistic similarity to inscribed statues of the queen. *Rogers Fund, 1935, 35.3.297*

28 Funerary Stela
Thebes, Deir el Bahri, Dynasty 18, ca. 1503–
1450 B.C.
Painted limestone; 17¾ × 12 in. (45 × 30.5 cm.)

This private-tomb stela is unfinished. The sculptor
—probably one of the artists of Tuthmosis III's
temple at Deir el Bahri, who may have made the
stela in his spare time—has carved only the
opening phrases of a prayer for offerings and
has left a blank space for the name and titles of
the deceased. The stela's purchaser would also
have had his own name, those of his two female relatives, and that of the son who officiates
at the offering table carved over the four figures
in the offering scene. The classic simplicity of the
composition is characteristic of the Tuthmoside
period. *Rogers Fund, 1923, 23.3.48*

29 Chair of Renyseneb
Middle Dynasty 18, ca. 1450 B.C.
Ebony with ivory; h. 34¹⁵⁄₁₆ in. (86.2 cm.)

The back of this wooden chair, belonging to the
scribe Renyseneb, is handsomely veneered
with ivory and further embellished by incised
decoration showing the owner seated on a chair
of identical form. This is the earliest surviving
chair with such a representation, and it is the
only nonroyal example known of any date. The
scene and accompanying text have funerary
import and would not have been usual for
furniture in daily use. If, as seems likely from its
solidity of construction, this chair was used by
Renyseneb during his lifetime, the design may
have been added following his death to make
the chair a more suitable funerary object. The
high quality of its joinery and the harmony of its
proportions testify to the skill of ancient Egyptian carpenters. The mesh seat has been restored according to ancient models. *Purchase,
Patricia R. Lassalle Gift, 1968, 68.58*

30 Sandals and Collar
Dynasty 18, ca. 1504–1450 B.C.
*Gold; l. of sandals 9⅞ in. (25 cm.), l. of collar
13½ in. (34.3 cm.)*

The fragility of this collar and pair of gold sandals would have prevented their being actually
worn, even for ceremonial occasions. They
were made as funerary objects for a woman of
the royal family during the reign of Tuthmosis III.
The sandals are replicas of leather ones com-
monly worn by Egyptian men and women. The
collar, reminiscent of jewelry the woman would
have worn during her lifetime, assures her the
use of precious objects in the afterlife. Five
rings of cylindrical beads are engraved in the
thin sheet of gold, while the outer band has a
flower-petal motif. The two falcon heads that
terminate the collar at shoulder level had attached loops to accommodate the cords that
secured the collar to the mummy wrappings.
*Fletcher Fund, 1922, 26.8.147; Fletcher Fund,
1920, 26.8.101*

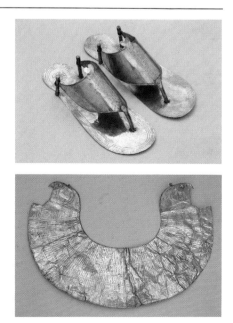

31 Sphinx of Amenhotpe III

Dynasty 18, ca. 1417–1379 B.C.
Faience; l. 9⁷/₈ in. (25 cm.)

Amenhotpe III ruled over a prosperous Egypt and a peaceful foreign empire. He erected numerous monuments on a colossal scale, which did not sacrifice artistic quality for the sake of size. His reign also saw jewel-like achievements in the minor arts. This inscribed faience sculpture with its fine blue glaze por-trays Amenhotpe III with a human head and hands and the forelegs and body of a lion. He wears a broad collar, bracelets, and the *nemes* headdress; in outstretched hands he holds jars of wine as offerings to a god. In its complete-ness and perfection of form this statuette is unique among ancient Egyptian statuary. *Purchase, Lila Acheson Wallace Fund, Inc. Gift, 1972, 1972.125*

32 Fragmentary Head of a Queen

Dynasty 18, ca. 1417–1379 B.C.
Yellow jasper; h. 5⁹/₁₆ in. (14.1 cm.)

This extraordinary fragment, polished to a mirror-like finish, is both sensual and elegant in expression, reflecting the sophistication of the court of Amenhotpe III, to whose reign it can be assigned on stylistic basis. When complete, this head probably belonged to a composite statue, in which the exposed flesh parts were of jasper and the remaining elements of other appropri-ate permanent materials. The use of yellow stone for the skin indicates that the person represented is female; the scale and superb quality of the work make it probable that she is a goddess or a queen of Amenhotpe III. The similarity of the full, curved lips with downturned corners to known representations of the Great Royal Wife, Tiye, suggests that it is she who is depicted here; this work may, however, repre-sent another important wife of Amenhotpe III, such as Sitamen. *Purchase, Edward S. Harkness Gift, 1926, 26.7.1396*

33 Sacrificing a Duck

Hermopolis(?), Dynasty 18, ca. 1373–1362 B.C.
Limestone; 9⁵/₈ × 21¹/₂ in. (24.5 × 54.5 cm.)

In what many scholars have seen as an attempt to limit the political, economic, and religious power of the Amun clergy, Amenhotpe IV, the son and successor of Amenhotpe III, severely curtailed the worship of Amen-Ra, previously the chief god of Egypt, and venerated exclu-sively the Aton, the power embodied in the sun disk. In about the sixth year of his reign, he changed his name to Akhenaton and moved the religious capital of Egypt from Thebes to the area of modern Tell el Amarna in Middle Egypt, where he founded the city of Akhetaton. This relief block, originally from Akhetaton, is carved in the mannered and expressive style peculiar to Akhenaton's reign. The king is shown making an offering of a pintail duck to the Aton, whose rays, ending in hands, stream down on him. One of the hands holds an ankh (the symbol of life) to the king's nose. *Lent by Norbert Schimmel, L.1979.8.2*

34 Pavement Fragment

Tell el Amarna, Dynasty 18, ca. 1373–1362 B.C.
Painted stucco; 16¾ × 20½ in. (42.5 × 52 cm.)

The painted walls and pavements of the royal palaces and private villas of Akhenaton's new capital city of Akhetaton are among the most attractive manifestations of Amarna art. The paintings have much in common with the approximately contemporary floor, wall, and ceiling paintings that decorated the palace of his father, Amenhotpe III, at Thebes. While retaining conventional principles of artistic organization, they reveal in general a greater freedom, naturalism, and feeling for space and a more subtle and harmonious palette than do the Theban tomb paintings of the same period. This pavement fragment, which depicts a walking duck surrounded by papyrus plants, is typical of the marsh scenes that decorated palace floors during late Dynasty 18. (See also no. 33.)
Rogers Fund, 1920, 20.2.2

35 Prancing Horse

Thebes, Late Dynasty 18, ca. 1379–1352 B.C.
Stained ivory with garnet; l. 6 in. (15 cm.)

The horse was a relative latecomer in Egyptian history. It was introduced during the Hyksos domination (ca. 1667–1570 B.C.), when new elements of power, notably the horse and chariot, were brought from the Near East. During the New Kingdom this animal became a familiar sight, and there were many portrayals of horses in the art of the time, particularly during the Amarna age. This small ivory handle of a light whip or fly whisk is a sensitively carved prancing or running horse stained reddish brown with a black mane. The eyes, one of which has fallen out, were inlaid with garnet. The lively carving of this piece, especially the gracefully arched back, typifies the spirit of the Amarna Period.
Gift of Edward S. Harkness, 1926, 26.7.1293

36 Funerary Stela of Ptahmose

Memphis(?), Early Dynasty 19, ca. 1320–1290 B.C.
Limestone; 56 × 27 in. (142.2 × 68.8 cm.)

This funerary stela shows a private official— Ptahmose, a royal scribe and overseer of the royal harem—worshiping the god Osiris, who is seated under an elaborate baldachin. A hymn to the god is inscribed, together with requests for offerings for Ptahmose. The variety of limestone used for this monument, as well as the form, style, and text, indicates that it was inscribed at Memphis during Dynasty 19. Stelae of this type were set up in the funerary chapels of the New Kingdom necropolis at Saqqara. The methodical clearance of this important cemetery—lost since the mid-1800s in drifting sand and only recently rediscovered—is currently providing a stylistic counterpoint to the better-known Theban monuments of the Ramesside Period. *Harris Brisbane Dick Fund, 1967, 67.3*

37   Ancestral Bust

Thebes, Deir el Medina, Early Dynasty 19,
ca. 1320–1237 B.C.
Painted limestone; h. 16¼ in. (41.3 cm.)

During the Ramesside Period busts of family
ancestors or members were set into wall niches
in the houses of Deir el Medina at Thebes or
placed in tombs or chapels there. This bust is
unusual because of its large size. It has well-
carved features and elaborate painted decoration,
which is exceptionally well preserved and appears to have undergone several revisions—
perhaps indicating a long period of veneration.
The brows and cosmetic lines are carved in
raised relief, and the earlobes have triangular
indications of piercing. Although the wig and
red-painted flesh suggest that this figure is
male, busts of this type appear to have been
rendered in a sexually ambiguous fashion. That
nearly all busts are anepigraphic has added to
this uncertainty. *Purchase, Fletcher Fund and
The Guide Foundation, Inc. Gift, 1966, 66.99.45*

38   Bowl

Tell Basta, Late Dynasty 19–Dynasty 20,
ca. 1216–1085 B.C.
Silver; diam. 8 in. (20.3 cm.)

In 1906 two rich hoards of silver and gold
objects were discovered in an ancient cache
near the temple of the cat goddess Bastet at
Bubastis (modern Tell Basta) in the eastern
Nile Delta. Among the most lavishly decorated
of these objects is this embossed silver bowl,
executed in repoussé and chasing techniques.
The outside of the bowl is decorated with lively
episodes borrowed in part from tomb scenes.
With a surprising amount of detail these tiny
scenes show a wide range of agricultural, pastoral, and hunting activities. Both the royal names
(Sety II and Tausert) and the private names and
titles inscribed on some of the pieces belonging
to the hoards indicate a late Dynasty 19–Dynasty
20 date for the majority of the objects. *Rogers
Fund, 1907, 07.228.20*

39   Amun

Dynasty 22, ca. 900 B.C.
Bronze with gold inlay; h. 6 in. (15.2 cm.)

Because monumental sculpture and architecture were not produced in quantity during the
Third Intermediate Period, the artistic quality of
the contemporary minor arts is all the more
striking. This outstanding bronze represents the
great god Amun with facial features and bodily
proportions consistent with a Dynasty 22 date.
Many details of the figure and dress of the god
are picked out with finely applied gold inlay, a
decorative technique widely practiced at this
time. He wears a broad collar and corselet of
scale armor, a finely pleated kilt held in place by
a decorated belt, and a crown, once overlaid
with gold, into which two tall plumes would have
been inserted. His hands once held divine symbols. *Harris Brisbane Dick Fund, 1955, 56.17*

40 Outer Coffin of Henettawy

Thebes, Deir el Bahri, Dynasty 21, ca. 1039–992 B.C.
Gessoed and painted wood; l. 79⅞ in. (203 cm.)

At the beginning of the Third Intermediate Period, ruling power was divided between a dynasty resident in the delta city of Tanis and the high priests of Amun at Thebes. During this unsettled period the individual private tomb was abandoned in favor of family tombs (or caches) that could be more easily guarded from thieves; often tombs that had already been robbed were reused for this purpose. Henettawy, a mistress of the house and chantress of Amen-Ra, was buried in such a tomb. Since her tomb, like most others of the time, was undecorated, the paintings on her coffin, with their emphasis on elaborate religious symbolism and imagery, replaced the wall decorations of previous periods and reflect a style and iconography developed during the late New Kingdom. Henettawy wears a plain tripartite wig with two sidelocks and elaborate funerary jewelry typical of the period. *Rogers Fund, 1925, 25.3.182*

41 Funerary Stela of Aafenmut

Thebes, Khokha, Dynasty 22, ca. 924–889 B.C.
Painted wood; 9 × 7¼ in. (23 × 18.2 cm.)

This small, exceptionally well-preserved wood stela was found in 1914–15 at Thebes by the Museum's Egyptian expedition during its clearance of a tomb containing the burial pit of Aafenmut, a scribe of the treasury. It was discovered along with some other small finds, which included a pair of leather tabs from a set of mummy braces bearing the name of Osorkon I, the second king of Dynasty 22. Solar worship is the theme of the stela's decoration: in the lunette the sun disk crosses the sky in its bark, while below the falcon-headed Ra-Harakhty, the Lord of Heaven, receives food offerings and incense from Aafenmut. The same episodes appear in a virtually identical style on the brightly painted coffins of the period. *Rogers Fund, 1928, 28.3.35*

43 Coffin of Udjaersen

Dynasty 26, ca. 656–525 B.C.
Gessoed and painted wood; l. 74³⁄₈ in. (189 cm.)

Udjaersen, the mistress of the house, was a daughter of a Theban priest and scribe. The shape of her coffin lid is typical of Theban coffins of the period, especially those of the priests of the local god Montu. The inner faces of Udjaersen's coffin feature two different renderings of the sky goddess Nut, accompanied by magical spells. The painting on the inner face of the lid, illustrated here, shows the nude goddess frontally, her stylized features echoing those of the Egyptian hieroglyph for the word "face." This portrayal of Nut is a symbolic rendering of the sun's journey during a twenty-four-hour day: she holds the sun between her hands preparatory to swallowing it (sunset); at the same time she is shown giving birth to the sun disk (dawn). *Purchase, 1886, O.C. 22*

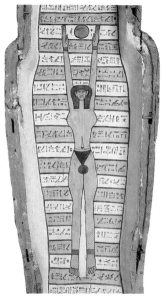

44 Funeral of Nespakashuty ▶

Thebes, Deir el Bahri, Early Dynasty 26, ca. 656–610 B.C.
Limestone with red ocher; 13³⁄₄ × 22⁷⁄₁₆ in. (35 × 57 cm.)

The vizier Nespakashuty took over the terrace of an old Middle Kingdom tomb tunneled into the north cliff at Deir el Bahri as the outer court of his own sepulcher. Work on his tomb was never finished, and many of the extant reliefs show varying degrees of completion, ranging from preliminary drawings in red ocher to finely carved raised reliefs. Several of these intermediate stages are preserved in this relief fragment depicting an episode from Nespakashuty's funeral, in which the barge bearing his coffin and the officiating mortuary priest clad in leopard skin is towed across the river to the necropolis on the west bank. There was a tendency during this late period of Egyptian art to draw on earlier styles and iconography. Theban tomb paintings of the New Kingdom were the models for this scene. *Rogers Fund, 1923, 23.3.468a*

42 Inner Coffin of Kharushere

Thebes, Sheikh Abd el Qurna, second half of Dynasty 22, ca. 825–715 B.C.
Painted wood; l. 73⁵⁄₈ in. (187 cm.)

An unusual and elaborate group of coffins was excavated in Thebes in 1885. This complete set comprises the outer, inner, and innermost coffins and a cartonnage containing the mummy of Kharushere, a doorkeeper of the house of Amun. The decoration of the innermost coffin, illustrated here, is divided into registers that depict scenes involving the funerary gods. The top register shows the deceased presented by Thoth to the "Lord of Eternity"; the second one represents Isis and Nephthys flanking a crowned *djed* column, a fetish of Osiris; and in the bottom register the bark of Sokar, an ancient mortuary divinity worshiped in the form of a falcon, is shown inside a shrine. *Purchase, Funds from Various Donors, 1886, 86.1.33*

45 Face of a Statue

Heliopolis, Late Dynasty 26, ca. 589–570 B.C.
Green basalt or diabase; h. 6¾ in. (17 cm.)

From an early period in Egyptian history Heliopolis, where this statue fragment originated, was the cult center of the sun-god Ra. Since the crown and other distinguishing characteristics have disappeared from the statue, it is impossible to know whether the subject is male or female and whether it is the face of a deity from one of the temples of Heliopolis or of a king or other royal personage. Because of the harmonious facial contours and subtle modeling, the serene smile, and the exquisite carving of eye and eyebrow, it was probably the product of a royal workshop and is representative of the end of Dynasty 26, probably the reign of Apries. The idealized sculptural style that was the hallmark of this era was dominant in Egyptian art during its five final centuries. *Gift of British School of Archaeology in Egypt, 1912, 12.187.31*

46 Neith

Dynasty 26–Dynasty 29, ca. 664–380 B.C.
Bronze inlaid with gold; h. 6⁷⁄₈ in. (17.5 cm.)

The war goddess Neith was worshiped in Lower Egypt as early as Dynasty 1. Neith rose to prominence as the divine patroness of the delta city of Sais, the place of origin of Dynasty 26. From that time until well into the Ptolemaic Period images of the goddess were produced in large numbers and dedicated in temples and cemeteries throughout Egypt. Certain stylistic features of this statuette may indicate a dating to the second half of Dynasty 26. Neith is depicted here in the traditional manner, wearing the red crown of Lower Egypt and a broad collar edged with pendants, both of which have been inlaid with gold in a decorative technique used to great effect in the Third Intermediate Period (no. 39) and later in the Late Dynastic Period. Both hands are pierced for the insertion of sacred emblems. *Purchase, Edward S. Harkness Gift, 1926, 26.7.846*

47 Anonymous Priest
Dynasty 27–Dynasty 30, ca. 525–342 B.C.
Green basalt; h. 18½ in. (47 cm.)

This virtually intact standing figure of a priest carrying a naos (shrine) with an image of Osiris was a type produced in large numbers during the Late Dynastic Period. These statues were individualized only by their texts. This figure, which lacks an inscription, is clad in the long, closely wrapped kilt with prominent fastening that was not depicted in Egyptian art until Dynasty 27, when the Persian kings ruled Egypt. The sculptor has produced a competent, yet uninspired, version of a common pattern, wherein this elderly official is portrayed in a smooth idealizing mode. The three disparate columns—rigid back pillar, irregularly contoured body of the priest, and boxlike shrine—have been artistically integrated without sacrificing their physical independence. *Rogers Fund, 1925, 25.2.10*

48 Panel from a Capital
Dynasty 30, ca. 380–342 B.C.
Cedar; 17⅝ × 10½ in. (44.7 × 26.6 cm.)

This finely carved panel would have been combined with three others to form the capital of a freestanding column of a shrine dedicated to the sky goddess Hathor. Although the cow's ears and long wig with two curled tresses are traditional attributes of Hathor, the smooth modeling of the face—with its slight double chin—and the meticulously carved brows and cosmetic lines clearly indicate a Dynasty 30 dating, at the end of pharaonic history. By this time Hathor had absorbed many of the symbols and epithets of less important female divinities; yet she retained her original identification with the various cow goddesses of the sky and the necropolis. *Gift of Mrs. Lucy W. Drexel, 1889, 89.2.214*

49 Anonymous Scribe

Memphis(?), Late Dynastic Period–Ptolemaic Period, 4th c. B.C.
Graywacke; h. 14⅛ in. (35.9 cm.)

Even during the Old Kingdom seated scribal statues were distinguished by lively facial expressions that contrasted with summarily carved bodies. In this head and torso from a much later example of the type the juxtaposition of the smooth contours of the bag wig and nearly featureless body and the vivid emotion of the face is particularly striking. The cheeks, chin, bags under the eyes, and bulge between the brows are fleshy in appearance and are balanced by incised brows, eyelids, frown lines, and crow's-feet. The work's plasticity of modeling and intensity of expression suggest that it is a forerunner of such so-called portraits as the Berlin "Green Head." *Rogers Fund, 1925, 25.2.1*

50 Anubis

Ptolemaic Period, ca. 332–30 B.C.
Gessoed and painted wood; h. 16½ in. (42 cm.)

This brilliantly painted sculpture is a fine example of Egyptian funerary art under the Ptolemies. The figure represents Anubis, the jackal-headed god of embalming and one of the principal tutelary deities who watched over dead Egyptians and their tombs. The god, standing on a painted rectangular base which represents the paneled facade of a tomb or palace, extends his hands in a gesture of protection. The fine carving and meticulous painting of this statuette are rendered even more striking by its unusual state of preservation. *Gift of Mrs. Myron C. Taylor, 1938, 38.5*

51 Coffin for a Sacred Cat

Ptolemaic Period, ca. 305–30 B.C.
Bronze; h. 11 in. (28 cm.)

The cat was long venerated as the sacred animal of Bastet, a goddess worshiped at the delta town of Bubastis. In 954 B.C. a family of Bubastite kings became the rulers of Egypt, and votive images of cats increased in popularity. In the fifth century B.C. the Greek historian Herodotus described the great annual festival of Bastet and her beautiful temple, near which mummified cats were interred in large cemeteries. This hollow figure served as a coffin for a mummified cat. The figure's smooth contours are complemented by a finely incised broad collar and a pectoral in the shape of a *wadjet* eye—the sacred eye of Horus. Holes for the attachment of earrings pierce the cat's ears. *Harris Brisbane Dick Fund, 1956, 56.16.1*

52 Taweret

Kena, Ptolemaic Period, ca. 332–30 B.C.
Glass; h. 4⅜ in. (11 cm.)

This particularly fine depiction of Taweret, the
patroness of women in pregnancy and childbirth,
shows the hippopotamus goddess standing upright and steadying a *sa* amulet, the symbol of
protection. The traditional tall, plumed crown
would have been attached to the vertical projection on top of her head. The texture and composition of this opaque glass figure differ markedly
from earlier Egyptian glass objects. Sculpture
made of glass was rare at any period of Egyptian history, which makes it difficult to date any
piece with confidence. Yet the statuette's turquoise color and the similarity of its sculptural
technique to other late Egyptian mold-made
figures suggest a date in the Ptolemaic Period.
*Purchase, Edward S. Harkness Gift, 1926,
26.7.1193*

53 Arsinoe II

Ptolemaic Period, after 270 B.C.
*Limestone with traces of gilding and paint;
h. 15 in. (38.1 cm.)*

Since the inscription on the back of this figure
refers to Arsinoe II as a goddess, it was probably made after her death in 270 B.C., when her
cult was established by her brother and husband,
Ptolemy II. The queen stands in a traditional
Egyptian pose, strictly frontal, with her left foot
advanced and right arm, hand clenched, at her
side. The statuette, one of only two known with
her name inscribed, is a fine example of the
tendency during the Ptolemaic Period to combine Egyptian artistic conventions with those of
the classical world; the style of her coiffure and
the cornucopia (a divine attribute) she holds are
Greek elements, while her stylized features and
garments and the back pillar are well-established
Egyptian conventions of the period. *Rogers
Fund, 1920, 20.2.21*

54   Temple of Dendur

Dendur, Early Roman Period, ca. 15 B.C.
*Aeolian sandstone; l. of gateway and temple
82 ft. (25 m.)*

The Temple of Dendur, an Egyptian monument in Nubia, would have been completely submerged by the lake formed by the construction of the Aswan High Dam (begun 1960); instead it came to the United States as a gift from the Egyptian government in recognition of the American contribution to the international campaign to save the ancient Nubian monuments. The temple was erected by the Roman emperor Augustus (63 B.C.–A.D. 14) during his occupation of Egypt and Lower Nubia. It honors the goddess Isis and—in a move to secure the loyalty of the local population—two sons of a Nubian chieftain, who were deified because they drowned in the sacred Nile. The temple, consisting of three rooms—pronaos, antechamber, and sanctuary—has been reassembled as it appeared on the banks of the Nile in a modern simulation of the entire temple site. The complex is a simplified version of the standard Egyptian cult temple, whose plan had remained fairly consistent for three thousand years. In the temple reliefs Augustus himself makes the offerings; however, he is represented in the traditional Egyptian manner with its related iconography. *Given to the United States by Egypt in 1965, awarded to The Metropolitan Museum of Art in 1967, and installed in The Sackler Wing in 1978, 68.154*

55   Mummy Shroud

Roman Period, 3rd c. A.D.
Tempera on linen; 39⅝ × 27¼ in. (100.6 × 69 cm.)

Under Ptolemaic and Roman rule Egyptian society was characterized by two distinct classes—native Egyptians and their foreign overlords. That this juxtaposition was also expressed in the arts is well illustrated by the painted linen shrouds of the Roman Period. The portraits of the deceased on these funerary objects were rendered in the classical Greco-Roman manner—including dress and hairstyle, the use of shading, and an illusion of depth—but they were surrounded by images of Egyptian deities and symbols in the hieratic and two-dimensional Egyptian style. This shroud painting portrays a toga-clad youth flanked by Horus falcons and, at the lower left, a figure of the goddess Isis. *Rogers Fund, 1908, 08.202.8*

SECOND FLOOR

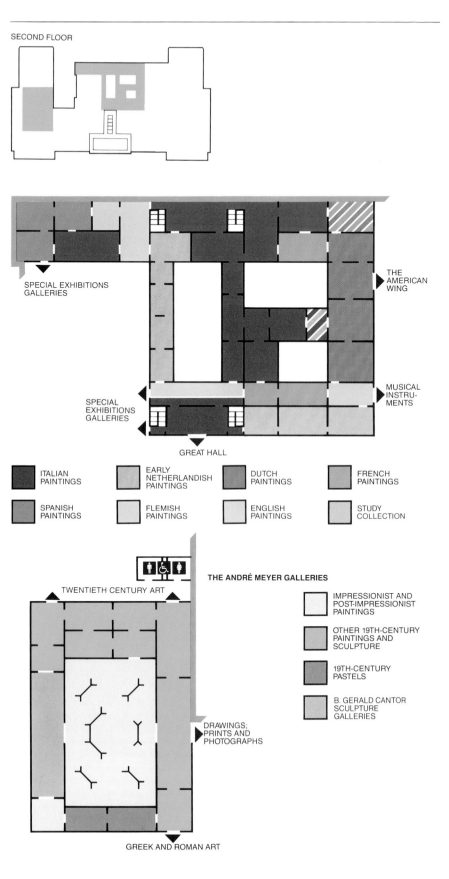

SPECIAL EXHIBITIONS
GALLERIES

THE
AMERICAN
WING

SPECIAL
EXHIBITIONS
GALLERIES

MUSICAL
INSTRU-
MENTS

GREAT HALL

ITALIAN
PAINTINGS

EARLY
NETHERLANDISH
PAINTINGS

DUTCH
PAINTINGS

FRENCH
PAINTINGS

SPANISH
PAINTINGS

FLEMISH
PAINTINGS

ENGLISH
PAINTINGS

STUDY
COLLECTION

THE ANDRÉ MEYER GALLERIES

TWENTIETH CENTURY ART

IMPRESSIONIST AND
POST-IMPRESSIONIST
PAINTINGS

OTHER 19TH-CENTURY
PAINTINGS AND
SCULPTURE

19TH-CENTURY
PASTELS

B. GERALD CANTOR
SCULPTURE
GALLERIES

DRAWINGS;
PRINTS AND
PHOTOGRAPHS

GREEK AND ROMAN ART

EUROPEAN PAINTINGS

The Museum's collection of European paintings numbers approximately three thousand works, dating from the twelfth through the nineteenth century. The Italian, Flemish, Dutch, and French schools are most strongly represented, but there are also fine works by Spanish and British masters.

The history of the collection is marked by extraordinary gifts and bequests. In 1901 the Museum received a bequest of almost seven million dollars from Jacob S. Rogers for the purchase of works of art in all fields. *The Fortune Teller* by La Tour and *Cypresses* by Van Gogh are only two examples from among many hundreds of works of art bought from this fund over the years. The bequest of Benjamin Altman in 1913 brought a number of major works to the Museum, including important paintings by Mantegna, Memling, and Rembrandt. In 1917 a bequest and funds for additional acquisitions were received from Isaac D. Fletcher. Velázquez's splendid portrait of Juan de Pareja was acquired in 1971 principally from the Fletcher Fund.

In 1929 the bequest of the H. O. Havemeyer Collection brought not only Old Masters, but also unrivalled works by the French Impressionists. Among the works owned by Mr. and Mrs. Havemeyer were El Greco's *View of Toledo,* the portrait of Moltedo by Ingres, many paintings and pastels by Degas, and Monet's *Poplars*. Michael Friedsam's bequest in 1931 strengthened the department's holdings of early French and Flemish paintings. The collection formed by Jules Bache, which included superb French eighteenth-century paintings and notable works by Crivelli, Holbein, and Titian, was deposited in the Museum in 1949.

In recent years Mr. and Mrs. Charles Wrightsman have presented many paintings of outstanding quality. Their gift in 1981—Rubens's portrait of himself, his wife, and their son—is an outstanding example of the discerning generosity that has made the Museum what it is today.

1   BERLINGHIERO, Lucchese, act. by 1228–
d. by 1236
Madonna and Child
Tempera on wood, gold ground; painted sur-
face 30 × 19½ in. (76.2 × 49.5 cm.)

The father of a family of painters in Lucca,
Berlinghiero was the most important Tuscan
artist of the early thirteenth century. He was
obviously familiar with Byzantine painting, examples of which he could have seen in Lucca and
Pisa, as both cities traded extensively with
Constantinople. The composition of this picture,
in which the Christ Child sits on the left arm of
the Madonna and lifts his right hand in blessing,
conforms to the Byzantine type known as the
Hodegetria, the "Indicator of the Way." It is one
of only three certain works by Berlinghiero.
Typical of him are the impeccable technique,
the manner in which physiognomical details
create a lively network of patterns, and the
expressive face of the Madonna. *Gift of Irma N.*
Straus, 1960, 60.173

2   GIOTTO, Florentine, 1266/76–1337
The Epiphany
Tempera on wood, gold ground; 17¾ × 17¼ in.
(44.9 × 43.7 cm.)

This picture, which shows the Adoration of the
Magi in the foreground and the Annunciation to
the Shepherds in the background, belongs to a
series of seven panels representing scenes
from the life of Christ. It seems to have been
painted around 1320, when Giotto was at the
height of his powers and enjoyed an unparalleled reputation throughout Italy. The Museum's
panel is characterized by a clear organization of
space—the hill is divided into a series of pla-
teaus and the stable is viewed as though seen
from slightly to the right of center—and a concern for simplified shapes that sets it apart from
the majority of works produced in the fourteenth
century. No less innovative is the manner in
which the eldest magus doffs his crown, kneels
down, and impetuously lifts the Christ Child
from the manger. *John Stewart Kennedy Fund,*
1911, 11.126.1

3 FRA FILIPPO LIPPI, Florentine,
ca. 1406–d. 1469
**Madonna and Child Enthroned, with Two
Angels**
*Tempera and gold on wood, transferred from
wood; 48¼ × 24¾ in. (122.6 × 62.9 cm.)*

The earliest dated painting by Filippo Lippi is a
Madonna and Child of 1437 in the Palazzo
Barberini in Rome. The present picture is about
contemporary with that work. It is the center of a
triptych, the lateral panels of which are in the
Accademia Albertina in Turin and show the four
Latin Fathers of the Church. The wall visible
in the background of the Museum's picture is
continued in the other panels, and all of the
figures are lit from the left, creating the effect of
a unified space. In his later works Filippo Lippi
frequently employed a bright palette and arranged the drapery in decorative patterns; here,
however, the forms are relatively simple and the
colors restricted. The scroll held by one of the
angels is inscribed with a verse from the Apocry-
pha (Ecclesiasticus 24:19), and the rose held
by the Virgin is probably an allusion to her
purity. *The Jules Bache Collection, 1949, 49.7.9*

4 FRA FILIPPO LIPPI, Florentine,
ca. 1406–d. 1469
Portrait of a Man and Woman at a Casement
*Tempera on wood; 25¼ × 16½ in. (64.1 ×
41.9 cm.)*

In Tuscany in the fifteenth century women were
invariably portrayed in profile, which was thought
to be the most flattering view. This painting,
datable about 1440, is the earliest example of
the type; as a double portrait it is even more
unusual and may have been painted to celebrate an engagement or marriage. The lady is
elaborately dressed in the French style and
wears a richly embroidered headdress with
scarlet lappets. The word picked out in pearls
on the sleeve seems to read *leal[ta]*, "fidelity."
The young man looking through the window
rests his hands on the coat of arms of the
Scolari family. The landscape is thought to
have been inspired by Flemish models. *Gift of
Henry G. Marquand, 1889. Marquand Collection, 89.15.19*

5 PESELLINO, Florentine, ca. 1422–d. 1457
Madonna and Child with Six Saints
Tempera on wood, gold ground; painted sur-face 8⅞ × 8 in. (22.5 × 20.3 cm.)

Although Pesellino's only documented work is a large altarpiece in the National Gallery, London, he specialized in delicately executed, small-scale paintings. This panel, painted in a miniature-like technique, is one of his finest works. It should be dated in the late 1440s and shows the influence of Fra Filippo Lippi in its figure types and lighting. The saints are, from left to right, Anthony Abbot, Jerome, Cecilia, Catherine of Alexandria, Augustine, and George. *Bequest of Mary Stillman Harkness, 1950, 50.145.30*

6 ALESSANDRO BOTTICELLI, Florentine, 1444/45–1510
The Last Communion of Saint Jerome
Tempera on wood; 13½ × 10 in. (34.3 × 25.4 cm.)

Here Saint Jerome is seen supported by his brethren in his cell near Bethlehem. Above the bed are two juniper branches, palms, a crucifix, and Jerome's cardinal's hat. The picture, which dates from the early 1490s, was painted for the Florentine wool merchant Francesco del Pugliese, who describes it in a will of 1503. Although pictures of Saint Jerome in his study, surrounded by ancient texts, were popular among humanists, the choice of this devotional subject, which is infrequently represented, may be related to the fact that Pugliese, like Botticelli's brother, was a supporter of Savonarola, the Florentine reformer and preacher. (See also Robert Lehman Collection, no. 8.) *Bequest of Benjamin Altman, 1913, 14.40.642*

7 ALESSANDRO BOTTICELLI, Florentine, 1444/45–1510
Three Miracles of Saint Zenobius
Tempera on wood; 26½ × 59¼ in. (67.3 × 150.5 cm.)

This picture is one of a series recounting miracles worked by Saint Zenobius, a fifth-century bishop and a patron saint of Florence. At the left the saint is shown restoring to life a dead youth whose funeral procession he has met. In the center he revives a man who was killed while bringing relics from Saint Ambrose (the relics

are shown in the open casket). In the background to the right Saint Eugenius receives water and salt blessed by Zenobius and then hastens across the piazza and revives a dead relative while the water. The series to which the picture belongs may have decorated a room in a religious confraternity in Florence. In these late works by Botticelli, the seductive grace and delicacy of his earlier paintings give way to a drier style, and the figures are charged with frenetic energy. *John Stewart Kennedy Fund, 1911, 11.98*

8 PIERO DI COSIMO, Florentine, 1462–1521?
A Hunting Scene
Tempera and oil on wood; 27¾ × 66¾ in. (70.5 × 169.5 cm.)

Francesco del Pugliese, the owner of Botticelli's *Last Communion of Saint Jerome* (no. 6), may have commissioned this and at least two further pictures by Piero di Cosimo illustrating the life of primitive man. In the present picture fire rages unchecked in the background, and

men, satyrs, and animals live a savage existence in a dense forest. Another, less well-preserved panel from the same series is in the Museum; it shows a higher state of culture. Piero di Cosimo was one of the most eccentric personalities of the early Renaissance, and this series permitted his marvelously fertile imagination full rein. *Gift of Robert Gordon, 1875, 75.7.2*

9 ANDREA DEL SARTO, Florentine,
1486–1530
The Holy Family with the Infant Saint John
Oil on wood; 53¹/₂ × 39⁵/₈ in. (135.9 × 100.6 cm.)

Among Andrea del Sarto's most famous pictures is this Holy Family, which he painted
about 1530 for the Florentine nobleman Giovanni
Borgherini. Here John the Baptist, a patron
saint of Florence, hands the globe to the infant
Christ, possibly symbolizing the transfer of Florence's allegiance from Saint John to Christ
himself. One of the masters of the High Renaissance, Andrea del Sarto was an exceptional
draftsman and preferred the rich, varied palette
that distinguishes this work. (See also The
Jack and Belle Linsky Collection, no. 4.)
Maria DeWitt Jesup Fund, 1922, 22.75

10   BRONZINO, Florentine, 1503–1572
Portrait of a Young Man
Oil on wood; 37⅝ × 29½ in. (95.5 × 74.9 cm.)

Bronzino is the foremost representative of the
sixteenth-century Mannerist style in Florence.
The elegance of this young aristocrat, clothed
in black and striking a self-consciously casual
pose, is highly characteristic of his work, as are
the bizarre ornaments on the furniture and the
cold, abstract forms of the architectural setting.
One of Bronzino's greatest portraits, it seems
to have been painted about 1540. *Bequest of
Mrs. H. O. Havemeyer, 1929. H. O. Havemeyer
Collection, 29.100.16*

13 SASSETTA, Sienese, ca. 1392–d. 1450/51
The Journey of the Magi
Tempera on wood; 8½ × 11¾ in. (21.6 × 29.8 cm.)

This panel, painted around 1435, was originally the upper part of a small *Adoration of the Magi;* the lower section, showing the Magi presenting their gifts to the infant Christ, is in the Palazzo Chigi-Saraceni in Siena. Sassetta was one of the most enchanting narrative painters of the fifteenth century, and although the Museum's picture is only a fragment, the sprightly, fashionable procession of the Magi, the sensitive feeling for light and atmosphere, and the stylized rendition of cranes flying across the sky have made this one of his most popular works. (See also Robert Lehman Collection, no. 5.) *Bequest of Maitland F. Griggs, 1943. Maitland F. Griggs Collection, 43.98.1*

11 SIMONE MARTINI, Sienese, act. by 1315–d.1344
Saint Andrew
Tempera on wood, gold ground; painted surface 22½ × 14⅞ in. (57.2 × 37.8 cm.)

No Italian Gothic painter possessed a greater descriptive ability and a more refined technique than Simone Martini. Both of these qualities have been brought to bear in this picture of Saint Andrew, one of five panels of a folding altarpiece to which a Madonna and Child and a Saint Ansanus in the Robert Lehman Collection also belonged. Especially remarkable are the rich patterning of the folds, modeled in green, of the pink cloak and the marvelously drawn hands. *Gift of George Blumenthal, 1941, 41.100.23*

12 PAOLO DI GIOVANNI FEI, Sienese, act. by 1369–d. 1411
Madonna and Child
Tempera on wood, gold ground; overall, with engaged frame, 34¼ × 23¼ in. (87 × 59.1 cm.)

Some of the most appealing images of the fourteenth century are based on the theme of the Virgin nursing her Child—the Madonna del Latte. Paolo di Giovanni Fei's remarkable painting, in which the solemn Virgin is portrayed frontally, while the head and the limbs of the lively Christ Child are aligned along a diagonal that crosses her torso, is among the most beautiful of these works. This picture is exceptional both for the tactility of the forms and the uncompromisingly regular brushwork with which they are described. No less exceptional are the almost perfect state of preservation and the original frame decorated with raised floral patterns, cabochon jewels, and glass medallions executed in a technique known as *verre églomisé.* The painting dates early in Fei's career, about 1380. *Bequest of George Blumenthal, 1941, 41.190.13*

14   GIOVANNI DI PAOLO, Sienese, act. by
1420–d. 1482
Paradise
*Tempera and gold on canvas, transferred from
wood; painted surface 17½ × 15⅛ in.
(44.5 × 38.4 cm.)*

In 1445 Giovanni di Paolo painted an elaborate
altarpiece for the church of San Domenico
in Siena, the main panels of which are now in
the Uffizi. There is reason to believe that both
this painting and the *Expulsion from Paradise*
in the Robert Lehman Collection (no. 6) come
from the predella of that altarpiece. Here a
company of saints—among them Augustine,
who embraces his aged mother, Monica, and
Dominic and Peter Martyr, who wear the black-
and-white Dominican habit—greet each other
or are welcomed by angels. In the upper right
an angel leads a young man into a golden light
that originally emanated from the city of Jerusalem. Although the composition derives from
Fra Angelico, Giovanni di Paolo transforms
Paradise into a fairy-tale land of oversized flowers
and stylized trees silhouetted against a gold
ground, and he has endowed the figures with
an intensity all his own. (See also The Jack
and Belle Linsky Collection, no. 1.) *Rogers
Fund, 1906, 06.1046*

15 PIETRO PERUGINO, Umbrian, act. by 1469–d. 1523
Saints John the Baptist and Lucy
Oil(?) on wood; each panel 63 × 26⅜ in. (160 × 67 cm.)

In 1505 Perugino, at the peak of his career, received the prestigious commission to complete the monumental high altarpiece for the Servite church of Santissima Annunziata in Florence. The freestanding altarpiece was double-sided: the Deposition of Christ faced the nave and the Assumption of the Virgin faced the choir. Each scene was flanked by two saints; the present pair seems to have stood on either side of the Deposition. These saints are shown in shallow niches illuminated from the left, and in a fashion typical of Perugino, they are conceived as mirror images. For their subdued coloring, subtle treatment of light, and refined conception these are among Perugino's most distinguished works. *Gift of The Jack and Belle Linsky Foundation, Inc., 1981, 1981.293.1,2*

17 RAPHAEL, Umbrian, 1483–1520 ▶
Madonna and Child Enthroned, with Saints
Tempera, oil, and gold on wood; main panel, painted surface, 66¾ × 66½ in. (169.5 × 168.9 cm.)

When Raphael began this celebrated altarpiece for the convent of Sant'Antonio at Perugia, he was barely twenty. He left for Florence in 1504 and probably completed it upon his return to Perugia the following year. His training under Perugino (no. 15) is evident in the conservative composition; the figures of Saints Peter and Paul are very skillfully modeled, however, and may reflect Raphael's study of works by Fra Bartolomeo in Florence. The most remarkable portions of the altarpiece are the predella scenes (no. 18) and the lunette, where the angels and cherub heads are positioned in the space with unsurpassed precision. The frame is contemporary, though not the original one. *Gift of J. Pierpont Morgan, 1916, 16.30ab*

16 LUCA SIGNORELLI, Umbrian, act. by 1470–d. 1523
Madonna and Child
Tempera and oil on wood; 20¼ × 18¾ in. (51.4 × 47.6 cm.)

A master of the nude, Signorelli was one of the most forceful draftsmen of the fifteenth century. He painted this picture about 1505, shortly after the completion of his famous fresco cycle in the cathedral of Orvieto. One of its most unusual features is the putti in athletic poses that are contained in the interlocked rings and acanthus borders of the gold background. The poses of some of these bear close comparison to figures at Orvieto. Adorning the upper corners are representations of Roman coins. *The Jules Bache Collection, 1949, 49.7.13*

18 RAPHAEL, Umbrian, 1483–1520
The Agony in the Garden
*Tempera and oil on wood; 9½ × 11⅜ in.
(24.1 × 29.8 cm.)*

Raphael's most engaging youthful works are his small narrative paintings. This one comes from the predella of the altarpiece for Sant'Antonio in Perugia (no. 17) and is executed with his characteristic delicacy. After the Last Supper Christ retired with the apostles to the Mount of Olives, and here he is seen praying while Peter, James, and John are fast asleep. The pose of each figure has been conceived so as to clearly define the space, and a preparatory drawing in the Morgan Library, New York, establishes the care that Raphael lavished on every detail. In 1663 the nuns of Sant'Antonio separated the predella scenes from the altarpiece and sold them to Queen Christina of Sweden. (See also Drawings, no. 3.) *Funds from various donors, 1932, 32.130.1*

19   ANDREA SACCHI, Roman, 1599–1661
Marcantonio Pasqualini Crowned by Apollo
*Oil on canvas; 96 × 76½ in. (243.8 ×
194.3 cm.)*

Marcantonio Pasqualini (1614–91) was perhaps
the leading male soprano (castrato) of his day
as well as a composer. He began his career at
the age of nine, and in 1630 he joined the Sistine
choir under the sponsorship of Cardinal Antonio Barberini. Like Sacchi, Pasqualini was a
member of the Barberini household, and he
was a principal singer in the operas performed
in the Barberini palace. Here he wears the tunic
of the Sistine choir and plays an upright harpsichord. Apollo, the god of music, holds a laurel
wreath over his head to signify his achievements,
while at the right is the satyr Marsyas, who had
unsuccessfully challenged Apollo in a musical
contest. The satyr's presence underscores
Pasqualini's triumph. Characteristic of Sacchi,
the leading classical painter in Rome in the
second quarter of the seventeenth century, are
the carefully balanced design of the work and
the intentional contrast between the richly painted
figure of Pasqualini and the smooth, enamel-
like treatment of Apollo. *Purchase, Enid A.
Haupt Gift, Gwynne Andrews Fund, and Purchase, 1871, by exchange, 1981, 1981.317*

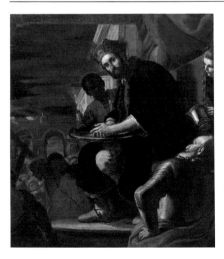

20   MATTIA PRETI, Neapolitan, 1613–99
Pilate Washing His Hands
*Oil on canvas; 81⅛ × 72¾ in. (206.1 ×
184.8 cm.)*

Preti, who was born in the remote town of
Taverna in Calabria, came to be one of the
most sought-after and innovative artists of the
second half of the seventeenth century. He
painted this picture in 1663, while he was decorating the vault of the church of San Giovanni in
Valetta for the Knights of Malta. It illustrates the
verses in the Gospel of Matthew (27:11–24) that
describe how Pilate, after hearing the accusa-
tions brought against Jesus, washed his hands
before the multitude, saying, "I am innocent of
the blood of this righteous person." Executed
with Preti's accustomed bravura, this is a picture of unusual psychological intensity. *Purchase,
Gift of J. Pierpont Morgan and Bequest of
Helena W. Charlton, by exchange, Gwynne
Andrews, Marquand, and Rogers Funds,
Victor Wilbour Memorial Fund, The Alfred N.
Punnett Endowment Fund, and funds from
various donors, 1978, 1978.402*

21 SALVATOR ROSA, Neapolitan, 1615–73
Self-Portrait(?)
Oil on canvas; 39 × 31¼ in. (99.1 × 79.4 cm.)

A man of many talents, Rosa was a distinguished painter, engraver, playwright, poet, and musician. During his residence in Florence, where he worked for the Medici, he became a close friend of Giovanni Battista Ricciardi, a professor of philosophy at the university of Pisa and a notable writer. The inscription on this enigmatic portrait states that it was painted by Rosa as a gift for Ricciardi. In the seventeenth century it was described as showing Ricciardi dressed as a philosopher, but it has subsequently been thought to represent Rosa himself. Regardless of the identification, this is a particularly poignant and mysterious work. The figure wears a cypress wreath, a symbol of mourning, and is writing on the skull in Greek: "Behold, whither, when." *Bequest of Mary L. Harrison, 1921, 21.105*

VENETIAN PAINTINGS

22 CARLO CRIVELLI, Venetian, act. by 1457–d. 1495
Pietà

Tempera on wood, tooled gold ground; overall 28¼ × 25⅜ in. (71.7 × 64.5 cm.)

This panel is presumed to have come from the uppermost tier of one of Crivelli's masterpieces, his altarpiece for the church of San Domenico at Ascoli Piceno, painted in 1476. Typical of Crivelli are the way in which the angular silhouettes are set against the elaborately tooled gold background and the clarity with which each form is described—even the bulging veins of Christ's arms and the wounds in his hands. Though Crivelli was a contemporary of Bellini (no. 23) and Mantegna (nos. 36 and 37), he evolved a highly personal and in some ways archaic style that seems to have been most appreciated not in his native Venice, but in the provincial region of the Marches, where he moved in 1468. *John Stewart Kennedy Fund, 1913, 13.178*

23 GIOVANNI BELLINI, Venetian, ca. 1430–d. 1516
Madonna and Child
Oil on wood; 35 × 28 in. (88.9 × 71.1 cm.)

In addition to the great altarpieces that Bellini created for churches throughout the Veneto, he also painted devotional images of the Madonna and Child for domestic settings. Despite their relatively modest dimensions and restrictive theme, these pictures invariably exhibit a remarkably fresh, inventive approach. In this painting, which dates from the 1480s, the Madonna is aligned with the vertical axis of the picture, but the cloth of honor introduces an asymmetry which at this date was extremely daring. Bellini filled the resulting void with an autumnal landscape of extraordinary beauty that contrasts with the warm colors of the figure group and at the same time contributes greatly to the still, poignant mood of the picture. The quince held by the Christ Child is a symbol of the Resurrection. (See also Robert Lehman Collection, no. 12.) *Rogers Fund, 1908, 08.183.1*

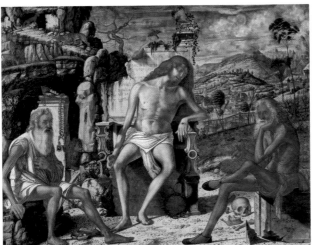

24 VITTORE CARPACCIO, Venetian, ca. 1455–1523/26
The Meditation on the Passion
Tempera on wood; 27¾ × 34⅛ in. (70.5 × 86.7 cm.)

Although Carpaccio's most famous pictures are the narrative cycles he painted for religious confraternities in Venice, his altarpieces and devotional paintings are no less distinguished. This picture (ca. 1510) is a masterpiece from the second group. To the right Job is seated on a marble block inscribed with his words, "I know that my redeemer liveth." According to Saint Jerome, who is portrayed at the left as a hermit, this passage refers to the Resurrection of Christ. The figure of the dead Christ is displayed on a broken marble throne, behind which a small bird, a symbol of the Resurrection, flies upward. The landscape—savage and barren on the left, pastoral and lush on the right—also alludes to death and life. In few other pictures by Carpaccio is the rich technique of Venetian painting employed to illustrate such a deeply serious theme and meditative mood. *John Stewart Kennedy Fund, 1911, 11.118*

25 TITIAN, Venetian, ca. 1488–d. 1576
Venus and the Lute Player
Oil on canvas; 65 × 82½ in. (165.1 × 209.6 cm.)

The Neoplatonic debate over whether Beauty is best perceived by the eye or by the ear seems to have inspired this ravishing picture in which Titian shows Venus reclining on a bed. She holds a recorder and a viola da gamba lies at her side, while a young man at the foot of the bed plays the lute. Cupid suspends a crown of flowers over the goddess's head while the young man turns to gaze at her—thus indicating the superiority of sight over hearing in the perception of Beauty. This picture, which dates from the 1560s, is the latest of five paintings by Titian of Venus serenaded by a musician. Typical of his late work is the marvelously free, open brushwork of the distant landscape, where satyrs and nymphs dance to the pipes of Pan. The head of Venus and the curtain, however, were probably left in an unfinished state by Titian and were completed by another hand. *Munsey Fund, 1936, 36.29*

26 TITIAN, Venetian, ca. 1488–d. 1576
Venus and Adonis
Oil on canvas; 42 × 52½ in. (106.7 × 133.4 cm.)

As often as not Ovid's *Metamorphoses* provided the inspiration for Titian's mythological paintings, but in this case no precise literary source has been found. The pose of Venus seems to have been inspired by that of a similar figure on a Roman sarcophagus relief. She embraces her lover, the hunter Adonis, who is about to depart on his fatal boar chase. Cupid is seen behind a rock protectively holding a dove,

as though forewarned of Adonis's imminent death. The beautiful landscape is lit by a golden ray of light emerging between the clouds, and a rainbow hangs over the lovers. Titian treated this subject a number of times, sometimes with the help of assistants, but the Museum's version appears to be completely autograph. Like *Venus and the Lute Player* (no. 25), it dates from the 1560s, but perhaps to an even greater degree it exemplifies Titian's unsurpassed mastery and inspired interpretation of classical mythology. *The Jules Bache Collection, 1949, 49.7.16*

27 PARIS BORDON, Venetian, 1500–1571
Portrait of a Man in Armor with Two Pages
Oil on canvas; 46 × 62 in. (116.9 × 157.5 cm.)

This striking portrait shows a high-ranking officer on the field of battle with two pages, one of whom holds his helmet while the other fastens the armor on his right arm. It may be identical with a portrait of Carlo da Rho that Bordon painted in Milan about 1540. Carlo da Rho, who died in an expedition against the Turks in 1559, is known to have been a commander of foot soldiers rather than cavalrymen, and indeed foot soldiers are shown in the background. Although Bordon was trained by Titian, his paintings have a somewhat mannered quality and show an attention to detail that relates him to North Italian traditions. *Gift of Mr. and Mrs. Charles Wrightsman, 1973, 1973.311.1*

28 TINTORETTO, Venetian, 1518–94
The Miracle of the Loaves and Fishes
Oil on canvas; 61 × 160½ in. (154.9 × 407.7 cm.)

On two occasions Christ fed a multitude with a few loaves and fishes. This painting depicts the miracle as recounted in the Gospel of John (6:1–14) and shows Christ handing Saint Andrew one of the five loaves and two fishes to be distributed to the crowd. The picture should be dated about 1545–50, and judging from the point of view from which the figures in the foreground are painted, it was intended to be hung fairly high. As in other paintings of this date by Tintoretto, the figures are painted with great assurance in a dazzling array of colors. Especially notable is the vast, circular space, dotted with the arched openings of tombs and animated with clumps of trees, which he has created around the central figures of Christ and Saint Andrew. *Francis L. Leland Fund, 1913, 13.75*

30 PAOLO VERONESE, Venetian, 1528?–1588
Mars and Venus United by Love
Oil on canvas; 81 × 63⅜ in. (205.7 × 161 cm.)

This work is one of five outstanding paintings by Veronese that were owned by Emperor Rudolf II in Prague. All illustrate abstruse allegories, and the exact meaning of the present picture has not been fully explained. It has been suggested that rather than being Venus, the woman symbolizes Chastity transformed by Love into Charity and that the horse held back by an armed cupid is an emblem of Passion Restrained. Regardless of its precise meaning, this is one of Veronese's masterpieces. When it was painted in the 1570s, Veronese was at the height of his powers, a marvelous colorist and the possessor of an unsurpassed representational technique. *John Stewart Kennedy Fund, 1910, 10.189*

29 PAOLO VERONESE, Venetian, 1528?–1588
Alessandro Vittoria
Oil on canvas; 43½ × 32¼ in. (110.5 × 81.9 cm.)

Alessandro Vittoria (1524/25–1608) was the greatest Venetian sculptor of the later sixteenth century. In this portrait he holds a model for one of his most famous statues, the Saint Sebastian carved in 1561–63 for the church of San Francesco della Vigna in Venice; a fragmentary antique torso rests on the table to the left. Notable for its restrained use of color, this portrait seems to have been painted several years after Vittoria collaborated with Veronese in 1560–62 on the decoration of the Villa Barbaro at Maser. *Gwynne Andrews Fund, 1946, 46.31*

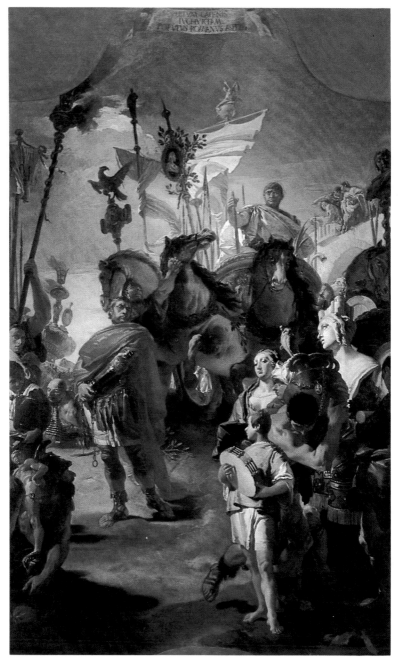

31 GIOVANNI BATTISTA TIEPOLO, Venetian, 1696–1770

The Triumph of Marius

Oil on canvas; 214¾ × 127¾ in. (545.5 × 324.5 cm.)

In about 1725 G. B. Tiepolo was commissioned by Dionisio Dolfin, the patriarch of Aquileia, to undertake frescoes in the archepiscopal palace at Udine. Concurrently he decorated the salone of the Ca'Dolfin, the patriarch's Venetian palace, with a series of ten large paintings of classical subjects. These irregularly shaped canvases were set into the walls of the salone and surrounded with elaborate fictive frames. The paintings were removed in 1870, and three of them are now in the Museum. The present picture shows the Roman general Gaius Marius in the victor's chariot while the conquered African king Jugurtha walks before him, bound in chains. A young boy playing a tambourine leads a group of Romans who carry the spoils of victory. The Latin inscription on the cartouche at the top translates, "The Roman people behold Jugurtha laden with chains"; on an oval medallion the date 1729 is visible. The deep, resonant colors and masterly drawing are typical of the thirty-three-year-old Tiepolo, who is shown at left, in front of the torchbearer. *Rogers Fund, 1965, 65.183.1*

32 GIOVANNI BATTISTA TIEPOLO, Venetian, 1696–1770

Allegory of the Planets and Continents

Oil on canvas; 73 × 54⅞ in. (185.4 × 139.4 cm.)

Tiepolo's greatest achievement was the decoration of the palace of Carl Philipp von Greiffenklau, prince-bishop of Würzburg, carried out between 1751 and 1753. The present picture is the model presented by Tiepolo on April 20, 1752, for the celebrated fresco over the staircase of the palace. It shows Apollo about to embark on his daily course across the sky. The deities around Apollo symbolize the planets, and the allegorical figures on the cornice represent the four continents of the world. Since the staircase measures over sixty by ninety feet, numerous changes were made between the model and the fresco. The model, however, shares with the completed ceiling the feeling for airy space, the beautiful colors, and the prodigious inventiveness that made Tiepolo the unexcelled decorator of the eighteenth century. (See also Drawings, no. 4.) *Gift of Mr. and Mrs. Charles Wrightsman, 1977, 1977.1.3*

---

33 GIOVANNI DOMENICO TIEPOLO, Venetian, 1727–1804

A Dance in the Country

Oil on canvas; 29¾ × 47¼ in. (75.6 × 120 cm.)

The son and valued assistant of Giovanni Battista Tiepolo, Giovanni Domenico especially excelled as a recorder of contemporary life. This canvas, painted about 1756, depicts a dance in the garden of a villa. The young man dancing with an actress wears the scarlet suit and red cap with black feathers traditionally associated with the commedia dell'arte character Mezzetino, and another figure wears the long-nosed mask and tall hat of Pulcinella. Of the countless conversation pieces produced in the mid-eighteenth century, this is one of the most effervescent and spontaneous, and it transmits an incomparably lively sense of the pleasures of aristocratic life in the Veneto. (See also Robert Lehman Collection, no. 42.) *Gift of Mr. and Mrs. Charles Wrightsman, 1980, 1980.67*

34 FRANCESCO GUARDI, Venetian, 1712–93
Fantastic Landscape
*Oil on canvas; 61¼ × 74½ in. (155.5 ×
189.2 cm.)*

This painting and its two companion works in
the Museum come from the castle of Colloredo
near Udine, where they were installed in an
eighteenth-century drawing room. They probably
date from the 1760s and are among Guardi's
finest imaginary landscapes. The light airy touch
with which they are painted and the feeling for
a saturated atmosphere are characteristic of
his best work. *Gift of Julia A. Berwind, 1953,
53.225.3*

NORTHERN ITALIAN PAINTINGS

35 MICHELINO DA BESOZZO, Lombard,
act. 1388–1450
The Marriage of the Virgin
*Tempera on wood, embossed and gilt halos
and ornament; 25⅝ × 18¾ in. (65.1 × 47.6 cm.)*

Of the great painter-illuminators who dominated
Lombard art in the early fifteenth century under
the patronage of the Visconti, the most famous
was Michelino da Besozzo. Little of his work
survives, and only two panel paintings by him
are known. This picture, which dates from about
1430, is laid out like an illumination, with the
principal figures placed beneath the curves of
the arch of the church, while the rejected suitors break their rods at the left. Typical of Michelino
are the elaborate drapery and the suitors' comi-
cal expressions. *Bequest of Maitland F. Griggs,
1943. Maitland F. Griggs Collection, 43.98.7*

36 ANDREA MANTEGNA, Paduan,
ca. 1430–d. 1506
The Adoration of the Shepherds
*Tempera on canvas, transferred from wood;
15¾ × 21⅞ in. (40 × 55.6 cm.)*

Mantegna was one of the great prodigies of
Italian painting, establishing his reputation when
he was barely twenty years old with the frescoes in the church of the Eremitani in Padua.

The Adoration of the Shepherds is among his
earliest paintings, but already his highly individual style is evident. The hard, precise drawing,
the astonishing clarity of even the smallest
details in the distant landscape, and the refined,
pure color are typical of his work as are the
intensely serious expressions of the figures.
Anonymous gift, 1932, 32.130.2

37 ANDREA MANTEGNA, Paduan,
ca. 1430–d. 1506
The Holy Family with Saint Mary Magdalen
*Tempera on canvas; 22½ × 18 in. (57.2 ×
45.7 cm.)*

In addition to the large altarpieces and decorations Mantegna painted for the Gonzaga palace
in Mantua between 1490 and his death, he
produced a number of comparatively small pictures for private devotion. Like the present
picture, these were frequently painted in tempera on a fine cotton support, and they are
exceptionally delicate in execution. This composition is based on classical funerary reliefs, which
seem to have dictated the physiognomical type
of Saint Joseph, the vaguely classical headdress of the Virgin, and the serious mood.
Bequest of Benjamin Altman, 1913, 14.40.643

38 COSIMO TURA, Ferrarese, act. by 1451–d. 1495
The Flight into Egypt
Tempera on wood; painted surface 15¼ × 15 in. (38.7 × 38.1 cm.)

This picture is one of three circular scenes illustrating the early life of Christ which have been supposed, without certain proof, to belong to Tura's masterpiece, the Roverella altarpiece, painted about 1474 for the church of San Giorgio fuori le Mura in Ferrara. Tura was the greatest Ferrarese painter and one of the most individual artists of the fifteenth century. In this work the gnarled figures, the eerie, barren landscape, and the unearthly pink of the morning sky are typical of his wonderfully imaginative approach to painting. *The Jules Bache Collection, 1949, 49.7.17*

39 CORREGGIO, School of Parma, act. by 1514–d. 1534
Saints Peter, Martha, Mary Magdalen, and Leonard
Oil on canvas; 87¼ × 63¾ in. (221.6 × 161.9 cm.)

This altarpiece seems to have been commissioned about 1517 by Correggio's compatriot Melchiore Fassi, who had a special devotion for the four saints shown. It is a relatively early work, in which the delicate, feminine beauty of the figures, the subtle treatment of light, and the emphatic use of shadow presage the achievements of Correggio's maturity. Saints Peter, Mary Magdalen, and Leonard hold their traditional attributes: Peter the keys of the gates of Heaven, Mary Magdalen the jar of ointment, and Leonard the fetters of prisoners released through his intercession. Saint Martha, however, is shown with unusual attributes—an aspergillum and the dragon she tamed with holy water. *John Stewart Kennedy Fund, 1912, 12.211*

40 MORETTO DA BRESCIA, Brescian, 1498–1554
Portrait of a Man
Oil on canvas; 34½ × 32 in. (87 × 81.3 cm.)

Although the sitter in this early portrait by Moretto was at one time thought to be a member of the Martinengo family of Brescia, this identification cannot be verified. There can, however, be no doubt that it is one of his most striking portraits. Moretto was, of course, familiar with the work of Titian, but he took a more realistic approach to painting, and some of the most beautiful passages in this work are details like the Turkish carpet, the hourglass (a symbol of the passing of time), and the black watered satin of the sitter's robes. *Rogers Fund, 1928, 28.79*

41 GIOVANNI BATTISTA MORONI, Lombard,
ca. 1524–d. 1578
Abbess Lucrezia Agliardi Vertova
Oil on canvas; 36 × 27 in. (91.4 × 68.6 cm.)

A pupil of Moretto da Brescia (no. 40), Moroni
was one of the most distinguished portraitists of
the sixteenth century. The inscription on this
portrait states that the sitter was the daughter
of the nobleman Alessio Agliardi of Bergamo
and the wife of Francesco Cataneo Vertova and
that she founded the Carmelite convent of
Sant'Anna in Albino, near Bergamo. In 1556
Lucrezia (b. 1490) named the convent benefici-
ary in her will, and it is probable that the portrait
was painted on this occasion. The date 1557
may be that of her death. The picture is one of
Moroni's finest, notable especially for the sever-
ity of its design, the lack of idealization of the
sitter's features, and the remarkable effect of
the hands resting on the ledge. *Bequest of
Theodore M. Davis, 1915. Theodore M. Davis
Collection, 30.95.255*

43 GUIDO RENI, Bolognese, 1575–1642
Charity
Oil on canvas; 54 × 41¾ in. (137.2 × 106 cm.)

Guido Reni was one of the leading painters in Bologna in the second quarter of the seventeenth century. Here the virtue Charity is shown with three baby boys—one at her breast, one sleeping in her lap, and one leaning against her shoulder. Charity's rose-red dress may have been intended as a reminder of Christ's sacrifice. The delicate and varied flesh tones, soft modeling, and gentle emotion are characteristic of Reni's late work at its best. The picture, which descended in the Liechtenstein family collection until the late nineteenth century, may have been purchased from the artist about 1630 by Prince Karl Eusebius von Liechtenstein. *Gift of Mr. and Mrs. Charles Wrightsman, 1974, 1974.348*

42 ANNIBALE CARRACCI, Bolognese, 1560–1609
The Coronation of the Virgin
Oil on canvas; 46⅜ × 55⅝ in. (117.8 × 141.3 cm.)

Carracci painted this celebrated picture shortly after he arrived in Rome in 1595. It seems to have been commissioned by Cardinal Pietro Aldobrandini, a nephew of Pope Clement VIII, and was singled out by early sources as one of the most distinguished works in the cardinal's collection. Despite its relatively modest dimensions, this picture is an example of Carracci's work at its best; especially notable are the rich use of color and dramatic lighting, the idealized figures, and the carefully constructed empyrean. *Purchase, Bequest of Miss Adelaide Milton de Groot (1876–1967), by exchange, and Dr. and Mrs. Manuel Porter and sons, Gift in honor of Mrs. Sarah Porter, 1971, 1971.155*

44   DOMENICHINO, Bolognese, 1581–1641
**Landscape with Moses and the
Burning Bush**
Oil on copper; 17¾ × 13⅜ in. (45.1 × 34 cm.)

Like his mentor Annibale Carracci (no. 42),
Domenichino was known not only for his large
narrative fresco cycles, but also for his idealized
landscapes of the Roman countryside. This
picture, painted about 1616, illustrates a passage in the Book of Exodus (3:1–6) that tells
how an angel of the Lord appeared to Moses in
the guise of a burning bush. Idealized representations like this exquisite work established the
vogue for classical landscapes and influenced
Claude Lorrain (no. 109). *Gift of Mr. and Mrs.
Charles Wrightsman, 1976, 1976.155.2*

45 EL GRECO, Spanish (b. Crete), 1541–1614
The Miracle of Christ Healing the Blind
Oil on canvas; 47 × 57½ in. (119.5 × 146 cm.)

In the Gospels there are three accounts of
Christ healing blind men. This picture seems to
follow Mark 10:46–52, which tells that the blind
Bartimaeus cried out for Christ's mercy and was
healed. Blindness is an age-old symbol of un-
belief, and particularly in the context of the
Counter-Reformation, the gift of sight should be
interpreted as emblematic of the true faith.

El Greco, born Doménikos Theotokópoulos
in Crete, received his training in Venice, reportedly in the workshop of Titian. He was in Rome
in 1570 and settled in Spain by 1577. *The
Miracle of Christ Healing the Blind* was probably painted shortly before his arrival in Spain. A
moving and highly individual picture, it illustrates the artist's mastery of the vocabulary of
mid-sixteenth-century Venetian painting. *Gift of
Mr. and Mrs. Charles Wrightsman, 1978,
1978.416*

46 EL GRECO, Spanish (b. Crete), 1541–1614
**Portrait of a Cardinal, probably
Don Fernando Niño de Guevara**
*Oil on canvas; 67¼ × 42½ in. (170.8 ×
108 cm.)*

This portrait has long been thought to represent
Cardinal Don Fernando Niño de Guevara (1541–
1609), the grand inquisitor who lived in Toledo
from 1599 to 1601, when he was appointed
archbishop of Seville. More recently he has
been identified as Don Gáspar de Quiroga
(d. 1594) or Don Bernardo de Sandoval y Rojas
(d. 1618). Both were cardinal archbishops of
Toledo. Whoever he may be, the sitter is portrayed as a man of power and uncompromising
religious fervor. This image should be interpreted as an ecclesiastical state portrait, intended
to express the authority not only of the individual,
but of his holy office. (See also Robert Lehman
Collection, no. 22.) *Bequest of Mrs. H. O.
Havemeyer, 1929. H. O. Havemeyer Collection,
29.100.5*

47 EL GRECO, Spanish (b. Crete), 1541–1614
View of Toledo
*Oil on canvas; 47¾ × 42¾ in. (121.3 ×
108.6 cm.)*

This view of Toledo, painted about 1597, is
El Greco's only true landscape. A city of great
antiquity, Toledo is the see of the primate archbishop of Spain and until 1561 was the capital of
the Spanish empire. The buildings are recognizable though interchanged, and the viewpoint is
identifiable. The foreground, irrigated by the
Tagus flowing beneath the Alcántara bridge, is
fertile and green; the distant landscape is barren and threatening. The sharp white light evokes
both the eerie beauty of the place and the
menace inherent in nature. *Bequest of Mrs.
H. O. Havemeyer, 1929. H. O. Havemeyer Collection, 29.100.6*

48 JUSEPE RIBERA, Spanish, 1591–1652
The Holy Family with Saints Anne and Catherine of Alexandria
Oil on canvas; 82½ × 60¾ in. (209.6 × 154.3 cm.)

Ribera, who was born in Valencia, moved to Italy as a young man and remained there for the rest of his life. In 1616 he joined the Accademia di San Luca in Rome; shortly thereafter he settled in Naples, a Spanish possession, where he was patronized by a succession of Spanish viceroys. Ribera was much influenced by Annibale Carracci (no. 42) and Caravaggio. This picture, one of his most celebrated late works, depicts the mystic marriage of Saint Catherine, but she is portrayed without her traditional emblems and she is not receiving a wedding ring from the Christ Child. *Samuel D. Lee Fund, 1934, 34.73*

49 DIEGO VELÁZQUEZ, Spanish, 1599–1660
Juan de Pareja
Oil on canvas; 32 × 27½ in. (81.3 × 69.9 cm.)

In 1648 Philip IV of Spain sent Velázquez to Italy to buy works of art for the Alcázar, the newly renovated royal palace in Madrid. While in Rome, then the center of the international art world, Velázquez painted two portraits which astounded his contemporaries: that of Pope Innocent X (Doria Pamphili Gallery, Rome) and that of his assistant, the painter Juan de Pareja (ca. 1610–70), a Sevillian of Moorish descent. This picture was exhibited at the Pantheon on March 19, 1650, and one connoisseur who viewed it is said to have remarked that while all the rest was art, this alone was truth. *Fletcher Fund, Rogers Fund, and Bequest of Miss Adelaide Milton de Groot (1876–1967), by exchange, supplemented by gifts from friends of the Museum, 1971, 1971.86*

50 BARTOLOMÉ ESTEBAN MURILLO, Spanish, 1617–82
Virgin and Child
Oil on canvas; 65¼ × 43 in. (165.7 × 109.2 cm.)

Murillo painted the Virgin and Child over and over again; his representations of the Virgin, supremely beautiful but always human, were sought after by Spanish ecclesiastics and pious families. This painting, which dates from the 1670s, hung in the private chapel of the Santiago family in Madrid until 1808. Palomino (*El Museo Pictórico*, 1715) described it as "enchanting for its sweetness and beauty." *Rogers Fund, 1943, 43.13*

51 FRANCISCO GOYA, Spanish,
1746–1828
Don Manuel Osorio Manrique de Zuñiga
Oil on canvas; 50 × 40 in. (127 × 101.6 cm.)

Not long after Goya was appointed painter to
Charles III of Spain in 1786, the conde de
Altamira seems to have asked him to paint
portraits of the members of his family, including
his son, who was born in 1784. Goya depicts a
fashionably dressed child holding a magpie on
a string, a favorite pet since the Middle Ages. In
the background three cats stare menacingly at
the bird, traditionally a Christian symbol of the
soul. In Renaissance art, the Christ Child is
often depicted holding a bird tied to a string,
and in the Baroque period, caged birds are
symbolic of innocence. Goya apparently intended this portrait as an illustration of the frail
boundaries that separate a child's world from
the forces of evil. (See also Robert Lehman
Collection, no. 23.) *The Jules Bache Collection,
1949, 49.7.41*

---

52 FRANCISCO GOYA, Spanish,
1746–1828
Majas on a Balcony
*Oil on canvas; 76¾ × 49½ in. (194.8 ×
125.7 cm.)*

This picture is one of a group of genre subjects
that Goya painted during the Spanish War of
Independence (1808–1814), when he received
no commissions from the court. Here he depicts
majos and *majas,* male and female members of
the Spanish working class who are easily recognized by their striking attire and flamboyant
behavior. The enthusiasm for *majaism* was such
that Goya's patrons sometimes chose to pose
in the guise of these dashing young Spaniards.
The shadowy figures of the two men with their
dark cloaks and hats inject something men-
acing and sinister into the scene. (See also
Drawings, no. 10, and Prints and Photographs,
no. 3.) *Bequest of Mrs. H. O. Havemeyer, 1929.
H. O. Havemeyer Collection, 29.100.10*

53   JAN VAN EYCK, Flemish, act. by 1422–d. 1441

The Crucifixion; The Last Judgment

Tempera and oil on canvas, transferred from wood; each 22¼ × 7¾ in. (56.5 × 19.7 cm.)

These two paintings are among Jan van Eyck's earliest surviving works; they probably date from shortly before the Ghent altarpiece (completed 1432)—that is, between 1425 and 1430. They are closely related to a group of miniatures in the manuscript known as the Turin-Milan Hours, which are attributed to the young Jan van Eyck. It cannot be established whether *The*

Crucifixion and *The Last Judgment* were originally planned as a diptych or formed the wings of a triptych or tabernacle. Every detail here is observed freshly and with equal interest—the Alpine landscape, the slender body of Christ, the great variety of onlookers and mourners and monsters and sinners. Perhaps more than any other works attributed to Jan, these pictures show him as the forerunner of realism in the North and as one of the most inspired practitioners of the newly invented technique of oil painting. *Fletcher Fund, 1933, 33.92ab*

54 ATTRIBUTED TO JAN VAN EYCK, Flemish, act. by 1422–d. 1441
The Annunciation
Tempera and oil on wood; 30½ × 25⅜ in. (77.5 × 64.5 cm.)

This panel is attributed by the Museum to Jan van Eyck and may be one of his early works; it has also, however, been ascribed to Jan's elder brother Hubert and to Petrus Christus, who is thought to have been active in Jan's workshop at the master's death. The symbolic juxtaposition of a Romanesque buttress on the right side of the portal with a Gothic buttress on the left is a reference to the transition from the era of the Old Testament to that of the New. *Bequest of Michael Friedsam, 1931. The Friedsam Collection, 32.100.35*

55 ROGIER VAN DER WEYDEN, Flemish, ca. 1400–d. 1464
Christ Appearing to His Mother
Tempera and oil on wood; 25 × 15 in. (63.5 × 38.1 cm.)

According to legend, the first act of the risen Christ was to visit his mother; the tears are still on her cheeks as he greets her. In the background is the Resurrection. The capitals show Old Testament events that prefigure Christ's triumph over death, and around the arch are scenes from the Virgin's later life. The restrained emotion and refinement of this picture are characteristic of Rogier, who was a student of Campin (Medieval Art—The Cloisters, no. 28) and the most influential painter active in the North in the fifteenth century.

This is the right wing of a triptych; the left wing, with the Nativity, and the central panel, showing the Pietà, are in the Capilla Real in Granada, Spain. *Bequest of Michael Dreicer, 1921. The Michael Dreicer Collection, 22.60.58*

56 ROGIER VAN DER WEYDEN, Flemish, ca. 1400–d. 1464
Francesco d'Este
Tempera and oil on wood; 11¾ × 8 in. (29.8 × 20.3 cm.)

Francesco d'Este (ca. 1430–after 1475) was an illegitimate son of Leonello d'Este, duke of Ferrara. He was sent to the court of Brussels for his military training in 1444 and seems to have spent the remainder of his life in the service of the dukes of Burgundy. This portrait was probably made about 1460, when Francesco was close to thirty. The aristocratic aloofness and elegance of the sitter are characteristic of Rogier's portraiture, but the white background is exceptional. The hammer and ring may be emblems of office or may allude to a tournament victory. The Este coat of arms is painted on the reverse of the panel. *Bequest of Michael Friedsam, 1931. The Friedsam Collection, 32.100.43*

57 PETRUS CHRISTUS, Flemish, act. by
1444–d. 1472/73
Portrait of a Carthusian
*Tempera and oil on wood; 11½ × 8 in.
(29.2 × 20.3 cm.)*

In its effect of realism this picture surpasses
even the masterful portraits of Christus's teacher,
Jan van Eyck (nos. 53 and 54). The sitter
whose personality is so powerfully projected
has been identified as a Carthusian lay brother.
On the sill of the simulated frame with the date
(1446) and his signature "carved" into it (*XPI* is
an abbreviation of the Greek form of *Christus*),
the artist has painted an astonishingly lifelike fly,
perhaps as a reminder of the ever-present
temptation of evil. (See also Robert Lehman
Collection, no. 14.) *The Jules Bache Collection,
1949, 49.7.19*

58 PETRUS CHRISTUS, Flemish, act. by
1444–d. 1472/73
The Lamentation
*Tempera and oil on wood; 10¼ × 14⅛ in.
(26.1 × 35.9 cm.)*

The sweeping curves formed by the body of
Christ with the Magdalen, Joseph of Arimathea,
and Nicodemus, and by the Virgin and Saint
John the Evangelist behind, make this one of
Christus's most expressive compositions. Typically, the doll-like figures in their enveloping
draperies are crisply drawn; the range of colors is restricted. The panel probably dates
from the 1450s. A larger version of the Lamentation (Musées Royaux des Beaux-Arts, Brussels)
was probably painted a few years earlier. *Gift of
Henry G. Marquand, 1890. Marquand Collection, 91.26.12*

59 JOOS VAN GHENT, Flemish, act. ca. 1460–d. ca. 1480

The Adoration of the Magi

Tempera on linen; 43 × 63 in. (109.2 × 160 cm.)

One of Joos's most beautiful compositions, this painting on fine linen (which accounts for the muted effect of the color) was probably executed in Ghent about 1467. Like other early works attributed to Joos, it shows the influence of his friend Hugo van der Goes, as well as that of Dieric Bouts. Sometime after 1469 Joos left Ghent for Italy, where he entered the employ of Federigo da Montefeltro, duke of Urbino; he remained there until the end of his life. *Bequest of George Blumenthal, 1941, 41.190.21*

60 HANS MEMLING, Flemish, act. ca. 1465–d. 1494

Tommaso Portinari and His Wife

Tempera and oil on wood; left 17⅜ × 13¼ in. (44.1 × 33.7 cm.); right 17⅜ × 13⅜ in. (44.1 × 34 cm.)

Tommaso Portinari, a Florentine who was the Bruges representative of the banking house of the Medici, married Maria Baroncelli in 1470, when she was fourteen and he was thirty-eight. Portinari loved Flemish art, and he commissioned from Memling at least one painting in addition to these portraits and from the Flemish painter Hugo van der Goes the famous Portinari altarpiece (Uffizi, Florence). The praying hands suggest that these panels were originally the wings of a triptych, possibly with a Virgin and Child in the center.

Memling was one of the great portrait painters of the northern Renaissance, and a large number of portraits by him survive. The nobility with which he invested his sitters and the classical poise of his compositions seem to have appealed particularly to members of the large Italian community in Bruges. (See also Robert Lehman Collection, nos. 15 and 16.) *Bequest of Benjamin Altman, 1913, 14.40.626,627*

61 HIERONYMUS BOSCH, Flemish, act. by 1480–d. 1516
The Adoration of the Magi
Tempera and oil on wood; 28 × 22¼ in. (71.1 × 56.5 cm.)

Bosch, who was active in 's Hertogenbosch in the northern Netherlands, is best known for his complex moral allegories with many small, fantastic figures. The Adoration of the Magi, which calls for an exotic cast of characters, seems to have had a special appeal for him. Because the figure types are rather awkward, the painting illustrated here is usually considered an example of Bosch's earliest style, but the landscape is similar to that in the larger and probably later Adoration of the Magi, which is the central panel of his Epiphany altarpiece (Prado, Madrid). *John Stewart Kennedy Fund, 1912, 13.26*

62 GERARD DAVID, Flemish, act. by 1484–d. 1523
The Rest on the Flight into Egypt
Tempera and oil on wood; 20 × 17 in. (50.8 × 43.2 cm.)

This is one of Gerard David's most beautiful and tender compositions and one of his rare "inventions." He painted at least two other variants, and the composition inspired numerous followers well into the sixteenth century.

63 JOACHIM PATINIR, Flemish, act. by 1515–▶ d. 1524
The Penitence of Saint Jerome
Tempera and oil on wood; central panel 46¼ × 32 in. (117.5 × 81.3 cm.); each wing 47½ × 14 in. (120.7 × 35.6 cm.)

The center panel of this triptych depicts the penitence of Saint Jerome; the baptism of Christ and the temptation of Saint Anthony are shown on the interior wings. On the exterior wings are painted Saint Anne with the Virgin and Child and Saint Sebald.

Patinir's emphasis on the natural setting over the narrative content of his paintings, as well as the probably true report that he furnished landscape backgrounds for other artists, has caused him to be regarded as the first landscape painter. In this panoramic view, so vast that we seem to see the curve of the earth, three saints are integrated in a setting that includes harbors, towns, a monastery, and a wilderness. *Fletcher Fund, 1936, 36.14a–c*

The lively little scene in the background—Mary and the Christ Child riding on a donkey with Joseph running after them—and the extensive landscape setting are indications of David's pioneering role in the development of genre and landscape painting in the Netherlands. (See also Robert Lehman Collection, no. 17; The Jack and Belle Linsky Collection, no. 6.) *The Jules Bache Collection, 1949, 49.7.21*

64 PIETER BRUEGEL THE ELDER, Flemish, act. by 1551–d. 1569

The Harvesters

Oil on wood; 46½ × 63¼ in. (118 × 160.7 cm.)

The casual truthfulness with which the peasants are painted, the convincing noonday heat and brilliant light, and the vast panoramic distance rendered with startling effectiveness are all characteristic of Bruegel. This is one of five remaining panels from a cycle devoted to the months. The original number of paintings in the series was either six, with two months represented in each picture, or twelve. *The Harvesters,* dated 1565, probably represents either the month of August or the two months of July and August. The other surviving paintings are *Hunters in the Snow, Return of the Herd,* and *The Dark Day* (all in the Kunsthistorisches Museum, Vienna) and *Haymaking* (National Gallery, Prague). *Rogers Fund, 1919, 19.164*

65 PETER PAUL RUBENS, Flemish,
1577–1640
**Rubens, His Wife Helena Fourment, and
Their Son Peter Paul**
*Oil on wood; 80⅜ × 62⅝ in. (204.2 ×
159.1 cm.)*

This magnificent, very personal work, which
dates from about 1639, is a life-size portrait of
the artist, his second wife, and their young son.
Rubens and Helena, the youngest daughter of
his old friend, the Antwerp merchant Daniel
Fourment, married in December 1630, when he
was fifty-three and she was sixteen. In this
picture, as in the famous *Garden of Love* (Prado,
Madrid) to which it is closely related, Rubens
celebrates his love for Helena, although here he
presents her as both wife and mother.

The picture has passed directly through three
exceptionally distinguished collections. According to tradition, the city of Brussels presented
the painting to the duke of Marlborough in 1704.
It remained at Blenheim Palace, the home of
the Churchills, for nearly two centuries. At the
famous sale of 1884, it was acquired by Baron
Alphonse de Rothschild. The painting left the
Rothschild collection in 1975 and shortly thereafter entered the collection of Mr. and Mrs.
Charles Wrightsman. (See also Drawings, no. 8;
The Jack and Belle Linsky Collection, no. 8.)
*Gift of Mr. and Mrs. Charles Wrightsman,
1981, 1981.238*

66   PETER PAUL RUBENS, Flemish,
1577–1640
Venus and Adonis
*Oil on canvas; 77¾ × 95⅝ in. (197.5 ×
242.9 cm.)*

Here, as in many of the paintings of the glorious
last decade of his career, Rubens has drawn
his subject from the *Metamorphoses* of Ovid.
Venus, assisted by Cupid, vainly tries to re-
strain her mortal lover Adonis from setting off for
the hunt, fearing that if he goes he may be
killed. The rich color, the superb technical ability,

the vitality and human warmth of Rubens's best
works are all united here.

When Rubens painted *Venus and Adonis*, he
had in mind similar pictures by Titian (no. 26)
and Veronese, but he designed it in a typically
Baroque manner. The great, turning figures
dominate the canvas in a huge triangle: Adonis,
pivoting on his spear, will in another instant
throw off the beautiful, entangling arms and be
on his way to his death. (See also Drawings, no.
8; The Jack and Belle Linsky Collection, no. 8.)
Gift of Harry Payne Bingham, 1937, 37.162

---

67   JACOB JORDAENS, Flemish, 1593–1678
**The Holy Family with Saint Anne, and the
Young Baptist and His Parents**
Oil on wood; 66⅞ × 59 in. (169.9 × 149.9 cm.)

This painting is the product of two widely separated periods in Jordaens's career. The Virgin
and Child, Saint Joseph, Saint Anne, and probably a version of the infant Saint John the Baptist
were painted in the early 1620s. A variant of the
painting in Munich attests to the intimate, domestic character of this first composition, painted
with the forceful contrasts of light and shade
typical of the artist's early works. In the 1650s
Jordaens enlarged the panel at the left, top,
and bottom, repainting the figure of Saint John
and adding his parents, Saint Elizabeth and
Zacharias, and an angel at the left. The globe
on which the Christ Child stands and the cartouche and inscription from the Epistle to the
Romans, "If the root be holy, so are the
branches," were also added at this time. In its
final state the painting has a somber balance
and a didactic character. *Purchase, 1871, 71.11*

68   ANTHONY VAN DYCK, Flemish, 1599–1641
Portrait of a Man, probably Lucas van Uffele
*Oil on canvas; 49 × 39⅝ in. (124.5 ×
100.6 cm.)*

This portrait belongs to a group of paintings
executed by Van Dyck in Italy between 1621
and 1627. The objects on the table—a celestial
globe, a recorder, a fragment of classical sculpture, and a red chalk drawing of a head—show
that the sitter was a man of learning and an art
collector. Van Dyck knew a number of wealthy
Flemish merchants and connoisseurs in Italy.
The identification of the sitter with Lucas van
Uffele (1583?–1637), a Flemish merchant and
collector living in Venice, is based upon an early
handwritten note on an impression of Wallerand
Vaillant's mezzotint after the painting. *Bequest
of Benjamin Altman, 1913, 14.40.619*

69   ANTHONY VAN DYCK, Flemish, 1599–1641
**Virgin and Child with Saint Catherine of
Alexandria**
Oil on canvas; 43 × 35¾ in. (109.2 × 90.8 cm.)

Between 1621 and 1627 Van Dyck lived in Italy.
Already an accomplished painter, he profited
much from his study of Italian artists. He was
chiefly interested in the North Italian painters,
particularly Titian, whose example helped form
the poetic and elegant style of the religious
pictures, mythological scenes, and portraits
Van Dyck painted later in Antwerp and in England. This painting was probably executed in
Antwerp shortly after his return from Italy, and it
reveals his study of Titian and also of Correggio
and Parmigianino. *Bequest of Lillian S. Timken,
1959, 60.71.5*

70   ANTHONY VAN DYCK, Flemish, 1599–1641
**James Stewart, Duke of Richmond
and Lennox**
*Oil on canvas; 85 × 50¼ in. (215.9 ×
127.6 cm.)*

In 1632 Van Dyck entered the service of King
Charles I of England; he was knighted the
same year. Van Dyck's portraits of Charles I
flatter a royal sitter who was actually not very
imposing. Possibly the same was true of James
Stewart (1612–55), Charles's cousin and protégé,
depicted here. Certainly Van Dyck has used all
his skills to give the duke elegance and a
commanding presence; the ratio of his head to
his body is one to seven, as in a fashion plate,
instead of one to six, the average in life. The
dog stretching its great body against its master
also emphasizes the height and aristocratic
bearing of the duke. *Gift of Henry G. Marquand,
1889. Marquand Collection, 89.15.16*

71 FRANS HALS, Dutch, after 1580–d. 1666
Portrait of a Man
Oil on canvas; 43½ × 34 in. (110.5 × 86.3 cm.)

Hals was a prolific portraitist, so one can assume that he provided what his unpretentious
bourgeois customers wanted: a good likeness,
without many sittings, at a reasonable price.
Probably few of them realized how much skill
was needed to produce his deceptively simple
pictures. The stable frontal pose of this portrait
is characteristic of Hals's work of the early
1650s. The flesh tones and mauve and green
ribbons play upon the gradations of black and
white in the costume. Viewed closely, all the
brushstrokes are visible. Yet, at a distance,
everything falls into place, the spectator's eye
unconsciously doing the work of making coher-
ent forms out of slashes and dashes. This
challenging technique impressed nineteenth-
century painters, especially Manet and Sargent.
*Gift of Henry G. Marquand, 1890. Marquand
Collection, 91.26.9*

72 HENDRICK TER BRUGGHEN, Dutch,
1588–1629
**The Crucifixion, with the Virgin and
Saint John**
Oil on canvas; 61 × 40¼ in. (154.9 × 102.2 cm.)

Ter Brugghen, who had studied in Rome, was
here influenced not only by the realism of
Caravaggio but also by the conventions of late
Gothic devotional imagery. He probably used
Dutch peasants as models for the Virgin and

Saint John. The intensity of Saint John's anguish,
expressed by his open mouth and twisted hands,
is made even more poignant by his plain face
and red nose. The compelling realism of the
corpse, with its green-toned face and belly, is
more disturbing than anything painted in Italy.
The strange, starry sky and the low horizon
heighten the impression of a supernatural event.
*Purchase, funds from various donors, 1956,
56.228*

73 REMBRANDT, Dutch, 1606–1669
The Toilet of Bathsheba
Oil on wood; 22½ × 30 in. (57.2 × 76.2 cm.)

In this scene from the Old Testament two servants attend Bathsheba while King David, barely discernible on the roof of his palace at the left, spies on her. Although the painting is dated 1643, the tactile quality of Bathsheba's drapery recalls Rembrandt's manner of the late 1630s. He may therefore have worked on the panel over several years. *Bequest of Benjamin Altman, 1913, 14.40.651*

75   REMBRANDT, Dutch, 1606–1669
Aristotle with a Bust of Homer
Oil on canvas; 56½ × 53¾ in. (143.5 × 136.5 cm.)

Rembrandt painted this picture for a Sicilian nobleman, Don Antonio Ruffo, his only foreign patron, who received it in 1654 and ten years later ordered from him two others, a Homer and an Alexander. In the *Aristotle,* dated 1653, three great men of antiquity are closely associated: Aristotle rests his hand on a bust of Homer, and he wears a gold chain with a medallion bearing the image of Alexander. The solemn stillness of the philosopher's study, the eloquence of the fingers laid on the head of the blind poet, and above all the brooding mystery in the face of Aristotle unite to communicate an image of great power. *Purchased with special funds and gifts of friends of the Museum, 1961, 61.198*

74   REMBRANDT, Dutch, 1606–1669
Flora
Oil on canvas; 39⅜ × 36⅛ in. (100 × 91.8 cm.)

A collector in Amsterdam owned a painting of Flora by Titian that Rembrandt certainly remembered when he painted his own in the 1650s. The model wears a great black hat with shiny leaves and pink flowers, a yellow apron that looks as if it were filled with light as well as blossoms, and a full-sleeved blouse that falls into elaborate folds. One can almost feel the joy with which Rembrandt worked on these folds— painting them white, but full of touches of pink, blue, and green. The sitter is certainly no goddess, and she is very different from Titian's lush Venetian beauties; she seems a real person —modest, gentle, and good—and Rembrandt's common-law wife, Hendrickje, is thought to have been the model for the painting. *Gift of Archer M. Huntington in memory of his father, Collis Potter Huntington, 1926, 26.101.10*

76 REMBRANDT, Dutch, 1606–1669
Self-Portrait
Oil on canvas; 31⅝ × 26½ in. (80.3 × 67.3 cm.)

Among Rembrandt's finest works are his self-portraits, which form an extraordinarily varied series extending the length of his career. Al-most one hundred are known. In this portrait of 1660 the artist suggests rather than defines his features and mood by means of clearly discernible superimposed brushstrokes. *Bequest of Benjamin Altman, 1913, 14.40.618*

77 REMBRANDT, Dutch, 1606–1669
Lady with a Pink
Oil on canvas; 36¼ × 29⅜ in. (92.1 × 74.6 cm.)

This portrait and its pendant, *Man with a Magnifying Glass* (also in the Museum), are datable between 1662 and 1665. The rich variety of reds and browns, the broad handling, and the thick impasto are familiar characteristics of Rembrandt's latest works. The sitter is clad in the exotic clothing common to a number of his later portraits of close friends and members of his family. The special meaning of these garments may be personal and thus lost to us. X-ray analysis has revealed the head of a child near the left hand of the woman, which was apparently painted out by the artist, perhaps after the child's death and before the completion of the portrait. The brightly lit carnation, which traditionally signifies love and constancy in marriage, may here allude to the briefness of life. None of the various identifications which have been proposed has proven to be absolutely convincing. *Bequest of Benjamin Altman, 1913, 14.40.622*

78 FRANS POST, Dutch, ca. 1612–d. 1680
A Brazilian Landscape
Oil on wood; 24 × 36 in. (61 × 91.4 cm.)

The first landscapist of the New World, Post arrived in Brazil in 1637 as a member of the scientific staff of Prince Johan Maurice van Nassau. His best paintings date from the decade after his return to Haarlem in 1644. He painted this large, well-preserved picture in 1650. Post's almost exclusive devotion to Brazilian scenery reflects the cosmopolitan interests of Amsterdam and Haarlem. Exotic landscapes and still lifes were of scientific as well as aesthetic interest; both concerns are addressed by Post, who combines textbook detail with the landscape style established in Haarlem. The figures in this picture are unusually prominent and interesting, but the exotic plants and the iguana at the lower right are among his favorite motifs. *Purchase, Rogers Fund, Gift of Edna H. Sachs and other gifts and bequests, by exchange, supplemented by Museum purchase funds, 1981, 1981.318*

---

79 GERARD TER BORCH, Dutch, 1617–81
Curiosity
Oil on canvas; 30 × 24½ in. (76.3 × 62.3 cm.)

Although Ter Borch worked in Deventer, outside the larger artistic centers of the United Provinces, he painted some of the most sophisticated genre pieces of his time. His paintings combine elegance and exquisite refinement of style with an extraordinary mastery of technique in the rendering of textures and light-touched surfaces. In his best work there is often, as here, an effect of seclusion and privacy and a very delicately implied wit. This picture is datable about 1660. (See also Robert Lehman Collection, no. 25.) *The Jules Bache Collection, 1949, 49.7.38*

80 AELBERT CUYP, Dutch, 1620–91
Starting for the Hunt
Oil on canvas; 43¼ × 61½ in. (109.8 × 156.2 cm.)

The sitters, the brothers Michiel (1638–53) and Cornelis Pompe van Meerdervoort (1639–80), are shown with their tutor and coachman. One of very few datable works by Aelbert Cuyp, this picture must have been painted just before Michiel's death in 1653. The two boys were members of a wealthy family residing in the area around Dordrecht, where the terrain is similar to the landscape represented in the background. They wear exotic costumes, perhaps of Persian inspiration, which are often found in portraits of members of the upper classes during this period. Cuyp's bright palette and refined manner are appropriate to the subject; the soft, fluid handling of the landscape contrasts with the colorful and elegant apparel. *Bequest of Michael Friedsam, 1931. The Friedsam Collection, 32.100.20*

81 PHILIPS KONINCK, Dutch, 1619–88
Wide River Landscape
Oil on canvas; 16¾ × 23¾ in. (42.5 × 60.3 cm.)

This panoramic view is a relatively early work. Koninck did not paint identifiable sites but constructed his flat landscapes from observations of nature. An exceptionally fine small painting, this picture was inspired by the somber color and high drama of Rembrandt's landscapes. *Anonymous gift, 1963, 63.43.2*

82 JAN STEEN, Dutch, 1626–79
Merry Company on a Terrace
Oil on canvas; 55½ × 51¾ in. (141 × 131.4 cm.)

Steen delighted in showing scenes of boisterous merrymaking. A prolific painter, he also owned a brewery and a tavern. The stout man sitting at the left, holding a jug, is a portrait of Steen himself. His foremost quality has been described as a natural lightheartedness, but he has depicted this scene of good-humored gaiety and noise with the most refined color and composition, centering on the tipsy fair-haired woman in the pale blue dress. (See also *The Jack and Belle Linsky Collection, no. 9.*) *Fletcher Fund, 1958, 58.89*

83 JACOB VAN RUISDAEL, Dutch, 1628/29–1682
Wheatfields
Oil on canvas; 39⅜ × 51¼ in. (100 × 130.2 cm.)

Better than any other Dutch painter, Ruisdael described in his landscapes—with their low horizons and wide vistas of sand and dunes —the look and feel of his country. In his paintings of the 1670s, such as *Wheatfields,* flat landscape subjects are characteristic, as are the converging lines of earth and sky and the alternation of shadow and sunlight. Ruisdael had numerous pupils and followers; Meindert Hobbema (no. 89) was his most famous disciple. *Bequest of Benjamin Altman, 1913, 14.40.623*

84 PIETER DE HOOCH, Dutch, 1629–84
Paying the Hostess
Oil on canvas; 37¼ × 43¾ in. (94.6 × 111.1 cm.)

Like Vermeer (nos. 85–87), Pieter de Hooch is best known for his depictions of interiors, in which he explores the play of light as it illuminates space and reflects off various surfaces. Here a soldier pays the hostess of an inn. While the subject is often found in De Hooch's paintings of the 1650s, the complex organization of space, the use of multiple sources of light, and the exceptionally large size of the canvas suggest a date in his later years. The decorative rendering of the soldier's garb may be due to the influence of French painting in Amsterdam, where De Hooch resided from 1670. This painting reflects a general trend in Dutch art of the 1660s and 1670s toward greater elegance and a more refined style. *Gift of Stuart Borchard and Evelyn B. Metzger, 1958, 58.144*

85 JOHANNES VERMEER, Dutch, 1632–75
Young Woman with a Water Jug
Oil on canvas; 18 × 16 in. (45.7 × 40.6 cm.)

The perfect balance of the composition, the cool clarity of the light, and the silvery tones of blue and gray combine to make this closely studied glimpse of an interior a very typical work by Vermeer. As Vermeer's paintings were few in number—fewer than forty universally accepted works have survived—and as they were not widely known, he was forgotten soon after his death. Almost two hundred years passed before the French critic Théophile Thoré rediscovered his work on a visit to Holland. Vermeer is now one of the most esteemed Dutch painters. The *Young Woman with a Water Jug* is characteristic of his early maturity, and it dates from the beginning of the 1660s. *Gift of Henry G. Marquand, 1889. Marquand Collection, 89.15.21*

86 JOHANNES VERMEER, Dutch, 1632–75
Portrait of a Young Woman
Oil on canvas; 17½ × 15¾ in. (44.5 × 40 cm.)

The portrait is the rarest of all Vermeer's subjects. In technique and lighting, this painting is closely related to Vermeer's most celebrated work, the *Portrait of a Girl* (Mauritshuis, The Hague), and seems to have been painted in the late 1660s. It is a subtle and delicate picture in which the artist explores the ambiguity of human expression with rare sensitivity. The work is remarkable for its simple yet highly sophisticated structure, subtlety of coloring, and haunting expressiveness. The painting reminded the French critic Thoré of that most enigmatic of all female portraits, Leonardo da Vinci's *Mona Lisa. Gift of Mr. and Mrs. Charles Wrightsman, 1979, 1979.396.1*

87 JOHANNES VERMEER, Dutch, 1632–75
Allegory of the Faith
Oil on canvas; 45 × 35 in. (114.3 × 88.9 cm.)

This is one of two pictures by Vermeer with explicit allegorical content. The woman is a personification of Faith and matches a description of Faith in Cesare Ripa's *Iconologia* (1593), in which the chalice, book, and globe are mentioned along with other attributes. Here Vermeer remains concerned with the depiction of objects, space, and light. The simplification and hardening of the light in this painting are characteristic of the artist's last style. The Museum's collection of five paintings by Vermeer is one of the most important in the world. *Bequest of Michael Friedsam, 1931. The Friedsam Collection, 32.100.18*

88 NICOLAES MAES, Dutch, 1634–93
Young Girl Peeling Apples
Oil on wood; 21½ × 18 in. (54.6 × 45.7 cm.)

This picture is one of a number of quiet scenes of women performing domestic tasks painted by Maes in the mid-1650s. In the distribution of light and shade, these paintings still show the influence of his teacher, Rembrandt. Later, Maes changed his style and increasingly concentrated on elegant portraits done in a courtly manner. *Bequest of Benjamin Altman, 1913, 14.40.612*

89 MEINDERT HOBBEMA, Dutch, 1638–1709
A Woodland Road
Oil on canvas; 37¼ × 51 in. (94.6 × 129.5 cm.)

The luxuriant foliage, the lively play of light and shadow, and the figures that animate this country scene give it a greater immediacy than the landscapes by Jacob van Ruisdael, who was Hobbema's teacher. This picture—with its windswept trees, fallen logs, and towering masses of moving clouds—is among Hobbema's most dramatic works. *Bequest of Mary Stillman Harkness, 1950, 50.145.22*

90 ALBRECHT DÜRER, German, 1471–1528
Virgin and Child with Saint Anne
Tempera and oil on canvas, transferred from wood; 23⅝ × 19⅝ in. (60 × 49.9 cm.)

Saint Anne, who was particularly venerated in Germany, is often represented with her daughter, the Virgin Mary, and the Christ Child. This picture was painted in 1519, the year that Dürer became an ardent follower of Martin Luther, and the emotional intensity of the image may be a reflection of his conversion. The motif of the Virgin adoring the sleeping Christ Child was probably inspired by the Venetian painter Giovanni Bellini (no. 23), whose art Dürer admired on his two trips to Italy. The monumental masses of the figures and the balanced composition attest to the impact that Italian art made on Dürer's native northern Gothic style. (See also Robert Lehman Collection, no. 43, and Prints and Photographs, no. 4.) *Bequest of Benjamin Altman, 1913, 14.40.633*

1 LUCAS CRANACH THE ELDER, German, 472–1553
he Judgment of Paris
empera and oil on wood; 40⅛ × 28 in. (102 × 1.2 cm.)

his painting shows Paris awarding a golden pple (here transformed into a glass orb) to enus, whom he judged more beautiful than Juno or Minerva. This myth was a favorite with Cranach and his large, prolific workshop. Painted about 1528, the sprightly narrative and decorative scene, if contrasted with Dürer's *Virgin and Child with Saint Anne* (no. 90) of a few years earlier, shows how oblivious Cranach was to the lofty monumental concepts of the southern Renaissance. *Rogers Fund, 1928, 28.221*

ANNO.1532.   ÆTATIS SVÆ 29

92 HANS HOLBEIN THE YOUNGER, German, 1497/98–1543
Portrait of a Member of the Wedigh Family
Tempera and oil on wood; 16⅝ × 12¾ in. (42.2 × 32.4 cm.)

During Holbein's second stay in England, he found many clients among the colony of German merchants in London. The arms on the ring worn by the sitter and the lettering on his book indicate that he is a member of a Cologne trading family named Wedigh; presumably he was their representative in England. He has sometimes been identified as Hermann Wedigh III (d. 1560), a merchant and a member of the Hanseatic trading company. This painting, dated 1532, demonstrates why Holbein is regarded as one of the world's greatest portraitists. The clarity of color, the precision of drawing, and the crisp, explicit characterization constitute a compelling expression of human personality. (See also Robert Lehman Collection, no. 21.) *Bequest of Edward S. Harkness, 1940, 50.135.4*

93 HANS BALDUNG GRIEN, German, 1484/85–1545
Saint John on Patmos
Tempera and oil on wood; 35¼ × 30¼ in. (89.5 × 76.8 cm.)

This work by Hans Baldung Grien, a major German religious imagist of the early sixteenth century, is one of the most important of the Museum's recent acquisitions. The picture exemplifies the qualities of Baldung both as a religious artist and as a landscape painter. The young Saint John, seated on the right, gazes tenderly at a vision of the Virgin, who stands on a crescent moon with the Christ Child in her arms. Behind Saint John stretches a romantic landscape, and at the lower left an eagle, the symbol of the Evangelist, is perched on top of a closed book.

This animal's imposing outline, the foreshortened book, and the powerful contrasts of black, turquoise, and gold make this one of the most arresting areas of the composition. The painting is almost perfectly preserved, and the highlights that are so important a feature of Baldung's pictorial language are intact. *Purchase, The Vincent Astor Foundation, The Dillon Fund, The Charles Engelhard Foundation, Lawrence A. Fleischman, Mrs. Henry J. Heinz II, The Willard T. C. Johnson Foundation, Inc., Reliance Group Holdings, Inc., Baron H. H. Thyssen-Bornemisza, and Mr. and Mrs. Charles Wrightsman Gifts; and John Stewart Kennedy Fund, Gifts of Henry W. Canon and J. Pierpont Morgan, and Bequest of Lillian S. Timken, by exchange, 1983, 1983.451*

94 ARNOLD BÖCKLIN, Swiss, 1827–1901
Island of the Dead
Oil on wood; 29 × 48 in. (73.6 × 121.9 cm.)

Böcklin painted five versions of *Island of the Dead* between 1880 and 1886. This painting, the first to be completed, resulted from a request made by the recently widowed Marie Berna. In Florence in 1880 she asked Böcklin to paint a picture on the theme of her bereavement. In a letter dated April 29, 1880, Böcklin wrote to her: "You will be able to dream yourself into the world of dark shadows until you believe you can feel the soft and gentle breeze that ripples the sea, so that you shy from interrupting the stillness with any audible sound." *Reisinger Fund, 1926, 26.90*

95 WILLIAM HOGARTH, British, 1697–1764
The Wedding of Stephen Beckingham and Mary Cox
Oil on canvas; 50½ × 40½ in. (128.3 × 102.9 cm.)

Hogarth, who is perhaps best known for his satirical prints, was also a gifted portraitist and observer of the English scene. Here he represents the marriage of Stephen Beckingham (d. 1756) and Mary Cox (d. 1738), which took place on June 9, 1729. The Beckingham family were members of the landed gentry, and Stephen Beckingham, like his father, was a barrister at Lincoln's Inn. The putti with the cornucopia, symbolizing plenty, and the portrait of Rev. Thomas Cooke, which borders on caricature, are rather surprising additions to this picture, which otherwise documents the occasion with due solemnity. *Marquand Fund, 1936, 36.111*

96 SIR JOSHUA REYNOLDS, British, 1723–92
Colonel George K. H. Coussmaker, Grenadier Guards
Oil on canvas; 93¾ × 57¼ in. (238.1 × 145.4 cm.)

Reynolds was the first president of the Royal Academy and the author of fourteen discourses on painting, which are classics of the theory of art. As a young man he spent two years in Italy, studying the works of the High Renaissance masters, especially Michelangelo, as well as Roman antiquities. These studies had a forma-tive influence on his own style.

In this portrait of 1782, Reynolds presents Colonel Coussmaker (1759–1801) in a pose of casual but studied negligence, the line of his body repeated in the curving neck of his horse. The summer before he painted the picture, Reynolds traveled to the Low Countries and profited by his observation of Rubens's works, especially in the creation of a free and painterly surface treatment. *Bequest of William K. Vanderbilt, 1920, 20.155.3*

97 GEORGE STUBBS, British, 1724–1806
**A Favorite Hunter of John Frederick Sackville,
later Third Duke of Dorset**
Oil on canvas; 40 × 49¾ in. (101.6 × 126.4 cm.)

Stubbs was largely self-taught, and except for a
trip to Rome in 1746, he spent his early years in
the north of England. For two decades from
about 1759, when he settled in London, he
commanded the field as an animal painter with
his coolly detached and meticulously accurate
and individual portraits of dogs and horses,
often with their owners, riders, or stablemen.
Despite the popularity of his paintings, Stubbs
attracted little critical notice in his lifetime. He
did, however, transform sporting art, and he is
now regarded as one of the most innovative
painters of his age. This picture, which dates
from 1768, shows a favorite hunter of John
Frederick Sackville, and it may be supposed
that the canvas was painted at Knole, the
Sackville family seat. *Bequest of Mrs. Paul
Moore, 1980, 1980.468*

98 THOMAS GAINSBOROUGH, British,
1727–88
Mrs. Grace Dalrymple Elliott
*Oil on canvas; 92¼ × 60½ in. (234.3 ×
151.2 cm.)*

This portrait was probably painted not long
before 1778, when Gainsborough sent it to be
exhibited at the Royal Academy, of which he
was a founding member. It is an excellent
example of his fashionable portrait style, which
he built upon his awareness of English likenesses
by Van Dyck (no. 70), modifying their monumental quality with the grace and elegance of
Watteau.

When very young, Mrs. Elliott (1754?–1823)
made an aristocratic marriage, which was followed by a slightly lurid romantic career in
London and during the French Revolution in
Paris. The marquess of Cholmondeley (who
commissioned this picture) and George IV were
among her admirers. *Bequest of William K.
Vanderbilt, 1920, 20.155.1*

99 SIR THOMAS LAWRENCE, British,
1769–1830
Elizabeth Farren, later Countess of Derby
Oil on canvas; 94 × 57½ in. (238.8 × 146.1 cm.)

The verve and freshness that make this portrait
so appealing are congruous with the youthful-
ness of Lawrence when he painted it in 1790.
The composition, the construction of the figure,
and the virtuosity and variety of the brushwork
are, however, extraordinary in an artist of relatively limited experience. Lawrence had been
admitted as a student at the Royal Academy in
1787, only three years before this portrait was
exhibited there.

Miss Farren (ca. 1759–d. 1829), a hugely
admired actress, retired from the stage in 1797
on becoming the second wife of the twelfth earl
of Derby. *Bequest of Edward S. Harkness,
1940, 50.135.5*

100 SIR THOMAS LAWRENCE, British,
1769–1830
The Calmady Children
Oil on canvas; 30⅞ × 30⅛ in. (78.4 × 76.5 cm.)

The children in this portrait, painted in 1823, are
Emily (1818–1906?) and Laura Anne (1820–94),
the daughters of Mr. and Mrs. Charles Biggs
Calmady of Langdon Hall, Devon. In composition this work shows the influence of sixteenth-
and seventeenth-century Italian paintings of the
Infant Jesus and Saint John the Baptist; its
circular form recalls the *Madonna della Sedia,*
Raphael's celebrated tondo. Exhibited at the
Royal Academy in 1824 and later engraved
under the title *Nature,* this portrait became one
of Lawrence's most popular paintings. The artist
himself declared: "This is my best picture. I
have no hesitation in saying so—my best picture of the kind, quite—one of the few I should
wish hereafter to be known by." *Bequest of
Collis P. Huntington, 1900, 25.110.1*

101   J. M. W. TURNER, British, 1775–1851
The Grand Canal, Venice
Oil on canvas; 36 × 48⅛ in. (91.4 × 122.2 cm.)

Venice, more than any of the other cities that he visited on his constant travels, provided Turner with congenial subject matter. This painting is a view from the Grand Canal at a spot near the church of Santa Maria della Salute, which can be seen at the right, looking toward the doge's palace and the exit to the sea. It dates from 1835, when Turner was at the height of his powers, and is a splendid expression of his ability to render solid architectural forms bathed in shimmering light and pearly atmospheric glow. When this painting was exhibited at the Royal Academy in 1835, it was well received as one of his "most agreeable works," though one critic cautioned Turner not to think "that in order to be poetical it is necessary to be almost unintelligible." *Bequest of Cornelius Vanderbilt, 1899, 99.31*

102   JOHN CONSTABLE, British, 1776–1837
Salisbury Cathedral from the Bishop's Grounds
Oil on canvas; 34⅝ × 44 in. (88 × 111.8 cm.)

Constable, in his day the preeminent painter of the English landscape, was a friend of Dr. John Fisher, bishop of Salisbury. Between 1820 and 1830 he repeatedly recorded the aspect of the great Gothic cathedral that presented itself to an observer standing in the bishop's grounds. Besides three sketches and a drawing, at least five paintings exist in various museums. All are very similar in composition. It seems likely that this one is the full-scale sketch for the second version of the picture, which is dated 1826 and is now in the Frick Collection, New York. *Bequest of Mary Stillman Harkness, 1950, 50.145.8*

103 JEAN CLOUET, French, act. by
1516–d. 1541
Guillaume Budé
*Tempera and oil on wood; 15⅝ × 13½ in.
(39.7 × 34.3 cm.)*

Jean Clouet, who was probably from the Netherlands, worked at the French court from 1516
and eventually became chief painter to King
Francis I. Budé (1467–1540) was a famous
humanist, the founder of the Collège de France,
the first keeper of the royal library, an ambassador, and chief city magistrate of Paris. This
portrait, which is mentioned in Budé's manuscript notes, is datable about 1536 and is Clouet's
only documented work. *Maria DeWitt Jesup
Fund, 1946, 46.68*

104 GEORGES DE LA TOUR, French,
1593–1652
The Fortune Teller
*Oil on canvas; 40⅛ × 48⅝ in. (101.9 ×
123.5 cm.)*

Georges de La Tour, who was born in the
independent duchy of Lorraine, established
himself by 1620 as a master at Lunéville, where
he remained for most of his career. Nothing is
known of his training or travels, but his patrons
included Henri II, duke of Lorraine, Richelieu,
and Louis XIII. Forgotten for two centuries,
La Tour is now recognized as an artist of great
brilliance and originality.

This picture, probably executed between 1632
and 1635, is one of his rare daylight scenes and
depicts a fashionably dressed young innocent
who is drawn into the snare of deceitful gypsies.
The subject of trickery, a common theme in
early seventeenth-century paintings, was popularized by Caravaggio and his followers.
La Tour may have known their work, and he may
also have been influenced by theatrical performances of his day. *The Fortune Teller* serves as
an object lesson, warning the unsuspecting of
the dangerous ways of the world. *Rogers Fund,
1960, 60.30*

105 GEORGES DE LA TOUR, French,
1593–1652
The Penitent Magdalen
*Oil on canvas; 52½ × 40¼ in. (133.4 ×
102.2 cm.)*

Georges de La Tour's candle-lit scenes, startlingly eloquent and austere, are among his
best-known works. This picture, probably painted
between 1638 and 1643, is one of four representations that La Tour did of the penitent
Magdalen, and it is unique in depicting her at
the dramatic moment of her conversion. The
elaborate silver mirror symbolizes luxury, while
the self-consuming candle reflected in it suggests the frailty of human life. The skull upon
which her clasped hands rest may stand for
peaceful acceptance of death. La Tour's extraordinary control of light—from near total darkness
to the bright flame—contributes to the pro-
foundly moving effect of this picture. The still
atmosphere has a warm cast that relates to the
paintings of northern followers of Caravaggio.
*Gift of Mr. and Mrs. Charles Wrightsman, 1978,
1978.517*

106 NICOLAS POUSSIN, French, 1594–1665
The Companions of Rinaldo
Oil on canvas; 46½ × 40¼ in. (118.1 × 102.2 cm.)

This picture represents an episode from *Jerusalem Delivered* (1580) by the Italian poet Torquato Tasso. Two Christian knights are about to slay the dragon that guards the palace of the pagan sorceress Armida. Their aim is to reach Rinaldo, their companion who is being held prisoner under Armida's spell, and to exhort him to rejoin the First Crusade. A female figure of Fortune, who has guided the knights to the island, looks on. *The Companions of Rinaldo* probably dates from the early 1630s. The Venetian influence evident in earlier paintings by Poussin is still present, but here the atmosphere is full of light and movement. *Gift of Mr. and Mrs. Charles Wrightsman, 1977, 1977.1.2*

107 NICOLAS POUSSIN, French, 1594–1665
The Rape of the Sabine Women
Oil on canvas; 60⅞ × 82⅝ in. (154.6 × 209.9 cm.)

Poussin, who settled in Rome at the age of thirty, found in antique history and mythology themes for his austere and noble art. Here he shows Romulus, ruler of the newly founded city of Rome, giving the prearranged signal with his cloak for the Roman soldiers to carry off the unmarried Sabine women. One mother has been seized by mistake; her two babies, with their old nurse, sprawl in the foreground. The Sabine men, duped into coming unarmed to what they thought would be a religious celebration, are put to flight. Poussin's choice of colors cannot be explained from an archaeological point of view and would seem to be expressive in purpose. *Harris Brisbane Dick Fund, 1946, 46.160*

108 NICOLAS POUSSIN, French, 1594–1665
Blind Orion Searching for the Rising Sun
Oil on canvas; 46⅞ × 72 in. (119.1 × 182.9 cm.)

According to classical mythology, the king of
Chios blinded the huge hunter Orion, who had
attempted to ravish his daughter. Told by an
oracle that the rays of the rising sun would
restore his sight, Orion walked eastward. Here
Cedalion, Orion's guide, stands on his shoulder;
at his feet Hephaestus, god of fire, points out
where the sun will rise; and from the clouds
Diana, goddess of the hunt, looks on.

Late in his career Poussin turned to landscape
painting, and this powerful and haunting vision
of Orion's story, executed in 1658, is one of his
greatest achievements. *Fletcher Fund, 1924,
24.45.1*

109 CLAUDE LORRAIN, French, 1600–1682
**The Trojan Women Setting Fire to
Their Fleet**
*Oil on canvas; 41⅜ × 59⅞ in. (105.1 ×
152.1 cm.)*

Claude Lorrain, like Poussin, was a French
painter who settled in Italy. He went to Rome
between 1612 and 1620 and remained there for
the rest of his life. Claude based a number of
his paintings on the poems of Vergil, who tells
the story of the Trojan women in the fifth book
of the *Aeneid.* Defeated by the Greeks in the
Trojan War, a band of Trojans, led by Aeneas,
set out to found a new city in Latium in Italy.
These legendary ancestors of the Roman people met with many adventures. In Sicily the
women, exhausted by seven years of wandering,
were inspired by Juno and Iris to burn their
"beautifully painted" ships, so that the exiles
would be forced to settle where they had landed.
Aeneas, however, prayed to Jupiter, who put
out the fires with a rainstorm. Claude's idealized
landscapes, in which he enhanced effects of
sunlight and atmosphere, transform Italian
scenery into a vision of the world of antiquity.
Fletcher Fund, 1955, 55.119

110 JEAN ANTOINE WATTEAU, French, 1684–1721

Mezzetin

Oil on canvas; 21¾ × 17 in. (55.2 × 43.2 cm.)

Mezzetin, whose name means "half measure," was a stock character of the commedia dell'arte, a form of improvisational theater of Italian origin; he acted as a confidential agent and sentimental lover, frequently engaged in the troublesome pursuit of unrequited love. Here he is shown singing before a verdant garden in which stands a marble statue of a woman with her back turned—an allusion to the insensible lover who turns a deaf ear to Mezzetin's romantic entreaties. Watteau made many paintings of actors and friends in theatrical costumes, but the sitter for this exquisite and wistful picture has not been identified. It was painted between 1718 and 1720, near the end of Watteau's short life.

Munsey Fund, 1934, 34.138

111   JEAN BAPTISTE PATER, French,
1695–1736
The Fair at Bezons
Oil on canvas; 42 × 56 in. (106.7 × 142.2 cm.)

The annual fair at Bezons, a village near Versailles, was the subject of several paintings by
Watteau and his followers, of whom Pater was
among the most gifted. Here Pater has placed
more than two hundred skillfully drawn figures
in a picturesque landscape that only vaguely
suggests the village. The stars of a troupe of
actors are dancing in a burst of sunlight; comics
and clowns, masked or in motley, cluster behind them. A feeling of decorous gaiety prevails.
The Jules Bache Collection, 1949, 49.7.52

112   JEAN BAPTISTE CHARDIN, French,
1699–1779
Boy Blowing Bubbles
Oil on canvas; 24 × 24⅞ in. (61 × 63.2 cm.)

Chardin, who was inspired by the seventeenth-
century Dutch masters, based this picture on a
familiar metaphor—human life is as brief as
that of a soap bubble. The balanced composition and the restricted color scheme contribute
to the effect of stillness and solemnity. In another second the bubble will break—and the
man and the child will outlive it only for an
insignificant length of time—but Chardin has
recorded this moment as if it were eternal.
Wentworth Fund, 1949, 49.24

113 FRANÇOIS BOUCHER, French, 1703–70
The Toilet of Venus
Oil on canvas; 42⅝ × 33½ in. (108 × 85.1 cm.)

Boucher's career is inextricably linked with that of his patroness, the marquise de Pompadour, mistress of Louis XV, and this picture, signed and dated 1751, is thought to have been commissioned as part of the decoration for Bellevue, her château near Paris. This painting and its companion piece, *Venus Consoling Love* (National Gallery, Washington), were installed there as overdoors in her *cabinet de toilette*. The winged putti and the doves are among the attributes of Venus as goddess of love, while the flowers allude to her role as patroness of gardeners, and the pearls to her birth from the sea. As a painter of nudes Boucher ranks with Rubens in the seventeenth century and Renoir in the nineteenth; among his contemporaries he had no equal. (See also The Jack and Belle Linsky Collection, no. 12.) *Bequest of William K. Vanderbilt, 1920, 20.155.9*

114 JEAN BAPTISTE GREUZE, French, 1725–1805
Broken Eggs
Oil on canvas; 28¾ × 37 in. (73 × 94 cm.)

Greuze had little interest in the mythological and historical subjects favored by his contemporaries. Instead, he was much influenced by Dutch genre painting and chose themes that allowed him to explore conflicting human emotions. This picture was one of four canvases, painted in Rome and representing figures in Italian costume, which Greuze sent to the Paris Salon of 1757. *Broken Eggs* and *The Neapolitan Gesture* (Worcester Art Museum, Massachusetts) were exhibited as a pair. The young woman of easy virtue seen here was thus contrasted with the chaste girl in the pendant, who mockingly rejects the overtures of her suitor. *Bequest of William K. Vanderbilt, 1920, 20.155.8*

115 JEAN HONORÉ FRAGONARD, French, 1732–1806
The Stolen Kiss
Oil on canvas; 19 × 25 in. (48.3 × 63.5 cm.)

Fragonard, who in 1752 won first prize at the Paris Academy, went to the French Academy in Rome in 1756 and remained there, traveling widely in Italy, until 1761. While he was in Italy, he painted this picture which was evidently commissioned by the bailli de Bréteuil, ambassador from Malta to the Holy See. It shows the influence of Fragonard's teachers, Boucher and Chardin (nos. 112 and 113). The controlled application of the paint and the smooth surface distinguish this early picture from his later works, in which the technique is freer and more spontaneous. *Gift of Jessie Woolworth Donahue, 1956, 56.100.1*

116 JEAN HONORÉ FRAGONARD, French, 1732–1806
The Love Letter
Oil on canvas; 32¾ × 26⅜ in. (83.2 × 67 cm.)

This picture exemplifies Fragonard's feeling for color, his sensitive handling of effects of light, and his extraordinary technical facility. The elegant blue dress, lace cap, and coiffure of the lady seated at her writing desk must have been the height of fashion. The inscription on the letter she holds has given rise to two different interpretations. It may simply refer to her cavalier, but if it should be read "Cuvillere," then the sitter would be François Boucher's daughter Marie Émilie (born 1740). She was widowed in 1769 and married, in 1773, her father's friend, the architect Charles Étienne Gabriel Cuvillier. *The Jules Bache Collection, 1949, 49.7.49*

117 JACQUES LOUIS DAVID, French, 1748–1825
The Death of Socrates
Oil on canvas; 51 × 77¼ in. (129.5 × 196.2 cm.)

The philosopher Socrates had been bitterly critical of Athenian society and its institutions. Accused by the Athenian government of denying the gods and corrupting the young through his teachings, he chose to die by his own hand rather than renounce his beliefs. David has portrayed him calmly reaching for the poisonous cup of hemlock while he discourses on the immortality of the soul. This picture was first exhibited at the Salon of 1787, on the eve of the Revolution. A tribute to the social criticism and stoical self-sacrifice of Socrates, it was full of political implication and was regarded as a protest against the injustices of the Old Regime. *The Death of Socrates* became a symbol of republican virtue and a manifesto of the Neoclassical style. *Wolfe Fund, 1931. Catharine Lorillard Wolfe Collection, 31.45*

118 JACQUES LOUIS DAVID, French, 1748–1825
Antoine Laurent Lavoisier and His Wife
Oil on canvas; 102¼ × 76⅝ in. (259.7 × 194.6 cm.)

The great David portraits are always richly informative about their sitters. Lavoisier (1743–94), a celebrated scientist and chemist, is represented with a number of scientific instruments, including two relating to his experiments with gunpowder and oxygen. The manuscript on which he is engaged may be that of the *Traité élémentaire de chimie,* which was published in 1789, the year after this picture was painted. The book was illustrated by his wife, Marie Anne Pierrette Paulze (1758–1836), who is said to have been a pupil of David; a portfolio of her drawings rests on an armchair at the left. One of David's greatest paintings, this is a key work in the development of eighteenth-century portraiture. *Purchase, Mr. and Mrs. Charles Wrightsman Gift, 1977, 1977.10*

119   ADÉLAÏDE LABILLE-GUIARD, French,
1749–1803
Self-Portrait with Two Pupils
Oil on canvas; 83 × 59½ in. (210.8 × 151.1 cm.)

Labille-Guiard was first apprenticed to a miniature painter and later, in 1769, studied the art
of pastel with Maurice Quentin de La Tour.
The rich palette and fine detail in this picture,
which is dated 1785, reflect her earlier training.
In 1783, when Labille-Guiard and Vigée-Lebrun
(no. 120) were admitted to the French Royal
Academy, the number of women artists eligible
for membership was limited to four, and this painting has been interpreted as a propaganda piece,
arguing for the place of women in the academy.
Labille-Guiard achieved a certain success at
court, and having painted a number of portraits
of the sisters of Louis XVI, she came to be
known as *Peintre des Mesdames*. She sympa-
thized with the Revolution, however, and unlike
Vigée-Lebrun she remained in France throughout her life. *Gift of Julia A. Berwind, 1953,
53.225.5*

121   J. A. D. INGRES, French, 1780–1867
Joseph Antoine Moltedo
Oil on canvas; 29⅝ × 22⅞ in. (75.3 × 58.1 cm.)

Ingres arrived in Rome in 1806 as a fellow of the
French Academy and remained there for fourteen years. He benefited from the patronage of
a number of Napoleon's official representatives
and painted many other members of the French
colony in Rome, as well as prominent English
visitors on the Grand Tour. The sitter here has
been convincingly identified as Joseph Antoine
Moltedo (b. 1775), a French industrialist who,
like Napoleon, was born in Corsica. Moltedo
served as director of the Roman post office
from 1803 to 1814. He appears to have been in
his thirties at the time this portrait was painted.
The Colosseum and the Appian Way are visible
in the background. Ingres has captured the
sitter's confident attitude; the technique is characteristically impeccable. (See also Drawings,
no. 5, and Robert Lehman Collection, nos. 26
and 45.) *Bequest of Mrs. H. O. Havemeyer,
1929. H. O. Havemeyer Collection, 29.100.23*

120   LOUISE ELISABETH VIGÉE-LEBRUN,
French, 1755–1842
Madame de la Châtre
Oil on canvas; 45 × 34½ in. (114.3 × 87.6 cm.)

In 1779 Marie Antoinette began to show a
strong interest in Vigée-Lebrun's work, and
during the next ten years the artist completed
many portraits of the queen and other court
figures. The sitter for this portrait, painted in
1789, was the daughter of Louis XV's *premier
valet de chambre* and the wife of the comte de
la Châtre. (She later married the marquise de
Jaucourt.) In her memoirs Vigée-Lebrun writes
that she favored the kind of plain white muslin
dress worn by Madame de la Châtre. The artist
wore such dresses herself, often persuaded her
sitters to wear them, and apparently admired
them for their classic simplicity. *Gift of Jessie
Woolworth Donahue, 1954, 54.182*

122 CAMILLE COROT, French, 1796–1875
The Letter
Oil on wood; 21½ × 14¼ in. (54.6 × 36.2 cm.)

In the 1850s and 1860s Corot sometimes painted models in his studio. He posed them against a dark background suggestive of contemporary interiors. In this painting, which is thought to date from about 1865, a simply dressed woman, her white chemise open to expose her shoulders, sits holding a letter. The motif and handling reflect an awareness of seventeenth-century Dutch painters, particularly Vermeer and De Hooch. Corot undoubtedly became acquainted with the work of both artists during a trip to Holland in 1854, and in the 1860s he must have been aware of the revival of interest in Vermeer's art. (See also Robert Lehman Collection, no. 27.) *Gift of Horace Havemeyer, 1929. H. O. Havemeyer Collection, 29.160.33*

123 EUGÈNE DELACROIX, French, 1798–1863
The Abduction of Rebecca
Oil on canvas; 39½ × 32¼ in. (100.3 × 81.9 cm.)

From the beginning of his career, Delacroix was inspired by the novels of Sir Walter Scott, a favorite author of the French Romantics. This painting, dated 1846, depicts a scene from *Ivanhoe:* Rebecca, who had been confined in the castle of Front de Boeuf, is being carried off by two Saracen slaves at the command of the Christian knight Bois-Guilbert, who has long coveted her. The contorted poses and the compacted space, which shifts abruptly from a high foreground across a deep valley to the fortress behind, create a sense of intense drama. Critics censured its Romantic qualities when the painting was shown in the Salon of 1846; nevertheless, it inspired Baudelaire to write: "Delacroix's painting is like nature; it has a horror of emptiness." *Wolfe Fund, 1903. Catharine Lorillard Wolfe Collection, 03.30*

24 HONORÉ DAUMIER, French, 1808–1879
The Third-Class Carriage
Oil on canvas; 25¾ × 35½ in. (65.4 × 90.2 cm.)

In 1839 Daumier began to depict groups of people in public conveyances and waiting rooms, and for more than two decades he treated this subject in lithographs, watercolors, and oil paintings. His characterizations of travelers document the period in the mid-nineteenth century when life in France was undergoing the im-

mense changes brought about by industrialization. Many of Daumier's canvases seem to have been executed between 1860 and 1863, when he stopped producing lithographs for the satirical newspaper *Le Charivari* to devote himself to painting. *The Third-Class Carriage* is believed to have been painted in 1863–65. *Bequest of Mrs. H. O. Havemeyer, 1929. H. O. Havemeyer Collection, 29.100.129*

125 THÉODORE ROUSSEAU, French, 1812–67
The Forest in Winter at Sunset
Oil on canvas; 64 × 102⅜ in. (162.6 × 260 cm.)

Rousseau was a leading member of the Barbizon school, a group of French landscape painters who worked mainly in the forest of Fontainebleau near the village of Barbizon. Rousseau began this ambitious canvas in the winter of 1845–46 and worked on it intermittently

for the next twenty years. He considered it his most important painting and refused to sell it during his lifetime. The ancient oaks towering above the tiny figures of the peasant women bent beneath their bundles of wood symbolize the grandeur of nature. Rousseau wished to create an imposing vision of the life of growing things, indestructible in their chaotic vitality and majestically dwarfing humanity. *Gift of P. A. B. Widener, 1911, 11.4*

126   JEAN FRANÇOIS MILLET, French,
1814–75
Haystacks: Autumn
*Oil on canvas; 33½ × 43⅜ in. (85.1 ×
110.2 cm.)*

This picture is from a series depicting the four
seasons that the industrialist Frederick Hartmann
commissioned in 1868. Millet, a member of the
Barbizon school, worked on the group intermittently during the next seven years. He completed *Spring* (Louvre, Paris) in 1873; by spring
1874 he reported that *Summer: Buckwheat*

Harvest (Museum of Fine Arts, Boston) and
Haystacks: Autumn were almost finished. *Winter:
The Woodgatherers* (National Museum of Wales,
Cardiff) was incomplete when he died.

Series of paintings depicting the seasons had
long been created by European artists, but
during the nineteenth century the subject grew
increasingly rare. After Millet, the only important French painter to undertake such a series
was Camille Pissarro, who was commissioned
to paint the four seasons in 1872. *Bequest of
Lillian S. Timken, 1959, 60.71.12*

127   GUSTAVE COURBET, French, 1819–77
Young Ladies from the Village
Oil on canvas; 76¾ × 102¾ in. (195 × 261 cm.)

Here Courbet shows his sisters walking in the
Communal, a valley near his native Ornans.
One of the girls offers either food or money to a
poor cowherd. This picture, which initiated a
series of paintings about the lives of women,
was painted during the winter of 1851–52. When
it was shown in the Salon of 1852, Courbet was

sure the critics, who had treated him harshly in
the past, would like the painting. It was, however,
attacked for its "ugliness," and the critics were
disturbed by the girls' common features and
countrified costumes, the "ridiculous" dog and
cattle, and the lack of unity and traditional
perspective and scale. The effects Courbet
worked hardest to achieve were those that were
most strongly attacked. *Gift of Harry Payne
Bingham, 1940, 40.175*

128 GUSTAVE COURBET, French, 1819–77
Woman with a Parrot
Oil on canvas; 51 × 77 in. (129.5 × 195.6 cm.)

Painted in 1865–66, *Woman with a Parrot* was one of two works that Courbet showed in the Salon of 1866. It is the best known of the series of nudes that he painted in the 1860s. The model's sensuality is emphasized by the exotic richness of details like the bird's bright plumage and the landscape and tapestry backgrounds. Critics censured Courbet's "lack of taste," as well as his model's "ungainly pose" and "disheveled hair." Like Manet's *Olympia* (1863; Louvre, Paris), Courbet's *Woman with a Parrot* was recognized as a real type, a courtesan of the demimonde. *Bequest of Mrs. H. O. Havemeyer, 1929. H. O. Havemeyer Collection, 29.100.57*

129 ROSA BONHEUR, French, 1822–99
The Horse Fair
Oil on canvas; 96¼ × 199½ in. (244.5 × 406.8 cm.)

The horse market of Paris was held on the tree-lined Boulevard de l'Hôpital, near the asylum of Salpêtrière, which is visible in the left background. Bonheur began this painting in 1852. Twice a week for a year and a half she went to the market to make sketches, dressed as a man so as not to attract attention. *The Horse Fair* was shown in the Salon of 1853. It is signed and dated, but the date is followed by the numeral 5, apparently because Bonheur retouched the painting in 1855. The repainted passages were the ground, the trees, and the sky—the passages that were criticized for their summary execution at the time of the Salon. *Gift of Cornelius Vanderbilt, 1887, 87.25*

130 GUSTAVE MOREAU, French, 1826–98
Oedipus and the Sphinx
Oil on canvas; 81¼ × 41¼ in. (206.4 × 104.8 cm.)

Moreau's interpretation of the Greek myth draws heavily on Ingres's *Oedipus and the Sphinx* (1808; Louvre, Paris). Both painters chose to represent the moment when Oedipus confronted the winged monster in a rocky pass outside the city of Thebes. Unlike her other victims, he could answer her riddle and thus saved himself and the besieged Thebans. This painting was extremely successful at the Salon of 1864; it won a medal and established Moreau's reputation. Critics offered a variety of interpretations of the theme: Oedipus was thought to symbolize contemporary man, and the confrontation between the Sphinx and Oedipus was believed to symbolize the opposition of female and male principles, or possibly the triumph of life over death. *Bequest of William H. Herriman, 1921, 21.134.1*

132   CAMILLE PISSARRO, French, 1830–1903
Jallais Hill, Pontoise
Oil on canvas; 34¼ × 45¼ in. (89.5 × 114.9 cm.)

In 1866 Pissarro moved to Pontoise, northwest
of Paris, where he lived until 1868. The lanes,
farm buildings, hillsides, and plowed and planted
fields of this hilly village on the Oise provided
the subject matter for a group of firmly structured works. Their strong brushstrokes and
broad, flat areas of color owe much to the example of Courbet and Corot, whose work was
on view in large, much discussed exhibitions
in Paris.

This picture, dated 1867, was exhibited in the
Salon of 1868. Émile Zola praised it, stating:
"There is the modern countryside. One feels
that man has passed, turning and cutting the
earth. . . . And this valley, this hillside embody a
simplicity and heroic freedom. Nothing could be
so banal were it not so great. From ordinary
reality the painter's temperament has produced a rare poem of life and strength." *Bequest of William Church Osborn, 1951, 51.30.2*

31   JULES BASTIEN-LEPAGE, French,
848–84
Joan of Arc
Oil on canvas; 100 × 110 in. (254 × 279.4 cm.)

After the province of Lorraine was lost to Germany following the Franco-Prussian War, the
French saw in Joan of Arc a new and powerful
symbol. In the fifteenth century this national
heroine had heard heavenly voices that urged
her to support the dauphin Charles in his battle
against the English invaders. In this picture,
which dates from 1879, Bastien-Lepage, a nave of Lorraine, shows Joan receiving her revela-
on in the garden of her parents. Behind her,
oating in supernatural light, are Saints Michael,
Margaret, and Catherine. The artist deliberately
endered the scene with as little archaeological
detail as possible, so that it would seem to be
aking place in Lorraine in his own time. As
ontemporary critics noted, his work is a combi-
ation of the solid drawing of academic art and
he emphasis on light effects introduced by the
lein air (open air) painters. *Gift of Erwin Davis,
889, 89.21.1*

133 HENRI FANTIN-LATOUR, French, 1836–1904
Still Life with Flowers and Fruit
Oil on canvas; 28¾ × 23⅝ in. (73 × 60 cm.)

In the early years of his career, Fantin-Latour painted various subjects, including allegory, still life, and portraiture, but he always worked in an unmistakably contemporary idiom. He was particularly successful with still-life and flower subjects, which occupied him throughout his life. Inspired by Chardin and Courbet, his approach was direct and naturalistic. Several paintings of flowers and fruit of 1865–66, including this example, are his first major still lifes. The special character of his work was described by Jacques Émile Blanche, a painter of the next generation: "Fantin studied each flower, each petal, its grain, its tissue, as if it were a human face. In Fantin's flowers, the drawing is large and beautiful, and it is always sure and incisive." *Purchase, Mr. and Mrs. Richard J. Bernhard Gift, by exchange, 1980, 1980.3*

134 ÉDOUARD MANET, French, 1832–83
The Spanish Singer
Oil on canvas; 58 × 45 in. (147.3 × 114.3 cm.)

Manet made his public debut at the Salon of 1861 with a portrait of his parents (Louvre, Paris) and *The Spanish Singer*. The paintings were well received, and the noted critic Théophile Gautier praised him as a gifted realist in the tradition of Spanish painters from Velázquez to Goya. As Gautier's own essays on Spanish culture had stimulated French printmakers to flood the market with illustrations of Spanish types, the theme of this picture was hardly novel. Yet, as Gautier observed, most of the illustrators romanticized their subjects, whereas Manet did not. Here the artist treats every detail with extraordinary finesse: the red shoulder strap, the rumpled trousers, the spent cigarette, and the soulful expression, captured in just two hours' work. *Gift of William Church Osborn, 1949, 49.58.2*

135 ÉDOUARD MANET, French, 1832–83
Woman with a Parrot
Oil on canvas; 72⅞ × 50⅝ in. (185.1 × 128.6 cm.)

Given his inclination to allude to the works of other painters, it is probable that Manet conceived this picture as a comment on the controversial nude exhibited by his rival Courbet at the Salon of 1866 (no. 128). While Courbet's picture is explicitly sexual, Manet's is discreet and spare. It has been suggested that this picture is an allegory of the five senses: smell (the violets), touch and sight (the monocle), hearing (the talking bird), and taste (the orange). The model is Victorine Meurent, who also posed for Manet's celebrated *Olympia* and *Le Déjeuner sur l'herbe* (both 1863; Louvre, Paris). *Gift of Erwin Davis, 1889, 89.21.3*

136 ÉDOUARD MANET, French, 1832–83
Boating
Oil on canvas; 38¼ × 51¼ in. (97.2 × 130.2 cm.)

Boating was painted during the summer of 1874, when Manet was working with Renoir and Monet at Argenteuil, a village on the Seine northwest of Paris. The high-keyed palette, the elevated viewpoint from which the water's sur-face rises up as a backdrop, and the artist's decision to celebrate the everyday pleasures of the middle class are in keeping with the Impressionist style recently developed by his younger colleagues. The cutting of forms at the edges of the picture reflects Manet's interest in Japanese prints. *Bequest of Mrs. H. O. Havemeyer, 1929. H. O. Havemeyer Collection, 29.100.115*

137 EDGAR DEGAS, French, 1834–1917
A Woman with Chrysanthemums
Oil on canvas; 29 × 36½ in. (73.7 × 92.7 cm.)

In a departure from tradition, most portraits by Degas were not formally posed. He wanted to depict his subjects in familiar and typical positions, often observing them in private, unguarded moments. In this painting, however, he may have relied as much on invention as on direct observation. When completed in 1858, this picture was a still life of flowers, strongly influenced by Delacroix's flower pictures of 1848–49; Degas added the figure of the woman in 1865. Like many of his ballet pictures, it may thus be an assortment of observations that were brought together first in his mind and then on canvas. (See also Drawings, no. 6.) *Bequest of Mrs. H. O. Havemeyer, 1929. H. O. Havemeyer Collection, 29.100.128*

138 EDGAR DEGAS, French, 1834–1917
Jacques Joseph Tissot
Oil on canvas; 59⅝ × 44 in. (151.4 × 111.8 cm.)

Tissot (1836–1902) was a friend of Degas's and a fellow artist, who fled France after having played an active role in the Commune of Paris in 1871. He spent ten years in England, where he was known as James Tissot, and achieved great success as a painter of fashionable women. In Degas's portrait, which dates from 1866–68, Tissot seems to have been interrupted while in the middle of a casual discourse on painting. On the wall of the studio are improvisations of works that Degas knew well: Old Masters, contemporary paintings, and oriental works. Their presence underscores Degas's, and presumably Tissot's, eclectic sensibility and willingness to consider the art of all periods in order to create a style anchored in tradition and appropriate to subjects taken from modern life. (See also Drawings, no. 6; European Sculpture and Decorative Art, no. 24; and Robert Lehman Collection, no. 31.) *Rogers Fund, 1939, 39.161*

39 EDGAR DEGAS, French, 1834–1917
Dancers Practicing at the Bar
Oil colors freely mixed with turpentine, on canvas; 29¾ × 32 in. (75.6 × 81.3 cm.)

Although this picture has a casually realistic appearance, Degas's fascination with form and structure is reflected in the analogy between the watering can (used to lay the dust on the studio floor) and the dancer at the right. The handle on the side imitates her left arm, the handle at the top mimics her head, and the spout approximates her right arm and raised leg. Compositional devices such as this bear out the artist's famous remark: "I assure you that no art was ever less spontaneous than mine. What I do is the result of reflection and study of the great masters; of inspiration, spontaneity, temperament . . . I know nothing." *Bequest of Mrs. H. O. Havemeyer, 1929. H. O. Havemeyer Collection, 29.100.34*

140   PAUL CÉZANNE, French, 1839–1906
Still Life: Apples and a Pot of Primroses
Oil on canvas; 28¾ × 36⅜ in. (73 × 92.4 cm.)

This painting, once owned by Monet, has been dated as early as 1880 and as late as 1894. Controversy about the date results in part from its quiet, almost static quality. The pattern of leaves against the background is unusual in Cézanne's work, as is the highly finished surface. But, with the exception of the primroses, the objects in the picture appear frequently in the

artist's still lifes: the scalloped table, the cloth pinched up in sculptural folds, and the apples nestled in isolated groups. When Cézanne visited Monet at Giverny in 1894, he met the critic Gustave Geffroy, to whom he explained in reference to his still lifes that he wanted to astonish Paris with an apple. He never did so during his lifetime, for his works were always considered unacceptable by Salon juries. *Bequest of Sam A. Lewisohn, 1951, 51.112.1*

141   PAUL CÉZANNE, French, 1839–1906
The Gulf of Marseilles Seen from L'Estaque
Oil on canvas; 28¾ × 39½ in. (73 × 100.4 cm.)

In the 1880s Cézanne executed more than a dozen closely related pictures of the panoramic view from the Provençal town of L'Estaque toward a low range of mountains across the Gulf of Marseilles. Pissarro and Monet independently adopted similar working methods. Their primary purpose, however, was to record transient effects of light, whereas Cézanne was interested in the variations in composition that re-

sulted when he changed his vantage point or slightly shifted his angle of vision. Here Cézanne contrasted the closely packed geometric forms of buildings in the foreground with the more scattered and irregularly shaped mountains. The composition is intriguing, for from the elevated position scale is distorted, and the nearby buildings seem comparable to the mountains in size. (See also Robert Lehman Collection, no. 30.) *Bequest of Mrs. H. O. Havemeyer, 1929. H. O. Havemeyer Collection, 29.100.67*

142   PAUL CÉZANNE, French, 1839–1906
Madame Cézanne in a Red Dress
Oil on canvas; 45⅞ × 35¼ in. (116.5 × 89.5 cm.)

This picture, which dates from about 1890, is one of twenty-seven portraits that Cézanne painted of his wife, Hortense Fiquet (b. 1850). These paintings are compositional studies based on the figure rather than portraits in the conventional sense. Here she does not sit comfortably in her chair but tilts to the right, echoing the axis of the fire tongs on the left and the curtain on the right. The flower that she holds seems neither more nor less real than those in the curtain at the right side of the painting. The reflection of a similar curtain is visible in the rectangular shape on the wall that we might not otherwise recognize as a mirror. The displaced image in the mirror is in keeping with the spatial dislocations evident in the artist's interpretation of the scene as a whole. *Mr. and Mrs. Henry Ittleson, Jr., Fund, 1962, 62.45*

143   PAUL CÉZANNE, French, 1839–1906
The Card Players
Oil on canvas; 25¾ × 32¼ in. (65.4 × 81.9 cm.)

The majority of Cézanne's works are landscapes, still lifes, or portraits. In 1890, however, he undertook this ambitious genre scene of peasants playing cards, possibly in emulation of Mathieu Le Nain (1607–1677), whose painting of the same subject was on view in the museum at Aix. The subject continued to interest Cézanne, and during the next years he painted five versions of the scene. In each of these he emphasizes the somber concentration of the participants. Expression and even personality have been suppressed by their interest in the cards. The pyramidal forms of the players can be compared to the apples turned in different directions in Cézanne's tabletop still lifes. *Bequest of Stephen C. Clark, 1960, 61.101.1*

144   CLAUDE MONET, French, 1840–1926
Terrace at Sainte-Adresse
Oil on canvas; 38⅝ × 51⅛ in. (98.1 × 129.9 cm.)

A prime mover among the artists who came to be known as Impressionists, Monet spent the summer of 1867 at the resort town of Sainte-Adresse on the English Channel. It was there that he painted this picture, which combines smooth, traditionally rendered areas with sparkling passages of rapid, separate brushwork and spots of pure color. The elevated vantage point and relatively even sizes of the horizontal areas emphasize the two-dimensionality of the painting. The three horizontal zones of the composition seem to rise parallel to the picture plane instead of receding clearly into space. The subtle tension resulting from the combination of illusionism and the two-dimensionality of the surface remained an important characteristic of Monet's style. *Purchased with special contributions and purchase funds given or bequeathed by friends of the Museum, 1967, 67.241*

145   CLAUDE MONET, French, 1840–1926
La Grenouillère
Oil on canvas; 29⅜ × 39¼ in. (74.6 × 99.7 cm.)

In 1869, when this picture was painted, Monet and Renoir were living near one another in Saint-Michel, a few miles west of Paris. They often visited La Grenouillère, a swimming spot with a boat rental and a café on the Seine, and each artist painted three views of the area. This example and the one by Renoir in the National-museum, Stockholm, are nearly identical in composition; they were undoubtedly painted side by side. Pursuing interests earlier defined in *Terrace at Sainte-Adresse* (no. 144), Monet concentrated on repetitive elements—the ripples on the water, the foliage, the boats, and the human figure—to weave a fabric of brushstrokes which, although emphatically brushstrokes, retain a strong descriptive quality. (See also Robert Lehman Collection, no. 28.) *Bequest of Mrs. H. O. Havemeyer, 1929. H. O. Havemeyer Collection, 29.100.112*

146 CLAUDE MONET, French, 1840–1926
Poplars
Oil on canvas; 32¼ × 32⅛ in. (81.9 × 81.6 cm.)

During the summer and fall of 1891 Monet painted a series of works depicting the poplars along the Epte River, about a mile from his house in Giverny. Some of these were painted from the banks of the river; others, such as this example, were painted from a boat. Lila Cabot Perry, an American who spent the summers of 1889–1901 in Giverny, wrote, "The Poplars series . . . were painted from a broad-bottomed boat fitted up with grooves to hold a number of canvases. [Monet] told me that in one of his Poplars the effect lasted only seven minutes, or until the sunlight left a certain leaf, when he took out the next canvas and worked on that." When fifteen paintings from this series were shown in Paris in 1892, some critics praised them for their naturalism, while others admired their abstract and decorative qualities. *Bequest of Mrs. H. O. Havemeyer, 1929. H. O. Havemeyer Collection, 29.100.110*

147 PIERRE RENOIR, French, 1841–1919
A Waitress at Duval's Restaurant
Oil on canvas; 39½ × 28⅛ in. (100.3 × 71.4 cm.)

In 1879 Edmond Renoir wrote that his brother Pierre was committed to art rooted in actual experience rather than contrived with the assistance of professional models wearing costumes. For this picture, painted about 1875, Renoir depicted a waitress whom he had met in a Parisian restaurant. Evidently he asked her to come to his studio to pose in her uniform, just as she looked while working. As he explained in a different context, "I like painting best when it looks eternal without boasting about it: an everyday eternity, revealed on the street corner: a servant-girl pausing a moment as she scours a saucepan, and becoming a Juno on Olympus." (See also Robert Lehman Collection, no. 29.) *Bequest of Stephen C. Clark, 1960, 61.101.14*

148 PIERRE RENOIR, French, 1841–1919
Madame Charpentier and Her Children
*Oil on canvas; 60½ × 74⅞ in. (153.7 ×
190.2 cm.)*

The well-to-do publisher Georges Charpentier and his wife entertained political, literary, and artistic notables on Friday evenings, and they welcomed Renoir to these gatherings. He was paid handsomely to paint this stunning group portrait, which is dated 1878. Though Renoir conveys the opulent ease of his subjects' lives, he made no attempt to capture their personalities.

Consequently, his portrait of this stylish family is closer in spirit to works by Rubens and Fragonard that he admired than to the more penetrating portraits of his colleague Degas (no. 138). Far more elaborately detailed than Renoir's other works of the 1870s, this painting marks the beginning of his important shift away from the classic Impressionist style, with which he had made his reputation only a few years before. *Wolfe Fund, 1907. Catharine Lorillard Wolfe Collection, 07.122*

IA ORANA MARIA

150 PAUL GAUGUIN, French, 1848–1903
Ia Orana Maria
Oil on canvas; 44¾ × 34½ in. (113.7 × 87.7 cm.)

This is the most important picture that Gauguin painted during his first trip to Tahiti (1891–93). The title is native dialect that translates, "I hail thee, Mary," the angel Gabriel's first words to the Virgin Mary at the Annunciation. In a letter written in the spring of 1892, Gauguin described the painting: "An angel with yellow wings who points out to two Tahitian women the figures of Mary and Jesus, also Tahitians. Nudes dressed in pareus, a kind of flowered cotton which is wrapped as one likes around the waist. . . . I am rather pleased with it." The only elements that he has taken from traditional representations of the Annunciation are the angel, the salutation, and the halos. Everything else is rendered in Tahitian idiom, except the composition which Gauguin adapted from a photograph of a bas-relief in the Javanese temple of Borobudur. *Bequest of Sam A. Lewisohn, 1951, 51.112.2*

◀ 149 HENRI ROUSSEAU, French, 1844–1910
The Repast of the Lion
Oil on canvas; 44¾ × 63 in. (113.7 × 160 cm.)

Rousseau had begun to paint imaginary scenes set in the jungle by 1891. This picture, which shows a lion devouring a jaguar, was probably first exhibited at the Salon d'Automne of 1907. The vegetation in Rousseau's jungle paintings is evidently based upon exotic plants that the artist had studied at the botanical garden in Paris, but disregarding their actual sizes, he invented forests that dwarf his figures of natives and animals. Reminiscent of Delacroix's studies of fighting lions, Rousseau's animals are often closely based upon photographs in a children's book that his daughter owned. Here the full moon partly visible beyond a hill intensifies the dreamlike character of the scene. *Bequest of Sam A. Lewisohn, 1951, 51.112.5*

151   VINCENT VAN GOGH, Dutch, 1853–90
Self-Portrait with a Straw Hat
Oil on canvas; 16 × 12½ in. (40.6 × 31.8 cm.)

This picture was probably painted toward the end of Van Gogh's two-year stay in Paris, from March 1886 to February 1888, not long before he departed to live and work in the Provençal city of Arles. The palette and directional brushstrokes are evidence of the influence of Divisionism, especially as represented by the work of Seurat (nos. 155 and 156) and Signac. Nevertheless, Van Gogh has clearly mastered the Neo-Impressionist current in his painting. This self-portrait reflects the bold temperament of the individual who in December 1885 wrote to his brother: "I prefer painting people's eyes to cathedrals, for there is something in the eyes that is not in the cathedral, however solemn and imposing the latter may be—a human soul, be it that of a poor streetwalker, is more interesting to me." *Bequest of Miss Adelaide Milton de Groot (1876–1967), 1967, 67.187.70a*

153 VINCENT VAN GOGH, Dutch, 1853–90
Cypresses
Oil on canvas; 36¾ × 29⅛ in. (93.3 × 74 cm.)

Van Gogh painted *Cypresses* in June 1889, not
long after the beginning of his year-long voluntary confinement at the asylum of Saint Paul in
Saint-Rémy. The cypress represented a kind of
perfect natural architecture in Van Gogh's canon
of pantheism: "It is as beautiful of line and
proportion as an Egyptian obelisk." The loaded
brushstrokes and the swirling, undulating forms
are typical of his late work. The subject posed
an extraordinary technical problem for the artist,
especially with regard to realizing the deep, rich
green of the trees. On June 25, 1889, he wrote
to his brother, "It is a splash of *black* in a sunny
landscape, but it is one of the most interesting
black notes, and the most difficult to hit off that I
can imagine." *Rogers Fund, 1949, 49.30*

152 VINCENT VAN GOGH, Dutch, 1853–90
Madame Ginoux (L'Arlésienne)
Oil on canvas; 36 × 29 in. (91.4 × 73.7 cm.)

Van Gogh stayed at Arles from February 1888
to May 1889, and this portrait was painted there
in late 1888 during the two-month period that
Gauguin spent with him. The two artists reportedly cajoled the reluctant *patronne* of the Café
de la Gare into posing by inviting her to have
coffee with them. The large areas of single
colors and the bold contours of the figure reflect
the influence of Japanese prints and medieval
cloisonné enamels. Van Gogh's highly abstract
use of line and color was undoubtedly approved
of by Gauguin, who, with their friend and fellow
artist Émile Bernard, advocated such synthe-
ses of form and color, in contrast to the empiri-
cism of Impressionism. *Bequest of Sam A.
Lewisohn, 1951, 51.112.3*

154 VINCENT VAN GOGH, Dutch, 1853—90
Irises
Oil on canvas; 29 × 36¼ in. (73.7 × 92.1 cm.)

In May 1890 Van Gogh was released from the asylum of Saint Paul in Saint-Rémy. His last month there was a period of relative calm and productivity, and he wrote to his brother: "All goes well. I am doing . . . two canvases representing big bunches of violet irises, one lot against a pink background in which the effect is soft and harmonious . . . the other . . . stands out against a startling citron background [with] an effect of tremendous disparate complementaries, which strengthen each other by their juxtaposition." The first picture is illustrated here (the background has faded considerably); the second is *Still Life: Vase with Irises Against a Yellow Background* (Rijksmuseum Vincent Van Gogh, Amsterdam). The entirely different effects achieved through slight alterations in his palette emphasize Van Gogh's interest in the symbolic meaning as well as the formal value of color. *Gift of Adele R. Levy, 1958, 58.187*

155 GEORGES SEURAT, French, 1859—91
Study for Sunday Afternoon on the Island of La Grande Jatte
Oil on canvas; 27¾ × 41 in. (70.5 × 104.1 cm.)

This painting, which dates from 1884, is Seurat's final sketch for his masterpiece depicting Parisians enjoying their day off on an island in the Seine (Art Institute of Chicago). As in the final work, the sketch juxtaposes contrasting pigments and depends on optical mixture—the phenomenon that causes two tones seen at a distance to form a single hue—to create the desired effect. Although there are only minor differences in compositional detail between this study and the final work, the pictures represent distinct stages in the development of Seurat's color theory. For the study he prepared the canvas with a red ground, upon which he applied layers of saturated colors in hatched strokes. He may have begun the larger version in a similar fashion, but eventually he chose a white ground and applied his paints in the small, discrete dabs characteristic of his Pointillist technique. (See also Drawings, no. 7.) *Bequest of Sam A. Lewisohn, 1951, 51.112.6*

156 GEORGES SEURAT, French, 1859−91
Invitation to the Sideshow (La Parade)
Oil on canvas; 39¼ × 59 in. (99.7 × 149.9 cm.)

This picture, painted in 1887−88, represents the *parade* of the Corvi Circus in the Place de la Nation in Paris. A *parade* is a sample entertainment performed on the street to entice passersby to purchase tickets. Using a fine brush, Seurat covered the canvas with precise, interspersed orange, yellow, and blue touches. Though his research in optics and perceptual psychology was highly scientific, the luminous shadows endow objectively observed forms with mystery. Figures seem to levitate in the moody gaslight, and railings suggest ramps that lead nowhere. In this world where nothing is certain to the eye, Seurat implies a parity between fact and fantasy. His contemporaries used the term *féerique* (enchanted) to describe pictures like this one, in which light imbues the commonplace with poetry. *Bequest of Stephen C. Clark, 1960, 61.101.17*

157 HENRI DE TOULOUSE-LAUTREC, French, 1864−1901
The Sofa
Oil on cardboard; 24¾ x 31⅞ in. (62.9 x 81 cm.)

Intrigued by erotic Japanese prints, as well as by Degas's small monotypes of brothel scenes (which were not intended for public exhibition), Lautrec set out to document the lives of prostitutes in a series of pictures executed between 1892 and 1896. Himself a social outcast because of his physical deformities, Toulouse-Lautrec was accepted by the prostitutes and keenly apprehended the dreary sadness of their lives. Since they were accustomed to being observed, these women made unaffected models, never compromising Toulouse-Lautrec's commitment to utter candor. At first he made sketches in the brothels; hampered by the insufficient lighting, however, he eventually had his models pose in his studio on a large divan.

The prostitutes often fell in love with one another, and Toulouse-Lautrec was sympathetic to lesbianism. Although the sexual attraction between the women is evident in this picture, their attentive affection is equally striking. *Rogers Fund, 1951, 51.33.2*

230

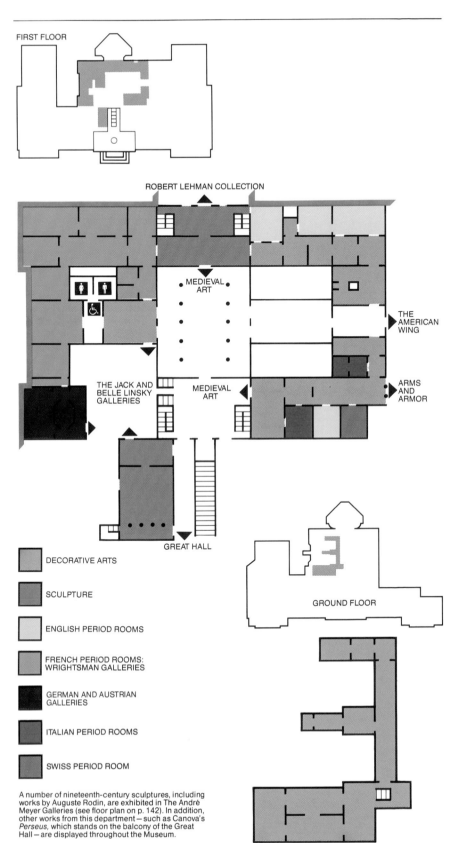

FIRST FLOOR

ROBERT LEHMAN COLLECTION

MEDIEVAL ART

THE AMERICAN WING

ARMS AND ARMOR

THE JACK AND BELLE LINSKY GALLERIES

MEDIEVAL ART

GREAT HALL

GROUND FLOOR

DECORATIVE ARTS

SCULPTURE

ENGLISH PERIOD ROOMS

FRENCH PERIOD ROOMS: WRIGHTSMAN GALLERIES

GERMAN AND AUSTRIAN GALLERIES

ITALIAN PERIOD ROOMS

SWISS PERIOD ROOM

A number of nineteenth-century sculptures, including works by Auguste Rodin, are exhibited in The André Meyer Galleries (see floor plan on p. 142). In addition, other works from this department — such as Canova's *Perseus*, which stands on the balcony of the Great Hall — are displayed throughout the Museum.

EUROPEAN SCULPTURE AND DECORATIVE ARTS

This department was established in 1907, as part of a reorganization of the Museum under the presidency of J. Pierpont Morgan, the renowned financier and art collector. Its creation coincided with Morgan's gift of more than sixteen hundred objects of French decorative art. At the outset the new department included collections of medieval, American, Islamic, Far Eastern, and primitive art, as well as musical instruments, but over the years these collections became the nuclei of independent departments. Today the department, one of the Museum's largest, is responsible for about sixty thousand works of art. These range in date from the beginnings of the Renaissance in the fifteenth century to the early twentieth century and cover eight areas: sculpture, woodwork and furniture, ceramics, glass, metalwork (including jewelry), horological and mathematical instruments, tapestries, and textiles. Although the purpose of the collections is to show the development of these various categories throughout Europe, the emphasis is on French, English, Italian, German, and Spanish art.

The department has distinguished holdings of Italian Renaissance sculpture, notably bronze statuettes, and French sculpture of the eighteenth century. Other major areas of strength are French and English furniture and silver, Italian majolica, and French and German porcelain. The department's collections also include entire rooms from palaces and great houses; among them are the sixteenth-century patio from Vélez Blanco, Spain; several salons from eighteenth-century French mansions; and two English Neoclassical rooms designed by Robert Adam. A comprehensive collection of textiles is open by appointment to scholars in the Textile Study Room.

SCULPTURE

1 ANTONIO ROSSELLINO, Florentine, 1427–79
Madonna and Child with Angels
Marble, with gilt details; 28³/₄ × 20¹/₄ in. (73 × 51.4 cm.)

Antonio Rossellino was trained in Florence in the workshop of his older brother, Bernardo. This Madonna and Child seems to have been carved about 1455–60, before the start of Antonio's first major independent work, the tomb of the cardinal of Portugal in the church of San Miniato, Florence, which he began in 1461. The relief has a certain naiveté in the densely packed surface decoration, which was to be eliminated by subtle changes in his later works. The exacting description of surfaces is extraordinary in sculpture at this or any other time: the halos and the Virgin's hem are picked out in gold, and the brownish mottled marble itself works in conjunction with the carving to make the piece wonderfully varied. *Bequest of Benjamin Altman, 1913, 14.40.675*

2 ANDREA DELLA ROBBIA, Florentine, 1435–1525
Madonna and Child
Glazed terracotta; 37³/₈ × 21⁵/₈ in. (95 × 55 cm.)

Andrea was the nephew and disciple of Luca della Robbia, developer of the blue and white glazes for terracotta sculpture with which the name della Robbia is associated. By the time he made the Lehman Madonna (ca. 1470–75), Andrea had for some years been chiefly respon-

sible for the output of the family shop in the Via Guelfa in Florence. Though he was a faithful follower of his uncle's style, his own personality emerged distinctly in works such as this, with its exceptionally high relief, in which he achieved monumental forms without sacrificing any of that sweetness and harmony of expression for which Luca is so admired. *Gift of Edith and Herbert Lehman Foundation, 1969, 69.113*

3 BARTOLOMEO BELLANO, Paduan,
ca. 1440–1496/97
David with the Head of Goliath
Bronze, partly gilt; h. 11¼ in. (28.6 cm.)

Bellano, the son of a Paduan goldsmith, is
recorded working with Donatello in Florence in
1456, and a clear point of reference for the
swaggering pose of this statuette is Donatello's
bronze nude *David* in the Bargello, Florence,

probably made in the 1440s. Bellano has clothed
his figure and has probably remembered Donatello's from some distance, long after his return
to Padua, for the closest parallels for the statuette in Bellano's works are to be found in his
highly picturesque bronze reliefs (1484–88) in
the choir of Sant'Antonio in Padua. *Gift of
C. Ruxton Love, Jr., 1964, 64.304.1*

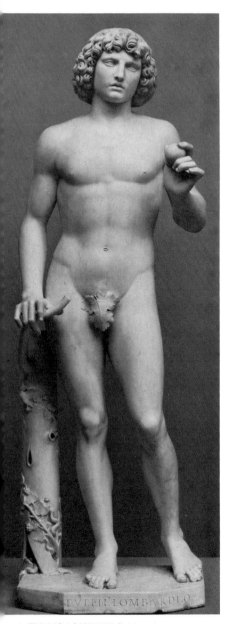

6 ANTONELLO GAGINI, Sicilian, 1478–1536 ▶
Spinario

Bronze; h. 34¼ in. (87 cm.)

The *Spinario* (*Boy Removing a Thorn*), datable about 1505, is an early work by Gagini, the leading Sicilian sculptor of his day, who virtually overnight created the Sicilian High Renaissance in sculpture. The original *Spinario,* a famous Hellenistic bronze in the Palazzo dei Conservatori in Rome, was one of the most frequently studied of all antiquities. Copies in many media exist, but no early one has the size and independent character of Gagini's, which has mellower, more rounded forms than the original, and clipped curls instead of a pageboy haircut. *Gift of George and Florence Blumenthal, 1932, 32.121*

5 ANTICO, Mantuan, ca. 1460–d. 1528
Paris

Bronze, partly gilt and silvered; h. 14⅝ in. (37.2 cm.)

Pier Jacopo Alari-Bonacolsi received the nickname Antico in acknowledgment of his reverent attitude toward classical antiquity. Most of his statuettes are small-scale replicas of ancient sculptures, but the prototype for his *Paris* has yet to be identified. The youth, holding a ring and an apple, looks as if he is about to choose the goddess Venus over Juno and Minerva, in the scene long familiar as the Judgment of Paris. The elegantly chased small details, smooth brown lacquer, and touches of both gilding (hair, apple) and silvering (eyes) are good indications of why Antico's bronzes are among the most sought-after of all early Renaissance statuettes. (See also The Jack and Belle Linsky Collection, no. 14.) *Edith Perry Chapman Fund, 1955, 55.93*

4 TULLIO LOMBARDO, Venetian, ca. 1455–d. 1532
Adam

Marble; h. 75 in. (190.5 cm.)

This figure belonged to the most lavish funerary monument of Renaissance Venice, that of Doge Andrea Vendramin, in the church of SS. Giovanni e Paolo. Lombardo is generally credited with the scheme of the monument as a whole (ca. 1490–95). Adam's pose is based on a combination of antique figures of Antinoüs and Bacchus, interpreted with an almost Attic simplicity. But the meaningful glance, the elegant hands, and the tree trunk are refinements on the antique. Remarkable for the purity of its marble and the smoothness of its carving, *Adam* was the first monumental classical nude to be carved since antiquity. *Fletcher Fund, 1936, 36.163*

8 ANDREA RICCIO, Paduan, ca. 1470–
d. 1532
Satyr
Bronze; h. 14⅛ in. (35.7 cm.)

This striding satyr, with its curvilinear contours
and masterly control of chasing, was executed
about 1507, at the height of Riccio's powers. He
had probably just completed his pair of Old
Testament bronze reliefs for Sant'Antonio in
Padua and had embarked on the model for
what was to be his greatest work, the bronze
paschal candlestick in the same church. The
candlestick includes satyrs among the many
nearly freestanding statuettes in its elaborate
decoration. *Rogers, Pfeiffer, Harris Brisbane
Dick and Fletcher Funds, 1982, 1982.45*

7 Rearing Horse
Probably Milanese, late 16th–early 17th c.
Bronze; h. 9⅛ in. (23.1 cm.)

This statuette is thought to be after a model by
Leonardo da Vinci (1452–1519). Leonardo's
longtime experimentations with equestrian movement included two planned sculptural monuments in Milan and the Battle of Anghiari fresco
in Florence, none of which survives, so that our
knowledge of his intentions is provided chiefly
by his drawings. We know from his notes, however, that small models were also part of his
preparation. The Milanese sculptor Leone Leoni
(1500–1590), who possessed many of Leonardo's
drawings, also owned a "horse in sculptural relief" said to be by Leonardo. Leoni may be the
author of the bronze statuette of a Horse and
Rider in Budapest which is based on Leonardo;
the horse is nearly identical in pose to the
Museum's statuette. The Budapest work is
fractionally larger and has greater
force than the present bronze.
The Museum's statuette may
also have been cast in Milan
but at a slightly later date.
*Rogers Fund, 1925,
25.74*

9 The Farnese Table
Roman, ca. 1565–73
Marble, alabaster, and semiprecious stones;
150 × 66¼ × 37¾ in. (381 × 165.3 × 95.9 cm.)

This monumental and sumptuous piece, after a
design by Jacopo Barozzi da Vignola (1507–
1573), proclaims the majesty of the Roman High
Renaissance. Vignola was connected with the
Palazzo Farnese in Rome as both an architect
and a designer; his principal original contribution was designing the fittings of the rooms of
the state apartment, for which this table was
made. The top of the table is an inlay of various
marbles and semiprecious stones. The two
"windows" in the center are of oriental alabaster,
and the piers are of carved marble. The lilies
(fleurs-de-lis) in the decoration of the top are
emblems of the Farnese family; the arms on the
piers are those of Cardinal Alessandro Farnese.
(See also no. 46.) *Harris Brisbane Dick Fund,
1957, 58.57*

10 GIOVANNI BOLOGNA, Florentine,
1529–1608
Triton
Bronze; h. 36 in. (91.5 cm.)

The *Triton* served originally as a fountain figure.
With its supple modeling in bold triangulations
and its brisk, vigorous chasing, especially to be
admired in the hair, this bronze is the earliest
example of the composition to survive and
should be dated to the artist's early maturity in
the 1560s. One example, presumably fairly
large like this one, was cast and sent to France,
along with a cast of Giovanni Bologna's celebrated *Mercury*. Known reductions of the *Triton*
composition show the streamlined simplifications
that mark the majority of the output of bronzes
after Giovanni Bologna's models as they increased in popularity in the course of the seventeenth century. *Bequest of Benjamin Altman,
1913, 14.40.689*

11 BATTISTA LORENZI, Florentine, 1527/28–1594
Alpheus and Arethusa
Marble; h. 58½ in. (148.6 cm.)

This work, Battista Lorenzi's masterpiece, illustrates a tale from Ovid. The wood nymph Arethusa, pursued by the river-god Alpheus, implored the goddess Diana to save her. Hearing her chaste plea, Diana quickly hid her in a cloud of mist and later transformed her into a fountain. Lorenzi's group (carved in Florence about 1570–80) shows Arethusa being overtaken by the river-god. It was erected in a grotto at the Villa Il Paradiso, belonging to Alamanno Bandini, sometime before 1584, when Raffaello Borghini mentioned it in his *Il Riposo*. The grotto combined water, statuary, and a theatrical setting in a lively manner that anticipated the Baroque. *Fletcher Fund, 1940, 40.33*

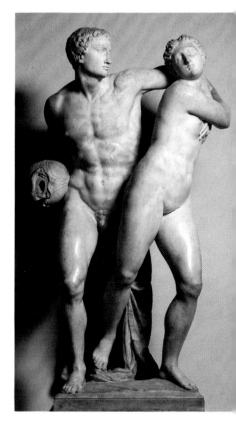

12 TIZIANO ASPETTI, Venetian, 1565–1608
Saint Daniel Being Dragged Before the Governor of Padua
Bronze; 19 × 29¼ in. (48.3 × 74.3 cm.)

The Counter-Reformation in Italy saw an increase in the literal depictions of the martyrdoms of saints. Here the spectacle of Saint Daniel being dragged by a horse is presented with the full repertory of classical and Renaissance poses and gestures. This relief is one of a pair that originally adorned the altar of the saint, commissioned in 1592, in the cathedral of Padua. *Edith Perry Chapman and Fletcher Funds, 1970, 1970.264.1*

13 GIAN LORENZO BERNINI, Roman, 1598–1680
Bacchanal: A Faun Teased by Children
Marble; h. 52 in. (132.1 cm.)

A prodigy of astonishing facility, the young Bernini was trained in the workshop of his father, Pietro, an important pre-Baroque sculptor. During this apprenticeship he executed a number of marble sculptures, which were recorded in his father's name. The present group is the most ambitious of these works and provides insights into the crucial shift in style that took place during the early seventeenth century. The subject is a somewhat mysterious one, having its origins, but no precise analogue, in the Bacchic revels of classical and Renaissance iconography. In his portrayal of the faun, Bernini revealed what would become a lifelong interest in the rendering of emotional and spiritual exaltation. *Purchase, The Annenberg Fund, Inc. Gift, Fletcher, Rogers, and Louis V. Bell Funds, and Gift of J. Pierpont Morgan, by exchange, 1976, 1976.92*

14 ANTONIO CANOVA, Roman, 1757–1822 ▶
Perseus with the Head of Medusa
Marble; h. 86⅝ in. (220 cm.)

Among the art treasures removed from Italy to France by Napoleon's army was the antique Vatican *Apollo Belvedere*. Between 1790 and 1800 Canova executed the first version of his *Perseus*, based on the *Apollo*. Perseus is shown carrying the head of Medusa, whom he has slain with the help of the goddess Athena. When the sculpture was exhibited in Canova's studio, it was acclaimed as the last word in the continuing purification of the Neoclassical style, and it was bought by Pius VII to replace the *Apollo Belvedere*. In 1804 a Polish countess commissioned another *Perseus*, the one shown here. This work, with refinements that perfect the first version, was completed about 1808. *Fletcher Fund, 1967, 67.110*

15 JOSEPH NOLLEKENS, British, 1737–1823
Bust of Laurence Sterne
Marble; h. including socle 21¾ in. (55.2 cm.)

This portrait bust of the British writer Laurence
Sterne is an early work (1765–66) by Nollekens.
At the time Sterne's novel *Tristram Shandy* was
appearing in installments and was all the rage
in England. Nollekens was an outstanding portrait sculptor, and his finest busts, such as
those of Sterne, William Pitt (an example also
in the Museum), and Charles James Fox, are
characterizations of a high order of sensitivity.
*Purchase, John T. Dorrance, Jr., Gift, in memory
of Elinor Dorrance Ingersoll, 1979, 1979.275.2*

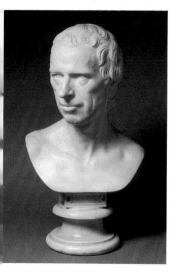

16 JUAN MARTÍNEZ MONTAÑÉS, Spanish,
1568–1649
Saint John the Baptist
Gilt and polychromed wood; h. 61 in. (155 cm.)

Montañés was a native of Seville, where he
was known as *El Dios de la Madera* for his
many retables which populate the churches
with magnificently polychromed wood figures.
This figure, which dates from about 1625–35,
came from the convent of Nuestra Señora de la
Concepción. It has for its compositional precedent
Montañés's own *Baptist* of the main altar in San
Isidoro del Campo at Santiponce, made between
1609 and 1613. The Museum's *Baptist* is, however, a fuller and more emotionally charged figure. In fact, it has been called Montañés's most
beautiful single figure. Its austere expression,
solid corporeality, and sharp colors give a disquietingly urgent impression of actuality and
conviction. *Purchase, Joseph Pulitzer Bequest,
1963, 63.40*

17 PIERRE ÉTIENNE MONNOT, French, 1657–1733
Andromeda and the Sea Monster
Marble; h. 61 in. (154.9 cm.)

When John Cecil, fifth earl of Exeter, commissioned this sculpture in Rome, he chose not an Italian but one of the French artists who dominated the field of Roman monumental sculpture at the time. Monnot shows Andromeda chained to a rock, lifting an imploring gaze heavenward, with the monster emerging from the waves. This coolly poised work of 1700, with its brilliant carving and psychological dissolution of spatial bounds, is a vivid example of the late Baroque in Rome. *Purchase, Josephine Bay Paul and C. Michael Paul Foundation, Inc., and Charles Ulrick and Josephine Bay Foundation, Inc. Gifts, 1967, 67.34*

---

18 JEAN LOUIS LEMOYNE, French, 1665–1755
Fear of Cupid's Darts
Marble; h. 72 in. (182.9 cm.)

In this lightly erotic group, a nymph reacts with a startled, self-protective gesture to the sudden appearance of Cupid, who is about to cast an arrow into her breast. The technique, in which the marble seems touched with flickering light, and the delicately off-balance pose are typically Rococo. Commissioned for Louis XV, this group was completed in 1739–40. *Purchase, Josephine Bay Paul and C. Michael Paul Foundation, Inc., and Charles Ulrick and Josephine Bay Foundation, Inc. Gifts, 1967, 67.197*

19 JEAN BAPTISTE LEMOYNE, French, 1704–1778
Bust of Louis XV
Marble; h. including socle 34¼ in. (87 cm.)

Lemoyne was the favorite sculptor of Louis XV, and for forty years he held a virtual monopoly on recording the benign royal features. He made a number of portrait busts of the king; many were destroyed during the French Revolution, as were Lemoyne's equestrian statues of the king in Bordeaux and Rennes. The Museum's bust is dated 1757, when Louis XV was forty-seven years old. *Gift of George Blumenthal, 1941, 41.100.244*

20 JEAN ANTOINE HOUDON, French, 1741–1828
Bust of Diderot
Marble; h. including socle 20⁷⁄₁₆ in. (52 cm.)

Houdon made over one hundred and fifty portrait busts of the great men and women of his age. He combined psychological perception with analytical realism to bring out the individual character of each sitter. Houdon executed a number of busts of the much-admired Denis Diderot—this one of 1773 was made for a Russian count—and of other leading Encyclopedists, such as d'Alembert, Rousseau, and Voltaire, which are masterpieces of portrait sculpture. *Gift of Mr. and Mrs. Charles Wrightsman, 1974, 1974.291*

22 ANTOINE LOUIS BARYE, French,
1796–1875
Theseus Fighting the Centaur Bianor
Bronze; h. 50 in. (127 cm.)

While better known for his animal sculpture,
Barye based a number of his works on classical
subjects. The subject of this one is an episode
from the battle between the Lapiths and Centaurs described in Book XII of Ovid's *Metamorphoses*. This bronze is reminiscent of
antique sculptural representations of the Lapiths
and Centaurs, for the sculptor must have known

the metopes from the Parthenon, at least in
reproduction. But the *Theseus,* first modeled in
1849, also reflects the underlying Romanticism
of Barye's vision. Like many Romantic artists
who were his contemporaries, Barye was fascinated by the primal energy of the animal world,
the violence of combat, and the elemental struggle for survival, here embodied in the death
struggle of the half-animal, half-human centaur
with the Greek hero Theseus. *Gift of Samuel P.
Avery, 1885, 85.3*

21   CLODION, French, 1738–1814
Relief with Satyresses and Baby Satyrs
Stucco; l. 157½ in. (400.1 cm.)

Three of the stucco reliefs that once embellished the courtyard of the Hôtel de Bourbon-Condé in Paris are in the Museum: two friezes and the lunette enclosing a circular window which is illustrated here. This series of bacchanalian scenes was created by Claude Michel, known universally as Clodion, about 1781–87. The lunette's two groups of satyr mothers with their young illustrate Clodion's unerring compositional skill, and even though the stucco is the enlargement of an idea first sketched in terracotta, one senses the delicate modeling of the original. *Ella Morris de Peyster Bequest, 1959, 59.24c*

23   JEAN BAPTISTE CARPEAUX, French, 1827–75
Ugolino and His Sons
Marble; h. 77 in. (195.6 cm.)

The subject of this intensely Romantic work is derived from Canto XXXIII of Dante's *Inferno*, which describes how the Pisan traitor Count Ugolino della Gherardesca, his sons, and his grandsons were imprisoned in 1288 and died of starvation. Carpeaux's visionary statue, executed in 1865–67, reflects his passionate reverence for Michelangelo, specifically for the *Last Judgment* of the Sistine Chapel in Rome, as well as his own painstaking concern with anatomical realism. *Purchase, Josephine Bay Paul and C. Michael Paul Foundation, Inc., and Charles Ulrick and Josephine Bay Foundation, Inc. Gifts, 1967, 67.250*

24 EDGAR DEGAS, French, 1834–1917
Little Fourteen-Year-Old Dancer
Bronze and muslin; h. 39 in. (99.1 cm.)

In the taut adolescent body of the little dancer, Degas has captured the mannered but still slightly awkward stance of the aspiring ballerina. The original work, now in the Louvre, was modeled in wax about 1880–81; its realism was heightened by the addition of ballet shoes, a bodice overlaid with a thin layer of wax, a tutu of muslin, and a horsehair wig tied behind with silk ribbon. The Museum's bronze was probably cast in 1922; the tinted bodice and slippers, augmented by a muslin skirt and silk hair ribbon, skillfully evoke the materials of the original sculpture. (See also Drawings, no. 6; European Paintings, nos. 137–139; and Robert Lehman Collection, no. 31.) *Bequest of Mrs. H. O. Havemeyer, 1929. H. O. Havemeyer Collection, 29.100.370*

26 ARISTIDE MAILLOL, French, 1861–1944
Torso of Île-de-France
Bronze; h. 42 ⅜ in. (107.5 cm.)

Maillol was primarily interested in representing the formal structure of the human figure, but he never ventured into the avant-garde world of abstraction. While influenced by Greek sculpture of the early fifth century, Maillol's female nudes are often recognizable as modern French women. Three versions of this torso were made between 1910 and 1921; this one is believed to be the second. *Edith Perry Chapman Fund, 1951; Acquired from The Museum of Modern Art, Gift of A. Conger Goodyear, 53.140.9*

25 AUGUSTE RODIN, French, 1840–1917
Adam
Bronze; h. 76¼ in. (193.7 cm.)

Adam shows the first man being roused to life slowly and with difficulty. Like Carpeaux (no. 23), Rodin drew upon Michelangelo's Sistine Chapel frescoes as a direct source of inspiration. In his *Adam* he combined elements from the *Creation of Man* in the Sistine Chapel and from the Christ of Michelangelo's *Pietà* in the Duomo in Florence. *Adam* was modeled originally in 1880, and for a time Rodin intended to incorporate the figure into his design for *The Gates of Hell,* the portal planned for a building in Paris that was never constructed. In 1910 the Museum commissioned this bronze from Rodin. *Gift of Thomas F. Ryan, 1910, 11.173.1*

FURNITURE AND WOODWORK

27 Room from Kirtlington Park
English, 1742–48
Wood, plaster, and marble; h. 20 ft. (6.09 m.), l. 36 ft. (10.97 m.), w. 24 ft. (7.32 m.)

Kirtlington Park, near Oxford, was built for Sir James Dashwood between 1742 and 1746 by William Smith and John Sanderson; the park was laid out by Lancelot ("Capability") Brown. This room, originally used for dining and now furnished as a drawing room, has its original overmantel painting by John Wooton, dated 1748. The spirited plaster decoration was designed by Sanderson and executed by an Oxford stucco-worker; the central panels at the four sides of the ceiling depict the seasons. The richly carved chimneypiece is of marble, the mahogany doors and shutters are equipped with their original gilt-bronze hardware, and the oak floor is also original. *Fletcher Fund, 1931, 32.53.1*

28 WILLIAM VILE, British, d. 1767
Coin Cabinet
Mahogany; 79 × 27 × 17¼ in. (200.7 × 68.6 × 43.8 cm.)

William Vile and his partner, John Cobb, created some of the finest pieces of English court furniture in the eighteenth century. Commissioned in 1758 by the Prince of Wales (later George III), this cabinet was completed in 1761. In all likelihood it was an end section of a tripartite piece of furniture. The other end section is in the Victoria and Albert Museum, London; the middle section, if it exists, has not been identified. There are 135 shallow drawers for coins and medals, allowing space for over six thousand items from the king's collection. The top door is carved with the star of the Order of the Garter, to which the Prince of Wales was elected in 1750. *Fletcher Fund, 1964, 64.79*

29 Tapestry Room from Croome Court
English, 1760–71
Wood, plaster, and tapestry; h. 13 ft. 10¾ in.
(4.23 m.), l. 27 ft. 1 in. (8.27 m.), w. 22 ft. 8 in.
(6.9 m.)

Robert Adam designed the Tapestry Room and
other interior architecture after he replaced
Lancelot ("Capability") Brown as architect to the
sixth earl of Coventry, whose country seat was
Croome Court, near Worcester. Designed in 1763,
the ceiling of this room, with its ornamented
wheel molding and garlanded trophies, is an
example of Adam's vigorous early style.

The tapestries on the walls and on the seat
furniture were woven at the Royal Gobelins
Manufactory, Paris, in the workshop of Jacques
Neilson. The medallions after designs by François
Boucher portray scenes from classical myths
symbolizing the elements. The borders were
designed by Maurice Jacques. Commissioned
in 1763, these tapestries were installed in 1771.
(See also no. 50.) *Gift of the Samuel H. Kress*
Foundation, 1958, 58.75.1a

30   Dining Room from Lansdowne House

English, 1765–68

Wood, plaster, and stone; h. 17 ft. 11 in. (5.46 m.), l. 47 ft. (14.31 m.), w. 24 ft. 6 in. (7.47 m.)

Robert Adam's style at its purest and best is seen in this room from Lansdowne House, the London residence of Lord Shelburne (later the marquess of Lansdowne). The feathery arabesques of griffins and putti, vases and trophies of arms, leaf garlands, sprays, rosettes, Vitruvian scrolls, and fan-shaped motifs are cast in plaster and constitute one of the glories of this room. The niches originally contained antique sculptures from Lord Lansdowne's collection, one of which, *Tyche,* still remains; the eight other niches hold plaster casts of Roman statues. The oak floor of the room is original. *Rogers Fund, 1931, 32.12*

31   Commode

English, ca. 1770–80

Satinwood, tulipwood, and other marquetry woods on oak with inlay of ivory; 37 × 59⅞ × 25⅜ in. (94 × 152 × 64.4 cm.)

The ornamental chests of drawers known as commodes originated in France in the late seventeenth century. In this piece each of the three doors opens upon a bank of four drawers, and the frieze is fitted with three drawers. The classical urns depicted in the marquetry on the sides and the floral garlands on the front resemble motifs that appear on a commode attributed to Thomas Chippendale, dated 1770, at Nostell Priory, Yorkshire. *Purchase, Morris Loeb Bequest, 1955, 55.114*

32 Savonnerie Carpet
French, 1680
*Knotted and cut wool pile; 29 ft. 9¾ in. ×
10 ft. 4 in. (9.09 × 3.15 m.)*

This carpet is one of a series of ninety-two
made for the *grande galerie* of the Louvre after
designs by Charles Lebrun (1619–90), *premier
peintre* of Louis XIV. In 1663 he was appointed
to supervise the Savonnerie manufactory, a
carpet-weaving works near Paris. He started

the designs for the Louvre in 1665, and the first
carpets were put on the looms in 1668. These
carpets, among the most extraordinary ever
made in Europe, have about ninety Ghiordes
knots per square inch. The carpet illustrated
here, one of the finest of the more than fifty
known to have survived from the series, was
delivered in 1680. *Gift of Mr. and Mrs. Charles
Wrightsman, 1976, 1976.155.14*

33 BERNARD II VAN RISEN BURGH, French,
act. ca. 1730–65
Commode
*Coromandel lacquer and ebony on oak;
marble top; 34 × 63 × 25¼ in. (86.4 × 160 ×
64.1 cm.)*

Van Risen Burgh was one of the great masters
of the fully developed Louis XV style in furniture.
In this commode, which was made about 1745,
he skillfully veneered the curving front and sides
with colorful panels from an incised Coromandel
lacquer screen. This type of lacquer derived
its name from the Coromandel coast, which
stretches north and south of Madras in south-

east India. In the late seventeenth and eighteenth centuries merchant ships stopped at
ports along this coast to pick up goods exported
.from China (such as the screen used in this
commode). The front panel of the commode
has scattered groups of oriental figures. Typically for the period, they are arranged without
regard for perspective. The side panels represent fantastic animals and are, like the front, set
within gilt-bronze Rococo mounts of exceptional vitality and inventiveness. *The Lesley and
Emma Sheafer Collection, Bequest of Emma A.
Sheafer, 1973, 1974.356.189*

34   GILLES JOUBERT,
French, ca. 1689– d. 1775
Writing Table
*Oak with red japanning,
gilt bronze; 31⁹/₁₆ ×
69¹/₄ × 36 in. (80.7 ×
175.9 × 91.4 cm.)*

This piece is documented by the number 2131, which is painted on its underside. It is identified under that number in the *Journal du Garde-Meuble,* the royal furniture registry, as the desk delivered by Joubert on December 29, 1759, for use by Louis XV in the *cabinet intérieur,* his favorite study at Versailles. Louis XV was surely consulted about the design and execution of this splendid red japanned writing table, which can thus be understood as an expression of the king's personal taste. *Gift of Mr. and Mrs. Charles Wrightsman, 1973, 1973.315.1*

35   *Grand Salon* from the Hôtel de Tessé
French, 1768–72
*Carved, painted, and gilded oak; h. 16 ft.
(4.88 m.), l. 33 ft. 7¹/₂ in. (10.25 m.),
w. 29 ft. 6¹/₂ in. (9 m.)*

The noble grace of the Louis XVI style is exemplified by the *grand salon* from the Hôtel de Tessé (the building still stands at no. 1 Quai Voltaire, Paris). The mansion was built in 1765–68 for Marie Charlotte de Béthune-Charost, comtesse de Tessé; the plans are attributed to the architect Pierre Noël Rousset. The interior decoration was probably completed in 1772, when final payment was made to the architect and contractor Louis Letellier.

Each of the four double doors is surmounted by a stucco relief of a pair of children holding a medallion of a dancing maiden. The four arched mirror surrounds contribute to the serenely Neoclassical effect of the room. *Gift of Mrs. Herbert N. Straus, 1942, 42.203.1*

36 Shopfront from No. 3 Quai Bourbon, Paris

French, ca. 1775
Carved oak; 13 ft. 1 in. × 20 ft. 4 in. (3.99 × 6.24 m.)

This Parisian shopfront, from the north bank of the Île Saint-Louis, stood on a site favorable to commerce, close to the junction of the Quai Bourbon and the Pont Marie, an early seventeenth-century bridge over the Seine. It was superimposed on the masonry of an existing seventeenth-century building, the modest outlines of which can still be seen. Chroniclers of late nineteenth- and early twentieth-century Paris drew attention to the charm and rarity of this isolated little shopfront, which was thought to be the only surviving eighteenth-century example in the city. By the time it was dismantled in World War I, the original painted surface had weathered to the bare oak, and the woodwork had suffered some losses. When the shopfront was restored at the Museum, the natural tone of the wood was retained. The missing elements were supplied in accordance with a measured drawing of the shopfront published in 1870. *Gift of J. P. Morgan, Jr., 1920, 20.154*

37 MARTIN CARLIN, French, act. 1766–85
Upright Secretary

Oak veneered with tulipwood and purplewood; porcelain plaques; white marble top; 47 × 31¾ × 14¾ in. (119.4 × 80.6 × 37.5 cm.)

This upright secretary with a fall front (*secrétaire à abattant*), signed by Carlin, is decorated with ten plaques of Sèvres porcelain. The veneered and marquetried wood surfaces of such pieces of furniture have faded in the course of years, but the porcelain plaques have retained their original brilliant coloration. These plaques have apple-green borders, and their white reserves are painted with naturalistic floral subjects, including baskets heaped with blooms and suspended from blue and violet ribbons. The plaques bear the date letter for 1773 and the designations of three flower painters (Xhrouet, Bulidon, and Noël). The chasing and gilding of the bronze mounts are of very high quality, contributing to the effect of rich ornamentation. *Gift of the Samuel H. Kress Foundation, 1958, 58.75.44*

38 Reception Room from the Hôtel de Cabris
French, 1775–78
Carved, painted, and gilded oak; h. 11 ft.
8½ in. (3.57 m.), l. 25 ft. 6 in. (7.77 m.),
w. 13 ft. 11 in. (4.24 m.)

The Hôtel de Cabris in Grasse, from which this
room was taken, is now the Musée Fragonard.
It was built between 1771 and 1774 for Jean
Paul de Clapiers, marquis de Cabris, after designs by a little-known Milanese architect, Giovanni Orello.

The paneling, dating from 1775–78, was

carved, painted, and gilded in Paris and was
installed in a small reception room on the main
floor. The four pairs of double doors are remarkable for the carved motifs of smoking incense-
burners, interlaced laurel sprays, and torches;
this decoration exemplifies the sobriety of the
Neoclassical style. The white marble chimneypiece, contemporary with the room, comes from
the Hôtel de Greffulhe in Paris. *Purchase,*
Mr. and Mrs. Charles Wrightsman Gift, 1972,
1972.276.1,2

39 GEORGES JACOB, French, 1739–1814
Armchair
Gilded walnut and embroidered satin; 40¼ ×
29½ × 30⅝ in. (102.2 × 74.9 × 77.8 cm.)

The Museum has a set of two armchairs (*fauteuils*
à la reine) and two side chairs (*chaises courantes*)
that were made about 1780 by Jacob; one of the
armchairs is illustrated here. The carved and
gilded frames show the extreme finesse of the
woodcarver's technique. The pieces are upholstered in white silk satin embroidered with colored
silks; the design is in the style of Philippe de la
Salle, the most prominent designer of woven
silk fabrics of the period. *Gift of the Samuel H.*
Kress Foundation, 1958, 58.75.26

40 JEAN HENRI RIESENER, French, 1734–1806
Upright Secretary
Japanese black-and-gold lacquer and ebony, veneered on oak; white marble top; gilt-bronze mounts; 57 × 43 × 16 in. (144.8 × 109.2 × 40.5 cm.)

This secretary and its companion commode, also in the Museum, stood in Marie Antoinette's private apartment at the Château de Saint-Cloud; her initials appear three times in the gilt-bronze frieze under the marble top. The opulent refinement of this secretary, made in 1783–87, is a direct response of the maker, Riesener, to the taste of his royal client. Cascading down the front are exquisitely chased gilt-bronze flowers, while fruits, wheat, flowers, and symbols of princely glory spill from the cornucopia mounts along the lower edge. The black-and-gold panels of Japanese lacquer reflect the queen's fondness for this material. *Bequest of William K. Vanderbilt, 1920, 20.155.11*

41 Coin Cabinet
French, ca. 1805
Mahogany with silver inlay and silver mounts; 35½ × 19¾ × 14¾ in. (90.2 × 50.2 × 37.5 cm.)

This cabinet is part of a set of furniture decorated with Egyptian figures, including a bed and a pair of armchairs, commissioned by Dominique Vivant Denon (1747–1825). The Parisian cabinetmaker Jacob-Desmalter executed the cabinet after a design by Charles Percier (1764–1838), probably suggested by Denon, and incorporated mounts by Martin Guillaume Biennais (1764–1843), whose workshop produced much of the best Empire silver and gilt bronze. The upper part of the cabinet is derived from the pylon at Apollonopolis (Ghoos) in Upper Egypt, which Denon saw while accompanying Napoleon's Egyptian campaign of 1798–99 and which is illustrated in his *Voyage dans la Basse et la Haute Égypte* (Paris, 1802). *Bequest of Collis P. Huntington, 1926, 26.168.77*

42 Corner Settee
German, 1766
Carved, painted, and gilded pine; covered in painted oriental satin (not original); 43 × 54½ × 25¼ in. (109.2 × 138.4 × 63.7 cm.)

The Rococo style in Germany was based on French prototypes and enriched by the native Baroque traditions. Fantasy seems to play over this extraordinary piece, made in Würzburg in 1766. It is part of a set of four side chairs, two armchairs, and two settees made by the cabinetmaker Johann Köhler for Seehof Castle, near Bamberg. *The Lesley and Emma Sheafer Collection, Bequest of Emma A. Sheafer, 1973, 1974.356.121*

43   DAVID ROENTGEN, German, 1743–1807
Rolltop Desk
Marquetry of satinwood, boxwood, white mahogany, ebony, and mother-of-pearl in panels of sycamore; cedar and oak carcass; brass and gilt-bronze mounts; 53½ × 43½ × 26½ in. (135.9 × 110.5 × 67.3 cm.)

This desk perfectly represents the inventive talents of its maker. The chinoiserie marquetry scenes have a painterly effect that Roentgen alone attained, using pieces of naturally colored exotic woods. His mechanical ingenuity is exemplified by the workings of the desk's lower section: when the key of the lower drawer is turned to the right position, the side drawers spring open; if a button is pressed on the underside of these drawers, each swings aside to reveal three drawers. Although Roentgen maintained his workshop at Neuwied, where this desk was made about 1780, his French clientele became so important that he opened an outlet in Paris and joined the Parisian guild in 1780. (See also The Jack and Belle Linsky Collection, no. 20.) *Rogers Fund, 1941, 41.82*

44   Patio from Vélez Blanco
Spanish, 1506–1515
Marble; h. 63 ft. (19.5 m.), l. 44 ft. (13.41 m.), w. 33 ft. (10.59 m.)

The richly carved Renaissance patio from the castle at Vélez Blanco, near Almería, is a jewel of Spanish and Italian architecture of the early sixteenth century. Its fundamental structure reflects the strongly Spanish, conservative taste of its architect in the asymmetrical layout, the use of Gothic gargoyles, the flat-timbered ceilings of the galleries, and the low, segmental arches. Yet the decorative details of the carved ornament are composed of Italian Renaissance motifs and were executed by carvers from northern Italy. A sumptuous array of fanciful flora and fauna appears on the spandrels and intrados of the arches, on the piers of the balustrade, and especially around the doors and windows. For all their elaboration, the motifs preserve the controlled clarity of form and organization, the vivid naturalism, and the bold three-dimensional quality characteristic of the early Italian Renaissance style. *Bequest of George Blumenthal, 1941, 41.190.482*

45 Study from the Palace of Duke Federigo da Montefeltro at Gubbio

Italian, ca. 1476–80
Intarsia of walnut, beech, rosewood, oak, and fruitwoods on walnut base; h. 15 ft. 11 in. (4.85 m.), l. 17 ft. (5.18 m.), w. 12 ft. 7 in. (3.84 m.)

This is a detail from a small room (*studiolo*), intended for meditation and study. Its walls are carried out in a technique of wood-laying known as intarsia; ingenuity has been lavished upon trompe-l'oeil images that seem to project from the flat paneling. The latticework doors of the cabinets, shown open or partly closed, are evidence of the great interest in linear perspective at the time. The cabinets contain objects reflecting Duke Federigo's wide-ranging artistic and scientific interests; the depictions of books recall his extensive library. *Imprese* (emblems) of the Montefeltro are also represented. This room may have been designed by Francesco di Giorgio (1439–1502) and others; it was executed by Baccio Pontelli (ca. 1450–92) with assistants. A similar room, still in situ, was carried out for the duke's palace in Urbino. (The Museum's room is not on view; it has been scheduled for reinstallation.) *Rogers Fund, 1939, 39.153*

46 FRA DAMIANO DA BERGAMO, Bolognese, ca. 1480–d. 1549

The Last Supper
Walnut, inlaid with various woods; 60¾ × 40⅞ in. (154.3 × 103.7 cm.)

This altarpiece (1547–48) was signed by Fra Damiano da Bergamo, whose workshop was at the convent of San Domenico in Bologna; it was designed by Jacopo Barozzi da Vignola (1507–1573). The heavy proportions of the architectural elements and the effects of depth, mass, and "surprise" are paralleled in the facade of a palazzo in Bologna that Vignola designed in 1545 for the humanist Achille Bocchi. This altarpiece was commissioned by Claude d'Urfé, the French ambassador to the Council of Trent. It was installed in the chapel of La Bastie d'Urfé, his château near Lyons. *Gift of the children of Mrs. Harry Payne Whitney in accordance with the wishes of their mother, 1942, 42.57.4.108*

47 Bookcase

Roman, ca. 1715
Walnut and poplar; 157 × 94 × 24 in. (398.8 × 238.8 × 61 cm.)

The stand and crest of this bookcase, one of a pair at the Museum, offered scope for an unknown sculptor to execute marvelously ebullient Baroque woodcarvings. The pair formerly stood in a wing added to the Palazzo Rospigliosi in Rome, where they were recorded in a 1722 inventory shortly after the wing was built. It is thought that the architect responsible for the new building, Nicola Michetti (d. 1759), may have supplied the design for the bookcases. *Gift of Madame Lilliana Teruzzi, 1969, 69.292.1*

48 Bedroom from the Palazzo Sagredo
Venetian, ca. 1718
Wood, stucco, marble, glass; h. 13 ft. (3.96 m.)

In design and workmanship this bedroom, consisting of an antechamber with a bed alcove, is one of the finest of its period in existence. The decoration is partly in stucco, partly in carved wood. In the antechamber fluted Corinthian pilasters support an entablature out of which amorini fly, bearing garlands of flowers. Other amorini bear the gilded frame of a painting by Gasparo Diziani, which depicts Dawn triumphant over Night. Above the entry to the alcove seven amorini frolic. Around the room runs a paneled wood dado with a red and white marble base. The unornamented portions of the walls are covered with seventeenth-century brocatelle. The bed alcove has its original marquetry floor. The stucco work was probably done by Carpoforo Mazetti and Abondio Statio. The amorini are beautifully modeled, and the arabesques of the doors are exquisitely executed. Everything unites to form a buoyant and joyful ensemble. *Rogers Fund, 1906, 06.1335.1a–d*

TAPESTRIES

49 The Bridal Chamber of Herse
Flemish, Brussels, ca. 1550
Wool, silk, and metal threads; 172 × 204 in. (436.9 × 520.7 cm.)

This tapestry is one of a set of eight that tell the story of the love affair between the god Mercury and Herse, daughter of Cecrops, king of Athens. Here Mercury enters her bedroom, so eagerly that his winged sandals fall from his feet. Several cupids attend him; one removes his hat and another takes off Herse's sandal. The splendid room is gorgeously furnished, with rich fabrics covering the walls and bed; Mercury has laid his golden staff, the caduceus, on an elaborately carved table. The figures in the borders represent Virtues and have no connection with the main scene; they were originally designed to frame tapestries after Raphael's cartoons of the Acts of the Apostles. Silver and silver-gilt threads are lavishly used throughout. In the lower borders, in gilt thread, are the letters BB for Brabant-Brussels and the weaver's mark of Willem de Pannemaker (fl. 1541–78). Another panel of the set is in the Museum and two are in the Prado. *Bequest of George Blumenthal, 1941, 41.190.135*

50 La Collation
French, Beauvais, 1762
Wool and silk; 130 × 102 in. (330.2 × 259.1 cm.)

This tapestry is from the first series (eight pieces) designed by François Boucher (1703–1770) for the Beauvais manufactory. The contemporary name for the series was *Fêtes italiennes,* and the first four designs, woven from 1736 on, do indeed show peasants, statues, and ruins like those Boucher might have seen in Italy; by the time the second four designs, including this convivial picnic, were first produced in the 1740s, however, the actors have become ladies and gentlemen enjoying themselves in the French countryside. The young men and their girls wear bright colors, and the parasol is a brilliant pink against the blue-green trees. The set to which this tapestry belongs is in the Museum; it is made up of six of the original designs with two others for narrow pieces added long after Boucher had ceased to work for Beauvais. The original purchaser and the entire history of the set are known; it is apparently the only one that has remained together. (See also no. 29 and European Paintings, no. 113.) *Gift of Ann Payne Robertson, 1964, 64.145.3*

GOLDSMITHS' WORK

51 Pendent Jewel: Prudence
Probably French (Paris), mid-16th c.
Gold, chalcedony, enamel, emeralds, rubies, a diamond, and a pendent pearl; 3½ × 2 in. (8.9 × 5 cm.)

The mirror and snake identify the subject of this jewel as Prudence, one of the Seven Virtues. Her image—white chalcedony carved in relief, combined with raised and tooled gold—is attached to a ground of enameled gold. The technique, a rare one, is a variety of *commesso.* In medium and style this Prudence is characteristic of a group of jewels traced to the court of the French king Henry II (r. 1547–59). *Gift of J. Pierpont Morgan, 1917, 17.190.907*

52 JEAN FRÉMIN, French, master 1738–d. 1786
Snuffbox
Gold; 3⅜ × 2¾ × 1⁹⁄₁₆ in. (8.6 × 7 × 4 cm.)

In the eighteenth century snuff constituted the most important part of the tobacco trade. In France snuff taking was enhanced among the nobility and gentry by the glitter and elegance of gold snuffboxes. By about 1740 the making of these *tabatières* became a specialized profession. This example was made in Paris by Jean Frémin in 1756–57, and its ample shape and uninterrupted decoration of enameled flowers are characteristic of the 1750s. The surface is worked in an extravagantly twisting trellis pattern, and the enamel is applied *en plein,* directly on the metal. *Gift of Mr. and Mrs. Charles Wrightsman, 1976, 1976.155.14*

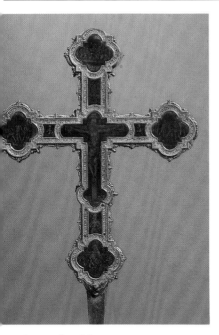

53 Processional Cross
Florentine, probably ca. 1460–80
Silver gilt, nielloed silver, and copper with traces of gilding; 21¾ × 12¾ in. (55.2 × 32.4 cm.)

An inscription on the base states that this cross was made for the convent of Santa Chiara in Florence. It is an extraordinary example of Florentine Renaissance metalwork incorporating within its silver-gilt frame a series of twenty silver plaques with nielloed scenes depicting the Passion of Christ and various saints. *Gift of J. Pierpont Morgan, 1917, 17.190.499*

54 FRANÇOIS THOMAS GERMAIN, French, 1726–91
Coffeepot
Silver; h. 11⅝ in. (29.5 cm.)

This coffeepot, made in Paris and dated 1757, was part of a service for the Portuguese court. Delightfully designed, with spiral flutes giving variety and movement to its surface, the coffeepot follows a familiar eighteenth-century style, but with rare distinction. The leaves and berries of the coffee plant decorate the finial, spout, and handle support. *Purchase, Joseph Pulitzer Bequest, 1933, 33.165.1*

55 JEAN BAPTISTE CLAUDE ODIOT, French, 1763–1850
Cruet
Silver gilt and glass; h. 15¹/₁₆ in. (38.2 cm.)

This cruet, one of a pair in the Museum, was made in Paris about 1817. It exemplifies Odiot's move away from the current flat decorative style to one that was boldly sculptural. Here the central figure is the focus of the design, as commanding by itself as it is a dramatic element in the overall composition. *Gift of Audrey Love in memory of C. Ruxton Love, Jr., 1978, 1978.524.1*

56   WENZEL JAMNITZER, German, 1508–1585
Relief with Allegorical Figures, Mounted as a Mirror Frame
Silver gilt; 11⅝ × 9⅛ in. (29.5 × 23.2 cm.)

Wenzel Jamnitzer was probably the greatest German Mannerist goldsmith, as well as an engraver, medalist, and maker of plaquettes and mathematical instruments. Born in Vienna, he became a master goldsmith in 1534 in Nürnberg, where his workshop included his brother Albrecht, his nephew Barthel, and his sons Wenzel II, Abraham, and Hans II. The design of this relief, with figures of Arithmetic, Geometry, Perspective, and Architecture, was adapted from the title page of the *Perspectiva Corporum Regularium,* Jamnitzer's second book on perspective, published in Nürnberg in 1568. The relief's use as a mirror frame seems to be of relatively recent date. *Gift of J. Pierpont Morgan, 1917, 17.190.620*

57   Automaton: Diana on a Stag
German, Augsburg, ca. 1620
Silver, partially gilt, encasing a movement of iron and wood; 14¾ × 9½ in. (37.5 × 24.1 cm.)

This automaton was used during luxurious drinking bouts, and some twenty other surviving examples of this composition attest to its popularity. When the stag's head is removed, the body serves as a drinking vessel. A mechanism in the base causes the automaton to roll about a tabletop in a pentagonal pattern and then stop; the person before whom it stopped had to drain the contents. This work was made by Joachim Fries (ca. 1579–1620); Diana's bow, quiver, and arrow are of later date. *Gift of J. Pierpont Morgan, 1917, 17.190.746*

59 SIMON PANTIN, British, d. 1731
Tea Kettle, Lamp, and Table
Silver; h. 40¾ in. (103.5 cm.)

Simon Pantin, a very successful London silver-smith of Huguenot origin, made this extraordi-nary set in 1724. Probably a special order for the wedding of George Bowes to the heiress Eleanor Verney, it is distinguished by its superb unity of design and its authority of execution, especially in the crisply engraved arms of its original owners. The tripod stand adopts the form of contemporary mahogany furniture. The plain faceted kettle is a late example of the Queen Anne style—the highpoint of English silver styles. *Gift of Irwin Untermyer, 1968, 68.141.81*

58 Spice Plate
English, ca. 1567–73
Silver and parcel-gilt; diam. 7¾ in. (19.7 cm.)

This is one of a set of twelve exquisite engraved plates in the Museum's collection which illus-trate stories about the Patriarchs from the Book of Genesis. Silverware decorated entirely with pictorial engraving and intended more for dis-play than use is the rarest of all early English silver. Only three sets of these plates, called "spice plates" and "demi-platters" in contempo-rary inventories, are known to have survived.

This plate shows the appearance of Mel-chizedek, "priest of the most high God," to Abraham. In this mystical event, one of many that marked the life of Abraham, Melchizedek blessed him and brought him bread and wine (Gen. 12 : 1–20). The Museum's set of plates is signed by the engraver PM, who has not been firmly identified. He was active in London be-tween 1567 and 1573 and may have been an émigré Protestant from the Continent. Here he used for a guide a woodcut illustration by Ber-nard Salomon in a version of the Bible pub-lished in Lyons in 1553. *Gift of C. Ruxton Love, Jr., 1965, 65.260.2*

60 The Fleet of Aeneas Arrives in Sight of Italy
French, Limoges, ca. 1530–40
Enamel painted on copper; 8¾ × 7¾ in. (22.2 × 19.6 cm.)

French Renaissance enamel designs were often based on contemporary woodcuts and engrav-ings. This plaque is one of seventy-four that are known to survive from a series illustrating the *Aeneid*. Like the rest of the series, it is based on the woodcut illustrations for an edition of Vergil's *Opera* printed by Johann Grüninger of Stras-bourg in 1502 and again in a Lyons edition of 1517. It is thought that the series, remarkable for its size and unity, might have been commis-sioned to decorate the walls of a small study of a French Renaissance patron, but the identi-ties of both patron and enamel painter are unknown. It has been tentatively suggested that the series might have been among the last works of Jean I Pénicaud, the painter com-monly known as the Master of the Aeneid. *Gift of J. P. Morgan, 1925, 25.40.2*

ENAMEL WORK

POTTERY

61 Dish
Italian, Faenza, ca. 1486–87
Majolica; h. 4⅛ in. (10.5 cm.), diam. 18⅞ in. (47.9 cm.)

This dish is decorated with the arms of Matthias Corvinus (1440–90), king of Hungary from 1458 to 1490, and Beatrix of Aragon, whom he married in 1476. It is one of a very small number of pieces surviving from a service of Italian majolica sent to Queen Beatrix by her sister Elenora. Painted in Faenza by an anonymous master in 1486 or 1487, this large plate documents the very best that could be done at that moment technically and artistically in the medium of majolica. The palette is still limited to blues, browns, greens, and aubergine, which are harmoniously juxtaposed and combined in the four bands of ornament surrounding the central scene—a lady combing the mane of a very subdued unicorn. The dish demonstrates the receptivity to the Italian Renaissance shown by the Hungarian court under the leadership of King Matthias. He brought Hungary fully into the sphere of the Renaissance by his knowledge and encouragement of all that was forward-looking in science, art, and literature. During his lifetime Hungary was one of those lands in the forefront of European cultural and intellectual life. *Fletcher Fund, 1946, 46.85.30*

62 NICOLA PELLIPARIO, Italian, 1475–ca. 1545
Dish with the Death of Achilles
Tin-glazed earthenware (faience); diam. 10⅜ in. (26.3 cm.)

Tin-glazed earthenware, a Near Eastern invention, is characterized by its opaque white glaze. Introduced to Italy by the early thirteenth century, it was produced in many Italian towns. The technique reached its highest development in north-central Italy during the sixteenth century, when a full range of colors had been developed for decorating the white surface.

Nicola Pellipario was the central figure of the school of majolica painting in Castel Durante, specializing in narrative subjects. Here his depiction of the death of Achilles, carried out with great delicacy of line and coloring, is based on a woodcut in an edition of Ovid's *Metamorphoses* (Venice, 1497). Polyxena, daughter of Priam, king of Troy, has lured Achilles to the temple of Apollo in Thymbra, where Paris is about to shoot him in the heel, his only vulnerable point. Of particular note is the temple interior, a display of Renaissance architecture with precisely calculated perspective. This dish dates from around 1520. *Purchase, 1884, 84.3.2*

63 ANTOINE SIGALON, French, ca. 1524–d. 1590
Pilgrim Flask
Tin-glazed earthenware (faience); h. with stopper 15 in. (42.6 cm.)

A pilgrim flask was slung from shoulder or saddle by a strap which passed through the slots on its body. The flattened shape was more practical for travelers than a rounded one. The form is of great antiquity in the Mediterranean area, but by the sixteenth century such bottles were also made in silver or fine pottery, clearly not intended for rough use on a journey. This flask was made by the French potter Antoine Sigalon, who learned the art of faience from immigrant Italian majolica workers. (In this tech-

64 Ewer
French, Saint-Porchaire, ca. 1530–50
White earthenware with inlaid clay decoration under a lead glaze; h. 10⁵/₁₆ in. (26.1 cm.)

Little is known about the small manufactory at Saint-Porchaire that produced highly elaborate pottery between 1524 and 1560. The products of the early, best period required much careful hand preparation after the basic shapes had been achieved by throwing on a wheel. This ewer, for example, has some sculptural decorations that were made in molds and then applied—the spout and handle, the festoons, the arcade of saints, and the lion masks. Other ornaments, which lie level with the surface, were made by pressing metal dies into the body and then filling the cavities with brown clay. Surviving examples of Saint-Porchaire ware, often with the devices or armorial bearings of royalty and members of the French nobility, demonstrate the clientele for this kind of domestic luxury ceramic. A distinct challenge in France to the colorful Italian majolica of the same period, Saint-Porchaire ware combines Gothic religious and Renaissance exotic ornament. *Gift of J. Pierpont Morgan, 1917, 17.190.1740*

65 Jug
German, Nürnberg, ca. 1550
Lead- and tin-glazed earthenware; h. 14 in. (35.6 cm.)

The "hafner" (potters) of Germany and Austria mainly built stoves with enclosed and tiled fireboxes and chimneys that might soar almost the full height of a principal room in a castle or abbey. This jug is an example of the occasional work which the hafner also produced. Against the curved tile set into the cutaway front of the jug two men attack each other with axes. The highly charged scene and the allegorical figures on the remaining three sides may refer to the Peasants' Revolt and the religious strife in sixteenth-century Germany. This jug was made in the workshop of Paul Preuning (fl. 1540–50), one of the most active of the hafner in producing such elaborately decorated and colored works. These wares combined the deeply colored lead glazes traditionally used by the hafner with the more recently imported white tin glaze. In a similar joining of old and new, traditionally thrown pots were ornamented with molded Renaissance figure decoration, which was derived from widely available printed sources. *Gift of R. Thornton Wilson, in memory of Florence Ellsworth Wilson, 1950, 50.211.202*

nique the lead glaze, similar to a thin coat of glass, was rendered opaque white by the addition of tin oxide.) Sigalon's atelier in Nîmes was one of the first to make fine tin-glazed earthenware in France.

The heraldic decoration on this flask is that of Count John Casimir of Bavaria. On each side of the coat of arms appear grotesques, taken from similar motifs in Italian majolica. Here, however, they are provided with emblems—the rosaries in their paws, for example—that ridicule the Roman Catholic Church. Sigalon was an ardent Huguenot, and this flask was undoubtedly made to commemorate the convocation of Protestant churches that met in Nîmes in February 1581. *Samuel D. Lee Fund, 1941, 41.49.9ab*

PORCELAIN

66 Ewer
Florentine, 1575–87
Soft-paste porcelain; h. 8 in. (20.3 cm.)

Inspired by imported blue-and-white Chinese porcelain, the grand duke Francesco de' Medici (1541–87) established a factory which produced the first surviving porcelain to have been made in Europe. The models and designs were borrowed from Near Eastern and Western as well as Chinese sources. The ewer is one of four examples of this so-called Medici porcelain in the Museum. *Gift of J. Pierpont Morgan, 1917, 17.190.2045*

67 Tea and Coffee Service
Italian, Doccia, ca. 1760–70
Hard-paste porcelain; h. of coffeepot 10½ in. (26.7 cm.)

Each piece of this large service is decorated in relief with scenes from Ovid's *Metamorphoses*, painted in bold enamel colors with gilt details.

This conjunction of a sculptural treatment of tablewares and classical subject matter was inspired by the personal taste of Carlo Ginori (1701–1757), who founded the Doccia factory in 1737. *Gift of George F. Baker, 1931, 31.132.1ab–33. The Charles E. Sampson Memorial Fund, 1973, 1973.134*

68 Potpourri Vase
French, Sèvres, 1757
Soft-paste porcelain; h. 17½ in (44.4 cm.)

This Sèvres vase (*vase vaisseau à mât*), in the soft pink known as *rose Pompadour*, is date-marked 1757. Its imaginative shape is regarded as an allusion to the single-masted vessel in the ancient coat of arms of the city of Paris. Along the shoulder is a series of "porthole" apertures, and at either end is a triton head. The intricately pierced cover suggests a mast; it is enclosed by four gilded rope ladders, and about its upper portion is the blue-and-gold pennant of France. The model is attributed to Jean Claude Duplessis (d. 1774), and the figure painting is in the manner of Charles Nicolas Dodin. *Gift of the Samuel H. Kress Foundation, 1958, 58.75.89ab*

69 Dish

Austrian, Vienna, ca. 1730–40
Hard-paste porcelain; 7 × 9⅛ in. (17.8 × 23.2 cm.)

This dish was made at the factory in Vienna directed by Claudius du Paquier (d. 1751). The motif that distinguishes his finest productions of the 1730s is the leaf-and-strapwork pattern, often interspersed with flowers and fruits, painted in iron red and other colors. Originating as a border ornament, strapwork emerges in its mature form as an entirely independent motif, and perfect harmony is achieved between the form of the piece and its painted decoration, each enhancing the other. *Gift of R. Thornton Wilson, in memory of Florence Ellsworth Wilson, 1950, 50.211.9*

70 Chinese Musicians

English, Chelsea, ca. 1755
Soft-paste porcelain; h. 14½ in. (36.8 cm.)

The technical difficulties of firing so large a soft-paste group were considerable, and this work is therefore among the most remarkable creations of Chelsea's Red Anchor period (1753–57). The modeler, Joseph Willems (ca. 1715–d. 1766), succeeded in harmonizing his exotic figures with Rococo ideals of beauty. Offering satisfying views from all sides, his group is ideally suited as a table centerpiece. It is apparently mentioned in the Chelsea Sale Catalogue of April 8, 1758: "A most magnificent LUSTRE in the Chinese taste, beautifully ornamented with flowers, and a large group of Chinese figures playing music." This description indicates that the model was also available for use as a candelabrum. *Gift of Irwin Untermyer, 1964, 64.101.474*

71 Bottle

German, Meissen, ca. 1715
Lacquered red stoneware; h. 6¾ in. (17.1 cm.)

The decoration on this bottle is attributed to Martin Schnell (ca. 1685–1740?), who came to Dresden from Berlin in 1710 as lacquerer to Augustus the Strong. He practiced his art not only on furniture and woodwork but, from 1712 to 1716, on the red stoneware then being produced at Meissen by J. F. Böttger (1682–1719). Much of the work attributed to Schnell is European in style, but the oriental landscape on a black ground of this bottle clearly demonstrates his familiarity with imported Japanese lacquer. *Gift of R. Thornton Wilson, in memory of Florence Ellsworth Wilson, 1943, 43.100.38ab*

72 Fountain

German, Meissen, ca. 1732
Hard-paste porcelain; 25⅟₁₆ × 18⅝₁₆ in. (63.7 × 46.6 cm.)

This fountain, modeled at Meissen by Johann Gottlob Kirchner (b. ca. 1706), was designed to hold rose water for the convenience of guests at a banquet. At the top, a figure of Neptune supports a reservoir in the form of a deep shell. His left foot rests upon the head of a dolphin, fitted with a dragon-head spigot of oriental silver. The supporting shaft of shellwork and rockery is braced by figures of a satyr and satyress. Their infant is sliding headlong toward a great shell basin painted with chinoiseries. *Gift of R. Thornton Wilson, in memory of Florence Ellsworth Wilson, 1954, 54.147.65a–c*

73 Goat and Suckling Kid

German, Meissen, ca. 1732
Hard-paste porcelain; 19⅜ × 25½ in. (49.2 × 64.8 cm.)

In 1732 Johann Joachim Kändler (1706–1775) completed the model for an Angora-goat group to be "left in the white" (glazed but unpainted). Depicting a nanny goat suckling her kid, the group is charged with energy and tenderness, and Kändler has invested familiar barnyard animals with aspects of nobility. Large compositions such as this group far exceed the normal capacity of the porcelain medium, as can be seen from the large fissures that developed in the first firing. But in his bold and simple manipulation of the surface, Kändler seems to have anticipated the inevitable firecracks, for they blend with the deep and wavy furrows in the shaggy coat of the nanny goat. A great modeler, he was the first to fully exploit porcelain as a medium for sculpture. *Gift of Mrs. Jean Mauzé, 1962, 62.245*

74 Lalage

German, Nymphenburg, ca. 1758
Hard-paste porcelain; h. 8 in. (20.3 cm.)

Franz Anton Bustelli (1723–63), the modeler of this figure, is best known for his representations of the characters of the commedia dell'arte. In addition to Harlequin and Columbine, Pantaloon and the Doctor, he also conceived models for characters whose names are known only from a single eighteenth-century German engraving. Lalage is one of these and has the dancing grace of pose and manner that characterizes all Bustelli's models. Portrayed here wearing a lozenge-patterned bodice, she represents a variant on the role of Columbine. *The Lesley and Emma Sheafer Collection, Bequest of Emma A. Sheafer, 1974, 1974.356.524*

**75   An Artist and a Scholar Being
Presented to the Chinese Emperor**
German, Höchst, ca. 1770
Hard-paste porcelain; h. 15⅞ in. (40.3 cm.)

This group, modeled by Johann Peter Melchior
(1742–1825), was made at the Höchst factory
about 1770. The exact source of the subject is
unknown, but the piece was probably inspired
by a French engraving, possibly Boucher's
Audience of the Emperor of China or Watteau's

Chinese Emperor. The emperor is backed by a
Rococo structure surmounted by a canopy hung
with bells. A court official presents an artist
wearing a laurel chaplet and a scholar holding
an open scroll. The group, an ambitious blend-
ing of chinoiserie with elements of the Rococo,
was a table centerpiece and would have been
surrounded by attendant figures. *Gift of R.
Thornton Wilson, in memory of Florence Ellsworth Wilson, 1950, 50.211.217*

76   Armorial Jardinière
Chinese, English market, ca. 1692–97
Hard-paste porcelain; diam. 13 in. (33 cm.)

In perfecting blue-and-white porcelain in the
fourteenth century, the Chinese developed one
of the most basic techniques of ceramic decoration: that of painting the designs "underglaze,"
or directly on the porcelain surface. The cobalt
oxide pigment, which is used for the design,
matures to a rich blue during the same firing
that fuses the ingredients of the ware itself.
Underglaze decoration has an agreeable directness and permanence that surface enameling,

however colorful, lacks. The first Chinese
porcelain to reach Europe was blue-and-white,
and it enjoyed instant and lasting favor. Its nov-
elty, economy, and dependability made it by far
the largest group of Chinese export wares made
for the West.

This large bowl belongs to the earliest known
set of armorial wares made for an English
patron. In a panel on one side are the arms of
Sir Henry Johnson, of Aldborough and Blackwall;
on the other sides are peonies and plants
growing by rocks. *Gift of Mr. and Mrs. Rafi Y.
Mottahedeh, 1976, 1976.112*

GLASS

77 Goblet
Venetian, ca. 1475
Glass, enameled and gilt; h. 8½ in. (21.6 cm.)

This goblet is probably from the workshop established in Murano by the Venetian glass-painter Angelo Barovieri (act. 1424–d. 1461). The decoration illustrates a popular Italian story. Vergil, the renowned poet, fell in love with Febilla, the daughter of the emperor of Rome. Enraged when she spurned him, Vergil magically caused all the fires in Rome to go out. The emperor had to agree to the remedy—Febilla was exposed in the marketplace until all the women of Rome had rekindled their fires with tapers lighted from a live coal magically placed in her body.

The decoration is one of the earliest surviving examples of work on a minute scale for enameling and gilding on glass. The composition was probably taken from a contemporary illuminated manuscript of the Venetian school. *Gift of J. Pierpont Morgan, 1917, 17.190.730*

78 FRANS GREENWOOD, Dutch, 1680–1761
Wine Glass
English flint glass; h. 8³⁄₁₆ in. (20.8 cm.)

In stipple engraving a diamond point is driven repeatedly into the glass surface, creating minute craters; very subtle effects are made possible by crowding or spacing the tiny dots. Of all the glass available in the eighteenth century, English flint glass was best able to withstand this process. The blanks Frans Greenwood used display characteristics of Newcastle on Tyne glasses, which were produced by several glasshouses operated there by the Dagnia family.

On this wine glass, which Greenwood engraved in Dordrecht in 1728, the River Meuse is personified as a goddess. The source for the decoration was probably a somewhat earlier Dutch engraving. Practiced by several generations of Dutch glass-engravers, stipple engraving seems to have been unique to Holland until it was revived in this century in England by Laurence Whistler. *Munsey Fund, 1927, 27.185.317*

79 Monteith
English, 1700
English flint glass; h. 6⅝ in. (16.8 cm.), diam. 12¼ in. (31.1 cm.)

Monteiths, filled with ice water, were used to cool wine glasses—the glasses were suspended in the water by their feet, which were placed in the notches of the rim. At the time this piece was made, monteiths were normally made in silver, and this is an unusually large object to be found in glass. It is engraved with the names and arms of William Gibbs and his wife, Mary Nelthorpe, and with inscriptions expressing moral sentiments in Italian, Hebrew, Slavonic, Dutch, French, and Greek. In the main decoration Cupid holds a bride by the hand and sings from a songbook while musicians assembled around a table play the lute, viola, and recorder. The piece was presumably made to mark the betrothal of William Gibbs and Mary Nelthorpe. It

is the Museum's earliest example of English flint glass, which was perfected late in the seventeenth century and immediately became a strong competitor to both Venetian and German clear glass since it had equal strength and greater inner "fire," or luminosity. *Bequest of Florence Ellsworth Wilson, 1943, 43.77.2*

STAINED GLASS

80   Jesus Rebukes the Storm

Belgian, probably Antwerp, ca. 1520–25
*Stained and grisaille-painted glass; h. 20 in.
(50.8 cm.)*

The Gospels of Matthew, Mark, and Luke re-
count that Jesus quelled a storm on the Sea of
Galilee. Mark (4:35–41) tells that Jesus "re-
buked the wind, and said to the sea, 'Peace! Be
still!'" This panel is attributed to Dirk Vellert
(act. 1511–44); he was reputed a great master
in his time, but few of his works in glass survive.
Recent research has identified as Vellert's a
number of medium-sized panels in the Museum
from the great cloister of the Carthusian monastery in Louvain. This glazing was started in about
1509 or 1510 by Louvain glaziers. In about 1517
the commission appears to have been transferred to a workshop in which Vellert was active.
The panel illustrated here shows Vellert's masterful execution of a design that is not in his own
vigorous style but in the static manner of the
original designer, who remains anonymous. *Gift
of Mr. and Mrs. Henry Goldman, 1944, 44.114.1*

IRONWORK

81   Reja from the Cathedral of Valladolid

Spanish, 1763
*Wrought iron, partially gilt, and limestone;
52 × 42 ft. (15.86 × 12.81 m.)*

This reja (choir screen) from the cathedral of
Valladolid, attributed to the Amezúa family of
Elorrio, was erected in 1763 and painted and
gilded in 1764. The decorative motifs—the *pie-
dras y gallones* (which imitate precious gems) in
the uppermost frieze, the small twisted columns
among the bars, and the markedly Rococo
ornamentation—are characteristic of the work
of Rafael and Gaspar Amezúa. There is great
formal clarity in the crestwork of the Valladolid
screen, and even the capricious Rococo scrollwork is clearly silhouetted in space. *Gift of The
William Randolph Hearst Foundation, 1956,
56.234.1*

HOROLOGY

82   Celestial Globe with Clockwork

Austrian, Vienna, 1579
Case: silver, partly gilded, and brass; movement: brass and steel; 10¾ × 8 × 7½ in. (27.3 × 20.3 × 19 cm.)

Described in an early seventeenth-century inventory of the Prague Kunstkammer of the Holy Roman Emperor Rudolf II (1552–1612), this globe houses a movement made by Gerhard Emmoser, imperial clockmaker from 1566 until his death in 1584, who signed and dated the globe's meridian ring. The movement, which has been extensively rebuilt in the course of its existence, rotated the celestial sphere and drove a small image of the sun along the path of the ecliptic. The hour was indicated on a dial mounted at the top of the globe's axis, and the day of the year on a calendar rotating in the instrument's horizon ring. The silver globe, with its exquisitely engraved constellations and its Pegasus support, is the work of an anonymous goldsmith who was probably employed in the imperial workshops in Vienna or possibly in Prague. *Gift of J. Pierpont Morgan, 1917, 17.190.636*

TEXTILES

83   Birth of the Virgin

Italian, last quarter of 15th c.
Silk and metallic threads on canvas; 12¾ × 19½ in. (32.4 × 49.5 cm.)

In the Middle Ages and the Renaissance, embroidery intended for use in a church was often extremely elaborate and sumptuous. Altar frontals and vestments were embellished not only with decorative patterns or heraldic and symbolic motifs but also with figural compositions. Among the latter the most popular subjects were those that allowed for a sequence of events, such as the lives of Christ, Saint John the Baptist, and the Virgin Mary. This panel may

have been part of an altar frontal which included other scenes from the life of the Virgin. The designer's talent and the embroiderer's skill are equally matched in this representation of the Virgin's birth. The believable interior space, which gives way to a glimpse of landscape through the doorway, is enlivened by patterned bedhangings, ceiling, and floor. The embroidery techniques include finely executed *or nué*, in which metallic threads are laid down and then worked over in silk, and split stitch, especially visible in the clothing and hair of the figures. *Gift of Irwin Untermyer, 1964, 64.101.1381*

84   Bookbinding with Representations of King David

English, 17th c.

Silk, silver, and silver-gilt metal threads on canvas; medallions embroidered in silk and metal threads on silk satin; 7 × 4½ in. (17.8 × 11.4 cm.)

The medallion on each cover of this bookbinding depicts King David: on the front he is shown playing his harp, while on the back he is seen with the instrument at his side. These representations have their source in printed book illustrations. Surrounding each medallion is an ornate frame; the remaining spaces of each cover are filled with birds, fruits, and flowers. Five large embroidered flowers decorate the spine. While the design of the medallions is not uncommon, the workmanship of the embroidery is of exceedingly fine quality, and the cover is in excellent condition. The binding encloses three books: *The New Testament* (London, 1633), *The Booke of Common Prayer* (London, 1633), and *The Whole Book of Psalmes* (London, 1636). Later inscriptions attribute ownership of the book to William Laud, archbishop of Canterbury (executed 1643). *Gift of Irwin Untermyer, 1964, 64.101.1294*

85   Coverlet or Bed Curtain

Flemish, Brussels, 1805–1815

Brussels bobbin lace with needlelace details; linen; 88 × 82 in. (223.5 × 208.3 cm.)

In subject and style this panel is an excellent example of the Neoclassicism in vogue in the early years of the nineteenth century. The central scene illustrates a subject very appropriate for lace intended to be used in the decoration of a bed: the myth of the goddess Diana and Endymion, the handsome sleeping shepherd with whom she fell in love. Technically, the lace is extremely intricate. The ground, known as *vrai réseau,* or *droschel,* was made with bobbins and was one of the marvels of the Brussels lace industry. The motifs were worked separately in needlelace and then applied onto the ground. This is a remarkably large piece for so delicate a medium, and its execution would have been enormously expensive because of the time, skill, and fine materials necessary to complete such a tour de force. *Gift of Mrs. Edward S. Harkness, 1944, 44.91.1*

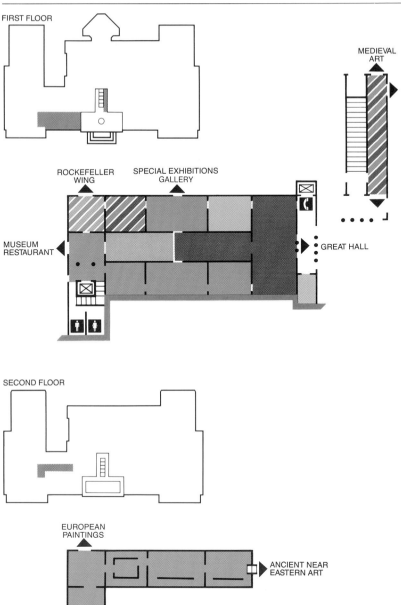

FIRST FLOOR

MEDIEVAL ART

ROCKEFELLER WING

SPECIAL EXHIBITIONS GALLERY

MUSEUM RESTAURANT

GREAT HALL

SECOND FLOOR

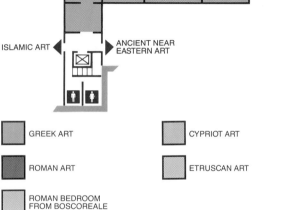

EUROPEAN PAINTINGS

ANCIENT NEAR EASTERN ART

ISLAMIC ART

ANCIENT NEAR EASTERN ART

GREEK ART

CYPRIOT ART

ROMAN ART

ETRUSCAN ART

ROMAN BEDROOM FROM BOSCOREALE

GREEK AND ROMAN ART

The Greek and Roman collections comprise the art of many civilizations and several millennia. The areas represented are Greece and Italy, but not as limited by modern political frontiers: much of Asia Minor on the periphery of Greece was settled by Greeks; Cyprus became increasingly Hellenized in the course of its long history; and Greek colonies sprang up all over the Mediterranean basin and on the shores of the Black Sea. In Roman art the geographical limits coincide with the political expansion of Rome. In addition, the collections illustrate the pre-Greek art of Greece and the pre-Roman art of Italy. The lower chronological limits are imposed by a religious event, the conversion of the emperor Constantine to Christianity in A.D. 337, which did not coincide with the fall of the Roman Empire and which did not bring about an immediate or complete change in art.

Although the Department of Greek and Roman Art was not formally established until 1909, the very first accessioned object in the Museum was a Roman sarcophagus from Tarsus, donated in 1870. Today the strengths of the vast collection include Cypriot sculpture, painted Greek vases, Roman portrait busts, and Roman wall paintings. The department's holdings in glass and silver are among the finest in the world, and the collection of archaic Attic sculpture is second only to that in Athens.

1 Seated Harp-Player

Cycladic, 3rd millennium B.C.
Marble; h. 11½ in. (29.2 cm.)

Little is known of the culture that flourished in
the islands of the Aegean Sea known as the
Cyclades. Artists of the twentieth century, however, have drawn our admiring attention to these
prehistoric masters of simplicity. Although most
Cycladic sculptures are of women, there are also
some of men, and in a few cases the sculptor
has abandoned the traditional pose to show
musicians. This seated harp-player, his head
thrown back in the classic attitude of performing
artists, is executed in astonishing detail despite
the primitive tools at the sculptor's disposal.
Rogers Fund, 1947, 47.100.1

2 Kouros (Statue of a Youth)

Attic, end of 7th c. B.C.
*Marble; h. without plinth 76 in. (193 cm.), h. of
head 12 in. (30.5 cm.)*

This kouros is the earliest Greek marble statue
in the Museum and one of the earliest stone
sculptures in Greek art. It probably stood on the
tomb of a young man, but its stance and expression are shared by cult statues of gods. Contact
with Egypt after the middle of the seventh century B.C. led Greek artists to create monumental
sculptures such as this one. Its blocklike form,
frontal pose, advanced left foot, and clenched
hands can be matched in Egyptian sculpture,
but departures from Egyptian style are equally
evident: the space between the elbows and waist
is cut away, and there is no supporting back
pillar. Anatomical details are still schematized.
Later, however, the body is rendered increasingly
realistically until classic perfection was achieved
in the second half of the fifth century B.C.
Fletcher Fund, 1932, 32.11.1

3 Grave Stele: Youth and Girl
Attic, ca. 540 B.C.
Marble; h. 166¹¹/₁₆ in. (423.3 cm.)

The Museum is rich in archaic grave reliefs made in Attica during the sixth century B.C. The most sumptuous (and most complete) is this stele of a youth and a girl, surmounted by a sphinx as guardian of the tomb. As is customary in archaic reliefs, the figures are shown in profile with the eyes frontal. The carving is relatively flat, but here, and on other stelai in the collection, the background is concave, so that the sculpture looks more rounded. The sphinx, worked separately, is carved in the round. Much of the original color is preserved under incrustation; Greek stone sculpture was never left the dead white favored by classicizing imitators. Paint was used to differentiate hair, nails, eyes, lips, drapery, armor, and other accessories. *Frederick C. Hewitt, Rogers, and Munsey Funds, 1911, 1921, 1936 and 1938; anonymous gift, 1951, 11.185*

4 Kore (Statue of a Girl)
Attic, late 6th c. B.C. (from Paros)
Marble; h. 41½ in. (105.4 cm.)

This statue of a maiden ("kore," in Greek) was found on the island of Paros in the Cyclades sometime before 1860. It was presumably a votive offering like the many korai found on the Acropolis in Athens. The right forearm was worked separately and is lost. The left leg is slightly forward, and the drapery is pulled tight across the thigh by the right hand which, together with most of the arm, is broken off and missing.

Many of the earliest Greek marble statues were made on the islands, and the island schools of Greek sculpture owed much to the excellent quality of the marble that was quarried there from prehistoric times. In style and execution this kore resembles one found on the Acropolis in Athens, which has also been attributed to Cycladic workmanship. *Gift of John Marshall, 1907, 07.306*

5 Wounded Warrior Falling Backward (*Volneratus Deficiens*)

Roman copy of a Greek bronze original of 440–430 B.C. by Kresilas
Marble; total h. 87 in. (221 cm.), h. without plinth 77½ in. (196.9 cm.)

This over-life-size warrior is shown with his right hand raised. A short mantle covers his left shoulder; his left arm is bent and must have carried a shield. His Corinthian helmet is pushed back on his head and his gaze is directed downward.

When first acquired, the statue was identified as Protesilaos, the first Greek to die at Troy. It was later remarked, however, that his right arm is not raised in an attitude of attack and that he is, in fact, wounded under his right armpit and supports himself on a spear. These observations bear out an identification of the statue with the *Volneratus Deficiens* by the renowned Greek sculptor Kresilas. *Frederick C. Hewitt Fund, 1925, 25.116*

6 Wounded Amazon

Roman copy of a Greek original of ca. 430 B.C.
Marble; h. including plinth 80¼ in. (203.8 cm.)

The Roman writer Pliny tells the story of the four sculptors (Polykleitos, Phidias, Kresilas, and Phradmon) who in a competition made statues of Amazons for the temple of Artemis at Ephesus. In the vote for the best, each artist put himself first, but Phidias, Kresilas, and Phradmon gave second place to Polykleitos, who thus won the prize. Although this anecdote may be apocryphal, Roman copies of three different types of Amazons are known, all after Greek originals. This statue is a copy after the one thought to be by Kresilas. The Amazon is wounded in her right breast where blood flows from a gash, yet her pose and expression reveal neither pain nor suffering. She embodies the classic ideal and represents an evolution of almost two hundred years from the earliest archaic marbles. *Gift of John D. Rockefeller, Jr., 1932, 32.11.4*

7 Grave Stele: Woman and Attendant

Attic, about 400 B.C.
Marble; h. as preserved 70¹/₁₆ in. (178 cm.), h. as restored 74 in. (188 cm.), w. 29¹³/₁₆ in. (75.8 cm.)

The dead woman is portrayed leaning against the pilaster of the architectural frame. With her right hand she fingers her mantle. A girl, perhaps a servant, approaches with a casket, perhaps her jewelry box. As often on Greek grave reliefs, the gaze of the two women does not meet, and the dead person is shown in a somewhat larger scale. The upper left corner of the relief is missing, but as the right acroterion is preserved, the restoration is certain. *Fletcher Fund, 1936, 36.11.1*

8 Old Market Woman

Greek, perhaps an original of the 2nd c. B.C.
Pentelic marble, restorations in plaster on face and breast; h. including base 49⁵/₈ in. (126 cm.)

The Hellenistic period spanned the three centuries between the death of Alexander the Great (323 B.C.) and the Battle of Actium (31 B.C.), which marked the beginning of the Roman Empire. In art the most creative centers were no longer on the Greek mainland but abroad, in Pergamon and Alexandria and on the island of Rhodes. Hellenistic art did not, of course, break with the past, but the conquest of the East brought with it a widening of horizons. Artists looked for new subjects and discovered *genre*, an excellent example of which is this realistic study of an old, tired woman going to market with her basket of fruits and vegetables and chickens. *Rogers Fund, 1909, 09.39*

9 Portrait of a Man

Roman, first quarter of 1st c. A.D.
Marble; h. 17½ in. (44.5 cm.)

Roman art is best represented in the collection by portrait sculpture, sarcophagi, wall paintings, and glass. Portraiture of the republican period in general relies upon the traditions of Etruscan and Italic funerary sculpture and is accordingly characterized by graphic realism. During the early imperial period a tendency toward more idealized likenesses becomes evident, drawing in part from Hellenistic portraiture. This striking portrait of a man is a transitional work, which reflects a persistent attention to realistic details. The sitter's unwrinkled face and the large size of the bust are, however, features of portraiture from the reigns of Augustus and his successor, Tiberius. *Fletcher Fund, 1926, 26.60.3*

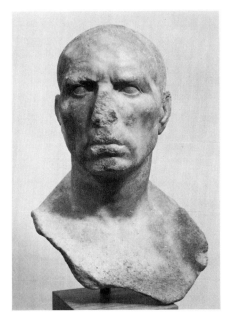

11 The Badminton Sarcophagus

Roman, A.D. 260–265
Greek marble; greatest h. 35 in. (88.9 cm.), greatest l. 87¾ in. (222.9 cm.)

Sarcophagi, literally "flesh eaters," were used for burial throughout antiquity. This one, in the shape of a tub, shows Dionysos and his followers. The young god is seated on a tiger; around him are satyrs and maenads and the horned god Pan. Four winged youths, in the front plane and in a larger scale, represent the seasons. They remind the viewer that time no longer touches the heroized dead, who now participate in the eternal feast, symbolized here by the Dionysiac festival. The relief uses classical tradition in many details, but the indications of space and scale and the relationships among the figures do not attempt to reflect reality. This masterpiece is representative of the end of classical antiquity and is a prelude to a sculptural tradition involving even greater abstraction.

The sarcophagus was brought from Italy to the collection of the duke of Beaufort at Badminton House in Gloucestershire in 1728. *Purchase, Joseph Pulitzer Bequest, 1955, 55.11.5*

10 Portrait Statue of a Roman Prince, probably Lucius Caesar

Roman, late 1st c. B.C. (said to be from Rhodes)
Bronze; h. 48½ in. (123.2 cm.)

The mixed nature of adolescence is neatly presented in this portrait: the subject has the body of a boy and the demeanor of a self-possessed young man. His hands are empty but probably once held objects connected with a religious ceremony. The richly decorated pallium he wears is a mark of wealth, and his features strongly suggest that he is a relative of the emperor Augustus. The most likely candidate is Lucius Caesar (17 B.C.–A.D. 2), the younger of the emperor's grandsons.

Augustan portraiture in general tempers the stark realism favored in preceding decades with graceful, classicizing modeling but, as this portrait attests, not at the expense of vivid characterization. *Rogers Fund, 1914, 14.130.1*

12 Portrait Statue of the Emperor Caius Vibius Trebonianus Gallus
Roman, A.D. 251–253
Bronze; h. 95 in. (240.6 cm.)

Much of the third century was a time of great uncertainty for the Roman Empire. This unrest is nowhere more evident than in portraits of the period. The frowns and furrowed brows of third-century rulers seem to reflect a fear of assassination as well as worry over problems of state: from 235 to 284 there were almost as many emperors as had ruled the empire in its first two and a half centuries, and many of them were killed in action or by their own troops. It is no wonder, then, that Trebonianus Gallus seeks to impress us with his renowned size and strength.

This statue recalls early imperial classicism through the use of heroic nudity and a pose then favored for commemorative statues of emperors. The allusion fails utterly, but there is poignancy in this backward glance at better times. *Rogers Fund, 1905, 05.30*

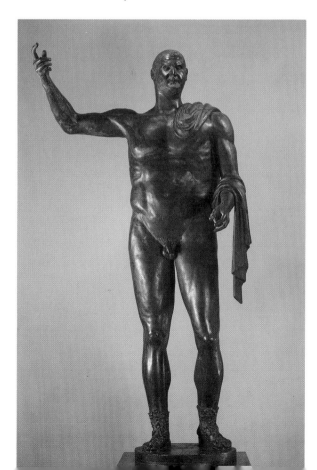

13 Colossal Head of Constantine
Roman, ca. A.D. 325
Marble; h. 37½ in. (95.3 cm.)

In the late third century A.D., Roman portrait sculpture tended to become less naturalistic and more geometric or blocklike in structure. In this head of Constantine this development is evident in the lines of the jaw, chin, and forehead and in the regular and symmetrical crown of hair. The upward gaze of the eyes with their transcendental seriousness is also characteristic of Roman portraiture of the third and fourth centuries A.D.

The head, which was once part of a colossal statue, probably showing the emperor seated, was known as early as the seventeenth century, when it was in the Giustiniani collection in Rome. The nose, lips, and chin and parts of the ears are restored. *Bequest of Mary Clark Thompson, 1926, 26.229*

14 Sarcophagus with Lid
Greek, Cypriot, 5th c. B.C. (from Amathus)
Limestone; l. 93⅛ in. (236.5 cm.)

From earliest times the art of Cyprus has reflected the island's position as a crossroads between East and West. This sarcophagus is Greek in form, in architectural ornament, and in details like the sphinxes at each end of the lid. Oriental are the "Bes" and "Astarte" figures decorating the short sides, the parasols in the chariot procession, and the horses' harnesses and other trappings. Made of the typical local limestone, the sarcophagus preserves an unusually large amount of added color. *The Cesnola Collection, Purchased by Subscription, 1874–1876, 74.51.2453*

15 Centauromachy, perhaps Herakles and Nessos

Greek, 8th c. B.C. (said to be from Olympia)
Bronze; h. of man 4⁷/₁₆ in. (11.3 cm.), h. of centaur 3⁷/₈ in. (9.9 cm.)

In this small bronze group, cast in one piece, a man confronts a centaur. Their feet are close together and they stand bolt upright: the action is limited to the arms that are locked in a wrestling pose. Clearly the man is a hero: he may be Herakles, but the absence of attributes makes a precise identification hazardous. The workmanship is Peloponnesian, and the group is said to have been found at Olympia, the great Greek sanctuary that has yielded so many bronze votive offerings. *Gift of J. Pierpont Morgan, 1917, 17.190.2072*

16 Head of a Griffin

Greek, mid-7th c. B.C. (found at Olympia)
Bronze; h. 10¹/₈ in. (25.8 cm.)

A feature characteristic of utilitarian objects made by the Greeks, whether in metal or clay, is the high quality of the workmanship and the often masterful decoration. This head of a griffin probably served originally as one of several attachments on a deep caldron. It was cast in the lost-wax technique and would have been attached to a neck made by hammering; the eyes would have been inlaid. Like the sphinx and other hybrid creatures, the griffin came to Greece from the East. It was particularly popular during the seventh and sixth centuries B.C., and as a protome it is one of the most typical types of vessel attachment. In its size, design, and execution, however, this example is exceptional. *Bequest of Walter C. Baker, 1971, 1972.118.54*

17 Herakles

Greek, late 6th c. B.C. (said to have been found in Arcadia)
Bronze; h. 5 in. (12.6 cm.)

This very sturdy Herakles is shown brandishing a short club. He stands with legs far apart, and the entire body is dominated by his well-developed muscles. As usual in Greek art, Herakles wears his hair short. Herakles was worshiped like a god, and many statuettes of him were dedicated as votive offerings. *Fletcher Fund, 1928, 28.77*

18   Athena Flying Her Owl
Greek, ca. 460 B.C.
Bronze; h. with owl 5¹⁵/₁₆ in. (15 cm.)

Athena, the patron goddess of Athens, could be considered present rather than remote, human rather than perfect and immortal. The combination of dignity and informality gives this small bronze its particular character. The goddess wears only a peplos that reveals the body beneath; her helmet has been pushed back in a moment of ease; she held a spear in her left hand, but with her right she is about to let fly an owlet, the bird sacred to her. While possibly influenced by a monumental statue, the artist has achieved great freshness and great sympathy for the patroness of the city and of craftsmen. *Harris Brisbane Dick Fund, 1950, 50.11.1*

19   Mirror Supported by a Woman Holding a Bird
Greek, 5th c. B.C.
Bronze; h. 15¹⁵/₁₆ in. (40.4 cm.)

Greek artists incorporated the human form into utilitarian objects of all kinds. This mirror is an example of exceptional quality. Made for the toilette of a lady of means, it shows a woman draped softly in a peplos, holding a pet bird. She serves as the support and handle for the mirror. *Bequest of Walter C. Baker, 1971, 1972.118.78*

20   Hermes
Late Hellenistic—early Roman, 1st c. B.C.–1st c. A.D.
Bronze; h. 11⁷/₁₆ in. (29.1 cm.)

By the end of the fourth century B.C. Greek statues had attained the stance and proportions that we call classic, and the idealized renderings of gods and goddesses, athletes and heroes, continued to be admired and copied for many centuries. The perfect proportions of this Hermes are echoed in other portrayals of the god. Especially well preserved, this large statuette counts among the finest of its period. *Rogers Fund, 1971, 1971.11.11*

21   Veiled and Masked Dancer
Greek, 3rd c. B.C.
Bronze; h. 8¹/₁₆ in. (20.5 cm.)

An innovation of Greek art in the fourth and third centuries B.C. was the characterization of specific subjects, which led to the development of such genres as portraiture and caricature. This bronze is remarkable in that its effect depends not on physical features of the figure but exclusively on the pose and on the treatment of the drapery. While the type of a long-robed dancer became established during the fourth century B.C., especially in terracottas, no surviving example can match the way folds are composed and articulated over the body of this figure, which is known as the "Baker dancer." *Bequest of Walter C. Baker, 1971, 1972.118.95*

22   Portrait Bust of a Child
Roman, first half of 1st c. A.D.
Bronze; h. 11½ in. (29.2 cm.)

Likenesses of children were not uncommon in the Roman imperial period, but they are usually made of marble or of less expensive materials. A portrait of one so young as this boy in a material so costly as bronze is highly unusual and indicates that he was especially wellborn. It has been argued that the sitter is Nero as a boy of five or six. The bust resembles other images of the future emperor at an early age, and the style of the work accords well with portraits from the 40s A.D. It is nonetheless difficult to identify portraits of children, particularly when there are so many who share the family traits of the Julio-Claudian house.

The bust was originally mounted on a hermlike base, probably of marble. *Purchase, Funds from various donors, 1966, 66.11.5*

25 Stirrup Jar
Mycenaean, 12th c. B.C.
Terracotta, h. 10¼ in. (26 cm.)

At the end of the Bronze Age, during the so-called Mycenaean period (ca. 1600–1100 B.C.), Greek influence in the Mediterranean extended from the Levant to Italy. The chief vehicle of this influence was trade, as ships sailed along the coast or from island to island bartering their products. One of the most characteristic types of Mycenaean vase, probably used for transporting and storing liquids like wine or oil, was the stirrup jar, named after the form of the handle at top. The marine decoration on this jar, featuring an octopus, is both typical and significant, for the sea was the ancient Greeks' chief source of livelihood. *Purchase, Louisa Eldridge McBurney Gift, 1953, 53.11.6*

24 Centaur
Etruscan or Campanian, 7th c. B.C.
Bronze; l. 5 ⅝ in. (14.3 cm.), h. 4½ in. (11.3 cm.)

In its raised arms this galloping centaur wielded an uprooted tree (now broken off and lost). As it is cast with a curving plinth, the statuette must have been soldered to the rim or shoulder of a bronze caldron, probably accompanied by other centaurs in similar poses. The elongated face and the treatment of the body (both the equine and the human parts) are typical of Etruscan sculptural tradition. *Gift of J. Pierpont Morgan, 1917, 17.190.2070*

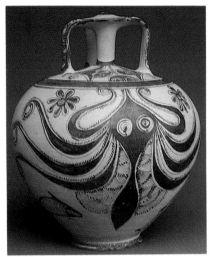

23 Chariot

Etruscan, late 6th c. B.C.
Bronze, h. 51½ in. (130.8 cm.)

Though familiar to us from representations of all kinds in ancient art, very few actual chariots survive because by the sixth century they were no longer used in warfare; the scenes in which they appear refer to an earlier mythological period. This chariot, found in a tomb in Monteleone, Italy, probably was made as a funerary offering. The richness and quality of the decoration, however, are exceptional. The pole issues from the head of a boar and ends in the head of a beaked bird. The axles and the yoke terminate in feline heads. The principal subjects on the three parts of the chariot box refer to the life of a hero, probably Achilles. In the center he receives armor from his mother, Thetis; on one side he engages in combat with another hero, possibly Memnon; on the other side he (or perhaps his apotheosis) appears in a chariot drawn by winged horses. While the style and subject depend on Greek sources, the interpretation is thoroughly Etruscan. *Rogers Fund, 1903, 03.23.1*

26 Sepulchral Vase

Attic, second half of 7th c. B.C.
Terracotta; h. 42⅝ in. (108.3 cm.)

This impressive vase was a funerary monument, the construction of the interior allowing for offerings to be poured to the deceased. The primary scene shows the deceased flanked by his household and mourners. The zone below, with warriors and chariots, suggests the dead man's chief pursuits in his lifetime. Because of the schematic rendering of the figures and the character of the ornament, this style of early Greek painting is called "geometric." *Rogers Fund, 1914, 14.130.14*

28 Trefoil Oinochoe (Wine Jug)

Corinthian, ca. 625 B.C.
Terracotta; h. 10¼ in. (26 cm.)

Some of the finest vases in the seventh century B.C. were made and painted in Corinth. The black-figure technique, which was invented there, enlivened the black silhouettes of figures by incised lines and added colors. This oinochoe is remarkably articulated. The animals and monsters are confined to a narrow zone in the middle of the vase. The sloping shoulder is given over to a scale pattern, and rosettes are painted in white on the neck and the mouth. The painter was obviously concerned with the overall appearance of the vase and the proper balance of dark and light areas. *Bequest of Walter C. Baker, 1971, 1972.118.138*

27 Black-Figured Amphora: Combat Between Herakles and the Centaur Nessos

Attic, second quarter of 7th c. B.C.
Terracotta; h. 42¾ in. (108.6 cm.)

The chief picture on this very large funerary vase depicts the combat between Herakles and the centaur Nessos. Herakles has seized the centaur by his hair and holds his sword at the ready. The centaur has let go of his weapon, a tree trunk, and sinks to his knees, pleading for mercy. The chariot of Herakles stands by. On the shoulder two horses graze peacefully, and on the neck a panther attacks a deer. As often in early archaic art, ornaments fill the background. They also frame the narrative frieze above and below and come into their own on the back of the vase, which is devoid of figures. *Rogers Fund, 1911, 11.210.1*

29 Kylix (Wine Cup)

Laconian, ca. 550 B.C. (found at Sardis)
Terracotta; h. 5 in. (12.7 cm.), diam. 7⅜ in. (18.8 cm.)

Laconian pottery was at its prime in the sixth century B.C. and was widely exported. This drinking cup was found in a tomb at Sardis, the capital of Lydia, together with Attic and Lydian vases; it is attributed to the manner of the Arkesilas Painter. The offset rim of the vase is decorated both on the inside and on the outside with ornaments, as are the outside of the bowl and the upper part of the stem. The figured decoration is limited to the tondo that displays a majestic sphinx. *Gift of the Subscribers to the Fund for Excavations at Sardis, 1914, 14.30.26*

30 Cosmetic Vase
East Greek, late 7th c. B.C.
Terracotta; h. 3⅞ in. (9.8 cm.)

This vase is an extraordinarily fine example of the unusual shapes and elaborate decoration that occur in Greek pottery of the late seventh and sixth centuries B.C. It is in the form of a recumbent ram with the head and neck worked separately and perforated, probably to hold an applicator. The main scene on the body shows a youth, who holds two winged horses, and two youths in a chariot. The other zones contain birds and animals, and the remaining free space is filled with geometric ornament. In the lively figures, varied color, and painstaking execution, the piece vies with the best early archaic miniature styles of Corinth or Athens. *Classical Purchase Fund, 1977, 1977.11.3*

31 NIKIAS (potter), Attic, mid-6th c. B.C.
Black-Figured Panathenaic Prize Amphora: Athena Polias
Terracotta; h. as restored (the foot is modern) 24⁵⁄₁₆ in. (61.8 cm.)

The composition on the obverse (illustrated here) is traditional in that it shows the statue of Athena Polias; the reverse shows three men sprinting. The amphora is inscribed: FROM THE PRIZES AT ATHENS and STADION RACE OF MEN. (The stadion was a race of nearly two hundred yards.)

Panathenaic vases were first created in the second quarter of the sixth century B.C. and continued well into Roman times. This amphora is among the earliest of those dated between 566 and 550 B.C., a period of some experimentation. The ornaments on neck and shoulder and the placement of the official prize inscription did not become established until the last quarter of the sixth century; in the early group no two amphorae are alike in these details. The prize vases were filled with oil from the sacred olive grove; each amphora holds one metretes (39.312 liters), which dictated a fairly uniform height. The presence of a potter's signature is rare, but not unique, though the potter Nikias is not known from any other vase. *Classical Purchase Fund, 1978, 1978.11.13*

32 LYDOS (painter), Attic, ca. 550 B.C.
Black-Figured Krater: The Return of Hephaistos
Terracotta; h. 22 in. (55.9 cm.)

This mixing bowl of impressive proportions offered the artist a broad surface to depict Hephaistos being escorted to Mount Olympus by Dionysos and his retinue of satyrs and maenads. Lydos conveys the exuberance of the procession so vividly that one can almost hear it.

The black-figure technique of vase painting, invented in Corinth, was perfected in Attica, and by the mid-sixth century B.C. Attic vases began to eclipse those made in other centers. Distinct styles emerged, and the development of individual artists can be observed. Some names of vase painters are known from their signatures; others remain anonymous and have been given names of convenience. Among the painters of Attic black-figured vases of the sixth century, Kleitias, Lydos, the Amasis Painter, and Exekias can be singled out as leaders, and all four are represented in the Museum. *Fletcher Fund, 1931, 31.11.11*

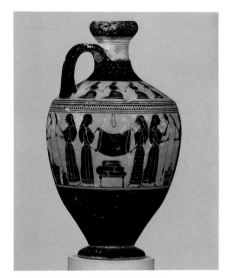

33 Lekythos (Oil Jug)
Attic, ca. 550 B.C. (said to be from Vari)
Terracotta; h. 6¾ in. (17.1 cm.)

Lekythoi were used for oil and are often found in tombs. This lekythos is attributed to the Amasis Painter. It may have been the property of a woman, as it shows several women and girls working wool—from spinning and carding to weaving and folding the finished cloth. On the shoulder girls dance on either side of a seated woman or goddess flanked by two standing youths.

Another lekythos by the Amasis Painter was acquired by the Museum in 1956. It is not only very close in shape, size, style, period, and scheme of decoration but also shares with this one the dancing girls on the shoulder. There the chief subject is a wedding procession, and it is tempting to think that the two vases were made for the same lady. *Fletcher Fund, 1931, 31.11.10*

34 EXEKIAS (painter), Attic, ca. 540 B.C.
Black-Figured Neck-amphora with Lid: On Each Side, Wedding Procession in a Chariot
Terracotta; h. 18½ in. (47 cm.)

Exekias is one of the greatest Attic black-figure vase-painters, and this neck-amphora, or storage jar for wine or oil, is one of his finest works. A wedded pair in a chariot is greeted by a woman (or a goddess), while a youth, perhaps Apollo, plays the kithara: the procession is about to start, led by the boy in front of the horses. The subject on the reverse is similar but without the boy; the kithara player is replaced by an old man or king. *Rogers Fund, 1917, and Gift of J. D. Beazley, 1927, 17.230.14*

35 ANDOKIDES PAINTER, Attic, ca. 530 B.C.
Red-Figured Amphora: Herakles and Apollo in the Struggle over the Delphic Tripod
Terracotta; h. 22⅝ in. (57.5 cm.)

Shortly after 530 B.C. the black silhouettes of the black-figured technique are replaced by figures left the color of the clay which on firing turns orange-red. These figures are set against a black background. Details are painted in glaze lines, and the added opaque colors, white and purple, are used only sparingly. The new technique appears first on vases by an anonymous painter called the Andokides Painter, since some of his works, like this amphora, are signed by Andokides as potter.

The struggle for the Delphic tripod also occurs on the pediment of the Siphnian treasury at Delphi with which many of the vases by the Andokides Painter are connected stylistically. As the dates of the Siphnian treasury are known approximately (ca. 530–525 B.C.), we thus have a reasonably accurate date for the beginning of Attic red-figure. *Purchase, Joseph Pulitzer Bequest, 1963, 63.11.6*

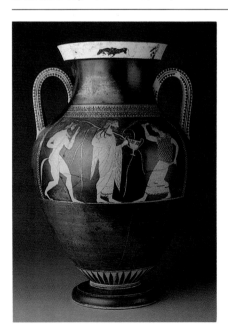

36 EPIKTETOS (painter), Attic,
ca. 520–510 B.C.
Red-Figured Plate: Boy on a Rooster
Terracotta; diam. 7⅜ in. (18.7 cm.)

This plate, signed by Epiktetos as painter, shows
the rare subject of a boy perched on a rooster,
his toes braced against the framing line, reserved in red, of the tondo border. It was found
in Vulci on the property of Lucien Bonaparte,
prince of Canino, in 1828, and twenty years later
passed into the collection of the second marquess of Northampton at Castle Ashby, where it
remained until 1980. The plates by Epiktetos
are all by the same potter and differ from other
contemporary plates in that they are not equipped
with two holes on the rim for suspension. Nine
complete plates by Epiktetos are known (of
which two are now lost), as are fragments of
three others. *Purchase, Classical Purchase
Fund, Schimmel Foundation Inc. and Christos
G. Bastis Gifts, 1981, 1981.11.10*

37 EUPHRONIOS (painter),
EUXITHEOS (potter), Attic, ca. 515 B.C.
**Red-Figured Calyx-krater: Sleep and Death
Lifting the Body of Sarpedon**
Terracotta; h. 18 in. (45.7 cm.)

If the amphora by the Andokides Painter (no.
35) may count as the earliest vase in the red-
figure technique, this krater signed by Euxitheos
as potter and by Euphronios as painter demonstrates how in less than half a generation the
new technique had been explored and mastered.
Diluting the black glaze introduces new subtleties:
the hair of Sarpedon is reddish-brown, lighter
than the hair and beard of Sleep (on the left).
Muscles and tendons can now be faithfully

rendered, and foreshortenings pave the way to
an understanding of corporeal perspective. This
krater is a masterpiece of composition, in full
harmony with the requirements of the shape, in
its movement of heads, arms, and legs, framed
by the two guards that flank the scene. The
alternation of black and red is carefully balanced and extends even to the pattern work on
the rim and to the area below the picture frieze.
All the figures are inscribed, their names painted
in added red, as are the artists' signatures.
*Purchase, Bequest of Joseph H. Durkee, Gift
of Darius Ogden Mills and Gift of C. Ruxton
Love, by exchange, 1972, 1972.11.10*

38 EUTHYMIDES (potter), Attic, ca. 510 B.C.
**Red-Figured Oinochoe (Wine Jug): The
Judgment of Paris**
Terracotta; h. as preserved 6⁷/₁₆ in. (16.3 cm.)

Here, as often in archaic art, Paris is shown running away in an effort to avoid judging which of
three goddesses—Hera, Athena, and Aphrodite
—is the most beautiful. Hermes restrains the
Trojan prince by seizing his lyre and is followed
by the three goddesses. Behind them Iris approaches, together with a seventh figure, Peitho,
who rushes up. Though there are many gaps
(only the heads of Athena, Aphrodite, and Iris
are fully preserved), the drawing is extremely
skillful, with great emphasis on the rich garments and on subtle variations in stance and
gesture. Euthymides, whose name appears as
the incised potter's signature on the foot, is
otherwise known only as the friendly rival of
Euphronios (no. 37). *Purchase, Leon Levy Gift
and Classical Purchase Fund, 1981, 1981.11.9*

39 BERLIN PAINTER, Attic, ca. 490 B.C.
**Red-Figured Amphora: Youth Singing and
Playing the Kithara**
Terracotta; h. 16³/₈ in. (41.6 cm.)

In the days of Euphronios (no. 37), it was
discovered that single figures gain much by not
being framed but by letting the black background merge with the black of the body of the
vase itself. This youthful citharoedus thus appears spotlighted against a darkened stage
formed by the entire vase. The swaying figure of
a young performer is the most impressive picture of ancient music that has come down to us
and makes us regret the more that Greek
music, like Greek painting, has been almost
completely lost. *Fletcher Fund, 1956, 56.171.38*

41 PENTHESILEA PAINTER, Attic, ca. 465–460 B.C.
Pyxis (Cosmetic Box) with Lid: The Judgment of Paris
Terracotta; h. with cover 6¾ in. (17.1 cm.)

The drawing on this pyxis is contemporary with the beginning of mural painting in Athens. Covering part of the vase with a white slip had been an Attic innovation half a century earlier, but polychromy (within the range of the ceramic colors) had not previously been attempted. Thus most conventional vase paintings resemble colored drawings, and it is almost impossible to speak of brushwork. Here, however, in such details as the rock on which Paris sits, outline drawing gives way to an imaginative rendering done exclusively with the brush. Some time-honored conventions, however, are retained, such as the common groundline and the avoidance of overlap in the composition. *Rogers Fund, 1907, 07.286.36*

40 Volute-krater (Bowl for Mixing Wine and Water)
Attic, ca. 450 B.C.
Terracotta; h. 25 in. (63.5 cm.)

The principal scenes on this volute-krater are the battle of Greeks and Centaurs at the wedding of Perithous (on the neck of the obverse) and the battle of Athenians and Amazons (on the body). Both subjects appear to reflect the great artistic creations of the middle of the fifth century: the sculptures of the west pediment of the temple of Zeus at Olympia and the wall paintings by Mikon in the Theseion and in the Painted Porch at Athens. The wall paintings are totally lost, but a score of contemporary Attic vases, unusually ambitious in their compositions if not always exceptionally well drawn, help us to visualize Mikon's great paintings. This volute-krater is attributed to the Painter of the Woolly Satyrs. *Rogers Fund, 1907, 07.286.84*

42 Column-krater (Bowl for Mixing Wine and Water): The Painting of a Marble Statue
Early Apulian, first quarter of 4th c. B.C.
Terracotta; h. 20¼ in. (51.5 cm.)

That Greek marble statues were not left as white as plaster casts but were tinted or painted is well known from ancient authors and from surviving sculptures, chiefly of the archaic period. This South Italian vase is unique in that it illustrates exactly how the paint was applied in what is called the encaustic technique. A statue of Herakles is about to be painted, and we observe the artist applying his emulsion of pigment and wax to the surface of the lion skin. After application, the painted surface was gone over with a red-hot iron so that the melted paint penetrated the stone. To the left of the statue an assistant or slave is heating several such rods in a charcoal brazier. Unbeknown to the artist who applies the finishing touches, Herakles himself approaches with an expression of critical curiosity. Zeus and Nike, seated above, complete the scene. *Rogers Fund, 1950, 50.11.4*

43 Woman Playing the Kithara

Roman, Boscoreale, 40–30 B.C.
Wall painting; 73½ × 73½ in. (186.7 × 186.7 cm.)

This painted panel, together with those exhibited beside it, comes from a villa near the town of Boscoreale. The figures painted on this section of the wall are a woman seated on a throne and a little girl standing beside her. The identities of these figures and those on the other panels from the villa's largest room have long been the subject of debate. They may be associated with Aphrodite and Adonis but are more likely members of the Macedonian royal family from the third century B.C. (See also no. 44.) *Purchase, 1903, 03.14.5*

detail

44 Cubiculum from Boscoreale

Roman, 40–30 B.C.

The Museum possesses the greatest assembly of Roman paintings to be seen outside Italy. One set includes most of the paintings from a villa at Boscoreale, about a mile north of Pompeii. Like Pompeii, the villa was buried by the eruption of Mount Vesuvius in A.D. 79, and it is for this reason that the paintings survived relatively intact. Among the paintings from Boscoreale is this complete bedroom decorated with rustic scenes and with complex architectural vistas that recall stage settings. (See also no. 43.) *Rogers Fund, 1903, 03.14.13*

45 Brooch with Tassels

East Greek, late 6th c. B.C.

Gold with glass beads; h. 2⅛ in.(5.5 cm.), l. of hippocamp 1¼ in. (3.3 cm.)

This tasseled gold brooch is part of a large group of East Greek works in gold and silver. A hippocamp (sea horse) in high relief is shown in profile, and three tassels, each composed of three strands of plaited gold chains, are suspended from its lower edge. The tassels, in turn, are equipped with pendants that terminate in glass beads. While no exact parallels for such hippocamp brooches are known, there is one in the form of a hawk in Berlin. *Purchase, Mr. and Mrs. Jan Mitchell Gift, 1966, 66.11.33*

46 The Ganymede Jewelry

Greek, late 4th c. B.C. (said to have been found in a tomb near Salonica)

Four gold fibulae: h. 1⁹/₁₆ in. (4 cm.); pair of gold earrings: h. 2⁵/₃₂ in. (5.5 cm.); pair of rock crystal bracelets with gold ram's-head finials: h. 3¹/₃₂ in. (7.7 cm.); gold ring with emerald: h. ⅞ in. (2.2 cm.); gold necklace: l.13 in. (33 cm.)

This very rich parure, presumably that of a woman, was found together in Macedonia sometime before 1913. These objects are among the finest pieces of Macedonian jewelry known. The pair of gold earrings belongs to a very small class of superbly crafted examples that have sculptural pendants. Although both show Zeus, in the guise of an eagle, carrying off Ganymede, the earrings are not identical. In one the head of Ganymede is turned to the left; in the other it is turned to the right. The upper part of each earring, hiding the loop, is decorated with acanthus palmettes. Equally rare is the pair of rock crystal bracelets, which terminate with gold finials of ram's heads with much detailed ornamentation on the cuffs. The rock crystal is grooved spirally, with a fine gold wire running along the groove. *Dick Fund, 1937, 37.11.8–17*

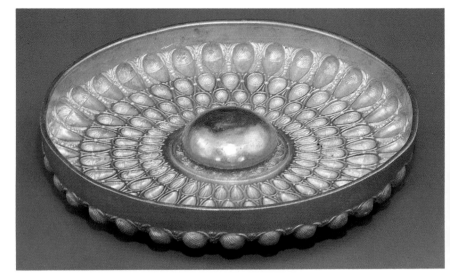

47 Phiale (Libation Bowl)
Greek, 4th c. B.C.
Gold; diam. 9¼ in. (23.5 cm.), h. 1⅜ in. (3.6 cm.)

Libations were one of the most common religious rituals, and many contemporary representations of these ceremonies are preserved (on painted vases, for example). The offering was poured from a phiale, a special type of shallow bowl that fits comfortably into the palm of the hand and has a hollow in the center for the fingers. Such bowls are known mainly from examples in clay, bronze, and silver, and this is one of only five Greek phialai of gold. It is decorated with three concentric rows of acorns and one of beechnuts; in the interstices appear bees and highly stylized filling motifs. It is of Greek workmanship but, interestingly, has incised on the underside a weight inscription in Carthaginian letters. One can imagine its being the prized possession of a Carthaginian living in or trading with a Greek community. *Rogers Fund, 1962, 62.11.1*

48 Scaraboid Gem: Archer Crouching, Testing His Arrow
Greek, late archaic period, ca. 500 B.C.
Chalcedony; ²¹⁄₃₂ × ⁹⁄₁₆ × ⁹⁄₃₂ in. (1.6 × 1.4 × 0.7 cm.)

This gem shows in masterly fashion the accomplishment of late archaic Greek art. The anatomy is fully understood and rendered correctly in spite of the difficult foreshortening. On the evidence offered by another chalcedony scaraboid in Boston, signed by Epimenes, this archer gem has been attributed to the same master, who was an Ionian, as the letter forms and the trappings on the horse of the Boston gem indicate. *Fletcher Fund, 1931, 31.11.5*

49 Head of a Sphinx

Corinthian, ca. 500 B.C.
Terracotta; h. 8⅛ in. (20.6 cm.)

Most terracotta sculptures of the archaic and classic periods that are known today are either architectural adjuncts like antefixes, revetments, and metopes or small votive figurines of animals and human beings found in sanctuaries and graves. That the Greeks, however, were equally good at making freestanding life-size terracotta statues has only recently become known thanks to excavations, especially in Corinth and at Olympia. This very fine female head is a Corinthian work as can be ascertained by the clay. It is slightly under life-size, but not out of scale when we think of it as a head of a sphinx that was shown seated. This would also explain the very pronounced angle at which the hair falls in back in a compact mass, without indication of locks or tresses. *Rogers Fund, 1947, 47.100.3*

50 Silver Treasure

Hellenistic, first quarter of 4th c. B.C.
Two deep bowls, three drinking cups with emblemata, a skyphos, a hemispherical bowl, an oinochoe, a phiale, a ladle, a small portable altar, a pyxis, an emblema, and two horns (perhaps from a helmet)

This rich treasure, acquired in two lots, should on the analogy of the famous Rothschild treasure be attributed to a Tarentine workshop of the early Hellenistic period. There is much gilding, and the stylistic unity of the objects is proved by the various figural adjuncts. The three theatrical masks that serve as feet of the two deep bowls (probably wine coolers) are echoed in the mask below the handle of the small oinochoe, and the ornaments of the drinking cups recur on the small altar. Perhaps the finest object in this hoard is the parcel gilt relief of the sea monster Scylla, who raises her arms to throw an enormous boulder at an unsuspecting seafarer. Of her three canine adjuncts that leap from her hips, two are feeding on an octopus and a fish, while the third is eyeing a dolphin. The altar, which bears a dedication "to the eight gods," is equipped with interchangeable containers for incense and other offerings. *Purchase, Classical Purchase and Rogers Funds, and Anonymous, Christos G. Bastis, Jerome Levy Foundation, Norbert Schimmel, Mrs. Vincent Astor, Mr. and Mrs. Martin Fried, Mr. and Mrs. Thomas A. Spears, Walter Bareiss and Mr. and Mrs. Howard J. Barnet Gifts, 1981, 1982, and 1983. 1981.11.15–22 and 1982.11.7–13*

SECOND FLOOR

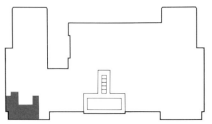

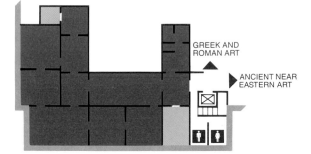

GREEK AND
ROMAN ART

ANCIENT NEAR
EASTERN ART

ISLAMIC ART

SYRIAN PERIOD ROOM
FROM DAMASCUS

THE HAGOP KEVORKIAN FUND
SPECIAL EXHIBITIONS GALLERY

ISLAMIC ART

Islam, the religion founded by Muhammad in A.D. 622, spread in succeeding generations from Mecca in Arabia to Spain in the west and to India and Southeast Asia in the east. The Museum's collection of Islamic art, which dates primarily from the seventh to the nineteenth century, reflects the diversity and range of Islamic culture. In 1891 the Museum received its first major group of Islamic objects, a bequest of Edward C. Moore. Since then the collection has grown through gifts, bequests, and purchases; it has also received important artifacts from the Museum-sponsored excavations at Nishapur, Iran, in 1935–39 and 1947. The Museum now offers perhaps the most comprehensive exhibition of Islamic art on permanent view anywhere in the world. Outstanding holdings include the collections of glass and metalwork from Egypt, Syria, and Mesopotamia, royal miniatures from the courts of Persia and Mughal India, and classical carpets from the sixteenth and seventeenth centuries. An eighteenth-century room from Syria introduces the recently installed complex of galleries and study areas. The organization of the collection as a separate department took place in 1963.

1 Ewer
Iranian, 7th c.
*Bronze, originally inlaid; greatest h. 19 1/16 in.
(48.5 cm.)*

Early Islamic metalwork developed under the
influence of the pre-Islamic traditions of the
ancient Near East and those of the late classical eastern Mediterranean world. This ewer's
shape, graceful elongated feline handle, and
decoration were inherited from the art of the
pre-Islamic Sasanian dynasty of Iran and
that of the preceding Parthian period. The
repetitive rhythm of its decoration,
probably based on stylized landscape
and plant motifs, reflects an Islamic
approach to design. Although the ewer
is made of bronze, its size and elegant
form suggest that it is an object of luxury.
Fletcher Fund, 1947, 47.100.90

2 Bowl
Iraqi, Abbasid period, 9th c.
*Earthenware, glazed and luster-painted; diam.
7 3/4 in. (19.7 cm.)*

The technique of luster painting on pottery was
one of the greatest contributions of Islamic
ceramists to pottery decoration. In this extremely difficult process, silver and copper oxides,
each mixed with a medium, were used to paint
designs on a vessel already covered with an
opaque glaze and fired. During a second firing
in a reducing kiln, oxygen was drawn out of
the metallic oxides, leaving the metal suspended on the surface to refract light and create a lustrous appearance. Shades of green
were obtained from silver and those of brown
from copper.

Originating as a means of decorating glass,
luster painting was first employed on pottery in
ninth-century Iraq. This innovation had a permanent influence on the pottery industry in general,
passing from Iraq to Egypt, North Africa, Syria,
Iran, and Spain, and from the Islamic world to
Italy, England, and America. On this bowl, which
exhibits the polychrome scheme found only in
the ninth century, the influence of Roman and
later millefiori glass is evident in the gridlike
decoration as well as in several of the motifs.
Rogers Fund, 1952, 52.114

3 Koran Leaf
Egyptian, 9th c.
*Ink, colors, and gold on parchment; l. 13 1/8 in.
(33.3 cm.)*

Despite its great variety, Arabic calligraphy can
be reduced to two basic categories: the angular
scripts, usually called Kufic (after the town of
Kufa in Iraq, where such scripts may have first
been put to official use), and the cursive scripts.

A handsome example of Kufic from the ninth
century—one of Arabic calligraphy's very finest
periods—is this Koran page, which typifies the
imposing grandeur and reverence for the written word that calligraphers succeeded in giving
the text. The style's horizontality, austerity, and
formality are emphasized by monumental scale:
not untypically, the whole top line is formed by a
single compound word. Other examples of the
period have as few as three lines on the page.

The text is written on parchment, which was
supplanted in the East by paper in the tenth
century. The vowel marks are red, yellow, and
green dots; some diacritics are in the form of
red diagonals, and the tenth-verse marker in the
margin is a triangle of six gold dots. *Gift of
Rudolph M. Riefstahl, 1930, 30.45*

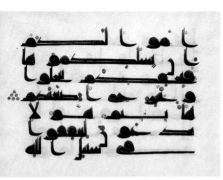

4 Beaker

Iranian or Iraqi, 9th c.

Glass, free-blown(?) and relief-cut; h. 5⅜ in. (13.6 cm.), diam. at lip 5⁹⁄₁₆ in. (14.2 cm.)

In many respects the glass produced by medieval Muslim craftsmen has never been surpassed. These artists continued pre-Islamic glass traditions as well as developing totally new departures for the medium. One such new technique was used to produce this beaker, whose ornament was created by cutting away the entire outer surface except for the design, which is then in relief. The technique as well as the design (palmettes, half-palmettes, and floral motifs on two scrolls between two horizontal ridges) bears a close resemblance to early Islamic carved rock crystal. In size, preservation, and fineness, this piece has few parallels in Islamic relief-cut glass. *Purchase, Rogers Fund and Jack A. Josephson, Dr. and Mrs. Lewis Balamuth, Mr. and Mrs. Alvin W. Pearson Gifts, 1974, 1974.45*

5 Bowl

Iranian or Transoxiana, Nishapur or Samarkand, 10th c.

Earthenware, slip-painted, incised, and glazed; diam. 18 in. (45.7 cm.)

Because of the sacred aspect of the Arabic language and the design potential of its various scripts, the use of calligraphy as a decorative element is prominent in all periods of Islamic art and in all media—on both secular and religious objects and buildings.

Perhaps the most outstanding examples of the use of calligraphy on pottery are to be found among wares from Nishapur and Samarkand. Now a small town, in the tenth century Nishapur was one of the great centers of Islamic art (it was totally destroyed by Mongol invaders in the early thirteenth century). The finest Nishapur ceramics were the slip-painted wares on which elegantly painted Arabic inscriptions are the main and frequently the only decoration. This bowl (the largest and perhaps the most important in the Museum) bears an inscription in Kufic script stating: "Planning before work protects you from regret; prosperity and peace." *Rogers Fund, 1965, 65.106.2*

6 Bowl

Egyptian, ca. 1000
Earthenware, glazed and luster-painted; diam. 10 in. (25.4 cm.)

From Iraq, the technique of luster painting on pottery spread to Egypt, where, in the Fatimid period (969–1171), the painters of lustered pottery employed a new style of animal and figural representation which displays more anatomical concern than that on Iraqi ware. Proof that artists were held in high esteem under the Fatimids is supplied by the number of signed works from this period—such identification was a quite sporadic practice until then. This luster-painted bowl with a powerful heraldic eagle bears the artist's signature beneath the left talon and again on the foot of the bowl. (See also no. 2.) *Gift of Mr. and Mrs. Charles K. Wilkinson, 1963, 63.178.1*

7 Pendant

Egyptian, Fatimid period, 12th c.
Gold, enamel, and turquoise; h. 1¾ in. (4.4 cm.)

The school of art centered in Egypt during the reign of the Fatimids from Cairo (969–1171) is noted for a surprising increase in the use of human and animal motifs. This period is also noted for a high level of craftsmanship. The goldwork is especially fine, with elaborate designs such as those on this pendant, which are constructed in filigree on a gold grid. The use of crescent-shaped ornaments was borrowed by the Fatimids from Byzantine art, as was the technique of cloisonné enamel (employed here for the birds in the center). This pendant would have been framed by strands of pearls or beads of precious or semiprecious stones, laced through the gold hoops around the edge. *Theodore M. Davis Collection, Bequest of Theodore M. Davis, 1915, 30.95.37*

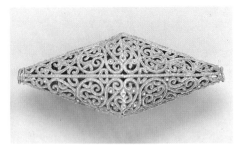

8 Gold Bead

Greater Syrian, 11th c.
Gold; l. 2 in. (5.2 cm.), greatest diam. ¹³⁄₁₆ in. (2 cm.)

Spanning more than a millennium, the history of Islamic jewelry is a long and illustrious one. The goldwork of the Fatimid period in Syria during the eleventh and twelfth centuries is the most accomplished and decoratively complex group within this history.

This biconical bead is one of only two such beads known. Constructed solely of filigree on a strip-support, with the paired twisted wires surmounted by grains of more than one size, the bead is totally covered with beautifully executed leaf scrolls, which unroll themselves along the full length of each of the bead's five sections. *Purchase, Sheikh Nasser Sabah al-Ahmed al-Sabah Gift, in memory of Richard Ettinghausen, 1980, 1980.456*

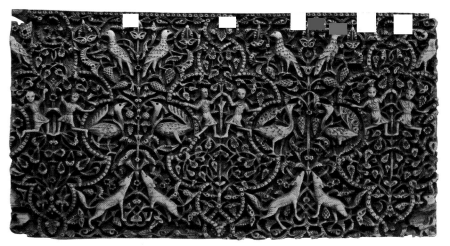

9 Plaque
Spanish, 11th c.
Ivory; 8 × 4¼ in. (20.3 × 10.8 cm.)

This plaque belongs to a group of eleventh-century ivories made in Spain during the reign of the Umayyads. Among the dynasty's most outstanding extant artistic achievements, most of these ivories were created for the royal family or its entourage, and many were made in the capital, Cordova, or in Madinat az-Zahra, the royal residence. Because of the Umayyads'

Syrian roots, it is not surprising that many of the motifs found on these ivories can be traced to that area. The leaf arabesques on this plaque are a stylized version of the vine-and-acanthus scroll so popular in late antique ornament. The prototypes for the animated figures can be found on early Islamic textiles from Syria or Egypt in which birds, animals, and human beings of similar character are also paired on either side of stylized trees. *John Stewart Kennedy Fund, 1913, 13.141*

10 Armlet
Iranian, first half of 11th c.
Gold sheet with applied twisted gold wire and granulation, originally set with stones; greatest diam. 4⅛ in. (10.5 cm.), h. at clasp 2 in. (5.1 cm.)

The pivotal pieces for the study of early medieval jewelry in Greater Iran are this armlet and its mate in the Freer Gallery of Art, Washington. Here each of the four hemispheres flanking the clasp bears at its base a flat disk of thin gold that was decorated by pouncing it over a coin bearing the name of the Abbasid caliph al-Qadir

Billah (991–1031). There are a large number of extant bracelets in both gold and silver that are analogous to this pair, although none is as fine or as elaborate.

Pre-Islamic jewelry forms can be seen in these bracelets, indicating continued conservatism and traditionalism in the art. Examples of coins and imitation coins on jewelry are quite numerous in the Byzantine period. The twisted effect of the shank must ultimately derive from Greek bracelets with similar shanks. *Harris Brisbane Dick Fund, 1957, 57.88a–c*

11 Incense Burner

Iranian, 1181/82
*Bronze, pierced and incised; l. 33½ in.
(85.1 cm.), h. 31½ in. (80 cm.)*

This unusually large and noble metal animal sculpture in the form of a lion belongs to a small group of incense burners with similar forms and shapes. The head is removable so that the in-cense can be placed inside, and the arabesque interlace on the body and neck is pierced to allow the aroma to escape. The Arabic inscriptions in Kufic script on the various parts of the animal as well as on three bosses provide the name of the emir who commissioned the work, its artist, and the date. *Rogers Fund, 1951, 51.56*

12 Ewer

Iranian, Khorasan, 13th c.
Bronze, silver, and gold; h. 15½ in. (39.4 cm.)

This outstanding example of bronze inlaid with gold and silver from the Seljuq period in Iran (1037/38–1258) epitomizes the fine metal workmanship characteristic of that time. The body of the ewer, which is covered with an elaborate interlace design with animal-headed terminals, is divided into twelve lobes, each topped by a pair of crowned harpies. Near the center of each lobe is a medallion enclosing a sign of the zodiac, generally shown with its ruling planet; the other motifs seem to reflect and support the astrological theme.

Several inscriptions on the shoulder and neck —all but one executed in human-headed Naskhi script—express good wishes to the owner, a common theme of the epigraphic decoration on Islamic metalwork in all periods. *Rogers Fund, 1944, 44.15*

13 Bowl

Iranian, 12th–13th c.
Composite body, stain- and overglaze-painted and gilded; diam. 7³⁄₈ in. (18.7 cm.)

In an attempt to increase the number of colors in their palettes, twelfth-century Iranian potters developed a technique now known as *mina'i* (enameled), in which stable colors were stain-painted in a lead glaze opacified with tin and, after a first firing, less stable colors were applied and the object was refired at a lower temperature. This technique enabled the artist to paint in a greater variety of colors with complete control, lending a miniature-like quality to the designs not found on other pottery types. Whether for practical or aesthetic reasons, this method was relatively short-lived.

In this brightly painted ceramic bowl, an enthroned ruler and his retinue of attendants, musicians, and mounted falconers surround the central astrological design—Saturn, Jupiter, Venus, Mercury, Mars, and the Moon around a rayed sun—which augurs good fortune for its owner. *Gift of the Schiff Foundation and Rogers Fund, 1957, 57.36.4*

14 Bowl

Iranian, Rayy, late 12th–early 13th c.
Composite body, glazed and luster-painted; diam. 8 in. (20.3 cm.)

Starting from around the time of the collapse of the Fatimid dynasty in 1171, luster-painted ware appeared in Iran as well as in Spain and Syria. While it seems quite certain that migrating Egyptian potters were responsible for bringing the technique to the latter two countries, their role in the appearance of luster-painted ware in Iran is less clear. Among the reasons given to support a connection between Egyptian and Iranian luster, particularly that from Rayy, are certain features characteristic of both wares, such as a central design reserved on a lustered ground, seen on this bowl from Iran, dated to the late twelfth–early thirteenth century. This feature, in addition to the monumental quality of the design and the clear distinction between foreground and background, is typical of pottery attributed to Rayy prior to its destruction by the Mongols in the 1220s. *Rogers Fund, 1916, 16.87*

15 Ewer

Iranian, Kashan, 1215/16
Composite body, painted and glazed; h. 8 in. (20.3 cm.)

In the twelfth century the potters in Seljuq Iran began making their vessels of an artificial paste and glazing them with an alkaline glaze consisting basically of the same ingredients as the body. Since designs painted under an alkaline glaze did not run during firing, this innovation allowed free painting under the glaze. Furthermore, since the body and glaze consisted of the same material, there was a complete fusion of the two during firing and therefore no later separation of the glaze from the body.

Surely one of the most beautiful examples of underglaze-painted ware made by Muslim ceramists is this double-walled ewer. The design includes pairs of winged sphinxes and harpies, together with deer, dogs, and hares, on a ground of carved and pierced arabesques. Incised Persian inscriptions surround the neck and lower body above a border of willow reeds. *Fletcher Fund, 1932, 32.52.1*

16 Bowl

Syrian, Raqqa, late 12th–early 13th c.
*Composite body, painted and glazed;
diam. 11¼ in. (28.6 cm.)*

Among the most accomplished animal paintings on Islamic ceramics are those of Syria in
the twelfth and thirteenth centuries, exemplified
by the present piece with its two peacocks set
off by plain bands with interstices containing
dot-lined areas filled with dotted scrolls. The
painted and incised silhouette-like birds are
related to the decoration of certain Fatimid
lusterware, and the background design derives
from Abbasid wares of Mesopotamia. The bowl
exhibits a marvelous combination of observation and artistic stylization; the decoration is
masterfully fitted to the form and surface.

   The glaze deteriorated badly during burial, in-
terfering with transparency and obscuring some
of the painting's details. The black is applied as
a stain to the white man-made body. This "artificial paste" body came into use in the Islamic
world in the late eleventh or twelfth century, representing a rediscovery of the paste or faience
bodies of the ancient world. *Bequest of Horace
Havemeyer, 1956, H. O. Havemeyer Collection,
56.185.6*

18 Pair of Doors

Egyptian, Cairo, probably second half of 14th c.
*Wood, inlaid with carved ivory panels; 65 ×
30½ in. (165.1 × 77.5 cm.)*

These doors of wood inlaid with carved ivory,
probably from a minbar (pulpit) in an Egyptian
mosque or madrasah, are outstanding examples
of the high achievement of the Mamluk craftsmen.
"Infinite" geometric design, prominent in Islamic art from the beginning of its history, reached
its height during the Mamluk period in Egypt
(1250–1517). No other artistic tradition has ap-
proached in number, sophistication, and complexity the geometric motifs of Islamic art, nor
does any other tradition rival the Islamic in the
importance given to such motifs. The Islamic
designer exercised greater freedom and imagination in his use of geometric structure than any of
his predecessors, and it is this fact, more than
any other, that explains the abundance and
diversity of patterns in Islamic art. *Edward C.
Moore Collection, Bequest of Edward C. Moore,
1891, 91.1.2064*

17 Mosque Lamp

Syrian, Mamluk period, second half of 14th c.
*Free-blown glass, tooled, applied foot, enam-
eled, and gilded; h. 10½ in. (26.7 cm.)*

In the Koran, God's light is likened to "a niche in
which is a lamp, the lamp is in a glass, and the
glass is as it were a brightly shining star." Because
of the vivid simile, this verse was often placed
on the richly enameled mosque lamps of the
Mamluk period. This example bears an inscription stating that it was made for the mausoleum
of a Syrian official (d. 1285) who had served as
bowman to the ruler (which explains the blazon
in the roundels). *Gift of J. Pierpont Morgan,
1917, 17.190.985*

19 Carpet

Egyptian, Cairo, last quarter of 15th c.
Wool (about 100 Senneh knots per sq. in.);
29 ft. 7 in. × 7 ft. 10 in. (9 × 2.4 m.)

In fineness, size, and preservation, this carpet is one of the most renowned of its type. Its design is seldom matched in carpets, and its color balance—primarily green and wine red—is marvelous, at once clashing and harmonizing.

This carpet belongs to a type now recognized not only as Egyptian but also as made in Cairo in the late fifteenth and early sixteenth centuries. The style combines motifs and compositions long out of usage (such as the papyrus plants with umbrella-shaped leaves) with contemporaneous designs. This particular carpet is unique among Mamluk rugs in having five major units. *Fletcher Fund, 1970, 1970.105*

20 Tympanum

Caucasian, probably Kubachi in Daghestan area, first half of 14th c.
Carved stone; 51 × 28¾ in. (129.5 × 73 cm.)

This monumental stone tympanum from the Caucasus shows the treatment of the human figure by Iranian artists in the early fourteenth century. The boldness of the relief carving, the naturalness of movement (the horse in midstride, the warrior using his whip), and the realism of the warrior's accouterments are effectively set off by the decorative approach to details and surface patterns. The artist's skill is also apparent in the way the horse and warrior fit into the space: the figures are carved to the correct scale but are not at all cramped by the semicircular shape of the tympanum. *Rogers Fund, 1938, 38.96*

21 Koran Leaf

Iraqi, Baghdad, Mongol period, 1307/1308
*Ink, colors, and gold on paper; 14½ × 20³⁄₁₆ in.
(36.8 × 51.3 cm.)*

Ahmad ibn as-Suwawardi al-Bakri was one
of the six outstanding disciples of Yaqut al-
Musta 'şimi (d. 1298), who gave the Arabic
cursive scripts their last refinement by cutting
the pen nib obliquely. This style of writing is
known as *muḥaqqaq*. The border text (in Kufic)
reads: "It is written: Baghdad, may God protect
her, in the months of the lunar year 707
[1307/1308 A.D.]." The *muhaqqaq* text reads:

> Ahmad ibn as-Suwawardi al-Bakri,
> praising God and blessing His Prophet
> Muhammad and his family and his
> companions, and submitting [himself to God].

The illuminator was Muhammad ibn Aybak.
Rogers Fund, 1955, 55.44

22 Yazdegerd I and the Water Horse That Killed Him

Iranian, Mongol period, early 14th c.
*Ink, colors, and gold on paper; 5 × 6¼ in.
(12.7 × 15.9 cm.)*

The legendary death of the Sasanian king
Yazdegerd I—who was said to have been kicked
by a horse that magically emerged from a
spring—is charmingly depicted in this leaf from
a dispersed manuscript of the *Shah-nameh*
(Book of the Kings) of Ferdowsi. The decoratively curving tree and the grassy verge of the
groundline, which rings the water, are traditional;
the fungus-like growths are derived from Chinese art and the costumes are Mongol. The
gestures of the figures at the left register aston-
ishment and dismay. *Cora Timken Burnett collection of Persian miniatures and other art objects,
Bequest of Cora Timken Burnett, 1957, 57.51.33*

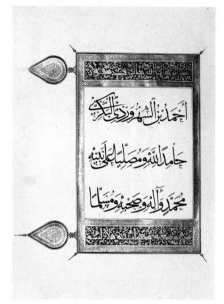

23 Jonah and the Whale

Iranian, late 14th–early 15th c.
*Illuminated manuscript; 12⁹⁄₁₆ × 18¹⁵⁄₁₆ in.
(32 × 48.1 cm.)*

One of the most popular prophets in Muslim
tradition was Jonah, and the story of his encounter with a whale was referred to in the Koran.
This story was retold in Muslim world histories
and was no doubt familiar to the general pop-
ulace. Here the whale, actually a carp, delivers
Jonah to the shore, where a gourd vine, custom-
arily depicted in Western medieval illustrations
of the subject, curves out and over his head.
The waves, made of neatly overlapping arcs,
are, like the fish, based on Chinese prototypes.
The painting, however, is characteristically
Persian, with its bright colors, strong outlines,
striking patterning of the angel's wings, and
decorative arrangement of the flowering plants.
Jonah modestly reaching for the clothes proffered
by the angel reinforces in a tangible manner the
Muslim belief in human dependence on the will
of God in every aspect of life. *Purchase,
Joseph Pulitzer Bequest, 1933, 33.113*

24 Mihrab

Iranian, Isfahan, ca. 1354
Mosaic tile, composite body, painted and glazed; h. 135 in. (342.9 cm.)

The most important element in any Muslim house of worship is the mihrab, or niche, which indicates the direction of Mecca. Because it is the focal point in the mosque, a great deal of attention has been devoted to its decoration throughout the Islamic world. This superb example, from the Madrasah Imami (theological school) in Isfahan (founded in 1354), is composed of small pieces of ceramic, each fired at a temperature that would bring out the brilliance of the glaze. These pieces were then fitted together to form

geometric and floral patterns and inscriptions.

There is a long history of glazed-ceramic architectural decoration in the Near and Middle East. Such decoration was first used in Islamic Iran in the twelfth century, when small, mono-chrome glazed tiles were set into walls of buildings in a very tentative manner. By the time this mihrab was made, whole walls were being covered with mosaics totally executed in small pieces. This highly exacting phase soon gave way to whole designs painted on larger tiles —a much quicker, easier way to cover large surfaces with patterned glazed ceramics. *Harris Brisbane Dick Fund, 1939, 39.20*

25 Koran Stand

West Turkestan, 1360
Carved wood; h. 51¼ in. (130.2 cm.)

The word of God as revealed to his prophet Muhammad is recorded in the Koran, the Muslim holy book. Very large, sumptuous Korans were too difficult to hold, and special stands were built for them. This stand (*rahleh*) was made by

Hasan ibn Sulayman of Isfahan for a madrasah (theological school), the name of which is partly obliterated in the inscription and the location of which is unknown. The stand's form is derived from a folding chair, and the decoration of the lower section, depicting a mihrab (no. 24), is exquisitely carved on three levels. *Rogers Fund, 1910, 10.218*

26 Ewer

Iranian, probably Herat, early Safavid period, early 16th c.
Brass, inlaid with gold and silver; h. 5½ in. (14 cm.)

The arabesque is the most distinctively Islamic of all forms of decoration. Invented and developed in the first centuries of Islam, it was used in a rich variety of forms and patterns in all areas of the Muslim world. Basically, it consists of vegetal ornament inorganically treated— tendrils terminating in bilateral leaves with more tendrils springing from their tips, in an infinite diversity of rhythmic repetitions.

In this Persian jug balanced arabesque designs in medallions punctuate a ground filled with arabesques. These are all inlaid in silver, with gold at the center of the medallions, the inlay shimmering against a brass ground darkened with bitumen. This dense design, with its counterplay of form and ornament, of movement and stability, of glittering and mat surfaces on a pleasing shape, shows the Islamic artist at his most successful. *Edward C. Moore Collection, Bequest of Edward C. Moore, 1891, 91.1.607*

27 Cross Guard

Iranian, Timurid period, 15th c.
Nephrite jade; l. 4⅛ in. (10.5 cm.)

Several jade objects of the Timurid period have terminals or handles with dragon's heads. The deep green of the nephrite of this cross guard, a color favored by the Timurids, accentuates the stylized fierceness of the mythical beast. The prototype for this object is found in metalwork of the period. The Timurids were partial to jade objects, and the Mughal rulers of India emulated their Timurid ancestors and made many objects in this hard stone. *Gift of Heber R. Bishop, The Heber R. Bishop Collection, 1902, 02.18.765*

28 Bahram Gur with the Indian Princess in Her Black Pavilion

Iranian, Herat, Timurid period, ca. 1426
Ink, colors, and gold on paper; 8⅝ × 4⅝ in. (21.9 × 11.7 cm.)

This painting illustrates an episode from the story of the Sasanian king Bahram Gur, the great hunter in the romantic epic *Haft Paykar* by the twelfth-century Persian poet Nizami. This miniature exemplifies the classic style of Persian painting, which reached full development in Herat under the patronage of the Timurid prince Baysonghor. The Timurid school excelled in purity and harmony of colors, delicacy of drawing, fine rendering of pattern and detail, and subtle balance of composition. Here the Persian artist characteristically shows every element in its most easily understood aspect. The pool and the bed are seen from a bird's-eye view, the human figures from a three-quarter view. Throughout there is an exquisite use of patterning. *Gift of Alexander Smith Cochran, 1913, 13.228.13, folio 23b*

29 The Feast of Sadeh

Iranian, Tabriz, Safavid period, ca. 1520–22
*Ink, colors, and gold on paper; painting 9¹/₁₆ ×
9½ in. (23 × 24.1 cm.)*

This miniature, from the great *Shah-nameh*
(Book of the Kings) made for Shah Tahmasp
(1514–76), was painted by Sultan Muhammad,
the first of several artists in charge of work on
the manuscript. The Feast of Sadeh celebrates
the discovery of fire by one of the early kings,
Hushang. The miniature is in the exuberant
style inherited from the Tabriz studio of the
White Sheep Turkoman rulers of the late fifteenth
century. A number of delightful beasts prowl or
rest among the rocks, which in some places
take the form of animal and human heads. Tree
branches and stumps twist and bend; the picture pulsates with the stirrings of an awakening
world. Hushang, with his jeweled wine cup, and
his courtiers would appear to be sophisticated
Safavids enjoying a picnic, were it not for the
leopard- and tiger-skin coats that some of them
wear—thus placing them in a time when only
animal skins were available as clothing. *Gift of
Arthur A. Houghton, Jr., 1970, 1970.301.2*

30 Compartment Carpet

Iranian, Tabriz, Safavid period, early 16th c.
*Silk and wool (about 550 Senneh knots per
sq. in.); 16 ft. 4 in. × 11 ft. 2 in. (4.9 × 3.4 m.)*

The carpets woven in Safavid Iran have a
greater affinity with miniature painting and manuscript illumination than with the angular, textile-
like patterns of earlier rugs from this country. In
fact, their designs are so close to the art of the
book that it seems quite probable that painters
were commissioned to execute the patterns for
the weavers to follow. This rug was probably
made during the period of Shah Isma'il (1502–
1524) in the northwestern region of the country.
The magnificent jewel-colored carpet, with its
elegant, curvilinear "compartments" based on a
geometric star pattern, is filled with creatures
borrowed from Chinese art, such as the dragon
and phoenix, and transformed into the Islamic
idiom. While the overall pattern is a continuous
repeat, the motifs in one half of the rug form a
mirror image of those in the other, so the design
is effective when viewed from either end. *Frederick C. Hewitt Fund, 1910, 10.61.3*

31 The Concourse of the Birds

Iranian, ca. 1600
Ink, colors, and gold on paper; 9¾ × 5½ in.
(24.8 × 14 cm.)

The painters of the School of Bihzad at Herat were unsurpassed in delicacy of drawing, pureness of color, and attention to detail. They incorporated the conventions of Persian painting developed in the fifteenth century (see no. 28). The innovations of this school were primarily a new interest in the everyday world coupled with a keener observation of both man and nature. When the manuscript of the *Mantiq at-Tayr* (The Language of the Birds) by the twelfth-century poet Farid al-din Attar came into the possession of Shah Abbas the Great (1557–1628), it had four miniatures from the time the manuscript was completed in 1483 in Herat and four blank spaces for other miniatures. Since the shah wished to present the manuscript to his family shrine, in about 1600 he had his own artists paint four miniatures to complete the book. Habib Allah, who painted *The Concourse of the Birds*, did his best to paint a miniature in a style that would be in harmony with the fifteenth-century illustrations of the manuscript. The birds that set out on a journey to seek a spiritual leader symbolize mankind in search of God. The crested bird at the far right, to which the other birds are listening, is a hoopoe (known in Iran as the *tajidar*, or "crown wearer"), which is said to have a special relationship with the supernatural world. *Fletcher Fund, 1963, 63.210.11 recto*

32 Dish

Iranian, Safavid period, 17th c.
Composite body, painted and glazed; diam.
17¼ in. (43.8 cm.)

Chinese blue-and-white porcelain began to exert a strong influence on ceramic production within the Islamic world in the late fourteenth century, an influence that persisted for at least two hundred and fifty years. In this dish a seventeenth-century Islamic artist followed Chinese prototypes in the bowl's color scheme and the drawing of the dragons, the wave patterns behind them and on the rim, and the lotus blossoms and leaf scrolls. In Chinese mythology, however, the dragons are beneficent symbols, quite contrary to the Iranian concept of fearsome, poison-breathing creatures, here locked in combat, fang and claw sunk into each other's body. But with the Iranian decorative sense the snakelike bodies create graceful, intertwined triangles, the twisted necks, turned heads, and looped tails forming a rhythmic counterpoise. This same dragon wreath appears on a number of sixteenth-century rugs and no doubt had more than a decorative meaning—most probably it symbolized power. (See also Far Eastern Art, no. 57.) *Harris Brisbane Dick Fund, 1965, 65.109.2*

33 Tughra of Sulayman the Magnificent

Turkish, Ottoman period, reign of Sulayman (1520–66)
Ink, colors, and gold on paper; 25⅜ × 20½ in.
(64.5 × 52.1 cm.)

There is no agreement among scholars concerning the underlying inspiration for the form of the Ottoman tughra (calligraphic emblem), which became largely standardized in general appearance at least as early as the fifteenth century. In any case it allowed calligraphers and illuminators to display their talents, particularly well exemplified by the present sumptuous example. Almost all of the orthographically functional lines of this tughra are concentrated in the area of dense activity at the lower right, which gives the name and patronymic of the sultan as well as the formula "ever victorious." The exaggerated verticals with their descending, swaying appendages, as well as the elaborate sweeping curves that form the large loops to the left and their extensions to the right, are essentially decorative. *Rogers Fund, 1938, 38.149.1*

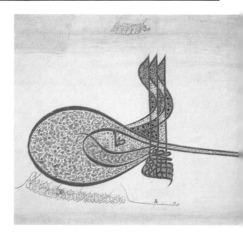

34 Bowl

Turkish, Iznik, Ottoman period, ca. 1535–45
*Composite body, slip- and stain-painted; diam.
15½ in. (39.4 cm.)*

The elements found in this unique piece of
blue-and-white Iznik ware were inspired by both
Chinese blue-and-white porcelain and celadon.
The shape, a rimless dish with curved sides,
and the patterns, particularly the interior square
grid and the exterior leaf scroll, have been
compared to Chinese models. However, the
color scheme, the technical composition of the
body, and the clear white ground and brilliant
glaze show the skills of the Iznik potters. *Bequest
of Benjamin Altman, 1913, 14.10.727*

35 Prayer Rug

Turkish, probably Bursa, Ottoman period,
late 16th c.
*Wool, silk, and cotton (about 288 Senneh knots
per sq. in.); 66 × 50 in. (167.6 × 127 cm.)*

This outstanding prayer rug, probably the most
famous in existence, is one of four types surviving among the Ottoman court prayer rugs, which
share the technical features of silk warps and
wefts with Senneh knots in colored wool and
white (and sometimes light blue) cotton, producing an especially light and supple rug. This rug
displays patterned columns supporting three
arches with a mosque lamp hanging in the
center. The favorite Turkish flowers, tulips and
carnations, are visible between the carefully
rendered column bases. Split palmette leaves
and small blossoms pattern the spandrels. In
the horizontal panel above the spandrels, four
domed buildings and varied flora appear between the curved crenellations.

The use of several delicate color tones (light
blue in particular) characterizes these court
rugs; the clarity of the drawing and the balance
of motifs, especially in the main border, reveal
the heights attained by the Ottoman court
designers and weavers. *Gift of James F.
Ballard, 1922, 22.100.51*

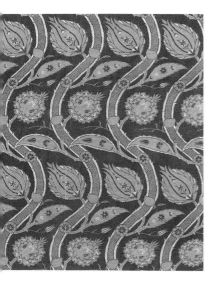

36 Textile Fragment

Turkish, Istanbul or Bursa, Ottoman period, second half of 16th c.
Silk and metallic threads; l. 48 in. (121.9 cm.)

In the sixteenth century Turkish imperial power reached its height in Asia and Europe. A correlation between this political eminence and the character of Turkish art may well be established by pointing to this boldly colored, monumental piece of silk, probably manufactured in Istanbul in the mid-sixteenth century. Its inner dynamics are established by the strong movements and countermovements of the large leaves and flowers and by the grandiose, sweeping verticals to which they are attached. The individual units combine the special qualities of several flowers (such as lotuses and tulips) and are further enriched by superimposed floral sprays. Highly decorative as this design is, it nevertheless evokes a natural setting. The parallel chevron lines in the curving verticals are an age-old symbol of water; hence the image of a garden with watercourses is readily evoked. *Purchase, Joseph Pulitzer Bequest, 1952, 52.20.21*

37 Nur ad-Din Room

Syrian, Damascus, Ottoman period, 1707
Marble floors, wood paneling, stained-glass windows; h. 22 ft. 1/2 in. (6.71 m.), l. from inside front entrance to back wall 26 ft. 4 3/4 in. (8.04 m.), w. 16 ft. 8 1/2 in. (5.09 m.)

This room, built in 1707, from the Nur ad-Din house in Damascus, is typical of traditional Syrian homes of the Ottoman period. The courtyard contains a fountain and flooring executed in richly colored marble. A high arch and a step lead to the raised reception area, where the master of the house welcomed guests. The wooden panels in both areas are lavishly painted, with raised designs, poetic Arabic inscriptions, and architectural vignettes. The warm colors are heightened with gilding. The open niches were used for books and other objects; the closed ones covered windows or served as closets or doors. The high stained-glass windows permitted tinted light to enter, while fresh air came through the lower grilled windows. Both ceilings are sumptuously ornamented, with decorated beams in the courtyard and a complex design in the reception area. *Gift of The Hagop Kevorkian Fund, 1970, 1970.170*

38 Dedicatory Inscription from a Mosque

Bengali, probably Malda district, Sultanate period, 1500
Schist; 45⅝/16 × 16⅛ in. (115 × 41 cm.)

This stone slab contains a dedicatory inscription from a mosque built by the Bengali prince Daniyal in 1500. The inscription begins with a maxim attributed to the Prophet Muhammad: "Whosoever builds a mosque for God, God will build for him a house in paradise." This saying is found in mosques throughout the subcontinent but rarely elsewhere.

This stone's special value is its superb calligraphy. "Rhythmic parallelism" is a particular quality of Indian calligraphy. Earlier examples show slow development toward more rhythmic forms, in which the vertical hastae become elaborated into a regular pattern, which is then interrupted by the strokes of other letters. This stone has sixty verticals of equal length, through which five "bows" are set. The pattern assumes an extraordinary harmony, and the inscription is among the finest from Bengal. *Purchase, Gift of Mrs. Nelson Doubleday and Bequest of Charles R. Gerth, by exchange, 1981, 1981.320*

39 Zanbur the Spy

Indian, Mughal period, reign of Akbar (1556–1605), ca. 1561–76
Ink, colors, and gold on cotton mounted on paper; 29⅛ × 22½ in. (74 × 57.2 cm.)

The first major work of the Mughal school—an illustrated copy of the *Dastan-i Amir Hamzeh* (The Story of Amir Hamzeh)—narrated the exploits of the Prophet's uncle Hamzeh (and another hero of the same name whose adventures were interwoven into this text). This manuscript consists of fourteen huge volumes (each about thirty by twenty-three inches). Each contains one hundred full-page paintings on cotton; many are scenes of violence and horror, but there are also quieter paintings, in which the artist portrayed his subject realistically in a peaceful setting. He did so in this picture, which shows a spy, Zanbur, bringing a maid named Mahiyya to town on a donkey. The houses and pavilions are more truthfully rendered than in contemporary Iranian miniatures. The high viewpoint and decorative quality stem from Persian models, but the increased realism and, through it, our more personal involvement are indicative of a new and different attitude. *Rogers Fund, 1923, 23.264.1*

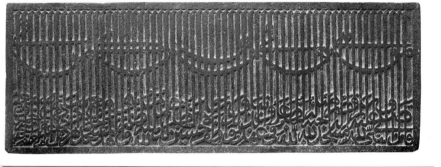

40 Shah Jahan on Horseback

Indian, Mughal period, reign of Shah Jahan
(1628–58)
*Ink, colors, and gold on paper; 10¹/₈ × 15⁵/₁₆ in.
(25.7 × 38.9 cm.)*

This magnificent equestrian portrait of Shah
Jahan (1592–1666) epitomizes the imperial
splendor of the "Grand Mogul," the epithet
used by Europeans when referring to rulers of
the Mughal dynasty. The richness and refinement
of the saddle, the saddlecloth, and the emperor's
own costume and arms, as well as the nobility
of his mount, are in perfect harmony with the
regal grandeur of his face. The work is a leaf
from the *Shah Jahan Album* and is attributed to
Bhag. *Purchase, Rogers Fund and The Kevorkian
Foundation Gift, 1955, 55.121.10.21*

41 Tent Hanging

Indian, Mughal period, reign of Shah Jahan
(1628–58), ca. 1635
*Red silk velvet and gold leaf; 18 ft. × 8 ft. 5 in.
(5.48 × 2.56 m.)*

In the lavish temporary encampments used by
Mughal emperors when traveling for reasons of
state or pleasure, the tents were lined with
beautiful textiles. This panel from the interior of
a tent complex, which was made about 1635,
probably for Raja Jai Singh I of Amber (Jaipur),
indicates the colorful ambience of such tent
cities. The velvet ground is intensified by glittering gold leaf. The panel has five compartments,
each containing a poppy plant under an arch,
with floral and leaf scrolls in the spandrels (a
typical pattern in Indian art). A floral-and-leaf
motif fills the narrow borders, and the large
main border shows poppy plants alternating
with miniature "trees" or stylized leaves. The
gold decoration was made by covering parts of
the design with an adhesive substance, then
placing gold leaf on top, rubbing and beating it
into the surface—the gold leaf remaining only
on the treated areas—and then burnishing the
surface. *Purchase, Bequest of Helen W. D.
Mileham, by exchange, Wendy Findlay Gift,
and funds from various donors, 1981, 1981.321*

GROUND FLOOR

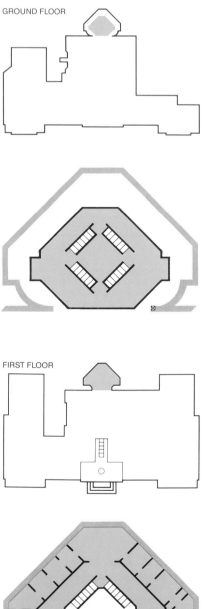

FIRST FLOOR

EUROPEAN SCULPTURE
AND DECORATIVE ARTS

ROBERT LEHMAN WING

ROBERT LEHMAN COLLECTION

The Robert Lehman Wing, which opened to the public in 1975, houses the extraordinary collection assembled by Mr. Lehman and his parents. Rich in Italian paintings of the fourteenth and fifteenth centuries, the collection also includes important works by early northern masters, including Petrus Christus, Memling, and the Master of Moulins. Among other strengths are Dutch and Spanish paintings, notably those by Rembrandt, El Greco, and Goya. French masterworks of the nineteenth and twentieth centuries include paintings by Ingres, Renoir, and the most important Post-Impressionists and Fauves.

This department is also known for its collection of drawings, among which are rare early Italian works, important sheets by Dürer, Rembrandt, and Flemish masters, a large group of French works, and close to two hundred eighteenth-century Venetian drawings. Periodic exhibitions present every aspect of this collection.

Renaissance majolica, Venetian glass, bronzes, furniture, and enamels form the core of an outstanding group of decorative arts. These works, like a large part of the Robert Lehman Collection, are exhibited in galleries designed to reflect the ambience of the Lehman house in New York.

1 FOLLOWER OF DUCCIO, Sienese,
first quarter of 14th c.
Madonna and Child; Crucifixion
Tempera on panel; each 15 × 10⅝ in.
(38.1 × 27 cm.)

The *Madonna and Child* and the *Crucifixion,*
which form a two-winged altarpiece, or diptych,
were painted about 1320 by a follower of
Duccio di Buoninsegna. The panels closely
reflect the influence of Duccio's *Maestà,* a
celebrated altarpiece (later broken up) that was

installed in the cathedral of Siena in 1311.
Here the painter simplified Duccio's large and
rich composition. Because of the reduced size
and scale, these two panels are more intimate,
much closer to the worshiper than the imposing
Maestà. The angels surround the throne in a
gently undulating circle rather than in hieratic
ceremonial rows. There is also a human tenderness in the way the Madonna is holding her
child and in his reaching for her cheek. *Robert
Lehman Collection, 1975, 1975.1.1,2*

2 UGOLINO DA NERIO, Sienese,
ca. 1296–1339/49
Last Supper
Tempera on panel; 13½ × 20¼ in.
(34.3 × 52.7 cm.)

This little rectangular panel is by Ugolino da
Nerio, the most gifted and individual follower of
Duccio. Ugolino painted an altarpiece (now
scattered) for the high altar of Santa Croce,
Florence; the *Last Supper* belonged to the
predella, which contained seven scenes from

the Passion of Christ. The elaborate coffered
ceiling and careful arrangement of food, wine,
and eating utensils illustrate the artist's love for
detail. It is also apparent in the richly tooled
halos of Christ and the apostles, where each
halo is decorated with a different pattern. The
panel can be dated shortly after 1321, since the
whole altarpiece is likely to have been commissioned after the church of Santa Croce was
opened for services in that year. *Robert
Lehman Collection, 1975, 1975.1.7*

3 AVIGNON MASTER, French(?), act. second quarter of 14th c.
Adoration of the Magi
Tempera on panel; 23¼ × 15⅛ in. (59 × 38.5 cm.)

This little picture, still in its original frame, shows Sienese influence. It was part of a series or of an altarpiece, two panels of which, the *Annunciation* and the *Nativity*, are in the museum at Aix-en-Provence, France. The dimensions of the three paintings are identical, as is their style. The delicately painted figures and the attention paid to the minutest details indicate that the artist was primarily a miniature painter, perhaps a French miniaturist who came under the influence of Simone Martini when Simone worked in Avignon. The panels were painted about 1345. *Robert Lehman Collection, 1975, 1975.1.9*

4 BARTOLO DI FREDI, Sienese, ca. 1330–1410
Adoration of the Magi
Tempera on panel; 78¾ × 47¼ in. (200 × 120 cm.)

Bartolo's *Adoration* is a work of his maturity and may be dated about 1380. The painting is a dramatic composition uniting the Holy Family, the richly attired, gift-bearing kings, and the realistically represented common people and horses. The contrasting colors are vivid and almost fantastic. The customary gold background has been replaced by a rocky landscape dotted with trees and shrubs. It can be seen that the top and the left side of the painting have been cut off. *Robert Lehman Collection, 1975, 1975.1.16*

5 SASSETTA, Sienese, ca. 1392–d. 1450/51
Temptation of Saint Anthony Abbot
Tempera on panel; 18⅝ × 13½ in. (47.3 × 34.3 cm.)

Part of a large polyptych, this panel has been dated shortly after 1444. Saint Anthony (ca. 250–350), who is considered the founder of monasticism, passed most of his life in the Egyptian desert, where he overcame many temptations. In this painting the Devil was shown between the saint and the rabbit on the left; this figure has, however, been painted over.

Sassetta depicts the desert in an almost surrealistic manner. The winding road first leads the eye to a strangely cubistic pink chapel, then toward the curving horizon where a boat floats on a lake or bay surrounded by mountains. Beyond this eerie landscape looms the sky, its blue, gray, and red cloud ribbons interrupted by a gold streak above the chapel and by two black birds. The style of the painting, its colors and technique, is strikingly different from that of Sassetta's Italian contemporaries. (See also European Paintings, no. 13.) *Robert Lehman Collection, 1975, 1975.1.27*

6   GIOVANNI DI PAOLO, Sienese, act.
by 1420–d. 1482
Expulsion from Paradise
*Tempera on panel; 17¹⁵⁄₁₆ × 20¹⁄₂ in.
(45.6 × 52 cm.)*

This extraordinary work, widely admired for its brilliant colors, curious iconography, and mystical vitality, is a fragment from the predella of an altarpiece probably painted about 1445 for the church of San Domenico in Siena (see European Paintings, no. 14).

Here an angel pushes Adam and Eve out of Paradise, while God points toward the place of their banishment; the arid, flat earth, surrounded by the concentric circles of the universe and framed in the outermost circle with the twelve signs of the zodiac. The earth is represented in the customary medieval manner in the form, roughly, of the letter T, with Europe and Asia forming the top bar and Africa the stem. The slender, nervous figures of the angel, Adam, and Eve and the wondrous details of the flora and fauna betray the artist's indebtedness to the International Gothic style and especially to Gentile da Fabriano and to French miniature painting. (See also The Jack and Belle Linsky Collection, no. 1.) *Robert Lehman Collection, 1975, 1975.1.31*

7   LORENZO MONACO, Florentine,
1370/72–1425/26
Nativity
*Tempera on panel; 8¹⁄₂ × 11³⁄₄ in.
(21.6 × 29.8 cm.)*

Lorenzo Monaco was probably the most important Quattrocento painter in Florence before Masolino and Masaccio. His original name was Piero di Giovanni, but on entering the Florentine monastery of Santa Maria degli Angeli in 1391, he took the name Lorenzo—hence Lorenzo Monaco, or Lorenzo the Monk. The monastery had a famous school of book-illuminators in which masters carried on the Sienese and Florentine traditions of miniature painting. Lorenzo Monaco mastered the technique of illumination here and turned to panel painting after leaving the monastery sometime before 1406.

The *Nativity* belonged to a predella of a still-unidentified altarpiece and is usually dated shortly before 1413. This panel, with its deliberately fantastic color and line, is an example of the artist's best work. *Robert Lehman Collection, 1975, 1975.1.66*

8 ALESSANDRO BOTTICELLI, Florentine,
1444/45–1510
Annunciation
*Tempera on panel; 9³/₈ × 14³/₈ in. (23.9 ×
36.5 cm.)*

One of the jewels of fifteenth-century Italian art,
this picture embodies the achievements that
made the art of Florence so famous and influential in the second half of the century. The
classical architectural setting is rendered in
perspective, one of the great discoveries of
Florentine artists. The tranquillity of the setting
contrasts with the colorful and vibrant figures of
the Virgin and the archangel Gabriel. They are
seemingly separated by the center row of pillars,
but subtle artistic devices draw them into a
unified composition. Their outlines are almost
mirror images of each other; the rays of light
coming through the doorway, which carry God's
message from heaven through the angel to the
Virgin, also tie the figures together with their
diagonals. The diagonals, along with the angel's
wings, cut the vertical and horizontal lines of the
painting and create an interplay of triangular
patterns. The complex composition, quality of
the drawing, and transparent colors are characteristic of Botticelli's late style, developed about
1490. (See also European Paintings, nos. 6
and 7.) *Robert Lehman Collection, 1975,
1975.1.74*

9 MASTER OF SAINT FRANCIS, Umbrian,
late 13th c.
Saints Bartholomew and Simon
*Tempera on panel; 18³/₄ × 8³/₄ in. (47.6 ×
22.3 cm.)*

This small panel was painted by an artist who is
called the Master of Saint Francis, after a portrait of Saint Francis in Assisi that he painted
between 1270 and 1280. The earliest painting in
the Robert Lehman Collection, it was part of an
altarpiece. Its style shows strong Byzantine influence, especially in the stiff facial lines and the
symmetrical arrangement of the beards. *Robert
Lehman Collection, 1975, 1975.1.104*

10 ROBERTO D'ODORISIO, Neapolitan, second half of 15th c.
Saints John and Mary Magdalen
Tempera on panel; 23 × 15⅝ in. (58.4 × 39.7 cm.)

This panel was originally the right wing of a diptych (the left wing, *The Dead Christ and the Virgin*, is in the National Gallery, London). It is a famous example of the Sienese and Florentine influence in Naples. The half-length figures with their narrow slit eyes and dramatic facial expressions and the small angels hovering over them represent the impact of Florentine art. The Sienese traits are the rich gold tooling of the halos and the strange scriptlike ornamentation (an imitation of Kufic characters in Arabic) framing the composition. The latest scholarly research attributes the diptych to Roberto d'Odorisio, a major artist of the Angevin court of Naples, and dates it around 1350. *Robert Lehman Collection, 1975, 1975.1.102*

11 LORENZO VENEZIANO, Venetian, act. 1356–72
Madonna and Child
Tempera on panel; 42½ × 25½ in. (108 × 64.7 cm.)

The Venetian love of luxury is evident in this large panel. The elaborate throne, the Madonna's sumptuous dress and mantle, and the gold, fur-lined robe of the Child demonstrate the richness of contemporary Venetian dress.

The goldfinch, perched on the Madonna's hand, is described in pious stories as a good omen in time of disease and plague; its appearance is especially associated with the recovery of sick children. This symbolic meaning and the presence of two donors—a merchant and a Franciscan friar—suggest that this panel may have been commissioned as a votive offering to give thanks for and to commemorate the Virgin's intercession at some grave time. Because of its rich colors, gentle emotions, and symbolism, this painting is considered an early work by Lorenzo, dating from about 1360. *Robert Lehman Collection, 1975, 1975.1.78*

12 GIOVANNI BELLINI, Venetian,
ca. 1430–d. 1516
Madonna and Child
Tempera on panel; 21⁵⁄₁₆ × 15⁵⁄₈ in. (54.2 × 39.8 cm.)

The Venetian master Bellini became known as the "painter of Madonnas." In this important early work (ca. 1460), the almost hieratic composition is coupled with a feeling of intense stillness. The former is mostly due to the Byzantine inheritance of Venetian painting; the latter comes mostly from the classical, sculptural modeling of the figures. Several elements contribute to the serenity of the painting: the dignified joining of the two figures, with the Child clasping his Mother's hand; the uninterrupted fall of drapery from the Madonna's headdress and the Child's tunic; and the quiet landscape, undisturbed by human or animal figures. The dramatic intensity and the strong plastic qualities of the figures reveal the influence of the great Paduan painter Andrea Mantegna, Bellini's brother-in-law. (See also European Paintings, nos. 23, 36, and 37.) *Robert Lehman Collection, 1975, 1975.1.81*

13 JACOMETTO VENEZIANO, Venetian,
act. 1472–98
Alvise Contarini; Nun of San Secondo
Panels; Contarini 4¹⁄₈ × 3 in. (10.5 × 7.7 cm.), Nun 3¹⁄₄ × 2⁹⁄₁₆ in. (8.3 × 6.7 cm.)

These small pictures are among the earliest and most famous examples of portrait painting, an art characteristic of sixteenth-century Venetian artists. The man is Alvise Contarini, a wealthy Venetian merchant; the identity of the nun, who wears the headdress of the Benedictine nuns of San Secondo, is unknown. Her décolletage is surprising, but life at San Secondo was so worldly that in 1515 the convent was subjected to reform by the patriarch of Venice.

The monumentality of these small portraits is achieved in part through the composition, with the sitters represented in three-quarter view. A profile view was then standard with Florentine and other Italian artists, and the three-quarter formula came to Venice through the influence of Flemish painters. Monumentality is also gained through the summary treatment of the faces, another Flemish trait. *Robert Lehman Collection, 1975, 1975.1.86,85*

14 PETRUS CHRISTUS, Flemish, act. by 1444–d. 1472/73
Saint Eligius
Oil on panel; 39 × 33⁷/₁₆ in. (99 × 85 cm.)

Tradition holds that this painting, dated 1449, was commissioned by a goldsmiths' guild to promote their trade under the protection of Saint Eligius, the patron saint of their craft. This picture, unusually large for a Flemish painting of this period, is dominated by three almost life-size figures. Saint Eligius, a metalworker and bishop who died in 660, is represented as a goldsmith. Because of the more than thirty depictions of jewels and other precious objects, this painting is one of the most important sources of knowledge of fifteenth-century goldsmiths' work. The almost total absence of representations of the saint or of goldsmiths prior to this painting indicates that the subject and the composition were new. As the representation of an everyday event, a genre scene, it might be called Petrus Christus's invention; as such it is the first of a long line of paintings showing goldsmiths and money changers. (See also European Paintings, nos. 57 and 58.) *Robert Lehman Collection, 1975, 1975.1.110*

15 HANS MEMLING, Flemish, act. ca. 1465–d. 1494
Annunciation
Oil on panel; 31 × 21⁵/₈ in. (78.8 × 55 cm.)

Memling was born in Germany but spent most of his life in Bruges, where he was a prolific and very popular artist. This painting, one of his masterworks, dates from 1482. Its serenity derives not only from the calm faces and quiet poses of the Virgin Mary and the archangel Gabriel but also from the cool, transparent colors. The room might be an ordinary bedroom in a wealthy burgher's house in Bruges. The everyday household objects have, however, a special significance. The brass candlestick and the half-filled glass bottle, for example, represent the shining glory and clarity of the Virgin, while the bouquet of lilies is a symbol of her purity. In using these objects as symbols, Memling followed the example of earlier Flemish painters such as Jan van Eyck and Robert Campin; the colors and the quiet drama of the composition reflect the influence of another Flemish predecessor, Rogier van der Weyden (see European Paintings, nos. 53–56, and Medieval Art—The Cloisters, no. 28). *Robert Lehman Collection, 1975, 1975.1.113*

16 HANS MEMLING, Flemish, act. ca. 1465–
d. 1494
Portrait of a Young Man
Oil on panel; 15¼ × 11⅛ in. (38.8 × 28.3 cm.)

Memling excelled in portraiture, continuing the
tradition of Jan van Eyck and Petrus Christus.
This picture, which dates from 1470–75, is one
of his finest male portraits. The identity of the
sitter is not known, but his features and dress
suggest that he may have been a member of
the large Italian colony in Bruges. (See also
European Paintings, no. 60.) *Robert Lehman
Collection, 1975, 1975.1.112*

18 JEAN FOUQUET, French, 1415/20–1480
Descent of the Holy Ghost upon the Faithful
Illumination; 7¾ × 5¾ in. (19.7 × 14.6 cm.)

This miniature is from a Book of Hours (a book
with prayers for the canonical hours of the day)
that belonged to Étienne Chevalier, treasurer of
France. It was illuminated by Jean Fouquet
after his return from Italy in 1448, most probably
in 1452. The Book of Hours, illustrated in luminous colors, its compositions enriched by the
subtle use of gold, united the achievement of
French and Italian art. This illuminated page
represents the descent of the Holy Spirit upon
the faithful, who are shown in medieval Paris.
This is the earliest known topographical view
of the city—an unusual setting for this scene.
The most famous monuments shown are the
facade of Notre-Dame, the Pont Saint-Michel—
a covered bridge at this time—and, beyond it,
the Petit Châtelet. The text at the bottom is
the beginning of the Vespers of the Holy Spirit.
Robert Lehman Collection, 1975, M 194

17 GERARD DAVID, Flemish, act. by 1484–
d. 1523
**Archangel Gabriel and the Virgin of
the Annunciation**
Oil on canvas; each 34 × 11 in. (86.4 × 28 cm.)

Reproduced here are the outer sides of the
wings of an altarpiece painted about 1500 by
Gerard David. The inner panels of these wings,
also in the Robert Lehman Collection, are *Christ
Bearing the Cross and the Crucifixion* and the
Resurrection with the Pilgrims of Emmaus. The
wings were split in the early nineteenth century;
it is not known when they were separated from
the central panel or whether the central panel
has survived. The four paintings from the wings
are in excellent condition and reveal the fine
details and careful brushwork characteristic of
this late medieval master. (See also European
Paintings, no. 62; The Jack and Belle Linsky
Collection, no. 6.) *Robert Lehman Collection,
1975, 1975.1.120*

19   MASTER OF MOULINS, French,
act. ca. 1480–1500
**Portrait of a Young Princess (Margaret
of Austria)**
*Tempera and oil on wood; 13½ × 9½ in.
(34 × 24 cm.)*

This portrait is believed to show Margaret of
Austria, the daughter of Emperor Maximilian I
and Mary of Burgundy, at the age of ten or
eleven, when she was betrothed to the king of
France, Charles VIII, and lived with the French
royal family at the château of Amboise. Her
marriage to Charles VIII was dissolved in 1491,
thus dating the painting to 1490–91. The somewhat sullen, pale face expresses the dignity
and social standing of the unhappy child bride
and contrasts strongly with the royal crimson of
the velvet robe, the pendant in the form of a
gold fleur-de-lis, and the elaborate headdress.
The painter of this well-composed panel seems
to have fused the Flemish and French traditions
of definition of form and clear precision. But as
an artist of a new generation he enlarged the
scope of the portrait by means of the deep
landscape, thus loosening its strict organization.
The painting is attributed to the Master of Moulins,
so called after a triptych he executed for the
cathedral of Moulins. *Robert Lehman Collection,
1975, 1975.1.130*

20   GERMAN MASTER, mid-15th c.
**Madonna and Child with a Donor Presented
by Saint Jerome**
Panel; 25 × 19 in. (63.5 × 48.3 cm.)

This German panel is a masterwork about
which very little is known. It may be dated by its
style and by the details of the costumes to
around 1450, and the facial types and the linear-
ity of the design point toward a region including
southern Germany and Switzerland. But the
sculptured bench shows the influence of Flemish
painters, and the prophets on the side of the
bench show some similarities to Burgundian
sculpture from about 1440. The delicate figures
of God and the two angels are direct borrow-
ings from Flemish and Burgundian goldsmiths'
work of the early fifteenth century. The three
trees on the grassy bank strongly resemble
those in Giovanni di Paolo's *Expulsion from
Paradise* (no. 6). Although the painter has not
been identified, he was probably a south German artist who may have traveled in Flanders
and Italy. *Robert Lehman Collection, 1975,
1975.1.133*

21 HANS HOLBEIN THE YOUNGER, German, 1497/98–1543
Erasmus of Rotterdam
Oil on wood; 7⅜ × 5¾ in. (18.7 × 14.6 cm.)

Holbein was introduced to humanist circles in Basel, Switzerland, in 1516, and he painted a number of portraits of humanists, including Erasmus (1466–1536), who became a close friend of the artist. Holbein executed many portraits of Erasmus, done at various times and for various purposes. This small likeness, with the arms resting on a parapet and the hands crossed, was probably painted after 1523. The "king of humanists" is represented in a dignified pose wearing a simple furred robe. The strong facial features have been somewhat softened, but they still transmit Erasmus's determined, unbending character. The *cartellino* in the upper left-hand corner is a seventeenth-century addition. Its inscription is illegible, but it might be the painted sign that was the mark of the collection of the earl of Arundel. (See also European Paintings, no. 92.) *Robert Lehman Collection, 1975, 1975.1.138*

22 EL GRECO, Spanish (b. Crete), 1541–1614
Saint Jerome as a Cardinal
Oil on canvas; 42½ × 34¼ in. (108 × 87 cm.)

El Greco was born Doménikos Theotokópoulos in Crete and received his early training there (probably in the Byzantine tradition). After studying in Venice and Rome, he settled in Toledo, Spain, about 1577. In this late painting, dated between 1600 and 1610, he presents Saint Jerome as an ascetic scholar and visionary. The frontality of this figure with its long head and beard demonstrates how strongly his Byzantine heritage influenced El Greco. There are five known versions of this composition, the finest of which are this one and that in the Frick Collection, New York. (See also European Paintings, nos. 45–47.) *Robert Lehman Collection, 1975, 1975.1.146*

23 FRANCISCO GOYA, Spanish, 1746–1828
The Countess of Altamira and Her Daughter
Oil on canvas; 76½ × 45¼ in. (194.3 × 114.9 cm.)

This double portrait is the third of four portraits that Goya painted of Count Altamira and his family between 1787 and 1789. (The fourth Altamira portrait is also in the Museum; see European Paintings, no. 51.)

This painting is a masterpiece both in its characterization and in its virtuoso use of color. Intensive study of the works of Velázquez and of the Venetian G. B. Tiepolo imbued Goya's art with a brilliant technique and breadth of style. His understanding of human nature shows in his portraits, and his free-flowing brushwork had an impact on the French Impressionists. *Robert Lehman Collection, 1975, 1975.1.148*

24 REMBRANDT, Dutch, 1606–1669
Portrait of Gérard de Lairesse
Oil on canvas; 44¼ × 34½ in. (112.4 × 87.6 cm.)

Painted in 1665, this portrait dates from
Rembrandt's last years. Gérard de Lairesse
(1641–1711), a painter well known in his time,
was notorious for his luxurious tastes and repul-
sive face. His almost-destroyed saddle nose,
swollen lips, and sullen expression were the
consequences of congenital syphilis. Rembrandt painted the young, brash, and unpleas-
ant Lairesse with compassion. He composed
the portrait to deemphasize the ugliness of the
face. The right hand is tucked into the robe,
perhaps to hide the sores that covered it; the
left hand is brought forward, counterbalancing
the ghostlike face. (See also no. 44 and European
Paintings, nos. 73–77.) *Robert Lehman
Collection, 1975, 1975.1.140*

25 GERARD TER BORCH, Dutch, 1617–81
Portraits of Jan van Duren and His Wife
Oil on canvas; 32 × 26 in. (81.3 × 66.1 cm.)

A pair of portraits by Ter Borch, which are both
in the Robert Lehman Collection, represent the
burgomaster Jan van Duren, a wealthy Dutch
burgher, and Margaretha van Haexbergen, his
wife. In these works, which date from about 1660,
the artist has portrayed the couple without flat-
tery. The faces mirror well-being and quiet con-
tentment, as do the dark clothes, brightened only
by the white of the collars and cuffs. Ter Borch
had traveled to Spain and had probably come
into contact with Velázquez. These solitary figures, represented with cool objectivity and on
a monotone gray background, reflect the influence of the Spanish painter. (See also
European Paintings, no. 79.) *Robert Lehman
Collection, 1975, 1975.1.141, 142*

26 J. A. D. INGRES, French, 1780–1867
Portrait of the Princesse de Broglie
Oil on canvas; 47¾ × 35¾ in. (121.3 × 90.8 cm.)

The princesse de Broglie (1825–60) was a great beauty and a highly respected woman, the embodiment of the best of the Second Empire aristocracy. Ingres began her portrait in 1851; after accepting the commission, he wrote to a friend that it would be his last except for that of his wife. Thus the painting completes Ingres's series of aristocratic portraits, and it incorporates his mastery, his bold use of color, and his understanding of female character.

The French poet Baudelaire remarked that Ingres "depicts women as he sees them, for it would appear that he loves them too much to wish to change them; he fastens upon their slightest beauties with the keenness of a surgeon; he follows the gentlest sinuosity of their line with the humble devotion of a lover."

Here the tranquillity of the princess's face, the resting arms, and the bluish gray of the background contrast with the shimmering dress, the damask chair, and the still-life arrangement of the evening wrap, gloves, and fan. This juxtaposition of background and foreground creates the inner tensions that make the painting so alive. (See also no. 45 and European Paintings, no. 121.) *Robert Lehman Collection, 1975, 1975.1.186*

27 CAMILLE COROT, French, 1796–1875
Diana and Actaeon
Oil on canvas; 61⅝ × 44⅜ in. (156.5 × 112.7 cm.)

This picture, dated 1836, was painted after Corot's second visit to Italy. The mythological story of the chaste goddess of the hunt, Diana, and her sudden discovery by Actaeon is set in a landscape of the Roman Campagna. This is the earliest landscape by Corot in which classical figures are introduced; the goddess and four bathing nymphs clearly show the influence of the seventeenth-century French painter Nicolas Poussin. The landscape looks as if Corot painted it on the scene; its deep, dense colors are naturalistic and somewhat different from the misty, silvery tones of his later, better-known paintings. That style may be recognized in the distant trees on the left side of the painting. This part was reworked by Corot almost forty years later, in 1874, when new owners of the painting asked him to do so. (See also European Paintings, no. 122.) *Robert Lehman Collection, 1975, 1975.1.162*

28 CLAUDE MONET, French, 1840–1926
Landscape near Zaandam
Oil on canvas; 17⁵⁄₁₆ × 26⅜ in. (44 × 67 cm.)

Monet was forced to leave Paris during the Franco-Prussian War of 1870, and after a stay in London he went to Zaandam on the advice of a friend, the painter Charles François Daubigny. The damp, dissolving atmosphere and the ca-

nals lined with colorful houses apparently were very appealing to Monet. This light and airy picture, painted in 1871, conveys how this experience helped give his palette a greater subtlety. His Dutch landscapes were greatly admired by his fellow artists. (See also European Paintings, nos. 144–146.) *Robert Lehman Collection, 1975, 1975.1.196*

9 PIERRE RENOIR, French, 1841–1919
oung Girl Bathing
il on canvas; 32 × 25½ in. (81.3 × 64.8 cm.)

1892–93 Renoir painted many similar nudes
young girls bathing. This painting, dated
892, probably exemplifies his method as he
escribed it in 1908: "I arrange my subject as I
ant it, then I go ahead and paint it; like a child I
ant a red to be sonorous, to sound like a bell; if
doesn't turn out that way, I put on more reds or
her colors till I get it. I am no cleverer than
at. I have no rules and no methods; anyone
an look at my materials or watch how I paint—
e will see that I have no secrets. I look at a
ude; there are myriads of tiny tints. I must find
e ones that will make the flesh on my canvas
e and quiver." The "sonorous reds" and the
nyriads of tiny tints" in this painting show
enoir's complete mastery of color. (See also
uropean Paintings, nos. 147 and 148.) *Robert
hman Collection, 1975, 1975.1.199*

PAUL CÉZANNE, French, 1839–1906
use Behind Trees on the Road to Tholonet
l on canvas; 26¾ × 36³/₁₆ in. (68 × 92 cm.)

is painting is an excellent example of
zanne's credo: "I try to render perspective
lely by means of color . . . the main thing in a
cture is to achieve distance. By that one
cognizes a painter's talent." The *House Bend Trees* (ca. 1885–86) was painted on the
tskirts of Aix, where Cézanne spent most of
s life. Apparently the mountainous landscape
Provence, with its tall trees and blue sky,
ovided the best surroundings for testing and
rfecting his revolutionary method. The trees
d the house behind them receive the most

summary treatment. The colors put on with
bold strokes are basic: the ocher reds, in accord
with his beliefs, have the same value in the right
foreground as on the roofs of the houses. The
basic principle of Impressionism—the representation of nature—is adhered to but in a different
manner. For instance, in Renoir's *Young Girl
Bathing* (no. 29), the artist's impressions are
broken up into "myriads of tiny tints," while
here they are compressed into larger forms of basic
colors. The former method eventually led to the
Pointillists (who painted in minute dots), while
Cézanne's very much influenced the Fauves.
(See also European Paintings, nos. 140–143.)
Robert Lehman Collection, 1975, 1975.1.160

31 EDGAR DEGAS, French, 1835–1917
Landscape
Oil on canvas; 20 × 24 in. (51 × 61 cm.)

The subject of this picture is unusual for Degas. Instead of the graceful ballet dancers and stylish ladies so closely associated with him, here is the peaceful town of Saint-Valéry-sur-Somme. This landscape was painted about 1898, when Degas stayed there with his painter friend Bra-

quaval. The colors are fresh and pastel-like, capturing the sunlit reds, ochers, and yellows of the houses. But the black contours of the houses and their roofs overlay a subtle network of geometric forms, perhaps an indication of the coming style of landscapes by Fauve artists. (See also Drawings, no. 6, and European Paintings, nos. 137–139.) *Robert Lehman Collection, 1975, 1975.1.167*

32 ANDRÉ DERAIN, French, 1880–1954
Houses of Parliament at Night
Oil on canvas; 31 × 39 in. (81 × 100 cm.)

Derain painted this strong Fauve canvas during his first visit to London in 1905. It is masterful in its composition and technique and most of all in its colors. The pictorial field is divided into two equal sections by the diagonal of the shoreline. The upper half is split again by the use of differing brushstrokes and colors: the short blue verticals and horizontals characterize the build-

ing; the wider, curving strokes the movement of the night sky. Derain repeated this pattern in the water of the Thames: the upper section, close to the shoreline, is done with parallel strokes, while the large expanse of the water with heavy barges is represented with long, flowing ones. This juxtaposition of rhythms and colors imbues the painting with an extraordinary sense of movement. (See also Twentieth Century Art, no. 4.) *Robert Lehman Collection, 1975, 1975.1.168*

PIERRE BONNARD, French, 1867–1947
Landscape in the South: Le Cannet
Oil on canvas; 25 × 28¼ in. (63.5 × 71.8 cm.)

Bonnard owned a villa in Le Cannet, a village above Cannes, and from his garden he could see the town's red roofs, the mountains, and the sea. In this luminous painting (1945–46), the garden is in late spring bloom; farther down are the red roofs. There is great freedom in this landscape, in the far-reaching vista and the brilliant colors. With hundreds of small brushstrokes the innumerable color spots are arranged into horizontal layers representing the shoreline, the shallow, then the deeper waters, and finally the distant sky. (See also Twentieth Century Art, no. 8.) *Robert Lehman Collection, 1975, 1975.1.158*

34 BALTHUS, French, b. 1908
Figure in Front of a Mantel
Oil on canvas; 75 × 64½ in. (190.5 × 163.8 cm.)

A self-taught painter, Balthus, like so many earlier French artists, made his pilgrimage to Italy, where he copied the frescoes of Masaccio and Piero della Francesca. The nude figure of a girl before a mirror and the intimacy of a bedroom interior are timeless themes of French art. In this picture, which was painted in 1955, the classical figure and the pure contour of the profile are undeniable echoes of Piero della Francesca's standing females, but without their gravity. The figure is rather light, like those of Matisse, and pliant, like those by Ingres. But the whole is totally mid-twentieth century. Some of the details are decorative, such as the wallpaper; some almost neorealistic, like the carving on the mantelpiece. The figure is painted with a discreet eroticism; the painter suggests the feline feeling permeating the body rather than its structure. The simplicity of his means counterbalances the complexity of his meanings. (See also Twentieth Century Art, no. 7.) *Robert Lehman Collection, 1975, 1975.1.155*

35 Aquamanile
Mosan school, ca. 1400
Bronze; h. 13³/₁₆ in. (33.5 cm.)

A strikingly bold composition, this aquamanile
(water vessel) is an exceptional piece of secular
sculpture, which represents an episode from a
popular medieval tale. It was said that Alexander the Great was so infatuated with his bride,
Phyllis, that he neglected affairs of state. The
dignitaries of the court sent his former tutor, the
philosopher Aristotle, to beg the king to return
to his duties. To avenge herself, Phyllis made
Aristotle fall in love with her and told him he
must prove his love by allowing her to ride on
his back. When Alexander demanded that Aristotle explain conduct so contrary to his own
advice, the philosopher replied, "If a woman
can make such a fool of a man of my age and
wisdom, how much more dangerous must she
be for younger ones? I added an example
to my precept; it is your privilege to benefit
by both." *Robert Lehman Collection,
1975, 1975.1.1416*

36 Plate with Hercules Slaying the Hydra
Italian, ca. 1515
Majolica; diam. 14¹/₂ in. (36.8 cm.)

This large plate represents an episode from the
Labors of Hercules: Hercules Slaying the Hydra.
The rich crimson luster and the rhythmical floral
border decoration indicate that the plate was
made in Deruta about 1515. The central composition is derived from elements taken from
many of the painter Antonio Pollaiuolo's designs.
The scene is well fitted into the center of the
plate; Hercules' raised arms and his stick curve
into the gold scale decoration of the well border.
The floral decoration, too, fills the background
well; it is present but does not overwhelm. The
pictorial center and the floral-wreath border
complement each other perfectly, not only in
design but also in color. The harmony of these
various elements gives this plate an unusual
beauty. Two other majolica plates in the Collection,
also depicting the Labors of Hercules, are based
on compositions by Pollaiuolo. *Robert Lehman
Collection, 1975, 1975.1.1038*

37 Plate with the Prodigal Son amid the Swine

Italian, 1525
Majolica; diam. 11¼ in. (28.6 cm.)

This brightly colored and brilliantly lustered plate has been attributed to Giorgio Andreoli (act. 1519–53), the most famous lusterer in Gubbio; his initials, with the date 1525, are painted on the back of the plate. The composition closely follows Albrecht Dürer's famous engraving, the *Prodigal Son amid the Swine*, usually dated to 1496. The print captured the essence of the biblical parable: the final humiliation and desperate prayer of the prodigal son when forced to eat from the trough of the swine. Italian artists especially admired this print, probably because it successfully blends pathos and genre details, such as the hungry, snorting pigs and the quaint German farmyard. The majolica painter defined the main areas with large masses of color set against each other. His mastery of color is shown best in the application of the luster. The strong outlines of the figures in the central group and the long vertical and horizontal lines on the timbered buildings provided him with an almost unlimited opportunity to display his virtuosity. *Robert Lehman Collection, 1975, 1975.1.1105*

38 Bowl with the Arms of Pope Julius II

Italian, 1508
Majolica; diam. 12¾ in. (32.4 cm.)

Technically and artistically this large bowl is one of the masterpieces of Italian majolica. The painted decoration is masterfully constructed from various elements. The center is occupied by the coat of arms of Pope Julius II (the oak tree of the Della Rovere family) crowned by the papal tiara and crossed keys (symbols of papal authority). Above a red hanging is the veil of Veronica with the Holy Face. This central part is surrounded by putti and satyrs. An inscription on the back states that the bowl was made in Castel Durante by the potter Giovanni Maria in 1508. Characteristic of his work are his distinctive colors: the soft, grayish blue, the light amber brown, and the beautifully drawn dark-blue contours. *Robert Lehman Collection, 1975, 1975.1.1015*

39 Plate with Conversion of Saint Paul

French, late 16th c.
Enamel; l. 20 in. (50.8 cm.)

The large oval plate of Limoges enamel, illustrating the Conversion of Saint Paul, is a signed work by Suzanne Court, who is the only known woman enameler of Limoges. There are no documents mentioning her, and the period of her activity can be dated only very loosely, to a few decades before 1600, which is the date assigned to this plate. The front and back are painted with the same virtuosity although in an entirely different manner. The front sparkles with the whites of arms, legs, and horses, as well as with the gold on the trappings and in the heavenly rays. The decoration of the wide rim resembles a jeweled collar, with centauresses, herms, and sphinxes painted with the precision of goldsmiths' work. On the verso, masks and herms are interwoven with a latticework of decoration in grisaille on a background of gold scrollwork. *Robert Lehman Collection, 1975, 1975.1.1233*

40 ANTONIO POLLAIUOLO, Florentine, 1429–98
Study for a Projected Equestrian Monument to Francesco Sforza
Pen and brown ink with light brown wash on paper; 11³/₁₆ × 9⁵/₈ in. (28.5 × 24.4 cm.)

This and the related study in the Graphische Sammlung, Munich, seem to be those owned by Vasari and described in his *Lives* as variant designs, found in Pollaiuolo's studio after his death, for the monument Ludovico Sforza proposed to commemorate his father, Francesco Sforza. The drawings presumably were executed between 1480 and about 1485—between Ludovico's accession as regent in Milan and Leonardo da Vinci's involvement in the ill-fated project. (Leonardo's clay model of 1493 was destroyed during the French occupation in 1499, and no bronze was cast.) *Robert Lehman Collection, 1975, 1975.1.410*

41 FRANCESCO DI GIORGIO, Sienese, 1439–1502
A Kneeling Humanist Presented by Two Muses
Pen and brown ink with brown wash and blue gouache on vellum; 7¹/₄ × 7⁵/₈ in. (18.4 × 19.4 cm.)

The versatile artist Francesco di Giorgio worked principally as an architect and designer of fortifications. The central figure in this drawing brings to mind the Saint Thomas in his *Nativity*, a signed painting of 1475 (Pinacoteca, Siena); similarly, the female figure on the left in the drawing is reminiscent of the saint in the right rear of the painting. It has been suggested that the trompe-l'oeil presentation of this drawing indicates that the artist had a sculptural project in mind; it is more likely, however, that the design was intended for a painting or, not impossibly, intarsia. (See also European Sculpture and Decorative Arts, no. 45.) *Robert Lehman Collection, 1975, 1975.1.376*

42 GIOVANNI DOMENICO TIEPOLO, Venetian, 1727–1804
Punchinello as a Dressmaker
Pen and brown ink, brown wash, over black chalk on paper; 12 × 16³/₄ in. (30.5 × 42.6 cm.)

The latest and most complete of all G. D. Tiepolo's various series of drawings is the Punchinello cycle of 104 drawings, which he titled *Divertimento per li Regazzi* (Entertainment for Children). The hero is a character from Italian comedy, but his history as illustrated by Tiepolo follows no known text. Here, in a Rococo interior, Punchinello fits a dress on his stocky client. His assistant carries off the old garments, which are made of striped Venetian stuff; the artist seldom fails to include a length of this fabric as a skirt, a waistcoat, a scarf, an oriental robe, or a camel's saddlecloth. (See also European Paintings, no. 33.) *Robert Lehman Collection, 1975, 1975.1.466*

43 ALBRECHT DÜRER, German, 1471–1528
Self-Portrait at Age Twenty-two
Pen and ink on paper; 14⅜ × 18¹¹/₁₆ in. (36.5 × 47.5 cm.)

One of Dürer's most important and revealing self-portraits, this drawing precedes the famous painted one in the Louvre. The hand seems to be a separate study; the pillow is related to those on the verso. The initials are not by the artist. (See also European Paintings, no. 90, and Prints and Photographs, no. 4.) *Robert Lehman Collection, 1975, 1975.1.862*

44 REMBRANDT, Dutch, 1606–1669
The Last Supper, after Leonardo da Vinci
Red chalks on paper; 14⅜ × 18¹¹/₁₆ in. (36.5 × 47.5 cm.)

This profound and magisterial drawing is one of the best demonstrations of Rembrandt's debt to the art of the Italian Renaissance. Since he had never been to Italy, Rembrandt used a Lombard engraving of Leonardo's fresco in Santa Maria delle Grazie in Milan. The study consists of two stages. The first, in hard chalk, is probably from the middle 1630s; the second stage, in broader strokes and with softer chalk, was probably added in the late 1640s or early 1650s. (See also no. 24; Drawings, no. 9; European Paintings, nos. 73–77; and Prints and Photographs, no. 2.) *Robert Lehman Collection, 1975, 1975.1.794*

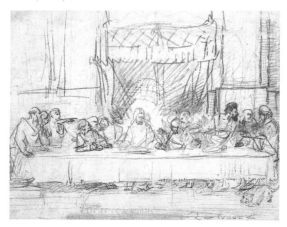

45 J.A.D. INGRES, French, 1780–1867
Study for "Raphael and the Fornarina"
Graphite on white wove paper; 10 × 7¾ in. (25.4 × 19.7 cm.)

This exquisite drawing is closely related to the painted *Raphael and the Fornarina* in the Fogg Museum in Cambridge, Massachusetts, which is the earliest surviving version from an original five. The painting is dated 1813 and was exhibited at the Salon of 1814. The drawing may therefore be dated around 1813. (See also no. 26; Drawings, no. 5; and European Paintings, no.121.) *Robert Lehman Collection, 1975, 1975.1.646*

FIRST FLOOR

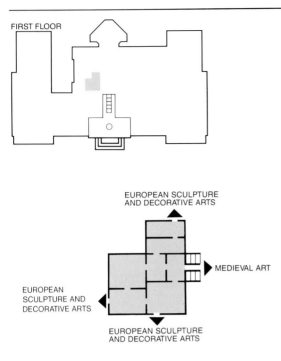

EUROPEAN SCULPTURE
AND DECORATIVE ARTS

MEDIEVAL ART

EUROPEAN
SCULPTURE AND
DECORATIVE ARTS

EUROPEAN SCULPTURE
AND DECORATIVE ARTS

THE JACK AND BELLE LINSKY COLLECTION

The Jack and Belle Linsky Galleries, opened in 1984, house a formerly private collection exceptional in its quality and its wide-ranging and highly personal yet discriminating interests. During their more than forty years of collecting, the Linskys were drawn to precious and luxurious objects—to the elegance of eighteenth-century French furniture as well as to a variety of European porcelains. Their love of works meticulously executed and carefully finished led them to gemlike paintings of the early Netherlandish and Italian schools in addition to sumptuous French and Spanish eighteenth-century paintings and fine medieval, Renaissance, and Baroque bronzes.

Highlights of the Linsky Collection include paintings by Lucas Cranach the Elder, Gerard David, Juan de Flandes, Rubens, and Boucher; more than two hundred Rococo porcelain figures, from such renowned factories as Meissen, Chantilly, Mennecy, and Capodimonte; exquisite furniture by such master *ébénistes* as Jean François Oeben and David Roentgen; jewelry and goldsmiths' work, such as James Cox's ingenious automaton; and thirty-seven bronze statuettes and utensils, among them a lively Romanesque monk-scribe astride a dragon and a standing satyr by Antico.

In the installation of the Linsky Galleries, the Museum has striven to create the atmosphere of intimacy the works of art demand and thus to preserve the essential quality of a private collection.

1 GIOVANNI DI PAOLO, Sienese, act. by
1420–d. 1482
The Adoration of the Magi
Tempera and gold on wood; 10⅝ × 9⅛ in.
(27 × 23.2 cm.)

Giovanni di Paolo was one of the most prolific
as well as individual artists of the fifteenth
century. This predella panel has long been
recognized as part of a remarkably inventive
series of scenes of the Infancy of Christ; its two
companion panels —*The Nativity* and *The Infant Christ Disputing in the Temple*—are in the
Fogg Art Museum, Cambridge, and the Isabella
Stewart Gardner Museum, Boston. The composition of this *Adoration* derives from Gentile da
Fabriano's great altarpiece *The Adoration of the
Magi*, painted in 1423 for the Sacristy at Santa
Trinità, Florence, and from that work Giovanni
di Paolo has taken the poses of the Virgin and
Child and of the first and second magi. Here,
however, he has simplified the costumes and
setting and brought a new intimacy to the scene
in the gesture of the youngest magus, who
tenderly embraces Joseph. The Metropolitan
has the largest collection of paintings by Giovanni
di Paolo outside Siena (see European Paintings, no. 14, and the Robert Lehman Collection,
no. 6). *The Jack and Belle Linsky Collection,
1982, 1982.60.4*

---

2 VITTORE CRIVELLI, Venetian, act. by
1465–d. 1501/1502
Madonna and Child with Two Angels
*Tempera and gold on wood; overall with added
strips 22½ × 16⅝ in. (57.2 × 42.4 cm.)*

Vittore Crivelli had the misfortune of being the
brother of a more inventive artist, and his reputation has suffered from the inevitable comparison—unfortunately so, for though Vittore's
later works were conceived under the influence
of Carlo (see European Paintings, no. 22), his
earlier paintings reveal quite independent gifts.
This panel, painted shortly after Vittore's move
from Dalmatia to the Marches in 1481, is among
his most beautiful works. At the top of the
picture is a swag of fruit composed of a pomegranate, emblem of the Church and of the
Resurrection; a plum, possibly an allusion to
fidelity or to Christ's Passion; and two pears
and an apple, which very likely symbolize Original Sin. On the parapet at the bottom are a
carnation, whose Greek name means "flower
of God"; two cherries, symbolic of Christ's blood;
and what is probably an open breviary. The
halos, crown, jeweled diadems, and the brocaded borders of the Virgin's clothes are in
raised, gilt relief (*pastiglia*). *The Jack and Belle
Linsky Collection, 1982, 1982.60.6*

3 FRA BARTOLOMEO, Florentine, 1472–1517
Portrait of a Man
Oil on wood; overall 15⅝ × 12⅛ in.
(39.7 × 30.8 cm.)

Vasari, in his life of Fra Bartolomeo, tells how the young artist transformed his work through the careful study of Leonardo's paintings. And, in the 1490s, Fra Bartolomeo was, aside from Leonardo, the most innovative painter in Florence. However, it was not just to Leonardo that he turned for inspiration. Flemish paintings were imported on a large scale in the second half of the fifteenth century, and their technical perfection and realism proved irresistible to Florentine artists. This portrait, as well as other works by Fra Bartolomeo, shows the influence of the Flemish painter Hans Memling—in the landscape and in the detailed physiognomic description. Yet the evocative treatment of the building and trees, the sense of atmosphere, and the lively figure who has set out for a walk are all Fra Bartolomeo's alone. These features foreshadow the extraordinary backgrounds of his mature work and testify to his exceptional sensitivity to nature.

Despite the posthumous inscription at the top, it has not been possible to identify the sitter, who was once thought to be a member of the Sassetti family of Florence. *The Jack and Belle Linsky Collection, 1982, 1982.60.8*

---

4 ANDREA DEL SARTO, Florentine, 1486–1530
Portrait of a Man
Oil on canvas, transferred from wood; 26¼ × 19⅞ in. (66.7 × 50.5 cm.)

From about 1514 until his death in 1530, Andrea del Sarto was one of the preeminent High Renaissance artists in Florence (see European Paintings, no. 9). Such was his fame that he was invited to France by Francis I, and in Florence he enjoyed the patronage and friendship of a number of leading citizens, yet fewer than a dozen portraits can be attributed to him with any degree of assurance. Typical of Sarto, the sitter here is posed with his torso in profile while his head is turned three-quarters toward the viewer. His simple attire—a blue-gray robe over a white shirt and a four-cornered *berretto* —suggests a scholarly occupation or, possibly, an ecclesiastical position, an impression reinforced by the small volume with yellow-edged pages that he holds. *The Jack and Belle Linsky Collection, 1982, 1982.60.9*

5 BACCHIACCA, Florentine, 1495–1557
Leda and the Swan
Oil on wood; overall 16⅞ × 12½ in.
(42.9 × 31.8 cm.)

Bacchiacca's celebrity in Florence in the second quarter of the sixteenth century was based on his carefully painted small narrative scenes that decorated furniture and rooms of patrician palaces. This charming and imaginative panel dominated by the nude figure of Leda seated on the swan is one such work, which, judging from the intentionally curved surface of the picture, must have been designed as part of a piece of furniture.

Leda, the wife of Tyndareus, king of Sparta, was said to have conceived on the same night children by her husband and by Zeus, who came to her in the form of a swan. The number of children—as well as who begat whom —varies from source to source. Here the three children at right can be identified as Castor, Pollux, and Helen, who is but partially hatched; the two children at left are Clytemnestra and Phoebe. The playfully lascivious detail of the swan nibbling Leda's breast derives from a print by the German artist Albrecht Dürer. Of Bacchiacca's five known pictures of Leda and the swan, this one is by far the most individual and accomplished. *The Jack and Belle Linsky Collection, 1982, 1982.60.11*

7 JUAN DE FLANDES, Flemish, ▶
act. in Spain by 1496–d. 1519
The Marriage Feast at Cana
Oil on wood; 8¼ × 6¼ in. (21 × 15.9 cm.)

The marriage feast is set at a sparsely laid table in an open loggia. Christ blesses the water being poured from a pitcher into one of four large pots by the wine steward, thereby enacting the first of his miracles, the changing of the water into wine. Seated at the table with Christ are the Virgin and the groom and bride, who are attended by the master of the feast. The man outside the loggia looking directly at the viewer is thought to be a self-portrait. Remarkably well preserved, this small panel painting is one of the great treasures of the Linsky Collection. It is one of forty-seven panels that were commissioned about 1500 by Isabella the Catholic, queen of Castile and León. Presumably the panels were intended for a portable altarpiece for personal devotion. Paintings by Juan de Flandes, who trained in Flanders, probably in Bruges, but whose activity is not known outside Spain, are exceedingly rare. *The Jack and Belle Linsky Collection, 1982, 1982.60.20*

6 Attributed to GERARD DAVID, Flemish,
act. by 1484–d. 1523
The Adoration of the Magi
Oil on wood; overall 27¾ × 28⅞ in. (70.5 × 73.3 cm.)

Gerard David, after the death of Hans Memling, became the most important painter of his day in Bruges. His style reveals the influence of his predecessor Memling and especially of the Ghent painter Hugo van der Goes, whose compositions he often copied. The architectural details in this *Adoration* reveal David's advanced awareness of Italian Renaissance developments.

The Adoration of the Magi was one of the most popular subjects for late fifteenth- and early sixteenth-century Flemish artists. The opulence of David's representation reflects the tastes of the prosperous bourgeois merchants and bankers who became the principal patrons of art at that time. (See also European Paintings, no. 62 and Robert Lehman Collection, no. 17.) *The Jack and Belle Linsky Collection, 1982, 1982.60.17*

8 PETER PAUL RUBENS, Flemish,
1577–1640
**Portrait of a Man, possibly an Architect or
Geographer**
Oil on copper; 8½ × 5¾ in. (21.6 × 14.6 cm.)

This small portrait of 1597 is Rubens's earliest
known dated work, and it is generally considered the best surviving example of Rubens's art
from his early years in Antwerp.

The painting's style of execution derives from
that of Rubens's teacher, Otto van Veen, while
the composition recalls portraits by Anthonis
Mor and his followers. In its strong modeling
and spatial effect, however, the painting anticipates Rubens's development in Italy (1600–1608).

The sitter has been variously described, on
the basis of the instruments he holds, as a
geographer, an architect, an astronomer, a goldsmith, and a watchmaker. The watch in his
hand, as in other sixteenth-century portraits,
serves here as a *vanitas* symbol, that is, as a
reminder of the brevity of life and of the relative
unimportance of worldly affairs compared to
spiritual being. Such a comment on the "vanity"
of life was recognized at the time as especially
appropriate to portraiture. (See also European
Paintings, nos. 65 and 66, and Drawings, no.
8.) *The Jack and Belle Linsky Collection, 1982,
1982.60.24*

9 JAN STEEN, Dutch, 1626–79
The Dissolute Household
Oil on canvas; 42½ × 35½ in. (108 × 92.2 cm.)

This large canvas is one of the finest examples of Jan Steen's extraordinary talent and represents a theme Steen treated frequently during the 1660s. An upper-middle-class family at home, in an advanced state of gastronomic gratification and, in the case of the master and lady of the house, inebriation, has finally finished dinner. The grandmother has fallen asleep, the man enjoys a pipe, and his wife another glass of wine. Both husband and wife are, in a sense, served by the maid, who suggestively joins hands with the man. At left, a young boy tickles the sleeping woman with a straw, while his older brother, dressed like a soldier, draws his sword to drive an old beggar from the door. Steen extols virtue by condemning vice through the use of parody. Signs and symbols, none of which could have escaped the understanding of contemporary viewers, litter the composition. The backgammon board and the lute with broken strings suggest discord and impending ill fortune, while contributing to the general atmosphere of idle pleasure, and the beggar at the door portends the state to which the revelers will be reduced. (See also European Paintings, no. 82.) *The Jack and Belle Linsky Collection, 1982, 1982.60.31*

10 LUIS EGIDIO MELÉNDEZ, Spanish, 1716–80
Still Life: La Merienda (The Afternoon Meal)
Oil on canvas; 41½ × 60½ in. (105.4 × 153.7 cm.)

Luis Meléndez was trained in Madrid, where his father, Francisco, was employed as a miniaturist in the service of Philip V. Though the younger Meléndez was never awarded a post at court and died in considerable poverty, he is now regarded as second only to Jean Baptiste Chardin among eighteenth-century still-life painters.

Meléndez's still lifes are of a uniquely Spanish type called *bodegon*, in which food, tableware, and kitchen utensils are represented. The format and the handling of space and light are typical of the artist, as is the meticulous rendering of textures and cubic volumes—here, of copper and pottery, of the pitted flesh of pears, the rough skin of a melon, and the smooth, luminous skins of grapes. The copper pot, the basket with handle, and the large bowl were studio props that Meléndez used repeatedly, in different combinations. This painting is the largest and most elaborate of some eighty-five still lifes by Meléndez known today. *The Jack and Belle Linsky Collection, 1982, 1982.60.39*

11 JEAN MARC NATTIER, French, 1685–1766
**Portrait of a Lady, called the Marquise
Perrin de Cypierre**
Oil on canvas; 31½ × 25¼ in. (80 × 64.1 cm.)

Nattier achieved considerable success as a
portraitist in mid-eighteenth-century Paris. He
was popular at the court of Louis XV and painted
the queen, Maria Leszczyńska, in 1748, but he
is perhaps best known for his likenesses of the
royal daughters, who sat for him on numerous
occasions. This portrait is a particularly fine
example of Nattier's style. The identity of the
sitter is not assured, but she may be Florimonde
Parat de Montgeron, wife of Jean Claude
François Perrin, seigneur of Cypierre. Nattier
often represented his subjects—mostly women,
whom he tended to depict in a flattering way—in
mythological or allegorical guises. The lady
here, however, is shown more naturally, wearing a white dress and a blue shawl and holding
a bouquet of flowers, her powdered hair coiffed
in tight curls. A direct, determined expression
gives her a certain individuality and suggests
that the portrait may be a good likeness. *The
Jack and Belle Linsky Collection, 1982,
1982.60.42*

12 FRANÇOIS BOUCHER, French, 1703–70
A View of the Campo Vaccino
Oil on canvas; 25 × 31⅞ in. (63.5 × 81 cm.)

Here Boucher gives us an imaginary evocation
of the Roman Forum, which had fallen to ruins
centuries before and which was known in the
eighteenth century as the Campo Vaccino (cow
field) because of the cattle that grazed there.
The painting, dated 1734, is perhaps the most
idyllic of the landscapes that were the fruit of
Boucher's Italian sojourn (1727–31). Boucher
had won first prize at the Académie Royale in
1723, and thanks to the generosity of an un-
named collector, he set off on his travels in
1727. He is thought to have spent most of his
time in Rome until 1731, and it is evident that
the city impressed him deeply. Unfortunately,
little of his work from this early period has
survived. Few of Boucher's pictures have the
spontaneity and freshness of this painting, which
was discovered in 1953 and is a major addition
to his oeuvre. (See also European Paintings,
no. 113, and European Sculpture and Decorative Arts, nos. 29 and 50.) *The Jack and Belle
Linsky Collection, 1982, 1982.60.44*

13 Monk-Scribe Astride a Dragon

Rhenish (Cologne?), third quarter of 12th c.
Brass, cast and chiseled; h. 9⅜ in. (23.8 cm.),
w. 7½ in. (19 cm.), d. 3⅝ in (9.2 cm.)

A young, beardless monk, tonsured and wearing a hooded habit, sits backward on a dragon. With head bowed, the monk is intent on what he is inscribing with the pen in his right hand; a correcting knife, or scraper, is poised in his left hand. The dragon on which he rides has richly feathered wings, crosshatched shoulders, furry legs, and vegetative extensions. Its tail, resting on a footlike support, is, in fact, a nubby stem beneath the lectern upon which the monk writes. The dragon's head and neck curl upward in an S curve and, with the crest, form a back support for the monk. Contrasting textures and patterns of points and engraved lines are used effectively throughout this distinctive medieval bronze. Since this figure probably came from a larger work, possibly a base for a cross or a candlestick, it provides an important insight into the nature of monumental church furnishings of the Romanesque period. *The Jack and Belle Linsky Collection, 1982, 1982.60.396*

14 ANTICO, Mantuan, ca. 1460–d. 1528
Satyr

Bronze; h. 12 in. (30.5 cm.)

More an evocation than a reiteration of an antique source, this satyr, who may once have held a lamp, shows Antico modeling with independence as well as with his usual lyricism. The statuette is admirable both for its graceful rightward sway and for the delicate attention to chasing throughout; the latter mark of excellence is only to be expected in bronzes by this goldsmith-sculptor. The eyes here are not silvered, as they are in many of Antico's bronzes; rather, he left them unlacquered, producing a fiery glint where the reddish exposed bronze contrasts with the surrounding dark lacquer. Antico not only revived the manner of the ancients in his coolly neoclassical statuettes and busts, but he also restored ancient sculptures, including one of the Dioscuri on the Monte Cavallo, Rome. (See also European Sculpture and Decorative Arts, no. 5.) *The Jack and Belle Linsky Collection, 1982, 1982.60.91*

15 JOHANN JAKOB KORNMANN,
b. Augsburg?–d. Rome after 1672
Bust of Paolo Giordano II Orsini, Duke of Bracciano

Bronze with silvered and gilt details; h. 7¼ in. (18.4 cm.)

This miniature bust, so charged with character, was long believed to be by Gian Lorenzo Bernini, the genius of the Roman Baroque. It is now known to be by the goldsmith and medalist Johann Jakob Kornmann, or Cormano, as he was known in Italy. Kornmann produced two other busts for Orsini closely similar to this one, which is nonetheless easily distinguished by the painstaking stippling of the corselet, the touches of gilding and silvering that the others lack, and its more forceful plasticity.

Orsini was duke of Bracciano from 1615 until his death in 1656, and while he was a great friend to musicians, his interest in the visual arts centered mainly on portraits of himself. Artists invariably seized upon his self-important but likable nature, manifested by his proud posture, pudgy features, and artfully flung-back hair. Such portraits are often described as verging on caricature, but in fact they—like this bust—are probably quite faithful records of the duke, who paraded through life as an opulent sort of *miles gloriosus. The Jack and Belle Linsky Collection, 1982, 1982.60.106*

16 After a composition by LEONHARD KERN,
German, 1588–1662
Nude Women Wrestling
Bronze; h. 8¼ in. (21 cm.)

Leonhard Kern was a prolific sculptor of wood and stone as well as ivory and bronze, and traveled widely, living briefly in Italy and reaching as far as North Africa on his journeys.

One of the most memorable compositions of the Northern Baroque, this model derives from an ivory by Kern in the Kunsthistorisches Museum, Vienna. The bronze artist has faithfully interpreted Kern's interplay of angles and delicate checks and balances, and has retained some, if not all, of the simple volumetric masses that typify Kern's carving style. The iconography of the work remains unexplained. Diana discovering the pregnancy of Callisto and a scene from Tasso's *Gerusalemme liberata* have been proposed as subjects. *The Jack and Belle Linsky Collection, 1982, 1982.60.120*

17 Ewer
Bohemian, Prague, ca. 1680; probably mounted in London, ca. 1810–19
Smoky crystal with enameled gold mounts set with diamonds; h. 9⅞ in. (25 cm.)

The Napoleonic Wars resulted in an enormous displacement of art of all kinds, and after the defeat of Napoleon in 1810, English collectors rushed to take advantage of the Continental markets from which they had long been excluded. Among them was the wealthy eccentric William Beckford, who bought this ewer (as a work by Cellini) to adorn his celebrated—and treasure-filled—neo-Gothic Fonthill Abbey. Made of a variety of crystallized quartz sometimes, and incorrectly, called smoky topaz, the ewer can be attributed to the Prague workshop of Ferdinand Miseroni and can be dated about 1680. The Renaissance-style mounts of enameled gold set with diamonds, however, are both different in style and far more elaborate than others made in Prague during this period. In fact, they are in all probability the early nineteenth-century product of a still unidentified London goldsmith whose neo-Renaissance design must have drawn heavily on the same sources that inspired the chinoiseries of the Royal Pavilion at Brighton. *The Jack and Belle Linsky Collection, 1982, 1982.60.138*

18   JAMES COX English, act. ca. 1749–83, d. 1791

Automaton in the Form of a Chariot Pushed by a Chinese Attendant and Set with a Clock
Gold, brilliants, and paste jewels; h. 10 in. (25.4 cm.)

A pair of automata, of which this is the surviving half, was commissioned from James Cox by the East India Company for presentation to the Ch'ien-lung emperor in 1766. Almost nothing is known of Cox before this date, but it is clear that he must have acquired a reputation in this genre, with which his name is regularly associated. From 1766 until 1772 Cox was preeminent in the vigorous but short-lived industry of manufacturing clocks and automata for the Chinese market, which he continued to supply at least until 1783.

This automaton is set in motion by levers that activate the whirligig held in the woman's left hand and the wings of the bird perched above the dial of the clock. A bell hidden beneath the lower tier of the parasol sounds the hours, and the entire mechanism is propelled by a spring and fusee device housed above the two central wheels. *The Jack and Belle Linsky Collection, 1982, 1982.60.137*

19   ANDRÉ CHARLES BOULLE, French, 1642–1732

Commode
Veneered on walnut with ebony and marquetry of engraved brass, inlaid on a tortoiseshell ground; gilt-bronze mounts; verd antique marble top; h. 34½ in. (87.6 cm.)

In 1708 André Charles Boulle, the most celebrated cabinetmaker of Louis XIV's reign, executed two "bureaux" for the bedroom of Louis XIV at the Palais de Trianon (known today as the Grand Trianon). A new invention in the history of furniture, the Trianon "bureaux" were a combination of the table and the newly emerging commode, with two drawers fitted under the top in a shape influenced by the Roman sarcophagus and by Jean Berain's engraved designs for bureaus. The drawers in Boulle's model required four extra tapered scroll legs for support. The result was a spectacular and opulent design, which became one of the most frequently repeated pieces of French eighteenth-century furniture. This lavish commode is similar in construction, in the quality of the bronze mounts, and in the engraved ornament on the inlaid brass to the Trianon prototypes (now at the Château de Versailles), and it appears to be an early version (ca. 1710–32) made in Boulle's workshop. *The Jack and Belle Linsky Collection, 1982, 1982.60.82*

20 DAVID ROENTGEN, German, 1743–1807
Commode
Veneered on oak and pine with tulipwood, sycamore, boxwood, purplewood, pearwood, harewood, and other woods; drawer linings of mahogany; gilt-bronze mounts; red brocatelle marble top; h. 35¼ in. (89.5 cm.)

Branded twice on the back with the mark of the Château de Versailles (a double V beneath a crown), this commode is recorded in a 1792 inventory as standing in Louis XVI's private apartments. Roentgen, who became the most successful cabinetmaker of the eighteenth century, also supplied large quantities of furniture for Catherine the Great and had workshops in Vienna and Naples as well as Paris and Neuwied —home of his first shop. His exquisite pictorial marquetry and intricate mechanical devices, such as elaborate locks and concealed buttons to open doors and drawers, appealed to collectors who could afford his high prices. Roentgen's flourishing career, however, was effectively ended by the Revolution, when his Neuwied workshop was destroyed.

The three marquetry scenes on the front of this fine example of Roentgen's work depict theatrical stages: those on the side are empty; that in the center is occupied by three figures from the Italian Comedy—Pantaloon, his daughter Isabella, and Harlequin. (See also European Sculpture and Decorative Arts, no. 43.) *The Jack and Belle Linsky Collection, 1982, 1982.60.81*

---

21 JEAN FRANÇOIS OEBEN, French, ca. 1721–63
Writing Table
Veneered oak with mahogany, kingwood, tulipwood, and marquetry woods; gilt-bronze mounts; h. 27½ in. (69.8 cm.)

Long recognized as one of Jean François Oeben's masterpieces, this table (ca. 1761–63) was made for his frequent and most important client, Mme de Pompadour (the main charge of her coat of arms, a tower, appears at the top of the gilt-bronze mount at each corner). The marquetry of the top—one of the finest panels in all of Oeben's furniture—was designed to reflect her interest in the arts, and depicts a vase of flowers as well as trophies emblematic of architecture, painting, music, and gardening. The table demonstrates Oeben's talents not only as a creator of beautiful furniture, but also as a mechanic, since an elaborate mechanism allows the top to slide back at the same time as the large drawer moves forward, thereby doubling the surface area. *The Jack and Belle Linsky Collection, 1982, 1982.60.61*

22 Kazan Tartar Woman

Russian, ca. 1780
Hard-paste porcelain; h. 9 in. (22.9 cm.)

Only two porcelain factories were in operation
in Russia during the eighteenth century, the
Imperial Porcelain Manufactory in Saint Peters-
burg and the Gardner factory at Verbilki, outside Moscow. About 1780 the imperial factory
began the production of a large series of figures
depicting Russian national types, of which fourteen are represented in the Linsky Collection.
Like most of the figures, this elegant woman
from Kazan is modeled from engravings published by Johann Gottlieb Georghi in his *Description of All the Peoples Inhabiting the
Russian State* (1774). The authorship of the
models themselves is not established, but some
may be attributable to Jean Dominique Rachette
(1744–1809), chief modeler at the factory from
1779 to 1804. Production of the series is believed to have continued until the end of the
century. *The Jack and Belle Linsky Collection,
1982, 1982.60.146*

23 Seated Chinese

French, Chantilly, ca. 1735
*Tin-glazed soft-paste porcelain; h. 10⅝ in.
(27 cm.)*

The principal French porcelain factories were
located either in Paris or its environs. One of
the earliest of these was founded by Louis
Henry Auguste, seventh prince de Condé, at
Chantilly, outside Paris, in 1725. The factory
continued production for seventy-five years under
a succession of proprietors, finally closing in
1800. Many of the works produced at Chantilly
were copied from Chinese specimens exported
to the West, and the authenticity of details such
as costume may be attributable to the artisans'
familiarity with oriental models, either directly
or indirectly. The brooding pose of this figure is
traceable to a Chinese model from the K'an-hsi
period (1662–1722) representing a Buddhist
ascetic, or lohan, in meditation. Here, however,
a new character has been imposed on the
figure by the introduction of cords that bind his
hands, transforming him into a captive. *The
Jack and Belle Linsky Collection, 1982,
1982.60.261*

24 Woman Dressed as a Persian

French, Mennecy, ca. 1760
Soft-paste porcelain; h. 9⅝ in. (24.4 cm.)

Porcelain was first made by the Chinese, and no comparable hard-paste porcelain was produced in Europe until the eighteenth century, although artificial, or "soft-paste," porcelain —the material of which this charming figure is made—was introduced somewhat earlier. The Mennecy factory where this figure was created began not in the town of that name but in Paris on the rue de Charonne in 1734. In 1748 the factory was relocated at Mennecy, but in 1773 it was again transferred, to Bourg-la-Reine, where it remained until it closed in 1806. Two variant models of this delightful figure —neither in oriental costume, however—have been recorded at auction. *The Jack and Belle Linsky Collection, 1982, 1982.60.367*

25 Augustus the Strong

German, Meissen, ca. 1713
Böttger stoneware; h. 4⁷⁄₁₆ in. (11.6 cm.)

Meissen, the first of the European hard-paste porcelain factories, was formally established in 1710 after five years of experimentation directed toward the rediscovery of porcelain. Sculpture was produced at Meissen from the beginning, but it was both experimental and somewhat tentative; it was not until the appointment in 1733 of Johann Joachim Kändler as chief modeler that the factory turned to the production of a wide repertoire of vividly modeled small sculptures. This small but powerful portrait of the founder of the Meissen factory reflects the early interest in sculpture at Meissen generated by such artists as Balthasar Permoser and Benjamin Thomae. This model, which has been attributed to Johann Joachim Kretzschmar (1677–1740) on stylistic grounds, is one of two representations of Augustus. *The Jack and Belle Linsky Collection, 1982, 1982.60.318*

26 Beggar

German, Nymphenburg, ca. 1760
Hard-paste porcelain; h. 6¾ in. (17.1 cm.)

Six major porcelain factories came into existence in Germany between 1746 and 1764. This quick succession was prompted by a number of circumstances: the demand for porcelain generated by the international success of Meissen, the easy availability of kaolin—a key ingredient —from Passau, and the constant movement between factories of technicians and artists. This plaintive figure was created Franz Anton Bustelli (1723–63) at the Nymphenburg factory, established in 1747 and still in operation today. The man and dog are but one element of a three-part composition described in the factory records in 1760 as "one beggarwoman with two children, 1 beggar with one dog, one messenger accompanying a young lady who gives alms to the beggarwoman." Porcelain figures were frequently paired or grouped for thematic purposes, but Bustelli's device of creating a narrative composition with three groups appears to be unique. (See European Sculpture and Decorative Arts, no. 74.) *The Jack and Belle Linsky Collection, 1982, 1982.60.227*

FIRST FLOOR

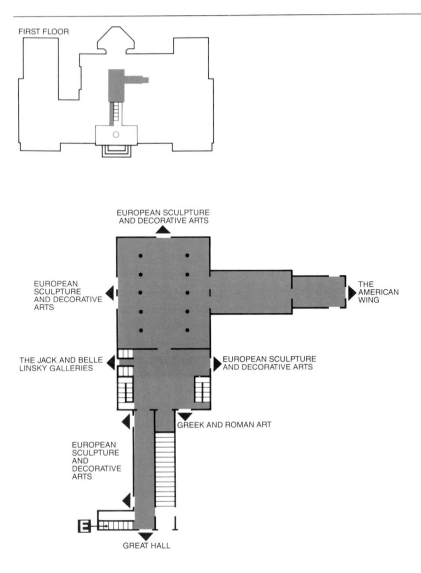

EUROPEAN SCULPTURE
AND DECORATIVE ARTS

EUROPEAN
SCULPTURE
AND DECORATIVE
ARTS

THE
AMERICAN
WING

THE JACK AND BELLE
LINSKY GALLERIES

EUROPEAN SCULPTURE
AND DECORATIVE ARTS

GREEK AND ROMAN ART

EUROPEAN
SCULPTURE
AND
DECORATIVE
ARTS

GREAT HALL

MEDIEVAL ART

MAIN BUILDING

The Middle Ages, the period between ancient and modern times in Western civilization, extends from the fourth to the sixteenth century—that is, roughly from the Fall of Rome to the beginning of the Renaissance. The Museum's collections cover the art of this long and complex period in all its many phases, including Early Christian, Byzantine, Migration, Romanesque, and Gothic. The Department of Medieval Art and The Cloisters, established in 1933, oversees not only the collection in the Museum's main building on Fifth Avenue, but also that of The Cloisters in northern Manhattan (see pp. 372–391).

A gift from the financier and collector J. Pierpont Morgan in 1917 forms the core of the more than four thousand medieval works of art now housed in the Museum's main building. The collection has grown through purchases as well as through gifts and bequests, most notably those from George Blumenthal, George and Frederic Pratt, and Irwin Untermyer. Among the strengths of the collection are Early Christian and Byzantine silver, enamels, glass, and ivories; Migration jewelry; Romanesque and Gothic metalwork, stained glass, sculpture, enamels, and ivories; and Gothic tapestries.

1 Sarcophagus Lid with the Last Judgment
Roman, late 3rd–early 4th c.
Marble; 16 × 93½ × 2¾ in. (40.6 × 237.3 × 7 cm.)

The parable of the separation of the sheep from the goats (Matt. 25:31–46) signifies the Last Judgment. This relief is the earliest surviving example of the image in Christian art. In the center Christ, dressed as a teacher-philosopher, sits on a rock and places his right hand tenderly on the head of a sheep, the first of eight that approach from the right. He repulses five goats on his left with his raised hand. Trees in the background create a pastoral-paradisiac setting, common in salvation imagery in Early Christian art. *Rogers Fund, 1924, 24.240*

2 Portrait Medallion of Gennadios
Alexandrian, second half of 3rd c.
Gold glass; diam. 1⅝ in. (4.2 cm.)

This bust portrait of a young man, perhaps made for use as a pendant, is drawn with a fine point on gold leaf applied to the surface of a deep sapphire-blue glass and sealed with a clear glass overlay; the rim is beveled for framing. The subject is identified by the inscription as "Gennadios, most accomplished in musical art." The grammatical variants in the inscription correspond to the Alexandrian dialect of Greek, and the technique of making portrait medallions of this type is also generally identified with that city. *Fletcher Fund, 1926, 26.258*

3 The Vermand Treasure
Provincial Roman, second half of 4th c.
Silver gilt and niello; left: l. 3¾ in. (9.5 cm.); center: l. 4⅞ in. (12.4 cm.); right: h. 1⅜ in. (3.5 cm.), diam. ⅞ in. (2.2 cm.)

A group of richly decorated silver mounts was among the objects unearthed from a military tomb in Vermand, near Saint-Quentin in northern France. The tomb must have been that of a chieftain of high rank, perhaps a Roman military officer or a barbarian in Roman service. Three of the pieces are illustrated here: the ring and two plaques for the spear shaft. They are decorated with vines and floral arabesques, cicadas, and fantastic animals.

The patterns belong to the repertory of Late Antique art, but the technique was a new method developed in the frontier regions along the Rhine and the Danube and used chiefly for the decoration of such military trappings. It is called chip-carving because the patterns, although not carved, are made up of wedge-shaped troughs like those left by the chips cut in woodcarving. The contrasts in the design are made more vivid by niello—a silver sulfide alloy set into the incised gilded silver. The Vermand find is the most distinguished example of chip-carving in existence. *Gift of J. Pierpont Morgan, 1917, 17.190.143–145*

4   Tomb Relief with the Traditio Legis
Roman, fourth quarter of 4th c.
Marble; 19⅛ × 52½ × 5¾ in. (48.6 × 133.4 × 14.6 cm.)

The very popular Early Christian image of the Traditio Legis (Christ giving the law to Peter) is depicted on this handsome relief which was probably made to face a tomb. In the right central niche Christ (his face missing) raises his right hand in proclamation and unfurls the scroll of the law toward Peter on his left. Paul is on Christ's right. The bottom half of the relief is

missing. Traces of arcades at the edges of the relief indicate that it had at least six, but most likely seven, niches with Christ in the center.

The relief is a finely carved example of Roman work produced under Eastern influence in the late fourth century. The figural style is clearly Theodosian in the strong and subtly molded, well-rounded bodies, the carving of the faces, and the delicate and intricate architectural decoration. *Gift of Ernest and Beata Brummer in memory of Joseph Brummer, 1948, 48.76.2*

5   Bust of a Lady of Rank
Constantinople, late 5th–early 6th c.
Marble; h. 20⅞ in. (53 cm.)

This bust, from the region of Constantinople, shows a young lady who wears an elegantly draped mantle over a tunic; her hair is covered by a snoodlike bonnet of the imperial type. The subtle and delicate modeling of her face still retains a feeling of naturalism in spite of the fixed gaze. The person represented probably enjoyed a high rank in the Byzantine court in the late fifth or early sixth century. *The Cloisters Collection, 1966, 66.25*

6   Bow Fibula

Ponto-Gothic, late 4th or 5th c.
Gold over silver core with almandine, mother-of-pearl, or enamel; l. 6¾ in. (17.1 cm.)

Bow fibulae were worn in pairs to secure a mantle. This type of fibula, with head and foot plates joined by an arched bow and a heavily gilded silver core decorated with cabochons, has been discovered mainly in Hungary and southern Russia. The closest parallels to this fibula are those from the Second Szilagy-Somlyo Treasure (Transylvania), from which this example may also come. This piece was probably made by the Goths in the late fourth century. The lack of documentary evidence in this period of migrations of "barbaric" tribes makes it impossible to be more precise. *Fletcher Fund, 1947, 47.100.19*

7   Steelyard Weight and Hook

Byzantine, first half of 5th c.
Weight: bronze filled with lead; hook: brass; 9⅛ × 4¼ in. (23.5 × 11 cm.); 5.04 lb. (2.29 kg. or 7 Byzantine litrae)

The weight is cast in the form of the bust of an empress (as yet unidentified). She is elaborately coiffed. The richness of her jeweled diadem, from which hang strands of pearls, is echoed in her four-tiered gem- and pearl-studded necklace. The bust is set on a plinth bordered with pearls and decorated with a guilloche pattern. Although governed by the hieratic style customary for Early Byzantine weights, the face, hair, jewelry, and clothing are sensitively and carefully modeled. When the weight was suspended by its hook, it could be moved along a ruled steelyard to establish the weight of the commodity hung from the opposite side. *Purchase, Rogers Fund, Bequest of Theodore M. Davis, by exchange and Gifts of George Blumenthal, J. Pierpont Morgan, Mrs. Lucy W. Drexel and Mrs. Robert J. Levy, by exchange, 1980, 1980.416a,b*

8   The Antioch Chalice

Early Christian, Syria(?), first half of 6th c.
Silver gilt; h. 7½ in. (19.1 cm.)

This early liturgical vessel, a plain cup of silver within an elaborate openwork cup of silver gilt, no doubt belonged to a wealthy parish—presumably the parish at Antioch on the Orontes River in Syria, near where it was reportedly discovered in 1910. Among the entwined grapevines are two representations of Christ—in one

he instructs his disciples; in the other he is enthroned above an eagle with outstretched wings, signifying the Resurrection. The vines and a basket of what may be loaves of bread are in accord with the chalice's eucharistic function. Soon after the chalice came to light, it was suggested that the inner cup was the Holy Grail, but the workmanship and design of the two pieces indicate that they were made in the sixth century. *The Cloisters Collection, 1950, 50.4*

10 Diptych of the Consul Justinian

Byzantine, Constantinople, 521

Ivory; each leaf 13¾ × 5¾ in. (35 × 14.5 cm.)

Justinian was appointed consul for the East in 521, six years before he became emperor, and had this diptych and others made for presentation to members of the senate to celebrate his consulship. In the center of each leaf is a medallion framing a running inscription addressed to the senator. Elegant in its simplicity, the medallion is composed of a simple pearl motif and a complex cyma carved with great care and precision. At the four corners of each leaf are lion's heads emerging from the center of lush acanthus leaves. The soft, plastic quality of the acanthus contrasts strongly with the abstract, geometric cyma. *Gift of J. Pierpont Morgan, 1917, 17.190.52,53*

9 Pyxis with the Holy Women at the Tomb of Christ

Syria-Palestine, 6th c.

Ivory; h. 4 in. (10.2 cm.), diam. 5 in. (12.7 cm.)

The subject of this pyxis is the visit of the Holy Women to the tomb of Christ; however, the two Marys, carrying censers, approach not a tomb but an altar. By substituting an altar for the actual tomb, the artist illustrated the popular belief that the altar symbolized the Holy Sepulcher. This association grew out of the Eastern belief in the presence of the crucified Christ on the altar during the celebration of the Eucharist. This scene is well suited for a pyxis which was probably used as a container for the host. *Gift of J. Pierpont Morgan, 1917, 17.190.57*

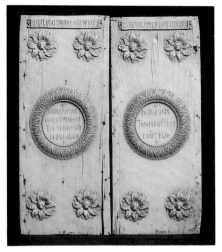

11 Pectoral

Byzantine, Constantinople(?), mid-6th c.
Gold and niello; h. including neck-ring 9⅜ in. (23.8 cm.)

This pectoral is part of a treasure said to have been found either at Antinöe or in Tomei, near Assiût. It is composed of a plain neck-ring attached to a frame set with a large central medallion flanked by coins and two decorative disks. The two ribbed rings at the bottom originally held a medallion. The coins represent emperors of the fourth to sixth centuries, portrayed for the most part in military dress. The latest coins date from the reign of Justinian. The central medallion shows on the obverse an emperor in military attire and on the reverse the figure of Constantinopolis, seated on a throne and wearing a helmet and tunic. She holds a globus cruciger and a scepter, and her left foot rests on the prow of a ship. This image reflects the passing of political primacy from Rome to Constantinople. *Gift of J. Pierpont Morgan, 1917, 17.190.1664*

12 Plate with David and Goliath

Byzantine, Constantinople, 628–630
Silver; diam. 19½ in. (49.5 cm.)

Ten silver plates of various sizes from the so-called Cyprus Treasure form a cycle showing scenes from the life of David. Six of these plates are in the Museum and four in the Cyprus Museum, Nicosia. They were made in Constantinople during the reign of Heraclius (610–641) and were perhaps intended as an imperial gift. The set was probably made for display. Its largest dish, which is illustrated here and which shows David fighting and slaying Goliath, may have been placed in the center, flanked or surrounded by the others of diminishing size. The series of images, as well as the classical style, may be based on earlier models; they appear to represent a conscious effort to keep alive the Hellenistic forms of antiquity. *Gift of J. Pierpont Morgan, 1917, 17.190.396*

13 Bow Fibula

Langobardic, first half of 7th c.
Silver gilt and niello; 6¼ × 3¾ in. (15.9 × 9.5 cm.)

This large bow fibula represents the work of the Langobards in Italy, which they occupied from 568 to 774. Unlike Frankish artists, who worked chiefly in bronze, the Langobards often produced jewelry in gold and silver. The design of the body of the bow fibula is composed of chip-carved zoomorphic forms. Two bird's heads project from each side of the body. Like the work of other barbarian tribes who gradually settled in western Europe in the so-called Migration period (fourth–seventh centuries), the art of the Langobards was dedicated to the ornamentation of weapons and other portable articles. Jewelry and weapons revealed the status of the barbarian warrior in a military society and were buried with him in his tomb. *Purchase, Joseph Pulitzer Bequest, 1955, 55.56*

14 Reliquary of the True Cross
Syria-Palestine or Byzantine, late 8th–early
9th c.
*Silver gilt, cloisonné enamel, and niello;
4 × 2⅞ in. (10.2 × 7.35 cm.)*

This reliquary's top and sides are decorated
with enamels of the Crucifixion and busts of
twenty-seven saints, including the twelve
apostles. Scenes of the Annunciation, Nativity,
Crucifixion, and Anastasis (Descent into Limbo)
are worked in niello on the underside of the lid.
Inside the reliquary is a cross-shaped compart-
ment that once held a particle of the True Cross
and perhaps other relics as well. On the lid
Christ is shown alive on the cross, wearing a
long tunic (colobium) of Eastern origin; he is
mourned by his mother and John. The extensive program of enameling stands at the beginning of the rich history of this technique in
Byzantine and Western art. *Gift of J. Pierpont
Morgan, 1917, 17.190.715*

**15 Christ Enthroned with Saints and
Emperor Otto I**
Ottonian, 962–973
Ivory; 5 × 4½ in. (12.7 × 11.4 cm.)

This dedication plaque shows Christ enthroned,
accepting a model of the church of Saint Mauritius in Magdeburg from Otto I (r. 962–973). It is
one of a series of nineteen known as the
Magdeburg ivories. All of identical size and all
having an unusual cutout geometric or floral
background, these ivories depict various New
Testament and symbolic scenes with a severe
monumentality like that of Ottonian wall painting.
Now dispersed in European and American collections, they once were part of a much larger
ensemble, conservatively estimated at forty-
four scenes, at the church of Saint Mauritius
(founded by Otto between 955 and 973). The
whole was probably a didactic embellishment
for an ambo (pulpit) or a chancel door. *Gift of
George Blumenthal, 1941, 41.100.157*

16   Plaque with the Crucifixion and the Stabbing of Hades
Byzantine, 10th c.
Ivory; 5 × 3½ in. (12.7 × 8.9 cm.)

This plaque's iconography is unusual among surviving Byzantine representations of the Crucifixion. While the Virgin, Saint John, the two angels, and the three soldiers dividing Christ's garment are frequent witnesses to Christ's death, the bearded reclining man who is stabbed by the cross is a most uncommon feature. He is Hades, ruler of the underworld.

After the devastations of the Iconoclastic Controversy (ca. 725–842), artists and scholars searched for earlier pictorial and literary sources to recreate a corpus of Christian imagery. The theme of Hades pierced by the cross, illustrating the victory of Christ over death and the forces of evil, was inspired by literary sources, particularly the *Hymn on the Triumph of the Cross* by Romanos the Melodist (d. 556), which was sung on Good Friday in the Byzantine church. *Gift of J. Pierpont Morgan, 1917, 17.190.44*

17   Enthroned Christ from a Pectoral Cross
Anglo-Saxon, early 11th c.
Walrus ivory; 5⁷⁄₈ × 2⁷⁄₁₆ in. (14.9 × 6.2 cm.)

This fragment of a pectoral cross shows Christ on one face and the Lamb of God and two Evangelist symbols on the other. It dates from the early eleventh century, but it is difficult to determine whether it was made in northern France or in England. The figure's posture and facial type—oval eyes (once inlaid with dark beads), drooping mustache, and divided beard—have parallels in English manuscripts and ivories. However, there are also clear stylistic affinities with some Saint-Bertin manuscripts created under English, or more specifically Winchester, influence. The French monasteries of Saint-Bertin and Saint-Vaast were closely connected to similar foundations in England, and the Winchester style not only dominated the ateliers of England but also had wide-ranging effects on the Continent, particularly in the area directly across the Channel. It may be that the cross was made at Saint-Bertin by an English artist or a Continental artist trained in England. *Gift of J. Pierpont Morgan, 1917, 17.190.217*

18   Plaque with the Journey to Emmaus and the Noli Me Tangere
North Spanish, probably León, early 12th c.
Ivory; 10⁵⁄₈ × 5⁵⁄₁₆ in. (27 × 13.5 cm.)

Two appearances of the risen Christ are represented on this plaque. The Gospel of Luke tells of the risen Christ traveling with two disciples on the road from Jerusalem to Emmaus. The Gospel of John describes the risen Christ's appearance to Mary Magdalen as she stood weeping at his tomb. Warning her, "*Noli me tangere* [Do not touch me]," he then told her to carry the news of his resurrection to his disciples.

A companion plaque with the Descent from the Cross and the Holy Women at the Tomb is divided between a private collection in Oviedo and the Hermitage, Leningrad. The animated carving of this ivory is characteristic of a number of Spanish Romanesque works of art. *Gift of J. Pierpont Morgan, 1917, 17.190.47*

19 Roundel of the Virgin
Byzantine, Constantinople, early 12th c.
*Cloisonné enamel on gold; diam. 3¼ in.
(8.25 cm.)*

This is one of nine medallions in the Museum
that came from an eleventh-century silver icon
of the archangel Gabriel (now destroyed) from
the Djumati monastery in Georgia (now part of
the U.S.S.R.). The medallions present an extended Deesis—the Virgin's and the saints'
intercession with Christ for the salvation of
humankind—a subject drawn from the Byzantine liturgy. Technically and stylistically accomplished, they are fine examples of Byzantine
cloisonné enameling. In this technique, strips,
or cloisons, are soldered onto the base to form
a system of cells that contains the glass flux
and prevents the various colors from running
into one another. Cloisonné enamels thus combine the luminosity of colored glass with the
shimmer of gold. *Gift of J. Pierpont Morgan,
1917, 17.190.675*

20 Châsse
Spanish, ca. 1170
*Copper gilt and champlevé enamel; 4⅞ × 7 ×
3⅛ in. (12.4 × 19.1 × 7.9 cm.)*

On the front plaques of this reliquary are the
symbols of the four Evangelists—the angel of
Matthew, the eagle of John, the lion of Mark, and
the ox of Luke. The other side represents Christ
between Mary Magdalen and Saint Martial (a
third-century bishop of Limoges) and the hand
of God flanked by two censer-bearing angels;
the narrow ends show Saints Peter and Paul.
Saints Mary Magdalen and Martial had a special cult in Limoges, and the châsse is known to
have been in the nearby town of Champagnat
in the nineteenth century. Stylistic elements
such as the floral ornament, however, point to a
Spanish atelier. *Gift of J. Pierpont Morgan,
1917, 17.190.685–687,695,710,711*

DNS LOQVIT VR MARIE

21 Plaque with the Three Marys at the Tomb of Christ
Rhenish, Cologne, ca. 1135
Walrus ivory; 8⅜ × 7¾ in. (21.3 × 19.7 cm.)

This plaque, its companion piece in the Museum (the Doubting of Thomas), and three others in the Victoria and Albert Museum, London, probably come from the same ensemble, possibly an ambo (pulpit) decorated with scenes of the Infancy and Passion of Christ. All are carved in walrus ivory, often used in lieu of elephant ivory in northern Romanesque art. The relatively small size of walrus tusks necessitated the use of three plaques for the central composition. The pricked drapery is a hallmark of the Cologne style, and the composition is close to that of an ivory plaque in the Schnütgen Museum in Cologne. Though stylized, the buildings in the background suggest contemporary Romanesque architecture. *Gift of George Blumenthal, 1941, 41.100.201*

22   Column Figure of an Old Testament King
French, Paris, ca. 1150
Limestone; 45¼ × 9¼ in. (115 × 23.5 cm.)

This column statue is from the old cloister of
the abbey of Saint-Denis outside Paris. A vast
program of construction and architectural decoration was carried out at Saint-Denis under the
direction of the extraordinary churchman Suger,
who was abbot from 1122 to 1151. This king is
the only complete column figure known to have
survived from that period. Like the head of King
David from Notre-Dame (no. 25), it has been
identified from early engravings. With the other
sculpture from the cloister, this Old Testament
king may have represented the royal genealogy
of Christ. *Joseph Pulitzer Bequest, 1920, 20.157*

23   Processional Cross
North Spanish, Asturias, late 11th–early 12th c.
*Silver, partially gilt on wood core, carved gems,
and jewels; 23¼ × 19 in. (59.1 × 48.3 cm.)*

The repoussé figure of Christ flanked by the Virgin and Saint John dominates the front of this
processional cross. Above him is a censing angel,
while at the bottom Adam rises from his tomb,
symbolizing the redemption of humankind. The
large crystal over the figure of Christ once
contained a relic. The reverse shows the Lamb
of God, surrounded by the symbols of the four
Evangelists. The reverse also bears a Latin
inscription which translates, "Sanccia Guidisalvi
made me in honor of Saint Salvador." Sanccia
is a woman's name; while she may have been
the donor, contemporary records do refer to
women artists working in Spain.

The cross comes from the church of San
Salvador de Fuentes in the province of Oviedo
and can be compared stylistically to other works
from that region. Details such as the filigree can
be compared to the silver-gilt bookcovers from
the cathedral of Jaca which are also exhibited
in the Medieval Treasury. *Gift of J. Pierpont
Morgan, 1917, 17.190.1406*

24   Virgin and Child
French, Auvergne, second half of 12th c.
Oak with polychromy; h. 31 in. (78.7 cm.)

This type of image of the Virgin and Child
enthroned was very popular in the Auvergne
region where this work was made. Mary was
thought of as the Throne of the New Solomon,
and as she became the Throne of Wisdom, the
Child on her lap became Divine Wisdom. To
convey these abstract ideas the statues had to
be formal and symmetrical, with a rigid frontality
and stylized forms and drapery. (See also Medieval Art—The Cloisters, no. 2.) *Gift of J. Pierpont
Morgan, 1916, 16.32.194*

25 Head of King David

French, Paris, ca. 1150
Limestone; h. 11¼ in. (28.6 cm.)

This is the only extant head from the jamb sculptures of the Saint Anne portal of the cathedral of Notre-Dame in Paris. It has been identified on the basis of engravings made of the portal before the destruction of its sculpture during the French Revolution. Carved in fine-grained limestone, the head has a polish that makes it look like marble. The deeply incised pupils of the large round eyes were originally inlaid with lead. The somewhat soft and fleshy cheeks contrast with the strong cheekbones and the intense eyes. This magnificent head is carved in the transitional style between Romanesque and Gothic and was possibly first intended for the basilica of Saint-Étienne which was being reconstructed after 1124 and before 1150 on the site of the cathedral. *Harris Brisbane Dick Fund, 1938, 38.180*

26 Panel with Censing Angels

French, Troyes, ca. 1170–80
Pot-metal glass; 18½ × 17⅜ in. (47 × 44 cm.)

The stained glass produced for the cathedral of Saint-Pierre in Troyes during the late twelfth century represents a major monument in the transition from the Romanesque to the Gothic style. This panel with censing angels is from a window of connected semicircles whose overall subject was the Dormition (Death) of the Virgin. (Also in the collection is the head of the Virgin from this window.)

The panel is painted with exceptional precision against a ground decorated with fine rinceaux. Stylistic links with Mosan enamelwork and illuminations from Champagne demonstrate that the Troyes artist had assimilated techniques, color relationships, and figure types not characteristic of other twelfth-century stained-glass painting. *Gift of Ella Brummer, in memory of her husband, Ernest Brummer, 1977, 1977.346.1*

◀ **27 Reliquary of Saint Thomas Becket**
English, 1175–80
Silver gilt, niello, and glass; 2¼ × 2¾ × 1¾ in.
(5.7 × 7 × 4.4 cm.)

The oblong front and back plaques show the
murder and burial of Saint Thomas Becket, the
archbishop of Canterbury who was killed in
1170 by four knights from the court of Henry II.
The front and back roof plaques contain half-
figures of angels, and the angel above the
martyrdom scene holds a child symbolizing
Becket's soul. The end plaques are filled with
foliate ornament, as are the roof plaques above
them. The reliquary's magnificent craftsmanship is evident in the beaded bands, hinges,
and floral decoration; the figures are delicately
drawn, and the bodies are modeled by sharply
drawn drapery folds. One of the earliest Becket
reliquaries, it is attributed to an English workshop active in the 1170s. *Gift of J. Pierpont
Morgan, 1917, 17.190.520*

28 Plaque with the Pentecost
Mosan, third quarter of 12th c.
*Champlevé enamel on copper gilt; 4½ ×
4½ in. (11.4 × 11.4 cm.)*

This plaque depicts the descent of the Holy
Spirit on the apostles, as related in Acts 2:1–4.
The hand of God appears to the apostles, who
are assembled within an architectural setting.
Only six apostles are shown; the others are
suggested by partially visible halos behind them.
Each one has a tongue of fire upon his head.
The Pentecost plaque is one of four in the
Museum from the same ensemble. *The Clois-
ters Collection, 1965, 65.105*

**29 Plaque with Applied Figure of
Saint James**
French, Limoges, 13th c.
*Champlevé enamel on copper gilt; 11⅜ × 5½ in.
(29 × 14 cm.)*

This plaque is one of six (the others are in
Paris, Leningrad, and Florence) which are
thought to have come from the altar of the
abbey of Grandmont in the Limousin region of
France. The ateliers of Limoges were known for
works of this type, in which gilded figures and
decorative elements were attached by rivets to
an enamel ground. The Grandmont plaques
are exceptional among these pieces for their
classicistic drapery and monumentality. Each
figure was cast and then finished by chiseling.
The eyes are formed by dots of dark blue
enamel, and small stones enhance details of
the robes. *Gift of J. Pierpont Morgan, 1917,
17.190.123*

30 Panel with Saint Vincent in Chains

French, Paris, ca. 1245
Pot-metal glass; 147 x 43½ in. (373.4 x 109.2 cm.)

This stained-glass panel is one of a series depicting episodes from the life of the deacon Vincent, the most celebrated of Spanish martyrs, who was executed in 304 at Valencia in the persecution under Diocletian. The series formed a window in the Lady Chapel of the Benedictine abbey church of Saint-Germain-des-Prés in Paris, where the relics of Saint Vincent had long been venerated. The abbey was rich in stained glass, notably the windows of the thirteenth-century Lady Chapel; almost all of these windows were destroyed in 1794 during the French Revolution. The Saint Vincent series was the most beautiful to survive. Other panels in North American collections are in The Cloisters, in the Walters Art Gallery, Baltimore, and in the Montreal Museum of Fine Arts. These panels are masterworks in the Gothic style. The bodies are elongated; the heads are expressive, drawn with great freedom and variety; the gestures are eloquent and emphatic. *Gift of George D. Pratt, 1924, 24.167*

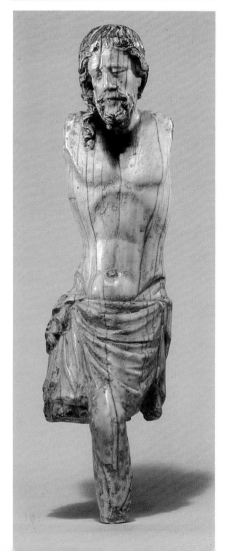

31 Corpus of Christ

French, Paris, third quarter of 13th c.
Ivory; h. 6½ in. (16.5 cm.)

The suffering Christ on the cross was a central theme in Gothic art. Carved in the round and intended for an altar cross, this masterpiece, probably from Paris, conveys the pathos and agony of Christ. In spite of the loss of arms and legs, the figure reveals a profound sensitivity to form and expression. The polychromy on the hair and on the facial features and body enhances the naturalism of the image. The powerful anatomical structure is remarkable for crucifixes of the Gothic period. The strict verticality of the corpus in Romanesque versions of the Crucifixion has been replaced by a subtly twisted posture. This magnificent corpus anticipates the more refined style of the court of the mid-thirteenth century, while retaining the main features of the Gothic classicism of the early part of the century. *Gift of Mr. and Mrs. Maxime L. Hermanos, 1978, 1978.521.3*

32 GIOVANNI PISANO, Italian, ca. 1245/50– after 1314 ▶

Lectern

Carrara marble; 28 × 23 in. (71.1 × 58.4 cm.)

This lectern in the shape of an eagle grasping an open book in its claws, with a polygonal bookrest, is believed to have come from the pulpit of the church of Sant'Andrea in Pistoia. The pulpit is by Giovanni Pisano and was completed in 1301. There is an aggressive bravura in the rendering of the feathers with strong, sweeping strokes of the chisel, almost horizontal in the legs, conveying a feeling of air and movement which is shared by the eagles carved by Giovanni Pisano in Siena and Perugia. *Rogers Fund, 1918, 18.70.28*

33 Aquamanile
German, Saxon, late 13th c.
Bronze; h. 12¼ in. (31.1 cm.)

This aquamanile in the form of a knight on horseback was made in Saxony in northern Germany. Aquamanilia were used by laymen to wash their hands at meals and by celebrants to wash their hands during the Mass. This example was surely intended for domestic use. The figure symbolizes the ideals of knighthood depicted in the popular medieval *romans courtois* (chivalric tales). *Bequest of Irwin Untermyer, 1964, 64.101.1492*

34 The Visitation
German, Constance, ca. 1310
Walnut, polychromed and gilded; 23¼ × 12 in. (59.1 × 30.5 cm.)

Soon after the Annunciation, when she learned of her miraculous conception of Jesus, the Virgin Mary visited her kinswoman Elizabeth, who was also expecting a child (John the Baptist). This representation of their joyous meeting comes from the Dominican monastery of Katharinenthal, in the Lake Constance region of present-day Switzerland. With the groups of Saint John and Christ in Antwerp and Berlin, the Metropolitan Visitation has been attributed to the circle of Master Heinrich of Constance. The crystal-covered cavities probably contained representations of the Christ Child and Saint John, a common German iconographic motif at that time. *Gift of J. Pierpont Morgan, 1917, 17.190.724*

35 Casket with Scenes from Romances

French, Paris, mid-14th c.
Ivory, with modern iron mountings; 4⅜ × 10 × 6⅛ in. (11.1 × 25.4 × 15.5 cm.)

This casket is exceptionally rich in carvings depicting chivalric scenes from medieval romances. Knights assault the castle of love and joust for their ladies' favors. Gawain and Galahad rescue maidens imprisoned in castles. Lancelot, in order to rescue Guinevere, crosses a raging torrent, using the blade of his sword for a bridge. Tristan and Isolde are spied upon from a tree by King Mark, but the king's reflection in a fountain reveals his presence to the lovers. Other popular themes—the unicorn captured by the lady; the hairy wild men of the forest—also are depicted. The front panel, which shows the fountain of youth and Phyllis with Aristotle, is a late nineteenth-century copy from a similar casket now in the Walters Art Gallery, Baltimore. *Gift of J. Pierpont Morgan, 1917, 17.190.173*

36 Virgin and Child

French, probably Vexin, 1300–1325
Limestone with polychromy; h. 62½ in. (158.8 cm.)

In this unusually large and imposing devotional statue, the Virgin holds the Child as if elevating him before the faithful. Her body forms a gentle curve, which is repeated in the parallel folds of her skirt. The subject of this sculpture was a frequent one in fourteenth-century French, German, and Netherlandish regions, and its widespread popularity as a votive image developed out of the intensity of belief in the cult of the Virgin at that time. Very few of these sculptures are preserved in the locations for which they were originally made, whether a parish church, a great cathedral, an aristocratic oratory, or a monastic chapel. Isolated examples intended for veneration in the open air, as at remote crossroad shrines, at town gateways, or on the exteriors of houses, have virtually vanished. Therefore, the preponderance of preserved examples—including this work—are without any historical clues as to their provenance, those responsible for commissioning them, and their original settings. On the basis of stylistic comparisons, the Vexin region, between Normandy and the Île-de-France, has been suggested as the most probable origin for this work. *Bequest of George Blumenthal, 1941, 41.190.279*

37 Clasp Decorated with Birds
French or Italian, possibly court of Avignon, second quarter of 14th c.
Silver gilt and translucent enamel; 2⅜ × 5 in. (6 × 13.7 cm.)

This type of double clasp was used to fasten a cape or mantle at the neck. The representation of birds and other small animals rendered in a lively and naturalistic way and enclosed within a lozenge is characteristic of works believed to have been produced in or imported to the papal court of Avignon about the third decade of the fourteenth century. Though the association of this clasp with Avignon must be tentative, the colors and design can be compared to those of a crozier in Cologne cathedral attributed to Avignon. *Purchase, The Cloisters Fund, Gifts of George Blumenthal, Mrs. Robert W. de Forest, J. Pierpont Morgan, and George D. Pratt, by exchange, and Mrs. Charles F. Griffith, Margaret L. Meiss, Eleanor Roach, and Anonymous Gifts, 1979, 1979.400*

38 Morse with Saint Francis of Assisi
Italian, Tuscany, ca. 1350
Copper gilt and translucent and opaque enamel; diam. 4¼ in. (10.8 cm.)

In this morse, or clasp for a cope, Saint Francis is shown receiving the stigmata, the wounds corresponding to those suffered by Christ. The closest iconographic parallels to this representation are the frescoes of the upper church of the basilica of Assisi. The morse departs from its prototypes, however, by presenting a nocturnal scene. The enamel technique differs completely from that seen in most other Italian and south European works of the fourteenth century. The artist was perhaps a Tuscan from Florence, who was drawn to Assisi when the basilica was being decorated. This octalobular morse could have been made for the ceremonial cope of one of the abbots. *Gift of Georges and Edna Seligmann, in memory of his father, Simon Seligmann, the collector of Medieval art, and of his brother René, 1979, 1979.498.2*

39 Basin with Horseman Spearing a Serpent
Spanish, Valencia(?), 1390–1400
Lustered earthenware; diam. 17¼ in. (43.8 cm.)

The earliest example of medieval lusterware in the collection, this basin displays both Islamic glazing technique and Gothic decoration. This combination is an expression of the meeting of the Christian and Islamic cultures that resulted from the gradual Christian reconquest of Muslim Spain. The figure in the middle—a horseman spearing a serpent—is perhaps inspired by representations of the legend of Saint George and the Dragon. Details are delineated by sgraffito (surface scratching). Although the shields around the rim are not identifiable coats of arms, they also appear on a contemporary piece in the Instituto de Valencia de Don Juan in Madrid. The representation of a large figure rather than the more usual floral or geometric decoration and the coloring of the Museum's basin make it exceptional. *Gift of George Blumenthal, 1941, 41.100.173*

40 The Annunciation Tapestry
Flemish(?), early 15th c.
Wool; 136 × 114 in. (345 × 290 cm.)

Seated on the right under an open edicule, Mary looks away from her book on the lectern to listen to the archangel Gabriel. He is holding a banner with the words "*Ave gracia plena* (Hail [Mary], full of grace)." In the sky, God the Father sends the infant Jesus bearing a cross down toward the Virgin; Jesus is preceded by the dove of the Holy Spirit. Two angels hold a coat of arms, which may be that of the patron. The cartoonist for the Annunciation clearly belonged to the Gothic International school. This work was probably woven in Arras, the most important center of tapestry weaving in the first half of the fifteenth century. The tapestry, however, was found in Spain, and the coat of arms has been called Spanish; whether the cartoon reflects a Flemish or a north Spanish design is still an open question. *Gift of Harriet Barnes Pratt, 1949, in memory of her husband Harold Irving Pratt (born February 1, 1877, died May 21, 1939), 1945, 45.76*

41 Saint Catherine of Alexandria
French, early 15th c.
Gold, ronde-bosse enamel, and jewels; h. 3¾ in. (9.5 cm.)

Saint Catherine of Alexandria, who is most likely a legendary rather than a historical figure, was said to have been a Christian princess executed by the Roman emperor Maxentius in the fourth century. She was one of the most popular saints in the medieval Church, and her relics were renowned for their miraculous powers. This statuette may have come from a reliquary where it and figures of other saints would have been integrated into an architectural ensemble. The craftsmanship of this piece is extremely fine, and the delicate modeling of the face approaches that of the enameled-gold Madonna of Toledo that was made for Jean, duc de Berry, before 1402. This statuette of Saint Catherine is said to come from a convent in Clermont-Ferrand. *Gift of J. Pierpont Morgan, 1917, 17.190.905*

42 Mourner from the Tomb of the Duc de Berry
French, Burgundy, ca. 1453
Alabaster; h. 15⅛ in. (38.4 cm.)

The tomb at Bourges of Jean, duc de Berry (1340–1416), was begun by Jean de Cambrai and completed by Étienne Bobillet and Paul de Mosselman. A realistic life-size effigy of the duke was placed on top of the sarcophagus, while on the sides were figures of mourners rendered in high relief under a series of arcades. These statuettes can be identified as relatives and allies of the deceased. The tomb was vandalized during the Revolution, and the mourner figures were destroyed or dispersed. Of the forty statuettes, twenty-five survive, including this one and two others in the Museum's collection.

The duc de Berry was a great patron, and the Museum has several works from his collection (see Medieval Art—The Cloisters, nos. 26 and 27). *Gift of J. Pierpont Morgan, 1917, 17.190.389*

43 Three Lords and Two Ladies
Flemish, ca. 1450
Wool; 122 × 99 in. (310 × 251 cm.)

This work is part of a set known as the Rose Tapestries. They were perhaps made for the French king Charles VII, whose colors were white, red, and green, and one of whose emblems was the rose tree. A royal connection is likely, for the tapestries are sumptuous, with metal threads not only in the clothes and jewelry but also, most unusually, in the leaves, buds, and open rose hearts. Woven in Arras or Tournai, the tapestries probably date from around 1450, since such details as the dark locks on the women's foreheads do not seem much in evidence before that time. *Rogers Fund, 1909, 09.137.1*

45 Crib of the Infant Jesus ▶
South Netherlandish, Brabant, 15th c.
*Wood, polychromed and gilt, lead, silver gilt,
painted parchment, and silk embroidered with
seed pearls, gold thread, tinsel, and translucent enamels; 12½ × 11 × 7³/₁₆ in. (35 × 28 ×
18 cm.)*

This extraordinary piece from Brabant is an
example of a reliquary crib known as a *"repos
de Jésus."* Such cribs seem to have been
popular devotional objects during the fifteenth
and early sixteenth centuries. They were venerated during Christmas festivities and may have
been given as presents to nuns taking their
vows. The Child (now missing) lay beneath the
silk coverlet decorated with the Tree of Jesse,
his head resting on the Lamb of God embroidered
on the pillow. Inside the bed is the case for the
relic. *Gift of Ruth Blumka as a memorial to her
late husband's ideals, 1974, 1974.121*

44 Virgin and Child
French, Poligny, ca. 1440–50
*Limestone, polychromed and gilt; 53¼ ×
41½ in. (135.3 × 105.4 cm.)*

This monumental yet touching work from the
Couvent des Clarisses in Poligny is distinguished
by the convincing naturalism of the figures and
the intimacy of their relationship. The emotional
immediacy and the heavy plasticity of the drapery are typical of Burgundian sculpture. The
group was originally bright with polychromy
and, like many medieval cult statues, was probably repainted more than once.

One of four Poligny sculptures exhibited, this
is the crowning work of the rich collection of
Burgundian sculpture in the Museum. *Rogers
Fund, 1933, 33.23*

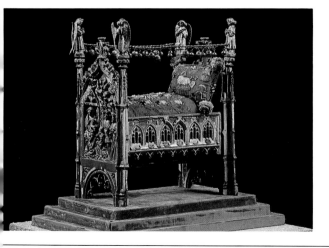

47 Holy Family

German, ca. 1500

Limewood with traces of polychromy and gilding; h. 31½ in. (80 cm.)

Carved in high relief and retaining its original polychromy, this Holy Family comes from an altar of the church of Gutenzell near Württemberg. The positioning of the figures—with the Virgin and Child facing the same direction and the Child raising his hand in blessing—suggests that they are from a larger composition of the Adoration of the Magi. The group has been associated with various important German masters working around 1500 and may be by Gregor Erhart. *Gift of Alastair B. Martin, 1948, 48.154.1*

46 Chair

North Italian, 15th c.

Oak; 32 × 28 × 17 in. (81.3 × 71.1 × 43.2 cm.)

This chair, decorated with Gothic tracery, is thought to come from the Piedmont region of North Italy. It is one of the earliest medieval chairs in the Museum's collection. Similar examples are preserved in the Collegiata di San Orso in Aosta. However, chairs such as this may equally have been intended for secular use. An illegible inscription in Gothic characters can be seen on the left stile. *Gift of George Blumenthal, 1941, 41.100.124*

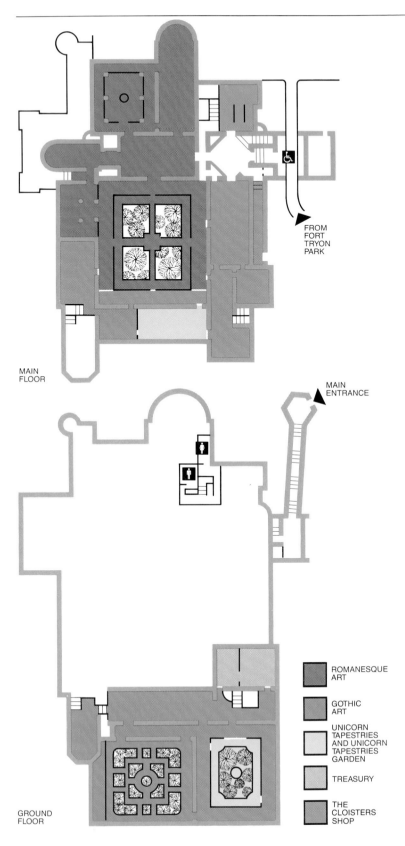

MAIN
FLOOR

MAIN
ENTRANCE

FROM
FORT
TRYON
PARK

GROUND
FLOOR

ROMANESQUE
ART

GOTHIC
ART

UNICORN
TAPESTRIES
AND UNICORN
TAPESTRIES
GARDEN

TREASURY

THE
CLOISTERS
SHOP

MEDIEVAL ART

THE CLOISTERS

The Museum's collection of medieval art is housed not only in the main building on Fifth Avenue (pp. 350–371) but also in The Cloisters. Located in Fort Tryon Park in northern Manhattan, a magnificent setting that overlooks the Hudson River, The Cloisters was opened in 1938. It incorporates elements of five medieval cloisters: Saint-Michel-de-Cuxa, Saint-Guilhem-le-Désert, Bonnefont-en-Comminges, Trie-en-Bigorre, and Froville. Much of the sculpture was acquired by George Grey Barnard (1863–1938), who was a prominent sculptor and an avid collector of medieval art. Barnard opened his original cloisters on Fort Washington Avenue to the public in 1914; through the generosity of John D. Rockefeller, Jr., they were acquired for the Museum in 1925. In addition to providing the grounds and building for the Barnard collection, Rockefeller contributed works of art from his own collection and established an endowment for future acquisitions.

Known particularly for its Romanesque and Gothic architectural sculpture, The Cloisters collection also includes illuminated manuscripts, stained glass, metalwork, enamels, ivories, and paintings. Among its tapestries is the renowned Unicorn series.

HOW TO REACH THE CLOISTERS

Subway: IND Eighth Avenue A train to 190th Street –Overlook Terrace. Exit by elevator, then take number 4 bus or walk through Fort Tryon Park to the Museum.

Bus: Madison Avenue bus number 4, "Fort Tryon Park–The Cloisters," stops at the door of the Museum.

Car: From Manhattan: Henry Hudson Parkway north to the first exit after the George Washington Bridge.

1   Plaque with Seated Saint John the Evangelist
Carolingian (court school), early 9th c.
Ivory; 7½ × 3⅝ in. (18.3 × 9.5 cm.)

The four Evangelists were among the most frequently represented images in Carolingian art. In this plaque John, accompanied by his symbol, the eagle, displays the opening text of his Gospel. The inscription along the top edge is from the writings of the early Christian poet Sedulius and translates: "Calling out, like an eagle, the word of John reaches the heavens." While inscribed in a later hand, it probably replaces an earlier original. This splendid plaque may have decorated the wing of a triptych. With the other Evangelists and their symbols, it would have framed a central image of Christ. The style—with deep layering of folds repeated across the surface—and the iconography closely link this ivory to manuscripts and ivories of Charlemagne's court school. *The Cloisters Collection, 1977, 1977.421*

2   Enthroned Virgin and Child
French, Burgundy, first half of 12th c.
Birch with polychromy; h. 40½ in. (102.9 cm.)

This sculpture comes from Autun in Burgundy; it is a moving example of the Throne of Wisdom type. Another example, from the Auvergne, is illustrated in this guide (Medieval Art—Main Building, no. 24). This Virgin is not quite so rigid and frontal as the one from the Auvergne: her head is slightly turned, and the linear treatment of the drapery at the "flying fold" near her right ankle suggests movement. The humanity of the subject has, however, been suppressed; the figure is virtually an abstract and refined icon. The repetition and variation of linear rhythms throughout serve to heighten the intensity of the image.

Traces of color can still be seen on the Virgin, and one of the original blue glass inlays for the eyes is still in place. *The Cloisters Collection, 1947, 47.101.15*

3 The Cuxa Cloister
French or Spanish, 12th c.
Marble

The Benedictine monastery of Saint-Michel-de-Cuxa, located at the foot of Mount Canigou in the Pyrenees, was founded in 878. Its cloister, seen here in part, was built in the twelfth century. In 1791, when France decreed the Civilian Constitution of the Clergy, Cuxa's monks departed; the monastery's stonework was subsequently dispersed. Since not all the capitals are at The Cloisters, the reconstruction is only a little over half the original size.

The boldly cut marble capitals show great variety of design. Some are fashioned in the simplest of block forms; others are intricately carved with scrolling leaves, pinecones, animals with two bodies and a common head (a special breed for the corners of capitals), lions devouring people or their own forelegs, lions restrained by apes, a leaping man blowing a horn, and a mermaid holding her tail. Some of the capitals suggest influences from Near Eastern textile designs with animal compositions. Others appear to derive from fables or the imaginative lore preserved in bestiaries. Many of the motifs represent Christian versions of the struggle between the forces of good and evil, but for the Cuxa artists, conveying the old meanings seemed to be less important than creating striking compositions.

The cloister garden is traversed by walks, which provided rapid access from one part of the monastery to another. As in most monasteries, a source of water occupies the center of the garden—here, an eight-sided fountain from a neighboring monastery, Saint-Genis-des-Fontaines. *The Cloisters Collection, 1925, 25.120.398, 399, 452, 547–589, 591–607, 609–638, 640–666, 835–837, 872c,d, 948, 953, 954*

4 Portion of a Crozier Shaft
Probably English, first half of 12th c.
Ivory; h. 11¼ in. (28.6 cm.), diam. 1⅜ in. (3.5 cm.)

A masterpiece of Romanesque art, this delicately carved cylinder formed the upper portion of a crozier. Croziers are rarely decorated with such an elaborate self-contained iconographic scheme. The shaft is divided into four bands depicting two principal realms—one celestial, the other terrestrial—each heralded by angels. At the top is Christ enthroned within a mandorla, and on the other side are the Virgin and Child in another mandorla. The two central registers are filled with angels dressed as deacons. The bottom register shows the installation of a bishop.

The figural style and technical virtuosity of the carving are almost without parallel in twelfth-century ivories. The entire surface is densely filled with richly animated figures. The chief characteristic of the style is the turbulence of the abundant drapery. *The Cloisters Collection, 1981, 1981.1*

5 Altar Cross

English, attributed to Bury Saint Edmunds, mid-12th c.

Walrus ivory; 22⅝ × 14¼ in. (57.5 × 36.2 cm.)

Carved on both sides, this cross has on it more than a hundred small figures and some sixty inscriptions in Latin and Greek. Despite the complexity of the religious content—eight scenes from the Old Testament and the New, the allegory of the Lamb of God, likenesses of twenty-one prophets, and symbols of the Evangelists —the over-all effect is one of simplicity and strength. The cross is attributed to the abbey of Bury Saint Edmunds, Suffolk, England, by reason of its relationship to a Bible "incomparably painted" by Master Hugo for that abbey. It may even be the cross in the choir that Master Hugo is said to have made for Ording, who became abbot of Saint Edmunds in 1148. *The Cloisters Collection, 1963, 63.12*

6 CIRCLE OF MASTER BIDUINUS, Italian, ca. 1175

Doorway

Marble; entire doorway 158 × 76 in. (401.3 × 193 cm.)

This lintel is part of a Romanesque doorway from the church of San Leonardo al Frigido near Massa-Carrara in Tuscany. Christ is repre-sented entering Jerusalem, accompanied by the apostles and by Saint Leonard of Aquitaine. As in several works by the well-known Tuscan sculptor Master Biduinus, with whom this carving is undoubtedly connected, this scene follows representations of Early Christian sar-cophagi, reflecting the revival of interest in Late Antique and Early Christian art that occurred in Tuscany during the twelfth century. *The Clois-ters Collection, 1962, 62.189*

7 Annunciation

Spanish, Fuentidueña, ca. 1160

Limestone; h. 89 in. (226.1 cm.)

The majestic apse in the Fuentidueña Chapel in The Cloisters is from the church of San Martín in the village of Fuentidueña, about seventy-five miles north of Madrid. This Romanesque monu-ment is believed to have been built in the mid-twelfth century, when the fortified town was still of strategic importance to the Christian kings of Castile in their war against the Moors. The apse stood intact while the rest of the church, which was poorly built, fell into ruins. The Annuncia-tion to the Virgin stands on the right of the apse, while a statue of Saint Martin appears on the opposite wall. Although much is missing from the figures, the work remains vigorous and lively. As the archangel Gabriel leans toward the Virgin, his drapery folds accentuate his forward motion. Mary listens intently, learning that she will miraculously conceive Jesus. Below this scene devils thrust damned souls into the jaws of Hell; the Nativity of Christ is represented on the capital above. *The Cloisters Collection, 1958, L.58.86*

8 Crucifix
Spanish, Palencia, second half of 12th c.
*White oak and pine with polychromy; 102½ ×
81¾ in. (260.4 × 207.6 cm.)*

According to tradition, this crucifix hung in the
convent of Santa Clara near Palencia. It is one
of the finest surviving examples of the Romanesque type. Wearing the golden crown of the
King of Heaven and triumphant over death, this
Christ contrasts sharply with crucifixes of later
dates, in which Christ, wearing the crown of
thorns, is shown in the full agony of his suffering.
The almost horizontal arms, stylized anatomy,
and flattened drapery folds give the sculpture
an impressive dignity. The figure, carved of
white oak, and the pine cross retain much of
their original paint. The gesso base over which
the paint was applied is thick, and at some
points it is molded to produce finer details than
could be achieved by carving. *The Cloisters
Collection, 1935, 35.36a,b*

9 Clasp
Mosan, ca. 1210
Gilt bronze; 2 × 3 in. (5 × 7.5 cm.)

On the right half of this clasp a crowned male
figure sits on a bench, his feet resting on a lion.
A kneeling male attendant places a hand on
the king's shoulder. On the left half is a seated
woman; she rests her feet on a basilisk with the
head of a monkey and the body of a dragon. She
too has an attendant seated at her side. This
piece may be a partial illustration of Psalm
91:13—"Thou shalt tread upon the adder and
the basilisk and trample under foot the lion and
the dragon"—a passage traditionally interpreted as the triumph of Christ and by Augustine
as the triumph of the Church.

  Many stylistic features, such as the drapery
drawn across the knees and the ornamental
motifs, point to the art of Nicholas of Verdun
and his school and to a date of about 1210.
The Cloisters Collection, 1947, 47.101.48

10 Scene from the Life of Saint Nicholas
French, Soissons, ca. 1200
Pot-metal glass with grisaille paint; 21½ × 15½ in. (54.6 × 39.3 cm.)

This panel, which has been traced to the early thirteenth-century glazing program at Soissons cathedral, illustrates a scene from the life of Saint Nicholas. A fourth-century bishop, Nicholas was a popular saint in western Europe, particularly in northern France, in the twelfth and thirteenth centuries, and a chapel was dedicated to him at Soissons in 1200. The rich, brilliant color of the glass and the small, tubular, molded folds of drapery are characteristic of this period, while the rectangular panels set in arcades are an innovation that would become the standard by the mid-thirteenth century. *The Cloisters Collection, 1980, 1980.263.3*

11 Panel with a Lion
Spanish, San Pedro de Arlanza, ca. 1220
Fresco mounted on canvas; 89 × 132 in. (226.1 × 335.3 cm.)

According to medieval bestiaries, lions sleep with their eyes open, and therefore they represent paragons of Christian watchfulness. This lion was one of a pair that watched over the entrance to the chapter house in the monastery of San Pedro de Arlanza. Fierce and oriental-looking, he stands between an arcade and a flowering tree and is the image of invincible power. Beneath him is a border of decorative fish. In its freedom of line the fresco is reminiscent of the calligraphy of manuscript illumination. *The Cloisters Collection, 1931, 31.38.1a*

12 Chalice
North European, 1222
Silver; 7¼ × 3⅝ in. (18.4 × 9.2 cm.)

This sacramental cup is distinguished by its spare ornamentation and represents a type that continued in Germany well into the thirteenth century. An inscription around its foot states that it was made by Brother Bertinus in 1222. As Bertinus has not been identified, the place of origin is unknown. The tight interlacing of animals and foliage indicates a knowledge of Mosan art of the early thirteenth century. *The Cloisters Collection, 1947, 47.101.30*

14 Standing Biblical Figure
Upper Rhenish, mid-13th c.
*Walnut, polychromed and gilded; h. 77 in.
(195.6 cm.)*

This monumental figure has been identified as
Saint James the Less, because of the distinctive cap and the similarity to representations of
Christ, whom James was thought to resemble.
However, the lack of any further qualifying attributes—such as a book usually carried by the
apostles—and the missing left arm make a
positive identification difficult. The right hand
seems once to have held a staff. The features
and the handling of the mustache and beard resemble sculptures from the Upper Rhine around
Constance. The large proportions suggest that
this was a freestanding figure placed in a niche
in a church or cathedral. While there may have
been other figures similarly placed, no companion pieces are known. *Fletcher Fund, 1928, 28.32*

3 Virgin
French, Strasbourg, 1247–52
*Sandstone, polychromed and gilded; h. 58½ in.
148.6 cm.)*

This polychromed sculpture of the Virgin, the
most important in the collection, was originally
set on the choir screen of Strasbourg cathedral.
Though the screen was destroyed in 1682, a
drawing of about 1660 records the position of
the Cloisters sculpture among others on the
face of the screen. The Virgin was once accompanied by the Christ Child, who was supported
by a rose(?) bush. The figure retains much of its
original polychromy. The breaking folds of the
drapery are indicative of the contemporary development of the court style in Paris. *The
Cloisters Collection, 1947, 47.101.11*

15 Diptych with the Coronation of the Virgin and the Last Judgment

French, Paris, ca. 1260–70
Ivory; h. 4⁷/₈ in. (12.4 cm.)

This diptych is exceptional not only for the depth and refinement of its carving, but also for its juxtaposition of scenes. While the Coronation of the Virgin and the Last Judgment often appear together on Gothic portal sculpture, they rarely do so in ivory carvings. Of further iconographic interest is the representation of a friar—members of mendicant orders played an active role in the religious life at court—guided to heaven by an angel and followed by a king and a pope. On the basis of comparisons to Parisian metalwork and monumental sculpture, this ivory has been dated to just after the mid-thirteenth century. *The Cloisters Collection, 1970, 1970.324.7a,b*

16 Dragon Aquamanile

German, 13th c.
Bronze; h. 8³/₄ in. (22.2 cm.)

Aquamanilia were made in imaginative, often playful forms. They held water for the washing of priests' hands during the celebration of the Mass, and they were also used in households for the washing of hands at meals. This dragon swallowing a man curves its tail over its winged body to form the handle. The water issues from a hole beneath the man's head. *The Cloisters Collection, 1947, 47.101.51*

17 Doorway

French, Burgundy, 1257–89
Limestone with traces of polychromy; 185 × 151 × 55 in. (469.9 × 383.5 × 139.7 cm.)

This doorway from the monastery church of Moutiers-Saint-Jean in Burgundy shows the High Gothic union of architecture and sculpture with the many separate elements combining to create a harmonious whole. The tympanum shows Christ crowning the Virgin while angels bearing candlesticks kneel at either side. The two large pier figures are thought to represent Clovis, the first Christian ruler of France, and Clothaire, his son and successor. Tradition has it that Clovis, in the year of his conversion (probably 496), granted the monastery a charter that exempted it in perpetuity from royal and ecclesiastical jurisdiction; this charter was said to have been confirmed by Clothaire.

As with most medieval sculpture, the stone was polychromed, and traces of paint can still be seen. *The Cloisters Collection, 1932, 32.147*

18   Altar Angel
French, late 13th c.
Oak; h. 29 in. (73.7 cm.)

This angel combines the monumentality of stone figures on cathedral portals of the thirteenth century with the delicacy and elegance of ivory carvings. Its mantle forms long, classical folds, and its pose may derive from classical models. This figure is one of a pair of altar angels in the collection that are believed to have come from the region around Pas-de-Calais in Artois. These two angels were originally polychromed and gilded and had wings. Angels of this type, holding candlesticks or carrying the instruments of Christ's Passion, were usually made in groups of four or six and were placed on top of columns around the altars of churches. *The Cloisters Collection, 1952, 52.33.1*

19   Tomb of Ermengol VII
Spanish; effigy: first half of 14th c.; sarcophagus and celebrants relief: mid-14th c.; assembled in 18th c.
Marble; greatest overall measurements 89 × 79½ × 35½ in. (226.1 × 201.9 × 90.2 cm.)

One double and three single engaged tombs in the Gothic Chapel belonged to members of the Urgel family of Catalonia and are among the finest surviving examples of sepulchral art of the Léridan school. Though the Urgels were patrons of the monastery of Bellpuig de la Avellanas, near Lérida, with which all but the effigy of a youth have long been associated, the figures have never been positively identified. They are thought to date from Ermengol X's rebuilding of the chapel in the early fourteenth century.

The effigy of the largest single-tomb ensemble —that of Ermengol VII (d. 1184), according to a tradition dating from the eighteenth century— is stylistically related to the other tombs but is more elaborate and refined. Ermengol is shown lying on the lid of the sarcophagus. Behind his effigy and carved from the same block of stone are rows of mourners. Above them, in separate and not so finely carved panels, clerics perform the funeral rite of absolution. The sarcophagus, somewhat later in date than the effigy, is ornamented with carved reliefs of Christ in Majesty and of the apostles. The tomb is not mentioned in monastic records until the mid-eighteenth century and may have been assembled at that time from parts of other tombs, accounting for the mixture of styles that characterizes its present arrangement. *The Cloisters Collection, 1928, 28.95*

20 Virgin and Child

English, London(?), ca. 1300
Ivory; h. 10¾ in. (27.3 cm.)

Ivory statuettes such as this, appearing at the height of the popularity of the cult of the Virgin, were devotional in nature and must have been intended for chapels and small oratories. In a complete change from the rigid frontality of Romanesque sculptures, such statuettes tended to emphasize an intimate and reciprocal tenderness between the Virgin and the Child. This is the finest of the very few extant English examples of the subject, even though the Christ Child, who at one time climbed up over the Virgin's left knee, is missing. It is a masterpiece for its unified clarity of vision, intense refinement, which is both pervasive and detailed, and impression of monumentality. The face of the Virgin is so exquisitely modeled and courtly that it may be regarded as one of the most beautiful images in all Gothic art. The Virgin's highly polished surfaces have taken on over the centuries an appealing dark reddish-brown patina. *The Cloisters Collection, 1979, 1979.402*

21 JEAN PUCELLE, French, act. ca. 1320–ca. 1350

Book of Hours of Jeanne d'Evreux

Tempera and gold leaf on parchment; 3½ × 2⁷/₁₆ in. (8.9 × 6.2 cm.)

This tiny book of hours, almost certainly made for Jeanne d'Evreux, queen of France, was illuminated between 1325 and 1328 by Jean Pucelle, whose style influenced Parisian manuscript illumination for nearly a full century. The only work entirely by Pucelle's hand, it contains twenty-five full-page miniatures, a calendar illustrating the signs of the zodiac, and numerous marginal drolleries, all painted in grisaille with touches of color. The two cycles of images illustrate the Infancy and Passion of Christ and the life of Saint Louis. Iconographic details of the Crucifixion scene (above left; folio 68v) point to the influence of Italy, and particularly the Sienese master Duccio. Pucelle's mastery is evident in the tightness of the drawing, the freedom in handling forms, and the degree of concentration and depth of expression in illustrations so restricted in dimension and color. *The Cloisters Collection, 1954, 54.1.2*

22 Virgin and Child

French, Île-de-France, first half of 14th c.
Limestone, polychromed and gilded; h. 68 in. (172.7 cm.)

Made in the Île-de-France, the region around Paris, this Virgin and Child is extraordinarily well preserved: the paint and gilding are almost intact, and most of the cabochons remain in the crown and borders of the garments. The Virgin is interpreted as the Queen of Heaven, regal, gracious, and serene, but more relaxed than earlier models. The figure swings in a graceful S-curve and the draperies are soft and pliant, characteristics of the style of the mid-fourteenth century. *The Cloisters Collection, 1937, 37.159*

23 Reliquary Shrine ("The Elizabeth Shrine")
French, Paris, 1340–50
Silver gilt and translucent enamel; h. 10 in.
(25.4 cm.), w. (open) 16 in. (40.6 cm.)

This reliquary shrine of the Virgin and Child, in the form of a miniature altarpiece with hinged wings, was made in Paris about 1345. It is believed to have been created for Queen Elizabeth of Hungary and possibly to have been bequeathed by her to the convent of the Poor Clares in Budapest, which she founded in 1334.

The translucent enamel scenes on the wings, front and back, are of a jewel-like brilliance. The architectural details are reminiscent of Gothic churches, notably the trefoil arches and the ribbed vaulting above the seated Madonna and her attendant angels. Since most of the scenes on the wings have to do with the Infancy of Christ, it seems probable that the angels once displayed relics associated with the Nativity in their small windowed boxes. *The Cloisters Collection, 1962, 62.96*

24 MASTER OF THE CODEX OF SAINT GEORGE, Italian, act. after 1310–1340s
The Crucifixion; The Lamentation
Tempera on wood, tooled gold ground; each panel 15⅝ × 10⅝ in. (39.7 × 27 cm.)

This small diptych is a late work (ca. 1340–45) by an Italian panel painter and illuminator known as the Master of the Codex of Saint George. His mature style is characterized by restraint and depth of emotion, harmony of mass and space, and elegant and refined use of color and detail.

The Lamentation is not mentioned in the Gospels; here the artist follows closely the description in the *Meditations on the Life of Christ*, a work by a thirteenth-century Franciscan known as Pseudo-Bonaventura: "Our Lady supports the head and shoulders [of Christ] in her lap, the Magdalen the feet at which she had formerly found so much grace. The others stand about making a great bewailing over him . . . as for a firstborn son." *The Cloisters Collection, 1961, 61.200.1, 2*

25 Emperor Henry II
Austrian, Lavanttal, ca. 1340
Pot-metal glass; 39 × 17¾ in. (99.1 × 45.1 cm.)

The three center windows in the apse of the Gothic Chapel contain glass from the church of Saint Leonhard in Lavanttal, built about 1340. The two complete windows, one with its original tracery lights, and parts from three others at The Cloisters illustrate scenes from the life of Christ and the Virgin and standing figures of saints. Together they constitute the most extensive collection of Austrian stained glass from a single church in a foreign country. Illustrated here is the Holy Roman Emperor Henry II; he and his wife, Cunegund, were the patron saints of the windows' donors. (The panels showing the donors are still preserved at Lavanttal.) *The Cloisters Collection, 1965, 65.96.3*

26 The Nine Heroes Tapestries: Julius Caesar
French, ca. 1385
Wool; 160½ × 91¾ in. (407.7 × 233 cm.)

Among the earliest Gothic tapestries to survive, the Nine Heroes Tapestries were made around 1385 and are attributed to the workshop of Nicolas Bataille in Paris. The theme of the heroes was popularized in a French poem of about 1312 in which three pagan, three Hebrew, and three Christian heroes were described. Illustrated here is Julius Caesar, identified by a double-headed eagle, his customary medieval coat of arms.

Medieval artists typically portrayed the ancients in contemporary dress, and the Nine Heroes are sumptuously clad and accoutered in the style of about 1380. The tapestries suggest the wealth and power of the French aristocracy; the small figures surrounding the heroes represent the members of a medieval court: bishops, cardinals, knights, ladies, musicians, spearmen, and archers. The arms displayed on most of the banners are those of Jean, duc de Berry; the prominence of his arms indicates that the tapestries were commissioned either by him or for him. *Gift of John D. Rockefeller, Jr., 1947, 47.101.3*

27 POL, JEAN, AND HERMAN DE LIMBOURG, act. ca. 1400–1416
The Belles Heures de Jean, Duc de Berry
French, Paris, ca. 1410
Tempera and gold leaf on parchment; 9⅜ × 6⅝ in. (23.8 × 16.8 cm.)

The exquisite paintings in this book of hours, in tempera and gold, were the first commission undertaken by Pol de Limbourg and his brothers for Jean, duc de Berry, one of the greatest art patrons and bibliophiles of the Middle Ages. (He also owned the Hours of Jeanne d'Evreux [no. 21] and the Heroes Tapestries [no. 26] in The Cloisters Collection.) Recorded in the duke's inventory of 1413 as a "belles heures," the book has ninety-four full-page miniatures, such as the Annunciation to the Virgin (f. 30) reproduced here, and many smaller ones, as well as calendar vignettes and border illuminations. The Limbourgs' style is characterized by meticulous detail, exquisite color, a degree of realism previously unknown in France, and a treatment of form and space that indicates a strong awareness of Italian painting traditions. (See also Medieval Art—Main Building, no. 42.) *The Cloisters Collection, 1954, 54.1.1*

28 ROBERT CAMPIN, Flemish, ca. 1378–1444
Annunciation Altarpiece
Oil on wood; central panel 25¼ × 24⅞ in. (64.1 × 63.2 cm.), each wing 25⅜ × 10¾ in. (64.5 × 27.3 cm.)

The central panel of this small triptych shows the Annunciation (the archangel Gabriel's announcement to the Virgin Mary that she would miraculously conceive Jesus Christ). Joseph, Mary's spouse, is seen in his workshop in the right panel; the donor, presumably Ingelbrecht of Mechelen whose coat of arms appears in the left window of the central panel, and his wife are shown kneeling in the left panel. This work (also called the Mérode Altarpiece) dates from about 1425 and is in the then-new Flemish technique of oil colors on wood panels. It is also innovative in showing the Annunciation occurring not in a portico or an ecclesiastical setting but in a middle-class room of the patron's own time. In all this Campin's art anticipates future developments in Flemish painting.

Although Campin clearly rejoices in his ability to paint real objects with beauty of form and texture, he is also guided by the symbolic needs of his subject. The laver and the Madonna lily in the vase are symbols of Mary's purity. The candle is a symbol of Christ; the candlestick represents the Virgin who bore him. *The Cloisters Collection, 1956, 56.70*

29 Windows with Saints

Rhenish, 1440–47
*Pot-metal glass; h. of entire panel 148½ in.
(377.2 cm.), w. of each window 28¼ in.
(71.8 cm.)*

In the Boppard Room are six panels of stained glass from the nave of the Carmelite church of Saint Severinus at Boppard-on-Rhine. These six lancets, placed three over three, originally constituted a single tall window, made and installed between 1440 and 1447. Following the secularization of the monasteries in the wake of the Napoleonic invasion of the Rhineland, all the stained glass was removed and dispersed. The Cloisters panels are the only series from the extensive cycle at Boppard to have survived intact and the only extant works by one of the

two Boppard masters. His figure style and wide use of white glass suggest that he was probably trained in Cologne.

The three lower lancets are shown here. The saints standing in elaborate canopied niches are, from left to right: Saint Catherine of Alexandria with the wheel and sword of her martyrdom; Saint Dorothea receiving from the Christ Child a basket of roses from the celestial garden; and Saint Barbara carrying her attribute, a tower. In the lancets above, Saint Servatius, bishop of Tongres, and Saint Lambert flank the central figure of the Virgin, around whom the iconographic program of the north nave was devised. The panels represent the most brilliant ensemble of Late Gothic glass in the United States. *The Cloisters Collection, 1937, 37.52.4–6*

30 Beaker ("Monkey Cup")

French, Burgundy, ca. 1425–50
*Painted enamel on silver and silver gilt;
h. 7⅞ in. (20 cm.), diam. 4⅝ in. (11.7 cm.)*

This rare and beautiful beaker, the work of Netherlandish or Franco-Netherlandish artists, was probably made for the Burgundian court. It is decorated with "painted" enamel, so called because the material was applied freely over the silver, without the grooves that separate the colors in champlevé enameling or the incised patterns that provide guidelines for the application of translucent enamels. Inside the beaker two monkeys, with their hounds, pursue two stags. One monkey has a hunting horn, the other a bow and arrow. The chase occurs against a stylized forest with a cloud band at the top. The exterior presents a favorite northern theme: monkeys rob a sleeping peddler of his wares and his clothing and frolic with their prizes in the beaker's elegant foliage scrolls. *The Cloisters Collection, 1952, 52.50*

31 GIL DE SILOE, Spanish, act. 1486–1505
Saint James the Greater
*Alabaster with traces of polychromy and gilding;
h. 18¹/₁₆ in. (45.9 cm.)*

In 1486 Isabel of Castile commissioned an
elaborate alabaster tomb for her parents, Juan II
of Castile and Isabel of Portugal. This star-shaped
tomb, still standing in the middle of the church
of the Carthusian monastery of Miraflores in
Burgos, was executed between 1489 and 1493.
The sculptor, Gil de Siloe, employed assistants
who were responsible for many of the monument's figures, but this statuette of the patron
saint of Spain must surely have been by him
alone. The carving of the entire piece, especially the fine details of the hands and face, is
masterful. Portrayed as a pilgrim, the saint has
a pilgrim's gourd hanging from his staff and
wears a hat adorned with the cockleshell and
the crossed staffs worn by the pilgrims to Santiago de Compostela. Traces of gold and polychromy remain on the figure's surface. *The
Cloisters Collection, 1969, 69.88*

32 One of the Three Magi
German, Swabian, ca. 1490
*Limewood, polychromed and gilded; h. 61½ in.
(156.2 cm.)*

In the Middle Ages, particularly in the Netherlands and Germany, the kings who brought the
Christ Child gifts of gold, frankincense, and myrrh
were thought to have descended from the three
sons of Noah and thus to represent the three
races of humankind. Here the Moorish king
opens a lidded cup, which resembles German
metalwork of the late fifteenth century. This
statue and similar ones of the two other Magi
were once part of the high altarpiece, with painted wings, in the convent of Lichtenthal in Baden-
Baden. The kings are especially appealing in
the elegance and vivacity of their poses and the
exceptional quality of their polychromy. *The
Cloisters Collection, 1952, 52.83.2*

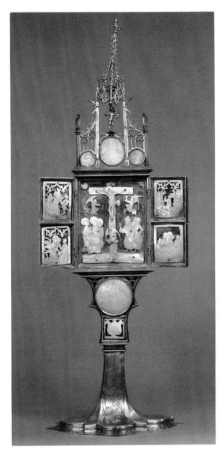

33 Tabernacle with Folding Wings

Austrian, Salzburg, 1494
*Silver, parcel-gilt, mother-of-pearl, and enamel;
h. 27⅜ in. (69.2 cm.), w. (open) 9⅞ in.
(25.1 cm.)*

This tabernacle is exceptional in its high artistic quality and its full documentation. According to the archives of the Benedictine monastery of Saint Peter of Salzburg, it was made in 1494 for Rupert Keutzl, abbot of the monastery, by the master goldsmith Perchtold. On the molding above the Last Supper is a Latin inscription which translates, "I stand by order of Abbot Rupert." On the base are shields with the arms of the monastery and of Abbot Rupert and the date 1494. The mother-of-pearl carvings are typically Austrian, but few examples are as successful as these, in which the polished silver background brings out the lively silhouettes. The scene of the Last Supper on the back is taken from an engraving by the Master J. A. M. Zwolle, whereas the Flagellation and the Taking of Christ are free copies of Schongauer engravings. *Gift of Ruth and Leopold Blumka (in commemoration of the Centennial of The Metropolitan Museum of Art), 1969, 69.226*

34 The Lamentation

Hispano-Flemish, ca. 1480–1500
*Walnut, with polychromy and gilding; 83 ×
48½ × 13½ in. (210.8 × 123.2 × 34.3 cm.)*

Originally the center of a large retable with painted wings, this polychromed Lamentation is an interesting example of Spanish workshop production at the end of the fifteenth century. The hands of several artists can be detected; different sculptors carved the frame and the figures, and different paints were used for the figures and the landscape. The debt to northern painting is evident in such figures as Saint John and the Magdalen wiping her eye, both of which are derived from Rogier van der Weyden (see European Paintings, no. 55). The gilded framework and brocaded sidewalls are, however, characteristically Spanish. *The Cloisters Collection, 1955, 55.85*

35 TILMAN RIEMENSCHNEIDER,
German, 1460?–1531
Seated Bishop
Limewood; h. 35⅞ in. (91 cm.)

Between 1475 and 1525 a school of limewood sculptors, known especially for their elaborate altarpieces, flourished in southern Germany. Riemenschneider, who also produced notable works in stone, was one of the first limewood masters; he had a large workshop in Würzburg from 1485 into the 1520s. Until the end of the fifteenth century it was usual for limewood sculptures to be painted; many still were long after 1500. As early as 1490, however, Riemenschneider produced works that were not polychromed but were finished with a brown glaze. This sculpture, which dates from 1495–1500, is one of the artist's few extant works in wood from the 1490s; it may have belonged to a monochrome retable. The figure may represent Saint Kilian or Saint Erasmus or perhaps one of the four Latin Fathers of the Church. The eyes—large, downturned, with the lower lid sharply marked—are characteristic of Riemenschneider's work, as are the handling of the drapery and the stance of the figure. *The Cloisters Collection, 1970, 1970.137.1*

36 The Unicorn Tapestries: The Unicorn at the Fountain
Franco-Flemish, ca. 1500
Wool; 145 × 149 in. (368.3 × 378.5 cm.)

This tapestry showing a unicorn surrounded by hunters at a fountain is the second in a series of seven representing the Hunt of the Unicorn. The first pictures the beginning of the hunt. The unicorn attempts to escape in the third, and in the fourth he defends himself. Only a small fragment of the fifth remains, illustrating the best-known part of the legend, which tells that the beast was captured when he rested his head in the lap of a virgin. The sixth tapestry shows the slain unicorn brought back to the castle, and in the seventh he is resurrected, enclosed in a garden under a pomegranate tree.

The legend of the unicorn was a popular parallel to the Passion of Christ: as the unicorn gave up his fierceness and was tamed by a maid, so Christ surrendered his divine nature and became human through the Virgin. The kneeling unicorn, dipping his horn into the water, alluded to the popular belief that the horn of the unicorn had the gift of purifying.

In view of their style and technique, these tapestries must have been woven in Brussels from a design by an artist familiar with French art. The mingling of Christian symbolism with flora and fauna associated with profane love and fertility suggests that the tapestries may have been designed to celebrate a marriage. However, the person who commissioned this superb ensemble and the occasion for which it was produced are unfortunately not known. *Gift of John D. Rockefeller, Jr., 1937, 37.80.2*

37 Playing at Quintain

French or Flemish, late 15th c.
Silver stain and grisaille paint on colorless glass; diam. 8–9½ in. (20.3–23.7 cm.)

Silver-stained roundels were widely used for the decoration of secular buildings in northern Europe at the end of the Middle Ages. In guild-halls they often depicted the guilds' crafts or patron saints. In private residences they usually illustrated scenes from the Bible or saintly legends; they were set in diamond-pane windows of clear glass, evidence of the new prosperity of the middle class.

This roundel is unusual in that it depicts a game known as quintain, in which the standing player attempts to topple his seated opponent. Developed from a tilting exercise for knights, the sport became a courting game in the fifteenth century and a common subject in late medieval secular art. *The Cloisters Collection, 1980, 1980.223.6*

38 The Death of the Virgin

German, Cologne, end of 15th c.
Oak; 69 × 79½ in. (175.3 × 201.9 cm.)

The Death of the Virgin was a popular subject in fifteenth-century art. Sculptural compositions were often indebted to Netherlandish paintings for composition and iconography, and this relief parallels several examples, including one by the Master of the Amsterdam Death of the Virgin in the Rijksmuseum, Amsterdam, and one by Petrus Christus in the Timken Gallery, Putnam Foundation, San Diego. The apostles are assembled at the Virgin's bed, as Saint Peter con-ducts the sacrament of extreme unction. The canopied bed and linenfold bench denote a fifteenth-century interior, while the censer held by one apostle resembles contemporary metal-work. In the doorway at the right the Legend of the Girdle is represented. Saint Thomas, who had not been at the deathbed, became convinced of the Virgin's Assumption only when her belt fell from the sky into his hands.

Originally the central scene of a polychromed altarpiece with two wings, this relief has been attributed to the Cologne workshop of Master Tilman. *The Cloisters Collection, 1973, 1973.348*

39 Ewer with Wild Man Finial

German, Nürnberg, ca. 1500
*Silver, silver gilt, and enamel; h. 25 in.
(63.5 cm.)*

This ewer with a wild man heraldic finial, one of
a pair in the Museum, is thought to have been
made in Nürnberg for Hartmann von Stockheim,
German master of the Order of Teutonic Knights
from 1499 to 1510. With the traditional attributes
of cudgel and armorial shield (now missing),
the wild man announced the ewer's ownership
and his protection of it.

The wild man was a literary and artistic invention of the medieval imagination. Thought to live
in remote forested regions, he was frequently
represented in German-speaking lands. The wild
man was originally regarded as brutish and irra-
tional, but he was transformed by Renaissance
humanism. Perceived as the embodiment of
legendary Germanic strength and endurance,
he became the standard by which man must
test his own mettle. *The Cloisters Collection,
1953, 53.20.2*

40 Eagle Lectern

South Netherlandish, Maastricht, ca. 1500
Brass; 79½ × 15½ in. (201.9 × 39.4 cm.)

Assembled from pieces cast separately, this
monumental work was made about 1500 in
Maastricht, possibly by the Belgian metal-caster
Aert van Tricht the Elder. The lectern rests upon
couchant lions and is topped by an eagle holding in his claws a vanquished dragon. The eagle's
wings support a large bookrack; a smaller rack,
possibly for the use of choirboys, is attached
below. Statuettes of Christ, saints, prophets, the
Three Kings, and the Virgin and Child appear
in the setting of mingled architecture and knotty
branches. Similar in type to lecterns still in parish
churches at Venraai and Vreren, this lectern is
believed to have come from the north side of the
high altar of the collegiate church of Saint Peter
in Louvain. *The Cloisters Collection, 1968, 68.8*

SECOND FLOOR

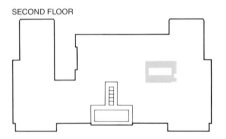

THE AMERICAN WING

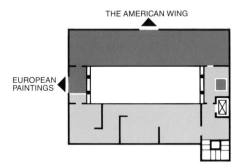

EUROPEAN
PAINTINGS

**THE ANDRÉ MERTENS GALLERIES
FOR MUSICAL INSTRUMENTS**

 WESTERN
MUSICAL INSTRUMENTS

NON-WESTERN
MUSICAL INSTRUMENTS

MUSICAL INSTRUMENTS

The Department of Musical Instruments, founded in 1942, preserves more than four thousand works from six continents, dating from prehistory to the present. A large part of the department's holdings came to the Museum in 1889, when Mrs. John Crosby Brown donated The Crosby Brown Collection of Musical Instruments.

The works in the Museum's collection, selected for technical and social importance as well as tonal and visual beauty, illustrate the history of music and performance. Of particular note are European courtly instruments from the Middle Ages and the Renaissance, the oldest extant piano, rare violins and harpsichords, instruments made from precious materials, and a fully equipped traditional violin-maker's workshop. The galleries, opened in 1971, display a representative selection of some eight hundred European, American, and non-Western works. Audio equipment enables visitors to hear music performed on these instruments, which are also used in gallery concerts and lecture-demonstrations.

2 ANTONIO STRADIVARI, Italian, 1644–1737
Violin
*Maple, spruce, various other materials;
l. 23⅝ in. (60.1 cm.)*

During the Baroque era (roughly 1600–1750), instrumentalists strove for clarity rather than for dynamic nuance. The supreme Italian luthiers valued warmth of tone above all, and their durable masterworks retain this quality after three centuries.

This Stradivari is the finest of all Baroque violins. Made in Cremona in 1691, it is unique in having been restored to its original appearance and tone. All other violins by this great master show later modifications aimed at exaggerating their loudness and brilliance, qualities remote from the maker's intent. This violin is robust but not shrill, its gut strings producing a sound ideal for chamber music. *Gift of George Gould, 1955, 55.86*

1 Late Medieval Stringed Instrument
North Italian, ca. 1420
Boxwood, rosewood; l. 14⅛ in. (36 cm.)

This appealing little cousin of the guitar was probably meant as a gift for the enjoyment and edification of a young woman. Its five strings would have passed over a low flat bridge, and the player would have used a plectrum to strum a chord or pick out a melody on one string at a time. This instrument may have been made to commemorate a betrothal. In Renaissance and earlier folklore, plucked instruments were frequently associated with Venus, with love and well-being, with springtime and vernal pursuits. The modestly garbed young couple on the back of this instrument, formally posed beneath a Tree of Life in which a naked Cupid draws his bow, seems to have nuptial implications. A number of familiar emblems drawn from sculpture, illumination, bestiaries, and other sources contribute to the imagery of courtship and betrothal. *Gift of Irwin Untermyer, 1964, 64.101.1409*

3   JOHANN WILHELM HAAS, Nürnberg,
1648–1723
Trumpet (left)
Silver; mouthpiece and cord not original; l. 28 in.
(71.2 cm.)
CHARLES JOSEPH SAX, Belgian, 1791–1865
Clarinet (right)
Ivory and metal; l. 26¾ in. (68 cm.)
Flute (bottom)
Saxon, 1760–90
Porcelain and metal; l. 24⅝ in. (62.6 cm.)

Unlike keyboard and stringed instruments, wood-
winds and brasses offer little area for decoration.
These examples are unusual in combining rare
materials with elegant ornament.

The silver trumpet with gold-washed mounts
dates from about 1700 and bears the engraved
arms of the king of Saxony in whose service it
probably sounded. Emblems of nobility, trum-
pets were played by an elite guild of musicians.

The ivory clarinet, made in Brussels in 1830,
has gilt lion-head keys and carries the arms
and motto of the princes of Orange.

The porcelain flute is embellished with a
colorful band of flowers that spirals between the
finger and embouchure holes, interrupted only
by gold-plated ferrules that connect the separate sections of tubing. Three center sections of
slightly different lengths can be interchanged to
adjust the pitch.

Trumpet: *Purchase, Funds from Various
Donors, 1954, 54.32.1;* clarinet: *Purchase, Funds
from Various Donors, 1953, 53.223;* flute: *Gift of
R. Thornton Wilson in memory of Florence E.
Wilson, 1943, 43.34*

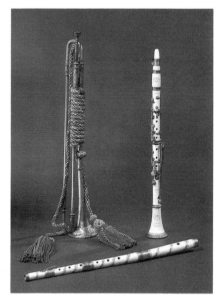

4   Chamber Organ
German, 18th c.
*Wood, metal, various other materials; h. 85½ in.
(217 cm.)*

Small pipe organs once served the same domestic functions as electric organs do today, furnishing popular musical entertainment and
accompanying private devotional services. This
colorful Baroque chamber organ reportedly came
from Castle Stein in Taunus, a region near
Frankfurt am Main. Its marbleized case has two
components: a cubic base containing the bellows and wind reservoir, fronted by a naive
painting of Saint Cecilia by Franz Caspar Hofer,
dated 1758, and an upper section holding the
keyboard, windchest, and pipes. Above the
cornice a carved gilded frame encloses two
unidentified coats of arms and the date 1700.
Another carved frame shades the tops of the
front rank of metal pipes. Two more ranks
within complete the tonal apparatus, which is
controlled by iron stop levers at the right of the
forty-five-note keyboard. The organist had to
play standing up, with another person inflating
the bellows by pulling a strap at the right side.
*The Crosby Brown Collection of Musical Instru-
ments, 1889, 89.4.3516*

5 Pentagonal Spinet
Venetian, 1540
Wood, various other materials; w. 54⁵/₁₆ in. (138 cm.)

In Renaissance Italy delicate spinets were the favored keyboard instruments of the aristocracy. Intended for amateur use, they were often richly decorated to charm the eye as well as the ear. One of the finest surviving spinets, this instrument was commissioned by the duchess of Urbino and was built by an unknown Venetian master. Over the keyboard is inscribed a humanistic appeal: "I'm rich in gold and rich in tone; if you lack goodness, leave me alone." ("Goodness" here means both personal virtue and musical skill.) Emblematic carvings bracket the arcaded keyboard, and intricate intarsia and pierced ornaments cover the front and the interior.

One of the oldest playable keyboard instruments, this spinet has been used in the Museum for concerts and recordings. Its brass strings are plucked by crow quills, and its lutelike tone especially suits the popular repertoire of its period, chiefly dances and variations on sacred and secular tunes. *Purchase, Joseph Pulitzer Bequest Fund, 1953, 53.6*

6 HANS RUCKERS THE ELDER, Flemish, ca. 1545–d. 1598
Double Virginal
Wood, various other materials; w. 74³/₄ in. (190 cm.)

This sumptuously painted virginal, made in Antwerp in 1581, is the oldest extant work by Hans Ruckers the Elder, head of a renowned family of Flemish harpsichord builders. Brought to Peru, it was discovered around 1915 in a hacienda chapel near Cuzco. Philip II of Spain and his wife Anne appear on gilt medallions over the right keyboard. When the high-pitched "child" at the left is placed above its "mother," both can be played by one person. The panel below the keyboards bears a Latin motto, which may be translated, "Sweet music is a balm for toil." *Gift of B. H. Homan, 1929, 29.90*

7 BARTOLOMMEO CRISTOFORI, Italian, 1655–1731
Piano
Wood, various other materials; l. 90 in. (228.6 cm.)

This, the oldest piano in existence, is one of three that survive from the workshop of Bartolommeo Cristofori, who invented the piano at the Medici court in Florence around 1700. The Museum's example is dated 1720 and remains in playable condition thanks to successive restorations that began in the eighteenth century. Outwardly plain, this piano is nevertheless a marvel of technology and tone. Its complex mechanism prefigures the modern piano's, but its keyboard is shorter and no pedals exist to provide tonal contrast. Instead, the compass comprises three distinct registers: a warm, rich bass; more assertive middle octaves; and a bright, short-sustaining treble. Intended chiefly for accompanimental use, Cristofori's invention was called *gravicembalo col piano e forte* (harpsichord with soft and loud), referring to its novel dynamic flexibility. Lodovico Giustini exploited its expressive qualities in composing the first published piano music (Florence, 1732), which was inspired by Cristofori's ingenious instruments. *The Crosby Brown Collection of Musical Instruments, 1889, 89.4.1219*

8 ERARD & COMPANY, London, ca. 1840
Piano
Wood, metal, various other materials; l. 97¼ in. (247 cm.)

The London branch of the famous Parisian firm of harp and piano makers built this magnificent piano for the wife of the third baron Foley. The keys and pedals seem scarcely to have been touched, so we can surmise that this fine instrument was kept merely as an emblem of culture and status. No other piano so richly decorated is known from the period. The marquetry of dyed and natural woods, engraved ivory, mother-of-pearl, abalone, and wire illustrates many musical scenes and trophies as well as animals, grotesque figures, floral motifs, dancers, Greek gods, and the Foley arms. This decor was executed by one George Henry Blake, of whom nothing is known. The mechanism, patented by Erard, is the direct ancestor of the modern grand "action," which allows great power and rapidity in technique; hence, Erard's pianos were favored by virtuosi such as Franz Liszt. *Gift of Mrs. Henry McSweeney, 1959, 59.76*

9 Bowl Drum
Ghanaian, 20th c.
Polychromed wood; l. 21 in. (53.4 cm.)

Many African tribesmen still make and play drums according to centuries-old methods, which are governed by complex rules and taboos. The carved decoration of the variously shaped wood bodies symbolizes their ritual functions. Drums may "reside" in huts where, representing deities or enclosing powerful fetishes, they receive offerings of food. A significant Ghanaian example is this polychromed bowl drum supported on the shoulders of two seated women. The depiction of writing and the drum's good state of preservation indicate a fairly recent origin for this evocative sculpture, symbolic of maternity. Presumably this cult drum was once an important furnishing of an Ashanti shrine; it must have lost its efficacy before leaving the cult's possession. *Gift of Raymond E. Britt, Sr., 1977, 1977.454.17*

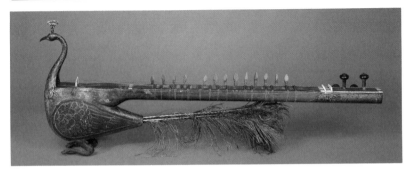

10 Mayuri
Indian, 19th c.
Wood, feathers, various other materials; l. 44⅛ in. (112 cm.)

A type of bowed sitar, the mayuri is one of many Indian instruments incorporating animal forms. Its Sanskrit name means "peacock." When it is played, the bird's feet stand on the ground, and the pegbox rests over the player's shoulder. Adjustable frets and wire strings lie along the fingerboard, above a tail of vivid feathers. Other kinds of sitars also employ avian materials, including eggshells, in their construction. *The Crosby Brown Collection of Musical Instruments, 1889, 89.4.3516*

11 Pi-pa

Chinese, Ming dynasty, 17th c.
*Wood, ivory, various other materials; l. 37 in.
(94 cm.)*

The term "pi-pa," originally a generic name
for Chinese lutes, describes the back-and-forth
motion of the player's right hand across the
strings. Lutes of various shapes and sizes
were mentioned as early as the Han dynasty
(206 B.C.– A.D. 220). The modern type shown
here, probably introduced by Central Asian
invaders by the sixth century A.D., reached
its zenith during the T'ang dynasty (618–907)
but is still heard in ensembles, accompanying
dramatic narrations and ballads, and in virtuo-
sic solo pieces with programmatic titles. The
extraordinary carved decoration of this example
includes 120 ivory plaques depicting animals,
flowers, people, and Buddhist emblems all symbolizing good luck, longevity, and immortality.
A bat, conventional symbol of good fortune,
appears at the end of the neck. Instruments of
such rare beauty were made as gifts for foreign
rulers and for use at court. The player of this
pi-pa certainly enjoyed high status as a musician.
*Bequest of Mary Stillman Harkness, 1950,
50.145.74*

12 Sesando

Indonesian, Timor, late 19th c.
Palm leaf, bamboo, wire; h. 22½ in. (57 cm.)

In Indonesia, sections of palm leaf (*Borassus
flabellifera*) are commonly sewn together to
make buckets for collecting sap. Here a similar
palm-leaf "bucket" forms the sound reflector for
a tubular bamboo zither with twenty wire strings
raised on short bridges. The elegant design is
practical and musically efficient: the fragile reflector can be cheaply replaced if damaged,
and the instrument is both lightweight and
resonant. The sesando is held vertically in front
of the player's chest, its opening toward his
body. The top is suspended from a strap around
the player's neck, and the bottom rests on his
lap. Fingers of both hands pluck the strings.
Tube zithers like this are also found in Mada-
gascar, where they were brought across the
Indian Ocean by sailors from the East. These
instruments play in ensembles accompanying
singing and dancing. Sesandos are seldom
seen in the West, where winter dryness cracks
their tropical materials. *The Crosby Brown Collection of Musical Instruments, 1889, 89.4.1489*

13 Shaman Rattle

Tsimshian Indian, around Queen Charlotte
Islands, British Columbia, 19th c.
Wood; l. 14 in. (35.5 cm.)

Chordophones, or stringed instruments, were
unknown in the Western Hemisphere before its
conquest by Europeans. Instead, over tens of
thousands of years Native Americans developed an astonishing variety of idiophones, drums,
and winds. Crisp-sounding rattles and non-
pitched single-head drums accompanied dance,
song, and ritual. Vivid bird-form rattles, such as
this one, are characteristic carvings from the
northwest coast of North America. These instruments embody totemic emblems and depict
animals conveying magical power to the sha-
man through their tongues. Particular colors
from natural pigments are essential to the rattles'
efficacy. *The Crosby Brown Collection of Musical Instruments, 1889, 89.4.615*

FIRST FLOOR

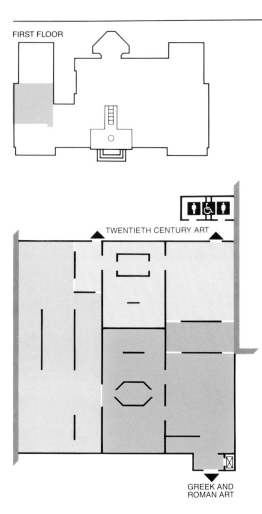

TWENTIETH CENTURY ART

GREEK AND
ROMAN ART

THE MICHAEL C. ROCKEFELLER WING

 ART OF THE PACIFIC ISLANDS

ART OF AFRICA

 ART OF THE AMERICAS

 SPECIAL EXHIBITIONS GALLERY

ART OF THE PACIFIC ISLANDS, AFRICA, AND THE AMERICAS

THE MICHAEL C. ROCKEFELLER WING

The arts of Africa, the Pacific Islands, and the Americas are displayed in The Michael C. Rockefeller Wing. Completed in 1982, this installation is the Museum's first permanent exhibition of art from these regions. About two thousand objects are on view in the wing, which unites the collection of the once-independent Museum of Primitive Art (established in 1954 by Nelson A. Rockefeller, later governor of New York), Nelson A. Rockefeller's own collection, and the objects acquired by the Metropolitan Museum during the last century. The wing is named for Governor Rockefeller's son Michael, who lost his life in 1961 while on an expedition to study the art and culture of the Asmat people of Irian Jaya (West New Guinea).

The African collection is especially strong in bronze sculpture from Benin (Nigeria) and wooden sculpture by the Dogon, Bamana, and Senufo of Mali. Major works from the Pacific area include sculpture from the Asmat, from the Sepik provinces of New Guinea, and from the island groups of Melanesia and Polynesia. From the Precolumbian cultures of Mexico and Central and South America come important holdings in gold, ceramics, and stone. A group of Eskimo and American Indian material represents the native arts of this country.

Founded in 1969, the Department of Primitive Art is the youngest of the Museum's curatorial departments. Its research facility—The Robert Goldwater Library, which includes a photograph archive—is available to scholars for consultation.

THE PACIFIC ISLANDS

2 House Pole Decoration

Polynesia, New Zealand,
Maori, early 19th c.
Wood; h. 43 in. (109.2 cm.)

The Maori used abundant architectural sculptured elements on the fences of their fortified villages, meeting places, and storehouses. The object shown here was probably part of a figural group carved on the inside of a beam that supported the porch roof of a large house. Another sculpture would have been placed symmetrically below this one; the characters represented were Mother Heaven (Papa) and Father Earth (Rangi). This figure sticks out its tongue; its right hand supports its chin, and its left hand is placed across its body. The eyes were originally inlaid with brilliant blue-green abalone rings. The sexual organs, illustrating the union of the divinities, were removed during the Victorian period. *The Michael C. Rockefeller Memorial Collection, Bequest of Nelson A. Rockefeller, 1979, 1979.206.1508*

3 Figure

Tonga Islands, Ha'apai Group, before 1868
Walrus ivory; h. 5¼ in. (13.3 cm.)

In the past the Polynesian peoples shared a language and many important elements of culture. The Polynesians believed in two great spiritual forces—tabu, a negative power, and mana, a positive one that pervaded not only human beings but material objects as well. For the individual, mana was derived partly from skill; it conferred a nearly divine status upon priests, chiefs, and carvers.

The majority of surviving Polynesian carving consists of elaborate utilitarian objects; figure sculpture—destroyed, in most areas, under early Western influence—is relatively rare. Small female figures were carved in the Tongan archipelago at least as early as the late eighteenth century, when some were collected on one of Captain Cook's voyages. A few were exported to the Fiji Islands, where this example was found. The figures are usually bored so that they can be suspended, probably on necklaces. Sometimes called "goddesses," they are thought to represent female ancestors. *The Michael C. Rockefeller Memorial Collection, Bequest of Nelson A. Rockefeller, 1979, 1979.206.1470*

1 Male Figure (probably the god Rogo)

Gambier Islands, Mangareva Island, 19th c.
Wood; h. 38¾ in. (98.4 cm.)

It is not known which of the numerous deities worshiped in the Gambier Islands is represented by this figure, but the god most often the subject of wood figures was Rogo, sixth son of Tagaroa and Haumea, the mythological first inhabitants of Mangareva. Rogo was the god of peace, agriculture, and hospitality in all of Polynesia, and he revealed himself in the form of a rainbow and as fog. On Mangareva Island he was invoked especially in rites connected with the cultivation of turmeric tubers. Most of the sculpture of Mangareva, where this object originated, was destroyed in April 1836 at the instigation of missionaries. Only eight figures have survived, six of them naturalistic and two of them highly stylized. *The Michael C. Rockefeller Memorial Collection, Bequest of Nelson A. Rockefeller, 1979, 1979.206.1466*

5 Funerary Carving
New Ireland, 19th–20th c.
Wood, paint, opercula; h. 100½ in. (255.3 cm.)

In New Ireland *malanggan* is the collective name for a series of ceremonies and the masks and carvings associated with them. The rituals, seldom practiced today, were held primarily in memory of the dead and were combined with initiation ceremonies in which young men symbolically replaced in society those who had died. The carvings, the most complex of all Oceanic works of art, were commissioned from recognized experts and embody images from clan mythology. They were displayed in special enclosures, sometimes in considerable numbers, during feasts honoring both the dead and the donors of the carvings, after which they were abandoned or destroyed. *The Michael C. Rockefeller Memorial Collection, Gift of Nelson A. Rockefeller, 1972, 1978.412.712*

4 Mask
Vanuatu, Malekula Island, 19th–20th c.
Vegetable compost on armature of tree fern, straw, paint, tusks, shells; h. 26 in. (66 cm.)

In Vanuatu (formerly New Hebrides) there were a number of men's societies that were known by different names although their structure was essentially the same. The societies were composed of many grades through which members ascended to sanctity and greatness by means of initiation rites, festivals, and pig sacrifices. Nimangki and Nalawan were two of the grade societies of south Malekula, and as elsewhere, each involved the making of figures and masks. This mask represents the mythical cannibal Nevinbumbaan, whose husband or son, Ambat Malondr, sits on her shoulders. Nevinbumbaan created the men's society Nimangki; her mask was worn at various stages of the Nalawan cycle. *The Michael C. Rockefeller Memorial Collection, Bequest of Nelson A. Rockefeller, 1979, 1979.206.1697*

6 Shield

Solomon Islands, probably Santa Isabel Island, 19th c.
Basketry, mother-of-pearl, paint; h. 33¼ in. (84.5 cm.)

The Solomon Islands form a double chain of seven large and many small islands. In these islands carvings were frequently made for canoe decorations and architectural use. Most carvings were painted black with touches of red; inlays of pearl shell were used instead of incised designs. A small number of shields —perhaps two dozen—exist that are painted completely and encrusted with shell pieces forming designs that represent a figure and several faces. All these decorated shields seem to have been made in the mid-nineteenth century —probably, in view of their fragility, as ceremonial objects. *The Michael C. Rockefeller Memorial Collection, Gift of Nelson A. Rockefeller, 1972, 1978.412.730*

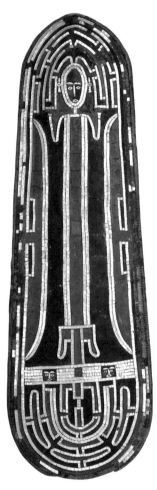

7 Mother and Child

Irian Jaya (New Guinea), Lake Sentani, Kabiterau village, Sentani people, 19th–20th c.
Wood; h. 36⅛ in. (91.8 cm.)

Lake Sentani, seventeen miles long, is surrounded by hills a few miles inland from Humboldt Bay. The six thousand people who lived along the lakeshore inhabited villages of pile houses built over the water. Considerable control was exercised by recognized chiefs and their immediate followers over economic activities (particularly trade with the people of Humboldt Bay) and over religion, which included a cult of flutes associated with mythical cassowaries. The privileged position of chiefs was reflected in their splendid longhouses, the posts of which were elaborately carved. The upper ends of shorter posts projected through the floors and were carved with figures in the round —exemplified by this object—some probably representing ancestors. *The Michael C. Rockefeller Memorial Collection, Bequest of Nelson A. Rockefeller, 1979, 1979.206.1440*

8 *Mbis* Pole

Irian Jaya (New Guinea), between the Asewetsj and Siretsj rivers, probably Per village, Asmat people, 20th c.
Wood, paint; h. 228 in. (579.1 cm.)

In southern Irian Jaya, approximately 10,500 square miles of flat, swampy terrain blanketed in jungle is the home of the Asmat, who number about 30,000 people. In Asmat belief, death was never natural; it was always caused by an enemy, and it created an imbalance in society that the living were called upon to correct by imposing death on the enemy. When a village suffered a number of deaths, it would hold the *mbis* ceremony. Carvings made specially for these events include *mbis* poles, the basic form of which is a canoe with an exaggerated prow that incorporates both ancestral figures and a phallic symbol in the shape of a winglike open-work projection. For each *mbis* ceremony several poles were displayed in front of the men's ceremonial house; they were kept until a successful headhunt had been carried out. The victims' heads were then placed in the hollow ends of the poles, and after a final feast the hunters abandoned the carvings in the jungle.
The Michael C. Rockefeller Memorial Collection, Gift of Nelson A. Rockefeller and Mary C. Rockefeller, 1965, 1978.412.1251

9 Mask

Papua New Guinea, Torres Strait, Mabuiag Island, 18th c.
Turtle shell, clamshell, wood, feathers, sennit, resin, seeds, paint, fiber; h. 17½ in. (44.5 cm.)

The islanders of the Torres Strait, between New Guinea and Australia, used turtle shell to construct masks, a practice found nowhere else in the Pacific area. Some are in human form or represent fish or reptiles, while others are a combination of attributes from all three. Turtle-shell effigies in these islands were first recorded in 1606 by the Spanish explorer Diego de Prado. Only two masks of the type shown here are extant; nothing is known of their use.
The Michael C. Rockefeller Memorial Collection, Purchase, Nelson A. Rockefeller Gift, 1967, 1978.412.1510

10 Figure
Caroline Islands, Palau Islands, 19th–20th c.
Wood, paint; w. 38 in. (96.5 cm.)

In the Palau archipelago of the Caroline Islands, men were grouped according to age and status. Each group had a clubhouse in which the men spent much of their time. The power and wealth of a village were reflected in the number of such structures. The clubhouses were impressive buildings, with high, pitched roofs that created large gables. The interior beams and the horizontal planks screening the gables were incised and painted with a multitude of scenes from legends. Large figures of women, often attached to the gables above the entrances, also illustrated legends. This figure was inspired by a tale about a promiscuous girl called Dilukai, whose angry father tied her in the position shown here as a lesson in chastity to the women of the village. Ironically, however, the clubhouses were frequently the temporary homes of prostitutes who were sent from other villages to gain wealth for their families. *The Michael C. Rockefeller Memorial Collection, Gift of Nelson A. Rockefeller, and Purchase, Nelson A. Rockefeller Gift, by exchange, 1970, 1978.412.1558a–d*

AFRICA

11 Mother and Child
Mali, Bougouni-Dioïla area, Bamana people, 19th–20th c.
Wood; h. 48⅝ in. (123.5 cm.)

Large figures like this one, found in only a few Bamana villages near Bougouni and Dioïla in southern Mali, appear in celebrations of the Jo society, an association of initiated men and women. They are distinct from other Bamana sculpture in that their forms are fluid and round rather than angular and cubistic. They wear elaborate coiffures, and scarification marks cover their faces, necks, and torsos. For annual Jo festivities and for fertility rites, the figures are removed from their shrines, washed, oiled, and adorned with beads and cloth and then displayed in groups. The central male and female figures in the group are seated on chairs; the woman holds a child. Attendant female figures are often shown as pregnant, and male figures hold objects used in Jo ceremonies, such as horns filled with medicines, and musical instruments. Figures of both sexes carry weapons and wear conical hats covered with amulets, emblems of their special power. *The Michael C. Rockefeller Memorial Collection, Bequest of Nelson A. Rockefeller, 1979, 1979.206.121*

12 Female Figure
Ivory Coast, Baule people, 19th–20th c.
Wood, paint, beads, cord; h. 25⅞ in. (65.7 cm.)

The Baule people of the central Ivory Coast live
in small farming villages that seldom have popula-
tions of more than five hundred. Baule artists
carve two types of figures. One kind is made to
honor and appease nature spirits, which are
hideous, filthy creatures that may possess men
and women and cause them to act in unproduc-
tive or antisocial ways. To please the nature
spirits, the figures carved for them depict beautiful human beings, with carefully coiffed hair and
decorative scarification marks. Though similar
in appearance, the other type of Baule figure
sculpture is dedicated to a different kind of
spirit, the spouse that a man or a woman had in
the other world before being born into this one.
Until it is honored with a shrine, a jealous or
dissatisfied spirit may cause difficulties for its
human partner. Both nature spirits and spirit
spouses are objects of personal devotion and
can bestow upon their devotees such blessings
as wealth and children. This particular figure
could have been made for either kind of spirit.
*The Michael C. Rockefeller Memorial Collection,
Bequest of Nelson A. Rockefeller, 1979,
1979.206.113*

14 Face from a Triple-Face Mask
Nigeria, Ibibio people, 19th–20th c.
Wood, paint; h. 23 in. (58.4 cm.)

This face, which seems to be a three-quarter
view, is actually a section of a helmet mask that
originally had three full faces. At one time the
mask was entirely covered with animal skin, a
technique that is characteristic of the art of
many ethnic groups living along the Cross
River in Nigeria and Cameroon. The sharp
delineation of the hairline, eyebrows, lips, and
circular scarification marks at the temples would
have been clearly visible beneath the taut skin,
which was held in place by tiny wooden pins.
Round pegs were inserted into the holes on top
of the head to represent hair, and wooden teeth
were driven into the mouth, enhancing the
mask's already lifelike appearance. The use of
multifaced, skin-covered helmet masks spread
east and west of the Cross River. This object, an
Ibibio work, was used at celebrations of Ikem, a
voluntary association that was founded at the
end of the nineteenth century. *The Michael C.
Rockefeller Memorial Collection, Gift of
Margaret Plass, 1955, 1978.412.287*

13 Head
Ghana, Fomena, Akan people, 17th c.(?)
Terracotta; h. 12⅜ in. (31.4 cm.)

Among the Akan peoples of southern Ghana
and the Ivory Coast, terracotta heads and figures
commemorate deceased members of the royal
family. Such terracottas were seen on graves
as early as the beginning of the seventeenth
century. To capture the essence of the individual depicted in this portrait head, the artist has
relied on details such as hairstyle, beard, and
scarification rather than distinctive facial features.
*The Michael C. Rockefeller Memorial Collection,
Gift of Nelson A. Rockefeller, 1964, 1978.412.353*

15 Pendant Mask
Nigeria, court of Benin, early 16th c.
Ivory, iron, copper; h. 9⅜ in. (23.8 cm.)

Benin is the best documented of the early kingdoms of tropical Africa. Portuguese explorers who visited the court in 1485 and other foreigners who later traveled there compared Benin favorably with Europe. The art of Benin is royal, created for a divine king and his court. Vast wealth, political stability, and the demand for an art that reflected the power of the kingdom assured the continuation of a five-hundred-year tradition of high artistic standards. The court's preoccupation with hierarchy is reflected in the attention to ornament—an indication of rank. The king of Benin probably wore this extraordinary mask at his hip during ceremonies commemorating his deceased mother. The delicate features of the mask may be those of a particular queen mother. The hair alternately takes the form of mudfish and bearded faces: mudfish symbolize wealth and royalty; the faces are images of the Portuguese. *The Michael C. Rockefeller Memorial Collection, Gift of Nelson A. Rockefeller, 1972, 1978.412.323*

16 Helmet Mask
Cameroon, Kom people, 19th c.
Wood, iron, copper, paint, wax; h. 20½ in. (52.1 cm.)

This mask was made in Kom, one of many kingdoms in the Cameroon grasslands. Above the larger-than-life-size face, four small disembodied arms support a flat disk pierced with holes that once held spears or feathers. The mask was worn tilted back, so that the wearer could look out below the chin or through the mouth. A feathered cloak or a gown of indigo-and-white cloth completed the costume. Artists in the Cameroon grasslands generally work in an exuberant, full-volumed style. In this mask, the gentle curves of the face, the slightly flared nostrils, and the lips parted as if to breathe or speak all contribute to a heightened feeling of vitality. The face was originally covered with a sheet of beaten copper, a material associated with political power and persons of high rank. The most important masks in the grasslands are the property of palace regulatory associations —groups of the king's advisers, princes, warriors, and other influential people—who use the supernatural power of the masks to reinforce their own authority as well as that of the king. *Purchase, Walter Annenberg, Ernst Anspach, Mrs. Vincent Astor, Charles B. Benenson, Mr. and Mrs. William W. Brill, Mr. and Mrs. J. Richardson Dilworth, Sigrid Galushka, Mr. and Mrs. Joseph Gerofsky, Marc and Denyse Ginzberg, Mr. and Mrs. Thomas B. Morgan, Mr. and Mrs. Milton F. Rosenthal, Mr. and Mrs. David T. Schiff, Gustave and Franyo Schindler, Faith and Martin Wright, Mr. and Mrs. Lester Wunderman and Anonymous Gifts, 1977, 1977.45*

17 Reliquary Head
Gabon, Fang people, 19th–20th c.
Wood, metal; h. 18¼ in. (46.4 cm.)

For the Fang people—inhabitants of the dense rain forests of Gabon, Equatorial Guinea, and southern Cameroon—the power of the dead to help the living was central to traditional religious beliefs. Each Fang family possessed a bark box containing the skulls of its ancestors, a practice that provided a sense of continuity with the past and the assurance of protection in the future. A carved head or figure mounted on top of each reliquary box guarded the sacred contents against the forbidden gaze of women and uninitiated boys. Reliquary figures and heads, blackened and glistening from ritual purifications with palm oil, exemplify through their forms the qualities the Fang admire in people—tranquillity, vitality, and the ability to hold opposites in balance. With its smooth, swelling forehead, sunken cheeks, and large eyes, this head combines qualities of both an infant's head and a skull, thus representing the spiritual link between the ancestors and future generations. *The Michael C. Rockefeller Memorial Collection, Bequest of Nelson A. Rockefeller, 1979, 1979.206.229*

18   Kneeling Figure
Zaire, Kongo people, 19th–20th c.
*Wood, bone, traces of cloth, other materials;
h. 11¼ in. (28.6 cm.)*

Among the Kongo people of Zaire, certain wood
sculptures are said to be endowed with life and
breath, vital qualities that set them apart from
other inanimate objects. They derive their power
from a spirit, often of an ancestor, that has been
captured in the object and that can be manipu-
lated to accomplish specific goals, such as
healing an illness or harming an enemy. The
spirit is induced to act by the addition to the
sculpture of diverse ingredients—leaves, special earths, parts of animals—whose names or
properties are symbolic of the desired result.
These materials are combined by a ritual expert,
who either inserts the mixture into cavities in the
sculpture or packs it around the head and the
torso. The encrusted material that once covered
the body of this figure is now lost, but the cap-
like mass at the head remains. Kongo wood
sculptures are further imbued with life through
their naturalistic features and active, often asymmetrical gestures. Here the artist has clearly
conveyed a sense of the body's bony structure
beneath the soft flesh. The figure kneels in the
posture of a hunter and probably once held a
rifle in its arms. *The Michael C. Rockefeller
Memorial Collection, Gift of Nelson A. Rockefeller, 1969, 1978.412.521*

19   Figure of a Warrior
Nigeria, Ijebu or Owo area, Yoruba people,
1455–1640
Bronze; h. 12¼ in. (31.1 cm.)

This figure is shown with the accouterments
and costume seen on figures of warriors in
Benin art. It carries a shield and a sword (with
blade missing) and wears a bell pendant, a
small woven cap with coral beads, and a stiff
leather skirt. The necklace is made of leopard's
teeth and glass beads and is a type that traditionally was filled with protective medicines and
worn into battle. The ribbing on the figure's chin
represents a beard, and the fine raised welts on
the forehead represent ornamental scars. A
thermoluminescence test of the intact clay core
places this figure between 1455 and 1640, the
early and middle periods of Benin art. However,
its spontaneous, somewhat rustic quality and
its vigor distinguish the figure from objects produced for the court of Benin during this time; it
was probably made in a Yoruba center that had
close ties to Benin. *Purchase, Edith Perry Chapman Fund, Rogers, Pfeiffer, Fletcher and
Dodge Funds, Gift of Humanities Fund, Inc., by
exchange, Mrs. Donald M. Oenslager Gift, in
memory of her husband, Geert C. E. Prins Gift
and funds from various donors, 1977, 1977.173*

THE AMERICAS

20 Stool with Female Figure
Zaire, Luba-Hemba people, late 19th c.
Wood; h. 24 in. (61 cm.)

This ceremonial stool is typical of sculpture made by the artist known as the Buli Master, after the town in eastern Zaire where two of the approximately twenty objects attributed to him were found. Brought to Europe about 1900, the Buli Master's sculptures were among the first works of traditional African art to be grouped and recognized as the creation of a single artist. Most Luba figures are full and round, their features idealized and ageless, but the Buli Master's works have an individuality and an emotional intensity that set them apart. Luba stools with caryatid figures were the exclusive prerogative of traditional rulers—kings and chiefs, clan heads, and the heads of extended families. The figures portray ancestors whose presence provides spiritual support for the ruler as well as physical support of his person. Most of the Luba people trace succession and inheritance through the female line; accordingly, the figures supporting chiefs' stools are usually female. *Purchase, Buckeye Trust and Charles B. Benenson Gifts, Rogers Fund and funds from various donors, 1979, 1979.290*

21 "Baby" Figure
Mexico, Olmec, 12th–9th c. B.C.
Ceramic; h. 13⅜ in. (34 cm.)

The Olmecs, who lived in the coastal swamps along the Gulf of Mexico around 1000 B.C., appear to have formalized many of the concepts that made possible the significant achievements of the ancient New World. Monumental basalt works, small jade objects, and carefully crafted ceramic figures and vessels are their chief sculptural legacy. The Gulf Coast near San Lorenzo and La Venta is so wet that only stone sculptures survive intact. Ceramic vessels in good condition come from drier areas, such as the central highland sites of Tlatilco and Las Bocas, where Olmec influence prevailed from about the twelfth to the ninth century B.C. Important Olmec ceramics are black, gray, or white. The most notable sculptural ceramics depict pudgy, nearly life-size human baby figures. White-surfaced and hollow, these figures may represent an early form of a Mexican deity and are the most "realistic" in Olmec art. *The Michael C. Rockefeller Memorial Collection, Bequest of Nelson A. Rockefeller, 1979, 1979.206.1134*

22 Seated Figure
Mexico or Guatemala, Maya, 6th c.
Wood; h. 14 in. (35.6 cm.)

Although in close proximity to one another and sharing many cultural traits, the Mexican and the Maya peoples were sufficiently different to represent distinct ancient cultures. Maya territory encompassed the Mexican states of Chiapas and Tabasco, those on the Yucatán Peninsula, the adjacent country of Guatemala, and parts of El Salvador and Honduras. The fame of Maya art rests on that produced in the southern lowlands, primarily in what is now the Petén district of Guatemala. This figure is reported to have come from the lowlands of the Mexico-Guatemala border, where wood objects do not survive well. It is a unique testament to wood sculptures otherwise lost to time and tropical rains. The mustachioed, elegantly dressed figure is seated in a ceremonial pose, the significance of which is not clear. Among the ancient Maya, gesture and posture had specific meanings, many of which are yet to be determined. *The Michael C. Rockefeller Memorial Collection, Bequest of Nelson A. Rockefeller, 1979, 1979.206.1063*

23 Panel: Eagle Devouring Human Heart
Mexico, Toltec, 9th–12th c.
Limestone, traces of paint; h. 27½ in. (69.9 cm.)

In the tenth century the Toltecs began a period of political rule in the central Mexican highlands that was to have an astonishing impact on the myths and history of subsequent Mexican peoples. The Toltecs came to be regarded as having had legendary prowess and learning and were revered by many, including the Aztecs, as legitimizing ancestors. It was in the Toltec city of Tula that the priest Quetzalcoatl rose to power. The historical persona of this venerated leader was later identified, in part, with the mythical deity Quetzalcoatl, the great culture hero of ancient Mexico. The Toltecs were renowned as artists, and today, through their extant work, they are known primarily as sculptors. Many relief panels showing eagles devouring human hearts decorated the temple of Quetzalcoatl at Tula. According to Mexican thought, the eagle represented the sun, which needed human hearts and blood to continue moving through the sky. The elaborate relief seen here is said to be from Tampico, in the Huastec area of Veracruz. *Gift of Frederick E. Church, 1893, 93.27.2*

24 Cihuateotl
Mexico, Aztec, late 15th–early 16th c.
Stone; h. 26 in. (66 cm.)

The Aztecs, a fierce warrior people, dominated Mexico at the time of the Spanish conquest in 1521. The Aztecs founded their capital, Tenochtitlán (now under downtown Mexico City), in 1325 and began their rapid rise to political power after a victory over the neighboring city of Azcapotzalco in 1428. Aztec-style sculptures proliferated in central Mexico, and when the Spanish arrived, thousands of carvings, particularly deity images, were scattered across the countryside. A Cihuateotl was a woman who died in childbirth, became a goddess, and brought disease and misfortune to mankind. Carved on the head of this sculpture is the Aztec date 1 House, one of the days on which these goddesses descended to earth. This figure probably came from Tenochtitlán, where four almost identical sculptures—now in the National Museum of Anthropology, Mexico City—were found. *Purchase, 1900, 00.5.30*

25 Figure Pendant
Colombia, Tairona, 14th–16th c.
Gold; h. 5½ in. (14 cm.)

The Tairona, who lived on the Caribbean side of Colombia in the Sierra Nevada de Santa Marta, were a fierce, bellicose people. They successfully resisted Spanish domination for almost one hundred years, succumbing only at the end of the sixteenth century. The legendary Tairona belligerence may be read into this pendant, although its pre-Hispanic significance is unclear today. The broad, stubby human figure with a headdress that intricately combines bird and animal heads and multiple spiral elements has a decidedly pugnacious air, its beady eyes glaring out from beneath the visor. The figure wears many jewels, a nose ornament, a lip plug in the lower lip, and two types of ornaments in each ear. Warrior or not, the figure was certainly meant as a depiction of someone rich and powerful. Podlike "rattles," one of which is now missing, were held in each hand. *Gift of H. L. Bache Foundation, 1969, 69.7.10*

26 Eagle Pendant
Costa Rica, Chiriquí, 11th–16th c.
Gold; h. 4⅜ in. (11.1 cm.)

The most well-known ancient American gold objects are eagle pendants. Made in such generalized forms that identification of species is only tentative, eagle pendants were common and apparently widely traded in the Panama–Costa Rica area during the last few centuries before the conquest. Early Spanish accounts mention such ornaments and, in fact, gave the pendants the name, *aguilas* (eagles), by which they have come to be known. Chiriquí eagles are among the most robustly designed of all the examples; they have a certain heaviness of material that corresponds well to their bulk and presence. This eagle has rattles in its bulbous eyes and holds a small animal and a double-ended snake in its large curved beak. The ancient Chiriquí area lay across the Panama–Costa Rica border, and objects in Chiriquí style thus may come from either country. *Bequest of Alice K. Bache, 1977, 1977.187.22*

27   Funerary Mask
Peru, Lambayeque, 10th–14th c.
Gold, paint, reconstructed overlays; h. 11½ in. (29.2 cm.)

Batán Grande, a twenty-one-square-mile area on the coast of northern Peru, contains at least fifty large cemeteries and many impressive architectural remains. Recent scientific excavations indicate that the site was in use almost continuously from the mid-second millennium B.C. until the late fifteenth century, when the Incas conquered the region. Batán Grande, which was apparently a religious center and a necropolis, became increasingly important in the tenth century, and during the centuries that followed, many objects made of precious materials were placed in burials there. Among these objects were large golden masks, sometimes called "death masks," that were long considered Chimu but are now thought to be Lambayeque. The Lambayeque style is noted for schematized faces with distinctive tear-shaped eyes. The Batán Grande masks were originally painted and ornamented in such a way that almost the entire golden surface—except the outline of the eyes and of the nose and an area of the chin—was hidden. The significance of the dense red color used on a number of the faces, including the one shown here, is not understood. *Gift and Bequest of Alice K. Bache, 1974 and 1977, 1974.271.35*

28   Feline-Head Bottle
Peru, Tembladera, 5th–4th c. B.C.
Ceramic; h. 12⅜ in. (31.4 cm.)

The Chavín era in Peru, dated to the middle centuries of the first millennium B.C. and named for a temple complex near Chavín de Huantar, was one of the most artistically inventive in the history of ancient South America. Many extant Chavín objects come from tombs in the coastal valleys of Chicama, Moche, and Jequetepeque; Tembladera is a burial site in the Jequetepeque. Chavín ceramic vessels, fired to muted tones of gray, black, and tan, are sculptural in form and have pleasingly finished surfaces, some highly polished, others painted with dusty, mat-textured paints in yellows and oranges. Chavín iconography is extremely complex. Considerable emphasis is placed on feline forms and on images based on various parts of the feline anatomy. Other animals frequently portrayed are alligators, serpents, and predatory birds. The representation of these jungle creatures may indicate influences from the areas of the Amazon to the east of the Andes. *The Michael C. Rockefeller Memorial Collection, Purchase, Nelson A. Rockefeller Gift, 1967, 1978.412.203*

29 Figure Holding Ceremonial Objects
Bolivia, Tiahuanaco, 4th–8th c.
Stone; h. 18⅜ in. (46.7 cm.)

Tiahuanaco, an ancient city that began to grow rich and powerful in the third century A.D., stands as a magnificent ruin in a small valley high on the great Andean plain of southern Peru and adjacent Bolivia. The temples and palaces of Tiahuanaco are at the heart of a city estimated to have reached a size of about one and one-half square miles. The religious and administrative buildings incorporated a great deal of carefully dressed stone, and the city center was embellished with impressively large, monolithic sculpture. Simple and frequently co-lumnar in form, Tiahuanaco sculpture is much celebrated, although its very intricate iconogra-phy is not well understood today. The columnar figures, which can reach as much as twenty-four feet in height, often represent men wearing short skirts and wide, elaborate belts. Caps or hats vary, as do the objects that the figures clutch tightly to their chests. *The Michael C. Rockefeller Memorial Collection, Bequest of Nelson A. Rockefeller, 1979, 1979.206.833*

30 Deer Vessel
Peru, Chimu, 14th–15th c.
Silver; h. 5 in. (12.7 cm.)

During the fourteenth and fifteenth centuries, the Chimu kingdom ruled the north of Peru from its capital at Chan Chan in the Moche Valley. The monarchs of Chan Chan amassed great wealth and constructed enormous walled com-pounds in which to protect it. So sizable were these royal compounds that they included—besides the storerooms—palace rooms, audi-ence courts, servants' quarters, and large multichamber burial platforms. The platform chambers contained so many objects made from precious metals that during the Spanish colonial times they were exploited as mines. In consequence, few works of precious materials can be traced to the royal mausoleums. This deer-shaped silver vessel is said to be from Chicama, the valley to the north of Chan Chan, and was part of a find of silver objects that included stirrup-spout and double vessels as well as tall beakers. Although three-dimensional animal-form vessels had been common on the north coast of Peru for about two thousand years prior to the making of this deer, the use of silver in their construction was rare. *The Michael C. Rockefeller Memorial Collection, Gift of Nelson A. Rockefeller, 1969, 1978.412.160*

SECOND FLOOR

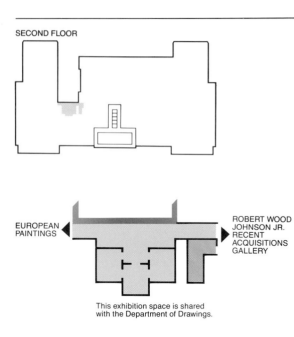

EUROPEAN
PAINTINGS

ROBERT WOOD
JOHNSON JR.
RECENT
ACQUISITIONS
GALLERY

This exhibition space is shared
with the Department of Drawings.

GALLERIES

PRINT STUDY ROOM
OPEN BY APPOINTMENT

PRINTS
AND
PHOTOGRAPHS

Few print rooms in the world house collections as varied and encyclopedic as those in the Museum's Department of Prints and Photographs. Founded in 1916, the department developed rapidly under its first curator, William M. Ivins, Jr. Both Mr. Ivins and his successor, A. Hyatt Mayor, were known for their extraordinary exhibitions and incisive writings, and they attracted remarkable gifts and bequests to the Museum: a collection of Dürer prints from Junius Spencer Morgan; Gothic prints and late Rembrandt prints from Felix M. M. Warburg and his family; and Rembrandt, Van Dyck, Degas, and Cassatt prints from the H. O. Havemeyer Collection.

The print collection includes major works by virtually every master printmaker, but its strengths are in fifteenth-century German, eighteenth-century Italian, and nineteenth-century French images. The extensive collection of photographs has at its core the works from the collection of Alfred Stieglitz that came to the Museum between 1928 and 1949.

The department's holdings are not confined to single printed images but also include more than twelve thousand books in which prints figure as illustrations. German and Italian books of the fifteenth century are particularly well represented, as are books on architecture, gardening, anatomy, costume, and calligraphy and volumes that commemorate lavish celebrations (fête books). The department's collection of designs for ornamentation from the late fifteenth century to the present is one of the most comprehensive in the world; it includes prints, drawings, and illustrated books. Ephemeral works, including trade cards, posters, and other commercial illustrations, form another notable collection.

The Print Study Room is open to scholars by appointment.

1 Virgin and Child

German, ca. 1430–50
Woodcut; hand-colored, heightened with silver and gold; 13 × 10 in. (33 × 25.4 cm.)

The earliest known woodcuts on paper date from about the first quarter of the fifteenth century. Very few, if any, were consciously made as works of art; instead their function and tradition determined their forms. This exquisitely tender Virgin and Child marks one of the high points of folk art. It is typical of the earliest devotional woodcuts that worshipers purchased at local shrines or during pilgrimages. Since such prints were too cheap and common to preserve, very few of the thousands that were made have come down to us. This unique impression is an exception of arresting beauty and majesty. *Gift of Felix M. Warburg and his family, 1941, 41.1.40*

2 REMBRANDT, Dutch, 1606–1669
The Three Crosses

Drypoint and burin; second state, printed on vellum; 15 × 17¼ in. (38.1 × 43.8 cm.)

One of the greatest painters, Rembrandt was also one of the greatest innovators in print-making; he reforged and reworked the techniques of etching, engraving, and drypoint until he had not only completely altered their aspect but also shown how they could deal with things that previously lay beyond their scope. Where earlier intaglio prints were translucent and in general rather bodiless, Rembrandt's have a structure and richness of surface that approximate oil painting. Moreover, they are illumined by an expressive power that never fails to pierce to the heart of things, whether the subject be, as here, a momentous scene from Scripture or the slightest study of still life. This drypoint is dated 1653. (See also Drawings, no. 9; European Paintings, nos. 73-77; and Robert Lehman Collection, nos. 24 and 44.) *Gift of Felix M. Warburg and his family, 1941, 41.1.31*

3 FRANCISCO GOYA, Spanish, 1746–1828
The Giant
Aquatint, first state; 11⅛ × 8⅛ in. (28.3 × 20.6 cm.)

Goya, the most bitter of satirists, often concealed his messages in disturbing and nightmarish images. His haunting *Giant* stands out as the most monumental and powerfully sculptured single figure among his shockingly dramatic etchings. More than any other print by Goya, it resembles the "black paintings" that the aging artist painted on the walls of his house near Madrid. One of the only six known impressions, *The Giant* announces not only nineteenth-century Impressionism, but also twentieth-century Surrealism and Expressionism. (See also Drawings, no. 10; European Paintings, nos. 51 and 52; and Robert Lehman Collection, no. 23.)
Harris Brisbane Dick Fund, 1935, 35.42

4 ALBRECHT DÜRER, German, 1471–1528
Design for Wallpaper: Satyr Family in a Vine
Woodcut on two blocks; each 21½ × 13¼ in. (54.6 × 33.7 cm.)

Dürer designed and produced these two purely ornamental woodcuts in what appears to have been a successful commercial venture. As a pair forming a single pattern—a bold vine reminiscent of textile patterns—they were made about 1515 and were meant to be pasted on a wall in multiple impressions. The satyr family, a most un-Gothic, un-German notion, is an antique motif that Dürer learned from Italian Renaissance artists, especially Jacopo de' Barbari, an engraver whom he met in Venice and knew later when Barbari lived in Nürnberg for several years. No other impressions of these blocks with a black background are known; these are early impressions, and in later ones the background was cut away to leave a white background for hand-coloring. These two impressions show the crisp, adroit cutting found in Dürer's most famous woodcuts. (See also European Paintings, no. 90, and Robert Lehman Collection, no. 43.)
Rogers Fund, 1922, 22.67.4,5

5 EDWARD J. STEICHEN, American, 1879–1973
The Flatiron
1909 print from 1904 negative; blue-green pigment gum-bichromate over platinum; 18¹³/₁₆ × 15⅛ in. (47.8 × 38.4 cm.)

The Flatiron was a very popular subject for photographers after its construction in 1902 on Madison Square in New York. Steichen's platinum prints of the building reflect the concordance of the arts prevailing at the turn of the century. At this time Steichen was as much a painter as a photographer, and he created in his photographs graphic equivalents of his paintings. The Museum's four versions of this subject, taken in 1904, are each in a different hue, achieved by applying a mixture of watercolor and light-sensitive gum arabic to the finished print. Steichen stretched the limits of photography—making exceedingly facile use of his materials—to create an artistic statement of exquisite beauty and delicacy that paralleled the aesthetics of American tonalist painting. *Gift of Alfred Stieglitz, 1933, 33.43.39*

6 CHARLES MICHEL-ANGE CHALLE, French, 1718–78
An Architectural Fantasy
Pen and brown ink drawing with brown, gray, and black washes; 16⅞ × 26³/₁₆ in. (43 × 66.7 cm.)

Trained in both architecture and painting, Challe in 1741 won the French Academy's Prix de Rome for painting. He went to Rome in 1742; he remained there, beyond the pensionnaire's usual three-year term, until 1749. In Rome his interests shifted from history painting to architecture and festival decoration. Challe and a number of his fellow pensionnaires were well acquainted with the work of Giovanni Battista Piranesi (1720–78) and were admitted to his studio. Piranesi's architectural fantasies, which include a mixture of extraordinary and grandiose ancient monuments disposed in ambiguous space, influenced the pensionnaires; the influence was mutual, and the young Frenchmen made their own contribution to the formation of Piranesi's style, especially his architectural fantasies.

After his return to France, Challe was in charge of designing theatrical productions for royal festivities. Under his direction architectural fantasies, such as this one which dates from 1746–47, were brought, if only temporarily, to realization. Through his work he participated in the radical change in direction of French architectural ideas at the end of the eighteenth century. *Edward Pearce Casey Fund, 1979, 1979.572*

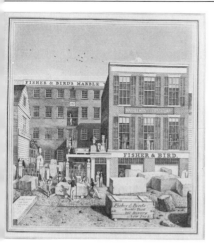

7 JOHN BAKER, American, act. 1831–41
Fisher & Bird's Marble Yard
Engraving; 9⅞ × 8¹³/₁₆ in. (25.1 × 22.3 cm.)

Merchants in the eighteenth and nineteenth centuries were as concerned about their "corporate" image as companies are today. In this tradecard (ca. 1837) for the firm of Fisher & Bird, the engraver John Baker has given the dusty and gritty marble yard an atmosphere of gentility. A fashionable couple inspects the premises, while a well-dressed man lounges in an upper doorway of the warehouse. Elegant urns, statuary, and pedestals can be seen in the showroom windows and on platforms in the yard. These elements contribute to the impression of good workmanship in the very best and newest taste. The format of Baker's engraving is somewhat larger than most tradecards and billheads, suggesting that it was intended for an advertisement in a merchants' directory or possibly as a label for finished goods. *The Edward W. C. Arnold Collection of New York Prints, Maps and Pictures. Bequest of Edward W. C. Arnold, 1954, 54.90.673*

8 GIOVANNI BATTISTA TIEPOLO, Venetian, 1696–1770
The Discovery of the Tomb of Punchinello
Etching; 9⅛ × 7⅛ in. (23.2 × 18.1 cm.)

Tiepolo, who was perhaps the finest draftsman of his age, made the most of the etching medium by insisting that it keep pace with his pen. He translated his rapid sketches in an etching style of the purest quality, marked by brittle lines dancing in light and short hatches packed into shadows.

This work is one of his *Scherzi*, a series of twenty-three etchings in which he combined the pageantry of Venice's festivals, the drama of its street theater, and the sparkle of sunlit lagoons. Scholars continue to puzzle over the colorful array of youths, sages, and sybils posed among the tombstones, skulls, and warriors' shields, but the fantastic tableaux were probably intended as diversions rather than lessons. (See also Drawings, no. 4, and European Paintings, nos. 31 and 32.) *The Elisha Whittelsey Collection, The Elisha Whittelsey Fund, Dodge and Pfeiffer Funds, Joseph Pulitzer Bequest, and Gift of Bertina Suida Manning and Robert L. Manning, 1976, 1976.537.17*

9 JULIA MARGARET CAMERON, British, 1815–79
Alice Lidell, 1872
Albumen photograph; 14¼ × 10¼ in. (36.2 × 26 cm.)

In the course of her productive life in photography (1865–79), Cameron portrayed many of the leading painters, poets, writers, and intellectuals of the day, including Tennyson, Browning, and Carlyle. Here, she arrested the original Alice of *Alice's Adventures in Wonderland.* Lewis Carroll first told this story on a river excursion and then published it in 1865, about seven years before this photograph was taken. Cameron posed many of her subjects as if they were subjects from biblical, classical, or Victorian literature in photographic equivalents of works by Pre-Raphaelite painters such as Rossetti and Watts. *David Hunter McAlpin Fund, 1963, 63.545*

10 EDGAR DEGAS, French, 1834–1917
The Fireside
Monotype in black ink; 16⁵/₁₆ × 23¹/₈ in. (50.2 x 64.7 cm.)

Between 1874 and 1893 Degas produced over four hundred monotypes. These unique prints, which the artist described as "greasy drawings put through a press," exemplify Degas's fascination with technical experimentation and his deep involvement in the representation of modern urban life. Treating the taboo subject of prostitutes in brothels, Degas created a series of monotypes showing nudes in dark hermetic interiors, among which *The Fireside* (ca. 1877–80) is monumental. Here, light blazing from a single source harshly describes the faceless women and furnishings of a *maison close*. Degas blanketed the plate with ink and used rags, brushes, and his fingers to extrapolate the shadowy forms. (See also Drawings, no. 6; European Paintings, nos. 137–139; and Robert Lehman Collection, no. 31.) *Harris Brisbane Dick Fund, The Elisha Whittelsey Collection, The Elisha Whittelsey Fund, and Douglas Dillon Gift, 1968, 68.670*

11 MARY CASSATT, American, 1845–1926
Woman Bathing
Drypoint and soft-ground etching printed in color; 14⁵/₁₆ × 10⁹/₁₆ in. (36.3 × 26.5 cm.)

In 1877, three years after her arrival in Paris, Cassatt was invited by Degas to exhibit with the Impressionists. Like Degas, she concentrated on the study of the human figure and in order to improve her draftsmanship took up the exacting technique of drypoint, drawing directly from models.

After viewing a large exhibition of Japanese prints at the École des Beaux-Arts in the spring of 1890, Cassatt began work on a set of ten color prints in conscious imitation of Ukiyo-e. *Woman Bathing*, which was executed in 1891, was one of this series. Transporting Utamaro's bathers and kimonos to French boudoirs, Cassatt converted the Japanese color woodcut medium to the intaglio processes with which she was familiar, and applied colors by hand to prepared metal plates. (See also American Paintings and Sculpture, no. 18.) *Gift of Paul J. Sachs, 1916, 16.2.2*

FIRST FLOOR

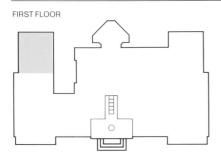

LILA ACHESON WALLACE WING

PAINTINGS

SCULPTURE. Sculpture is also displayed in The Iris and B. Gerald Cantor Roof Garden.

DESIGN AND ARCHITECTURE

THE GIOCONDA AND JOSEPH KING GALLERY; PRINTS, DRAWINGS, PHOTOGRAPHS

THE BERGGRUEN KLEE COLLECTION

THE HELEN AND MILTON A. KIMMELMAN GALLERY FOR SPECIAL EXHIBITIONS

SECOND FLOOR

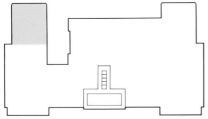

Note: The Iris and B. Gerald Cantor Roof Garden, which is reached by stairway from the fourth floor, is open during the summer months.

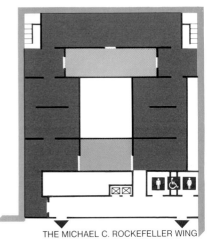

THE MICHAEL C. ROCKEFELLER WING

Note: These galleries are located on the mezzanine between the first and second floor. Handicapped visitors can reach the mezzanine by elevator from the first or second floor.

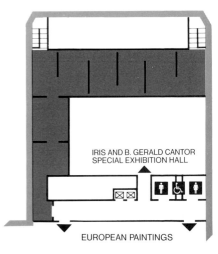

IRIS AND B. GERALD CANTOR SPECIAL EXHIBITION HALL

EUROPEAN PAINTINGS

TWENTIETH CENTURY ART

LILA ACHESON WALLACE WING

The Department of Twentieth Century Art surveys paintings, works on paper, sculpture, and decorative art from 1900 to the present. Since its inception the Museum has had a continuous if at times tenuous contact with contemporary art. In 1906 George Hearn, a trustee of the Museum, established a fund in his name for the purchase of art by living American artists; a second fund, in the name of his son Arthur Hoppock Hearn, was established five years later. Today these funds continue to be a main source of income for departmental purchases. The collection has also grown through gifts and through bequests, most notably Georgia O'Keeffe's gift from the estate of Alfred Stieglitz in 1949 and the bequest of Scofield Thayer in 1982.

In 1967, with the establishment of the Department of Twentieth Century Art, the Museum made a focused commitment to collecting the art of this century. Although such European artists as Picasso, Bonnard, and Kandinsky are represented by important works, the strength of the collection is decidedly American. Of particular interest are the paintings by The Eight, the modernist works of the Stieglitz circle, Abstract Expressionist and Color Field paintings, and the collections of Art Nouveau and Art Deco furniture and metalwork.

The Lila Acheson Wallace Wing, opened in 1987, provides permanent exhibition space for the Museum's collections of twentieth-century art. This wing displays selections from more than eight thousand paintings, sculptures, works on paper, and objects of design and architecture created by American and European artists.

1 HENRI MATISSE, French, 1869–1954
Seated Nude
Pencil on paper; 12 × 9⅛ in. (30.5 × 23.2 cm.)

Seated Nude, probably executed in 1908, was
included in the 1910 exhibition of Matisse's
drawings and of photographs of his paintings,
mounted by Alfred Stieglitz in his Gallery 291.
Among the artist's best-known drawings, it demonstrates the classical clarity of his line. Here the
line is used in a sculptural manner to achieve
repeated, rich contours; this work is thus related
to the sculptural forms with which Matisse started
to experiment at this time. Some of his other
drawings have a more simplified line, a Pointillist broken line, or his famous arabesque line.

Three drawings from the 1910 exhibition were
given to the Museum later that year; the Metropolitan was thus the first public institution to
accept works of art by Matisse. *The Alfred Stieglitz
Collection, 1949, 49.70.8.*

2 MAURICE PRENDERGAST, American
(b. Newfoundland), 1859–1924
Central Park
Oil on canvas; 20¾ × 27 in. (52.7 × 68.9 cm.)

Prendergast's palette was influenced by that of
the French Post-Impressionists, and here we see
his highly individual style of placing patterns of
pure bright colors with broad brushstrokes. The
composition is built up into a decorative mosaic
or tapestry-like surface in which people and landscape are interwoven in the richly painted surface
of vertical trees and horizontal paths. Like most
of the artist's works, this picture is undated; it was
probably painted around 1908–1910. Prendergast's oils were based on his watercolors, and his
many watercolor sketches attest to his superb
mastery of that medium.

A member of The Eight, Prendergast participated in that group's historic 1908 exhibition at
the Macbeth Galleries, New York. The Eight depicted mundane themes peculiar to the American
urban environment of crowded streets, parks,
dance halls, and theaters, and the exhibition was
attacked by critics who preferred traditional academic and sentimental paintings stressing moral-
istic values. *George A. Hearn Fund, 1950, 50.25*

3 PABLO PICASSO, Spanish, 1881–1973
Gertrude Stein
Oil on canvas; 39⅜ × 32 in. (100 × 81.3 cm.)

This portrait of the American writer Gertrude
Stein was begun during the winter of 1905–1906.
Pablo Picasso was twenty-four years old and
had been working in Paris for five years. Stein
posed for Picasso on some eighty occasions,
but he had great difficulty with the head. After a
trip to Spain in the fall of 1906, he painted in a
new head. The masklike face with its heavy-
lidded eyes reflects Picasso's recent encounter
with African, Roman, and Iberian sculpture.
The massive quality of the figure (which accurately reflects Stein's body) shows the artist's
transition from the ethereal slender figures of
the previous five years (the so-called Blue and
Rose periods) to the sturdy cubistic forms that
immediately preceded the formal breakthrough
of the *Demoiselles d'Avignon*. It is said that in
response to the observation that Stein, who
was then thirty-two years old, bore little resemblance to the portrait, Picasso replied simply,
"She will." *Bequest of Gertrude Stein, 1946,
47.106*

4 ANDRÉ DERAIN, French, 1880–1954
The Table
Oil on canvas; 38 × 51⅝ in. (96.5 × 131.1 cm.)

Together with Henri Matisse and Maurice de
Vlaminck, André Derain was one of the group of
artists dubbed the Fauves (Wild Beasts), whose
use of bold, garish colors and aggressive forms
jolted the French art world during the first decade of this century. By 1910, however, Derain,
as well as Matisse, came under the influence of
the newly emergent Cubists. *The Table* (1911)
shows Derain at this transitional period. While
his palette includes blues and reds, their intensity and brilliance have been drastically reduced.

The firm modeling of the table, draperies, and
pottery contrasts vehemently with Derain's Fauve
works, in which form was suggested by daubs
of pure pigment that rarely correlated "realistically" with nature. The somewhat unsystem-
atic perspective of this composition obliquely
quotes the Cubist fracturing of form and space,
but in the final analysis *The Table* probably
illuminates the Cézannesque roots of Cubism
more directly than the contemporary work of
Picasso and Braque. (See also Robert Lehman
Collection, no. 32.) *Wolfe Fund, Catharine
Lorillard Wolfe Collection, 1954, 54.79*

5 AMEDEO MODIGLIANI, Italian, 1884–1920
Juan Gris
Oil on canvas; 21⅝ × 15 in. (54.9 × 38.1 cm.)

Modigliani, who left Italy for Paris in 1906, is said to have met the Spanish artist Juan Gris at the apartment of Gertrude Stein in 1909–1910. This portrait was done in 1915 when Modigliani was thirty and Gris twenty-seven. Although he was undoubtedly influenced by the Cubist painters, Modigliani also worked in sculpture briefly under the tutelage of Constantin Brancusi (no. 33). The ovoid head and the simply defined features in this portrait reflect Brancusi's own series of heads done between 1910 and 1917. Modigliani also drew directly on African sculpture for his emphatically geometric forms. After 1915, when he stopped doing sculpture, Modigliani's oeuvre consisted mainly of painted nudes and portraits. He produced a prodigious body of work before dying of tuberculosis at the age of thirty-five. *Bequest of Miss Adelaide Milton de Groot (1876–1967), 1967, 67.187.85*

6 GEORGES BRAQUE, French, 1882–1963
Le Guéridon
Oil with sand on canvas; 75 × 27¾ in. (190.5 × 70.5 cm.)

The period 1919–20 was a transitional one in the career of Braque. Approaching the age of forty, he had resumed painting after serving in the army during World War I. Braque's work began to show the reemergence of naturalistic elements, while retaining many of the formal innovations of Cubism. This still-life composition, *Le Guéridon* (The Small, Round Table) of 1921–22, is typical of this period. Braque retains the Cubist palette of greens, beiges, and whites with a prominent use of black. The pictorial space is compressed to the front of the picture plane, and the tabletop is tilted to display the still-life arrangement of fruits, pipes, newspapers, and musical instruments. The fragmented geometric forms and flat patterned shapes are related to the collage technique first explored by Braque and Picasso some ten years earlier. Braque did no fewer than fifteen *Guéridons* between 1921 and 1930. This painting is probably the earliest of the series and was exhibited at the Salon d'Automne in November 1922. *Jointly owned by The Metropolitan Museum of Art and Mrs. Bertram Smith, 1979, 1979.481*

7 BALTHUS, French, b. 1908
The Mountain
Oil on canvas; 98 × 144 in. (248.9 × 365.8 cm.)

The Mountain was completed in 1937, three years after Balthus had his first one-man exhibition at the age of twenty-six. The ambition and accomplishment of this composition demonstrate his precocity. His strong simplified forms show the influence of Piero della Francesca and Georges Seurat, and the cultivated awkwardness of his figures indicates his debt to Gustave Courbet. *The Mountain* has been considered Balthus's answer to Courbet's *Young*

Ladies from the Village, painted almost a century before (see European Paintings, no. 127). Like Courbet, Balthus depicts a landscape that he has known since childhood. The indolent adolescent girls find corresponding echoes in the mountains behind them. This work is the masterpiece of Balthus's early period. (See also Robert Lehman Collection, no. 34.) *Purchase, Gifts of Mr. and Mrs. Nate B. Spingold and Nathan Cummings, Rogers Fund and The Alfred N. Punnett Endowment Fund, by exchange, and Harris Brisbane Dick Fund, 1982, 1982.530*

8 PIERRE BONNARD, French, 1867–1947
The Terrace at Vernon
Oil on canvas; 57¾ × 76½ in. (146.7 × 191.3 cm.)

As a young artist, Bonnard came under the influence of Gauguin's ideas about representing things symbolically in strong patterns and color. Bonnard and his friend Édouard Vuillard also adapted the lyrical elements of a Renoiresque Impressionism and Pointillism to their quiet everyday scenes, which have come to be termed "Intimist." These influences remain evident in

The Terrace at Vernon, which he began in 1920 and reworked in 1939. This painting of his house in the Seine Valley reveals an intricate spatial organization. Bonnard differentiates the foreground space from the background by the dramatic vertical of the huge tree trunk. On the right he frames pockets of space around the figures. Thus the viewer can isolate areas of the composition and discern an orderly progression through this heroically proportioned work. (See also Robert Lehman Collection, no. 33.) *Gift of Mrs. Frank Jay Gould, 1968, 68.1*

9   MAX WEBER, American (b. Russia),
1881–1961
Athletic Contest
*Oil on canvas; 40½ × 55¼ in. (102.9 ×
140.3 cm.)*

As a young man in New York, Max Weber studied with Arthur Wesley Dow, later Georgia O'Keeffe's teacher, who stressed structure and harmonious spacing. Later, in Paris (1905–1908), he absorbed the lessons of Fauvism, Cubism, and Futurism. Returning to New York in 1909, Weber stayed somewhat aloof from organized activities: his association with Alfred Stieglitz,

champion of American modernism, was unhappy and short-lived (1910–13), although he was included in two exhibitions at Stieglitz's Gallery 291; in 1913 he declined to participate in the famous Armory Show. Between 1912 and 1918 Weber painted some of his most advanced abstractions. *Athletic Contest* (1915) is a kaleidoscopic scene of figures in action, rendered in a Futurist idiom of simultaneous views, overlapping planes, and swirling vortices. These athletes appear to be engaged in a variety of sporting events in an outdoor setting.
George A. Hearn Fund, 1967, 67.112

---

10   MARSDEN HARTLEY, American, 1877–
1943
Portrait of a German Officer
Oil on canvas; 68¼ × 41⅜ in. (173.4 × 106 cm.)

Hartley painted his most startlingly advanced and integrated abstractions during the first years of World War I while living in Berlin (March 1914–December 1915). *War Motifs,* his German military series, are intensely powerful canvases in an Expressionist vein; they reflect not only his revulsion at the wartime destruction, but also his fascination with the energy and pageantry that accompanied the carnage. *Portrait of a German Officer,* painted in November 1914, shows Hartley's assimilation of both Cubism (the collage-like juxtaposition of visual fragments and the hieratic structuring of geometric shapes) and German Expressionism (the coarse brushwork and the dramatic color). The condensed mass of images (badges, flags, medals) evokes a collective psychological and physical portrait of the officer. There are also specific references to Hartley's close friend Karl von Freyburg, a young cavalry officer who had recently been killed in action: K.v.F. are his initials, 4 was his regiment number, and 24 his age.
The Alfred Stieglitz Collection, 1949, 49.70.42

11 STUART DAVIS, American, 1894–1964
Edison Mazda
Oil on cardboard; 24½ × 18⅝ in. (62.2 × 47.3 cm.)

Edison Mazda (1924) is a transitional piece in Davis's stylistic development, balanced between his early representational works and the abstract compositions that characterize his mature style. Davis incorporated into his paintings everyday objects and settings, particularly those related to the modern consumer-oriented world: a 75-watt Edison Mazda light bulb—reflecting the windows of the artist's studio—a wine goblet, and an artist's portfolio. The objects are geometrically simplified and flatly organized in a manner influenced by Cubism. Variations in decorative patterning differentiate overlapping planes, as variations in color do in Davis's later paintings. Three years after completing *Edison Mazda*, Davis produced his first truly abstract compositions, the *Eggbeater* series, one of which is also in the Museum's collection. *Purchase, Mr. and Mrs. Clarence Y. Palitz, Jr. Gift, in memory of her father, Nathan Dobson, 1982, 1982.10*

12 ARTHUR G. DOVE, American, 1880–1946
Ralph Dusenberry
Oil on canvas with pasted ruler, wood, and paper; 22 × 18 in. (55.9 × 45.1 cm.)

In this witty portrait, completed in 1924, Dove affixed to the painted canvas a few carefully chosen objects that convey an impression of the subject's personality and activities, in much the same way that Marsden Hartley (no. 10) and Charles Demuth (no. 14) did in their painted "portraits." This is one of twenty-five assemblages Dove constructed between 1924 and 1930 while living on a houseboat in Long Island Sound. It exemplifies his assertion that "good art" results from a simple motif, "a few forms and a few colors." The characterization of his houseboat neighbor Ralph Dusenberry is achieved with a minimum number of elements, selected for their textural interest as much as for their symbolic meaning. Two pointed wooden shingles form an abstracted head, with painted eye and pipe-smoking mouth. They also allude to Dusenberry's life on the water and his great swimming ability. The starred flag may be a boat pennant; the wooden ruler may be an allusion to Dusenberry's architectural career; the printed hymn is one he often sang when drunk. *The Alfred Stieglitz Collection, 1949, 49.70.36*

13   GEORGIA O'KEEFFE, American, b. 1887
Black Abstraction
Oil on canvas; 30 × 40¼ in. (76.2 × 102.2 cm.)

Georgia O'Keeffe was the only woman among
the American modernists who rallied around
Alfred Stieglitz, and she and Stieglitz were married in 1924. For more than six decades she
produced highly original paintings, almost exclusively of landscape, floral, and skeletal motifs,
which are depicted in both a representational
and an abstract manner. *Black Abstraction,*
painted in New York in 1927, was inspired by a
medical operation she had that year. O'Keeffe
recalls that while fighting the effects of anes-
thesia, she tried to reach up to a bright skylight
that seemed to whirl and become ever smaller.
The canvas is filled by three dark concentric
rings, in front of which is a graceful white V,
perhaps her extended arms. At its vertex is a
small, bright spot, the disappearing skylight.
The mood is tense and ominous, and there is a
sense of whirling into deep space. This painting
shows the effective combination of subjective
emotion and abstract forms that characterizes
O'Keeffe's best work. *The Alfred Stieglitz Collection, 1949, 69.278.2*

14   CHARLES DEMUTH, American, 1883–1935
I Saw the Figure 5 in Gold
*Oil on composition board; 35½ × 30 in. (90.2 ×
76.2 cm.)*

Charles Demuth was among the group of American modernists who exhibited regularly at Alfred Stieglitz's Gallery 291. Although Demuth
was influenced by Cubism and Futurism, his
choice of urban and industrial subjects, his sense
of scale, and his directness of expression were
American. In the 1920s Demuth produced a
series of poster-portraits, honoring his contemporaries, which were inspired by Gertrude Stein's
word-portraits. *I Saw the Figure 5 in Gold* (1928)
is the most accomplished of the group. It was
dedicated to the artist's friend, the American
poet William Carlos Williams, whose "The Great
Figure" inspired the painting's title and imagery.
Demuth's painting, however, is not a representational illustration of the poem but rather an
abstract impression of the No. 5 fire engine
clanging through the lamp-lit streets of the darkened, rainy city. Scattered words and initials
refer to the artist and the poet. *The Alfred Stieglitz
Collection, 1949, 49.59.1*

15   GEORGE BELLOWS, American, 1882–1925
Tennis at Newport
Oil on canvas; 40 × 43¼ in. (101.6 × 109.9 cm.)

The annual tennis tournament at the Newport Casino in Rhode Island was an important sporting event and social occasion. In 1919 Bill Tilden and William Johnson were the star players. However, in this depiction of their match, painted in that year, Bellows emphasizes the setting rather than the game. Although the players are seen in the foreground, it is the spectators strolling about the grounds and lingering on the lawn who divert our attention. Bellows draws our eye into the composition by means of the strong diagonal of the sunlight that streams from behind the building and through the trees. Although never formally associated with The Eight, Bellows has a broadly painted, spontaneous style that bears a strong relationship to that of Robert Henri (Bellows's teacher at the Art Students League) and his fellow members of The Eight, particularly William Glackens and John Sloan. *Bequest of Miss Adelaide Milton de Groot (1876–1967), 1967, 67.187.121*

16   EDWARD HOPPER, American, 1882–1967
Tables for Ladies
Oil on canvas; 48¼ × 60¼ in. (122.6 × 153 cm.)

Hopper isolated and transformed familiar aspects of the American scene. The waitress and cashier in *Tables for Ladies* (1930), each lost in thought, are typical elements of his sparsely peopled compositions. Here the artist contrasts the solitude of the two female figures with the couple conversing in the background. Hopper has lavished much attention on the rich buffet, and its opulence contrasts with the stark presentation of the figures. *Tables for Ladies* reflects the artist's long-standing interest in observing people in restaurant settings. This compositional type was a favorite of nineteenth-century French painters and was continued in this century by many of Hopper's contemporaries. Although Hopper's paintings give the impression of tremendous attention to detail, the paint surface is loosely treated and the descriptive means are quite economical. *George A. Hearn Fund, 1931, 31.62*

17 GRANT WOOD, American, 1892–1942
The Midnight Ride of Paul Revere
Oil on composition board; 30 × 40 in. (76.2 × 101.6 cm.)

Grant Wood was the most self-consciously primitive artist of his generation. His exaggerated, precise depiction of reality was strongly influenced by the realist style that appeared in Germany between the two world wars. Known as Neue Sachlichkeit (New Objectivity), this art was a reaction to modernism and a call for a new order in the aftermath of World War I. Wood's style also has much in common with that of his American contemporaries, the so-

called Precisionist artists. But while these artists, who included Georgia O'Keeffe and Charles Sheeler, were primarily interested in more formal and abstract concerns, Wood was preoccupied with celebrating American regional life and history. In *The Midnight Ride of Paul Revere* (1931), Wood gives a bird's-eye view of the New England landscape on the historic night of April 18, 1775. The topographical and architectural elements, which are rendered in almost obsessive detail, dwarf the minuscule human figures. *Arthur Hoppock Hearn Fund, 1950, 50.117*

18 JACOB LAWRENCE, American, b. 1917
Pool Parlor
Gouache on paper; 31 × 22¾ in. (78.7 × 57.8 cm.)

Lawrence's work is imbued with his concern for social issues and historical events, particularly as these affect black Americans. This concern is evident in *Pool Parlor* (1942), which won a purchase prize in the Museum's exhibition "Artists for Victory" (1942). It is one of Lawrence's few compositions that is not part of a series, a form of narrative vehicle that the artist used to explore the range of his ideas on a subject. The flat, geometric shapes and the restricted palette of *Pool Parlor* are characteristic of Lawrence's early style. He exaggerates the limbs, features, and postures in order to reinforce the narrative of the painting. The diagonal positioning of the cue sticks and randomly placed cigarettes creates a zigzag pattern which leads the eye through the entire composition. This simple, flat style later gave way to more complicated linear play and more three-dimensional modeling. *Arthur Hoppock Hearn Fund, 1942, 42.167*

19 CHARLES SHEELER, American,
1883–1965
Water
Oil on canvas; 24 × 29⅛ in. (61 × 74 cm.)

Sheeler made industrial America the subject of his art, and *Water* (1945) exemplifies his technical mastery. A depiction of the power generators of the Tennessee Valley Authority, it is a dispassionate view of a gigantic machine environment. It also suggests a utopian view of the power of industry to better the lives of the masses of American people. The stately, dignified structure celebrates the formal geometry and gleaming materials of American architecture and design of the 1930s. Sheeler developed a style based on the visual means of photography; this "Precisionist" technique emulates the camera's detached observation of the world. Sheeler himself worked as a photographer and was employed for a time in this capacity at the Museum. *Arthur Hoppock Hearn Fund, 1949, 49.128*

20 THOMAS HART BENTON, American,
1889–1975
July Hay
Egg tempera, methyl cellulose, and oil on Masonite; 38 × 26¾ in. (96.5 × 67.9 cm.)

In 1907, after studying at the Art Institute of Chicago, Benton went to Paris where for five years he was involved in the avant-garde movements of Cubism and Synchronism. Upon his return to the United States, Benton rejected abstraction and "internationalism" to concentrate on creating a native American art. But we can always sense behind his work an effort to emulate the Old Masters, and his style was strongly influenced by El Greco. Benton's tendency to cast the ordinary American in a heroic mold is evident in *July Hay* (1943). He uses a strong contrast of light and dark tones to emphasize the sculptural modeling of the forms. Like Grant Wood, Benton was a student of traditional techniques; he worked primarily in egg tempera, which he finished in delicate glazes that enhance the brilliance of the colors. We may glimpse in Benton's rhythmic expressionist style a foreshadowing of the early work of Jackson Pollock, his best-known pupil. *George A. Hearn Fund, 1943, 43.159.1*

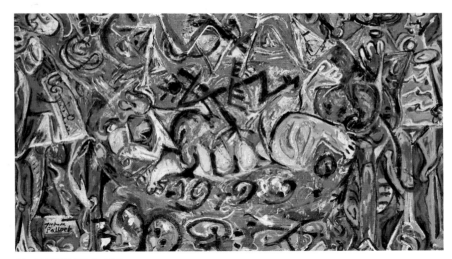

21   JACKSON POLLOCK, American,
1912–1956
Pasiphaë
Oil on canvas; 56⅛ × 96 in. (142.6 × 243.8 cm.)

Pollock's early masterpiece *Pasiphaë* (1943) summarizes the iconographic and stylistic concerns in his art in the early 1940s. The title refers to the mythological story of Pasiphaë who, under a curse from Poseidon, falls in love with a white bull and gives birth to the legendary Minotaur. Amid the swirl of lines and forms in this painting, one can discern two totemic figures, perhaps more, flanking a reclining female nude.

Other faces and torsos emerge from the intricate fabric of sharp, angular slashes and meandering arabesques. The energetic, almost brutal gestural application of paint anticipates by several years the Abstract Expressionist movement of the late 1940s and 1950s, of which Pollock's large "poured" paintings are innovative landmarks. *Pasiphaë* also marks a transition to the mural-size painting and allover imagery that characterize his later work. *Purchase, Rogers, Fletcher and Harris Brisbane Dick Funds and Joseph Pulitzer Bequest, 1982, 1982.20*

22   ARSHILE GORKY, American (b. Armenia),
1904–1948
Water of the Flowery Mill
Oil on canvas; 42¼ × 48¾ in. (107.3 × 123.8 cm.)

Gorky's biomorphic abstractions, produced in New York in the 1940s, reflect the liberating influence of Surrealist automatism and anticipate the gestural calligraphy of Abstract Expressionism. His work, however, remained tied to the traditional values of Western painting—relatively moderate-sized easel paintings, based on carefully planned and presketched compositions. Gorky's vocabulary reached mature refinement

in the mid-1940s and is exemplified by his masterpiece, *Water of the Flowery Mill* (1944), a landscape of exquisite color, poetic brushwork, and compositional complexity. Although not easily deciphered, the painting's images are based on those observed in nature and depict a specific setting, the remains of an old sawmill on the Housatonic River in Connecticut. After Gorky visited there in 1942, the Connecticut terrain became, in his late paintings, a surrogate for his native Armenia, whose presence pervaded his early work. *George A. Hearn Fund, 1956, 56.205.1*

23 WILLEM DE KOONING, American (b. The Netherlands), b. 1904
Attic
Oil, enamel, and newspaper transfer on canvas; 61⅞ × 81 in. (157.2 × 205.7 cm.)

The gestural dynamism and allover imagery of *Attic* (1949), de Kooning's early masterwork, exemplify the radically new visual language espoused by the Abstract Expressionist painters in New York during the late 1940s and 1950s. The painting culminates a series of complex black-and-white abstractions, begun in 1946, that explore the positive-negative relationships of form and space. The web of white shapes is so dense that the black background on which they are situated virtually disappears. De Kooning's almost exclusive use of black and white was determined in part by the availability of inexpensive commercial enamel paint. Although his palette is severely restricted, de Kooning displays virtuosity in his sensuous and expressive handling of paint, surface, and line. In the works that immediately followed *Attic,* de Kooning resumed his use of full color. *Jointly owned by The Metropolitan Museum of Art and Muriel Kallis Newman, in honor of her son Glenn David Steinberg, the MURIEL KALLIS STEINBERG NEWMAN Collection, 1982, 1982.16.3*

24 CLYFFORD STILL, American, 1904–1980
Untitled
Oil on canvas; 61¾ × 44½ in. (156.8 × 113 cm.)

Although Still was a major figure in the New York School after 1950, his style developed in the late 1940s on the West Coast. This untitled painting, which was executed in 1946, is an early example of the color-field abstractions for which he is best known. Eliminating all representational imagery and any sense of illusionistic space, Still concentrated on the physical aspects of painting. The dense surface is activated by a proliferation of jagged interlocking areas of color, which are applied with a palette knife in short, energetic strokes. Still's deep, somber colors compress the space of the composition frontally. Typically, there is no central focus but rather an allover activation of the surface. Underlying rhythms permeate the composition, effecting what the artist called "a living spirit." *George A. Hearn and Arthur Hoppock Hearn Funds, 1977, 1977.174*

25 ROBERT MOTHERWELL, American,
b. 1915
Elegy to the Spanish Republic, 70, 1961
Oil on canvas; 69 × 114 in. (175.3 × 289.6 cm.)

Since 1950 Motherwell has created more than one hundred variations of *Elegy to the Spanish Republic*. Although these works were initially inspired by the Spanish Civil War, their real subject is a meditation on life and death. Although specific paintings may express an individual spirit or "tone of voice," they are related to one another by similarities in composition: the horizontal white canvas is rhythmically divided by two or three freely drawn vertical bars and punctuated at various intervals by ovoid forms. These structural elements are almost exclusively painted in funereal black. The *Elegies* of the 1960s reflect Motherwell's Abstract Expressionist ties in their gestural, painterly treatment of forms, their rapid execution, and their integration of accidental effects, such as spattered paint. *Elegy to the Spanish Republic, 70, 1961* was executed on the floor, rather than on an easel, in the manner of Jackson Pollock's "poured" paintings. *Anonymous Gift, 1965, 65.247*

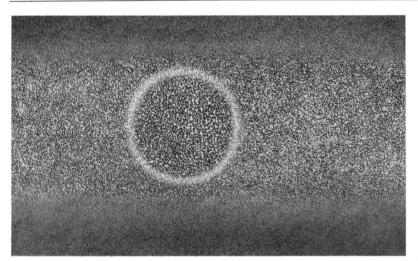

26 RICHARD POUSETTE-DART, American,
b. 1916
Presence, Ramapo Horizon
Acrylic on canvas; 72 × 120 in. (182.9 × 304.8 cm.)

Although he is often grouped with the Abstract Expressionists with whom he exhibited in the 1940s, Pousette-Dart developed his mature work in relative isolation. He stood apart from these artists by his contemplative, calculated process and his wish to express a spiritual content in painting. Elliptical and circular shapes take on symbolic and mystical qualities in his work. *Presence, Ramapo Horizon* is one of several paintings done in 1975, inspired by the landscape of the Ramapo Mountains around the artist's studio in Suffern, New York. The composition is divided into three lateral bands: a wide center zone, energized by stippled paint and articulated by a slightly off-center ring of light, and two thinner bands that halo it top and bottom. Allusions to spiritual and psychological states and to celestial motifs characterize his work. *George A. Hearn Fund, 1982, 1982.68*

27   ELLSWORTH KELLY, American, b. 1923
Blue Red Green
Oil on canvas; 91 × 82 in. (231.1 × 208.3 cm.)

Kelly's precisely rendered paintings utilize a few flatly painted abstract forms of intense, bold color. His six-year stay in Paris (1948–54) directed his art toward the biomorphic abstractions of Jean Arp and the late paper cutouts of Matisse, rather than to the gesturalism of Abstract Expressionism. Kelly's close-up scale and oversize canvases, however, expressed contemporary concern with flattening the picture space to focus attention on the formal elements of color and shape. *Blue Red Green* (1962–63) creates a tense ground-space relationship between the incomplete, irregular ellipse and the rectangular field it bisects. The rectangle can be viewed as a flat plane or as a slightly receded background. Kelly explores the same visual vocabulary and concerns in his sculpture. *Arthur Hoppock Hearn Fund, 1963, 63.73*

28   FRANK STELLA, American, b. 1936
Marrakech
Fluorescent alkyd on canvas; 77 × 77 in. (195.6 × 195.6 cm.)

Stella's first mature paintings of the late 1950s and early 1960s continued in the nonfigurative, nonillusionistic direction forged by the Abstract Expressionists. However, like many of his contemporaries, Stella later rejected the emotional, gestural approach of this school and produced canvases that were more controlled and structured and that emphasized the painting's existence as an object. Commercial fluorescent paint was flatly applied; compositions, drastically simplified to a few elements (stripes and arcs), were symmetrical and deduced from the format of the canvas, which was sometimes shaped. *Marrakech* (1964) is one of Stella's "Moroccan" paintings of 1964–65; these works are characterized by their square format and their consideration of color as a primary pictorial element. Later works in the series employed as many as ten colors. *Gift of Mr. and Mrs. Robert C. Scull, 1971, 1971.5*

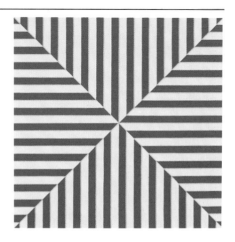

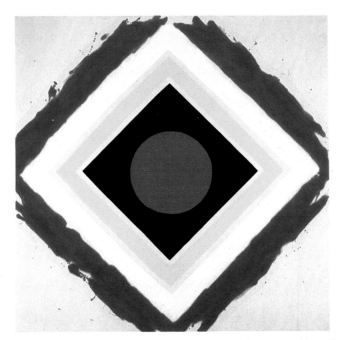

29   KENNETH NOLAND, American, b. 1924
Magic Box
Acrylic on canvas; 96 × 96 in. (243.8 × 243.8 cm.)

Influenced by Helen Frankenthaler's work, Kenneth Noland and Morris Louis began to stain raw canvases with diluted pigment in the early 1950s. By literally uniting paint and support into one plane, this technique created spatially flattened images. Noland's early mature works were square canvases, dominated by centered, frontal, geometric images, particularly concentric rings; these paintings eschewed illusionistic references and forced both artist and viewer to focus on formal elements (color, size, and shape). *Magic Box* (1959) is a variant on the target motif, using squared bands instead of rings. The square canvas is contrasted with both the circular red bull's-eye and the colored diamond bands. As in Noland's other early works, hard-edged painting is combined with freehand brushwork. The painterly outer band creates an unexpected sense of motion in an otherwise static composition. *Purchase, Anonymous Gift, 1977, 1977.8*

30   DAVID HOCKNEY, British, b. 1937
Mount Fuji and Flowers
Acrylic on canvas; 60 × 48 in. (152.4 × 121.9 cm.)

In the early 1960s Hockney joined other young artists working in England (R. B. Kitaj, Allen Jones, and Richard Hamilton, among others) in creating figurative art that incorporated modern abstraction without sacrificing content. His subsequent work in paintings, drawings, and prints maintained a narrative focus even when it showed stylistic affinities to Pop Art (early 1960s), naturalism (mid-1960s–1970s), and inventive colorism (late 1970s–1980s). Apart from his innovative theater designs, Hockney's subjects are autobiographical, depicting friends and travel experiences (particularly from his lengthy and numerous stays in the United States). *Mount Fuji and Flowers* (1972) was painted in London after a two-week visit to Japan. Disappointed by the country, Hockney nevertheless painted a scene of classical beauty, perhaps reflecting the cliché image of oriental tranquillity and unspoiled nature that the artist had expected to find. The images are derived from a postcard of Mount Fuji and a flower-arrangement manual, rather than direct observation. *Purchase, Mrs. Arthur Hays Sulzberger Gift, 1972, 1972.128*

31 ROY LICHTENSTEIN, American, b. 1923
Stepping Out
Oil and magna on canvas; 86 × 70 in. (218.4 × 177.8 cm.)

Since his Pop Art canvases of the 1960s Roy Lichtenstein has recycled imagery from our everyday culture, often rendering it in the benday dots of the comic strips. More recently, subjects are borrowed from the masterpieces of art history. In *Stepping Out* (1978), the dapper young man, dressed in straw hat and high-collared shirt, relates directly to figures in Fernand Léger's 1944 painting *Three Musicians* (Museum of Modern Art, New York). The disjointed, seductive, blonde female companion at the left is a synthesis of Surrealist imagery, such as that used by Picasso in the 1930s. Although these characters are presented in a witty manner, Lichtenstein's attention to composition is studied and structured. The painting exemplifies his very individual style: color is bright and limited to the three primaries plus black and white; paint is applied in a flat, hard-edged manner; and forms are thickly outlined in black. *Purchase, Lila Acheson Wallace Fund, Inc. Gift, Arthur Hoppock Hearn Fund, Arthur Lejwa Fund in honor of Jean Arp, The Bernhill Fund, Joseph H. Hazen Foundation, Inc., Samuel I. Newhouse Foundation, Inc., Walter Bareiss, Marie Bannon McHenry, Louise Smith and Stephen C. Swid Gifts, 1980, 1980.420*

32 JAMES ROSENQUIST, American, b. 1933
House of Fire
Oil on canvas; 78 × 198 in. (198.1 × 502.9 cm.)

Painted twenty years after Rosenquist's first Pop Art canvases, *House of Fire* (1981) exudes the same dynamism that characterized his best work of the 1960s. The elimination of visible brushwork and the use of commercial materials exemplify American Pop Art. Images are disquietingly juxtaposed and realistically rendered. The exact meaning of this allegorical triptych is elusive. In the central panel a bucket of molten steel, supernatural in its radiance, descends through a partly open window. Intruding from the right are fiery red and orange lipsticks aligned like a battery of guns. At the left a brown paper bag overflowing with groceries is unexpectedly turned upside down. Allusions to war, sex, violence, industry, and domesticity may be drawn from the images. The painting can also be interpreted as a metaphor for modern American society, a society filled with contradictions. *Purchase, George A. Hearn and Arthur Hoppock Hearn Funds and Lila Acheson Wallace Gift, 1982, 1982.90.1a–c*

33 CONSTANTIN BRANCUSI, French (b. Romania), 1876–1957
Sleeping Muse
Bronze; h. 6¾ in. (17.1 cm.)

Working in Paris during the early 1900s, Brancusi rejected academic sculptural traditions in favor of abstraction. His subjects relied on organic forms, particularly the human figure. The sleeping head, one of Brancusi's first thematic cycles, occupied him for twenty years. Early versions depict a particular individual sleeping; later works abstract the human face to its most simplified form, an ovoid. Although *Sleeping Muse* (1910) is recognizable as a head, it achieves what Brancusi called the "essence" of the inner form. The face of Baroness Renée Irana Frachon is reduced to a slender V denoting eyebrows and nose, a small mouth, and the suggestion of closed lids. This head is one of four bronzes cast in 1910 from a marble of the previous year; each version was individually worked and varies in size and surface treatment. *The Alfred Stieglitz Collection, 1949, 49.70.225*

34 ALEXANDER ARCHIPENKO, American (b. Ukraine), 1887–1964
The Gondolier
Bronze with black paint; h. 34¾ in. (88.3 cm.)

Archipenko arrived in Paris from the Ukraine in 1908, and during the next decade he created his most original sculptures, which anticipated other artists' similar application of Cubist theory to three-dimensional form. His works of 1913–14, exemplified by *The Gondolier*, are the major achievements in his oeuvre. This bronze is one of several reduced casts made by the artist in 1961 from the original 1914 plaster. Archipenko used the figure, usually female, to explore compositional rhythms and relationships between solid and void, concave and convex. Here the central axis is formed by the gondolier's head, torso, and right leg. In opposition is the strong diagonal line of the oar and the left leg, which are fused into a single element. *Gift of Ernst Anspach, 1964, 64.2*

35 ALBERTO GIACOMETTI, Swiss, 1901–1966
Annette VI
Bronze; h. 25⅞ in. (65.7 cm.)

This bronze bust, which was executed in 1962, near the end of Giacometti's life, represents a major achievement in an innovative career that spanned forty years. During the early 1930s, his sculptures were inspired by Surrealism. His unique vision of reality subsequently found true expression in the exaggeratedly elongated figures that typify his oeuvre. The works produced during the last ten years of Giacometti's life, however, reflect a transition in style toward more substantially rendered figures. *Annette VI* is one of ten portrait busts modeled after his wife which he created between 1960 and 1964. The works in the series are compelling psychological and physical presences. Emphasis is given to the subject's eyes, which have a lifelike gaze. *Jointly owned by The Metropolitan Museum of Art and Mr. and Mrs. Joseph Zimmerman, 1981, 1981.491*

36 ANTOINE PEVSNER, French (b. Russia), 1886–1962
Column of Peace
Bronze; h. 53 in. (134.6 cm.)

In 1920 the Constructivist artists Antoine Pevsner and his brother Naum Gabo published the *Realist Manifesto* in Moscow. In it they proclaimed that sculpture should be abstract rather than representational and that it should interact with the surrounding space, suggesting the dimension of time. These principles continued to guide Pevsner's creation of the majestic *Column of Peace* (1954) thirty-four years later. In this piece ridges made in the bronze reflect light, producing highlights and shadows that articulate the forms and planes. The graceful extension of four turned columns creates a strong sense of upward movement and growth. From one view the rods open out like a flower, exploring the play between solid and void; from another the piece retracts into a compact, thrusting, vertical mass. *Gift of Alex Hillman Family Foundation, in memory of Richard Alan Hillman, 1981, 1981.326*

37 DAVID SMITH, American, 1906–1965
Becca
Stainless steel; 113¼ × 123 × 30½ in. (287.7 × 312.4 × 77.5 cm.)

This century's most influential American sculptor, Smith was a master of the welded-metal technique. He was trained as a painter (1927–32), and his subsequent sculptural work was paradoxically frontal in its orientation, almost two-dimensional, and often calligraphic, paralleling concerns of postwar American painting. His early constructions of the 1930s were influenced by the works of Julio González and by Picasso's iron sculptures. Smith's landscape-inspired works of the 1940s and 1950s were open "drawings in metal." The art of the last fifteen years of his life was characterized by monumental pieces utilizing overlapping rectangular plates of highly polished steel. *Becca* (1965), named after one of Smith's two daughters, exemplifies the bold simplicity and remarkable grace of these forms. The surface is covered with elaborate scribblings that resemble brushstrokes. *Purchase, Bequest of Miss Adelaide Milton de Groot (1876–1967), by exchange, 1972, 1972.127*

38 ISAMU NOGUCHI, American, b. 1904
Unidentified Object
Black basalt; h. with base 18½ ft. (5.63 m.)

Noguchi's prolific output over a career of more than sixty years traverses a wide range of styles and media. He has created both large-scale environmental works (primarily gardens, playgrounds, and plazas) and traditional sculpture, large and small, as well as theatrical designs. His emphasis has always been on the artist's ability to control medium and space, create order, supply focus, and integrate a sense of the surrounding place. *Unidentified Object* (1979) was carved in the artist's studio in Japan; it now stands on Fifth Avenue at the south end of the Museum. Its massive columnar shape, recalling ancient menhirs like those at Stonehenge, has been articulated by the subtle modeling of the cavities. *Gift of The Isamu Noguchi Foundation, Inc., 1981, 1981.131*

39 ÉMILE GALLÉ, French, 1846–1905
Hanging Cabinet
Birch and rosewood; 48 × 40 × 12 in. (121.9 × 101.6 × 30.5 cm.)

A revolutionary style known as Art Nouveau swept Europe at the turn of the century, transforming the decorative arts and architecture. Artists, stimulated by imports brought west in the newly opened trade with Japan, abandoned historical models to seek inspiration through observation of nature. Gallé was the first major exponent to infuse glass and furniture with the lyricism of the new style. Organizing the École de Nancy, he rallied colleagues to develop form and ornament from the flora of their native Lorraine. Gallé used a common wildflower for the motif of the silhouette and structural supports of this cabinet, and he depicted the butterflies attracted to the flowers in wood marquetry on the cabinet door. *Anonymous Gift, 1982, 1982.246*

40 *History of Navigation* from the *Normandie*
French, 1934
Reverse-painted glass; 20 ft. 5 in. × 29 ft. 5¾ in. (6.22 × 8.99 m.)

The liner *Normandie* was the last great expression of French Art Deco. The elegance of this style had won acclaim in the Paris Exposition of 1925. Such luxury could not survive the Depression, and only subsidy by the French government made possible the extravagance of the *Normandie.*

The Museum's mural, now installed in the Museum Restaurant, was one of four covering the corners of the liner's Grand Salon (a detail is shown here). Jean Dupas (1882–1964), who designed these works, chose the history of navigation as his nominal subject, but the profusion of quasi-historical vessels and mythical creatures was clearly not meant to tell a story but to create an overwhelming effect. The murals were executed by Charles Chapigneulle in 1934. Their mirror-like brilliance was achieved by an unusual technique of glass decoration. Segments of the scene were painted on the reverse of panels of plate glass and overlaid with gold and silver leaf. *Gift of Dr. and Mrs. Irwin R. Berman, 1976, 1976.414.3*

ACKNOWLEDGMENTS

My first thanks must go to Saul P. Steinberg whose generous support made the publication of this guide possible. I am also most grateful to Daniel Berger, who brought this project to Mr. Steinberg; his advice and support have been invaluable.

This book, the product of many hands, embodies the spirit of willing cooperation I found throughout the Museum. I extend my warmest thanks to all the staff members who worked with me; among them are: John K. Howat, Lewis I. Sharp, Morrison H. Heckscher, Frances Gruber Safford, Natalie Spassky, Doreen B. Burke, Alice Cooney Frelinghuysen, R. Craig Miller, Terese Bienfait Blake, Kristine Schassler, Don E. Templeton, Gary Burnett, George Asimakis, and Benjamin Zibit of The American Wing; Prudence O. Harper, Oscar White Muscarella, Holly Pittman, Mary M. Pernot, and James Vogler of Ancient Near Eastern Art; Helmut Nickel, Stuart W. Pyhrr, and Howard Sloan of Arms and Armor; Stella Blum, Paul M. Ettesvold, Jean R. Druesedow, and Irja Zimbardo of the Costume Institute; Jacob Bean, Helen B. Mules, and Calvin D. Brown of Drawings; Christine Lilyquist, Cathleen A. Keller, Maureen Limond, Louis Kunsch, and Donald Fortenberry of Egyptian Art; John Pope-Hennessy, Katharine Baetjer, Charles S. Moffett, Keith R. Christiansen, Walter Liedtke, Polly J. Sartori, and Michael O'Brien of European Paintings; Olga Raggio, James Parker, James David Draper, Jessie McNab, Clare Vincent, Clare Le Corbeiller, Johanna Hecht, William Rieder, Katherine Bernacki, and Rose Whitehill of European Sculpture and Decorative Arts; Wen Fong, Martin Lerner, Suzanne Valenstein, Alfreda Murck, Maxwell Hearn, Barbara Ford, Yasuko Betchaku, Marise Johnson, Tasia Pavalis, and Stuart Edelson of Far Eastern Art; Dietrich von Bothmer, Joan R. Mertens, Maxwell L. Anderson, and Mary Eigsti of Greek and Roman Art; Stuart Cary Welch, Marie Lukens Swietochowski, Marilyn Jenkins, Carolyn Kane, Annemarie Schimmel, Martha Deese, and Marcel G. Berard of Islamic Art; George Szabo and the staff of the Robert Lehman Collection; William D. Wixom, Carmen Gómez-Moreno, Margaret E. Frazer, Charles T. Little, Katharine R. Brown, and Barbara Drake Boehm of Medieval Art; Jane Hayward, Timothy Husband, and Carl Koivuniemi of Medieval Art—The Cloisters; Laurence Libin, J. Kenneth Moore, Susan J. Snyder, Helmut Hauser, and Stewart Pollens of Musical Instruments; Douglas Newton, Julie Jones, Susan Vogel, and Kate Ezra of Art of the Pacific Islands, Africa, and the Americas; Colta Ives, Janet S. Byrne, Weston J. Naef, and David W. Kiehl of Prints and Photographs; William S. Lieberman, Lowery S. Sims, Ida Balboul, Lisa Messinger, Anne Lantzius, and Vito Luongo of Twentieth Century Art; Ashton Hawkins, Carol Moon Cardon, Patricia F. Pellegrini, and Tanya Maggos of the administrative staff; Merribell Parsons and Michael O'Brian of Education Services; Mark D. Cooper, Walter J. F. Yee, Sheldan Collins, Lynton Gardiner, Gene C. Herbert, Alexander Mikhailovich, Kenneth Campbell, Luis Almodovar, Brock Elgart, Gerald Leitner, Islam Sultani, and Wanda Williams of the Photograph Studio; Margaret P. Nolan, Priscilla F. Farah, Donna C. Smidt, Mary F. Doherty, Diana Kaplan, Deanna Cross, and Kathleen James of The Photograph and Slide Library.

In the Editorial Department Amy Horbar, Naomi Godfrey, Rebecca Hantin, Katherine Balch, and Stephen Sechrist made substantial contributions. Finally I must thank Hugh J. Howard for his good cheer and encouragement.

K. H.

INDEX

Photographic Credits

Richard Cheek: American Decorative Arts, nos. 4, 11; Federico Arborio Mella: Islamic Art, nos. 19, 30; Otte Nelson: Islamic Art, no. 35; Stan Ries: Egyptian Art, no. 24; Malcolm Varon: Drawings, no. 1; Islamic Art, nos. 28, 31; Robert Lehman Collection, nos. 1, 4, 5, 10, 11, 12, 13, 21, 23, 25, 28, 30, 31, 32, 37, 39, 40, 41; Medieval Art—The Cloisters, no. 11.

All other photography was done by the Museum's Photograph Studio.